ALLIANCE CAPITALISM AND GLOBAL BUSINESS

Placing the evolution of alliance capitalism in the context of the globalizing economy, John Dunning explores the consequences of the economic and political events of the past twenty years for the economic jurisdiction of firms, markets and nation states, their impact on the structural organization of firms and on the domestic policies of national governments. Other key issues discussed include:

- global restructuring and alliance capitalism
- the interaction between trade and integration
- a re-evaluation of the costs and benefits of FDI
- the competitiveness of firms and countries
- the spatial dimensions of globalization

The volume includes some personal reminiscences by the author about the evolution of his ideas and writings over the last thirty years and a comparative look at US and Japanese FDI in Europe. The volume also includes an evalution of the current, and likely future, foreign MNE activity in Japan. The volume concludes with some forward-looking insights by the author into the paradoxes at the contemporary globalizing economy and of how these might be managed or resolved.

Professor John H. Dunning is currently State of New Jersey Professor of International Business at Rutgers University 1996–7 and is also Professor Emeritus at the University of Reading. He also holds an honorary Professorship in International Business at Beijing's University of International Business and Economics. He is past President of the International Trade and Finance Association, and of the Academy of International Business. He has published extensively on international direct investment and the multinational enterprise, and on industrial and regional economics.

ROUTLEDGE STUDIES IN INTERNATIONAL BUSINESS AND THE WORLD ECONOMY

1 STATES AND FIRMS
Multinational Enterprises in Institutional Competition
Razeen Sally

2 MULTINATIONAL RESTRUCTURING, INTERNATIONALIZATION AND SMALL ECONOMIES
The Swedish Case
Thomas Andersson, Torbjörn Fredriksson and Roger Svensson

3 FOREIGN DIRECT INVESTMENT AND GOVERNMENTS
Catalysts for Economic Restructuring
Edited by John Dunning and Rajneesh Narula

4 MULTINATIONAL INVESTMENT AND ECONOMIC STRUCTURE
Globalization and Competitiveness
Rajneesh Narula

5 ENTREPRENEURSHIP IN A GLOBAL CONTEXT
EDITED BY SUE BIRLEY AND IAN MACMILLAN

6 THE GLOBAL STRUCTURE OF FINANCIAL MARKETS
An Overview
Edited by Dilip K Ghosh and Edgar Ortiz

7 ALLIANCE CAPITALISM AND GLOBAL BUSINESS
John H Dunning

ALLIANCE CAPITALISM AND GLOBAL BUSINESS

John H. Dunning

Routledge
Taylor & Francis Group
LONDON AND NEW YORK

To my past and current Ph.D. students

First published 1997
by Routledge
2 Park Square, Milton Park, Abingdon, Oxfordshire OX14 4RN

Simultaneously published in the USA and Canada
by Routledge
711 Third Avenue, New York, NY 10017

First issued in paperback 2014

Routledge is an imprint of the Taylor and Francis Group, an informa business

Typeset in Garamond by Pure Tech India Ltd, Pondicherry

British Library Cataloguing in Publication Data

A catalogue record for this book is available from the British Library

Library of Congress Cataloging in Publication Data
Dunning, John H.
Alliance capitalism and global business / John H. Dunning.
p. cm.
Includes bibliographical references and index.
1. Strategic alliances (Business) 2. International business enterprises—Management. 3. Investments, Foreign.
I. Title. HD69.S8D86 1997 658.1′6—dc20 96–25974 CIP

ISBN 13: 978-1-138-87937-9 (pbk)
ISBN 13: 978-0-415-14828-3 (hbk)

CONTENTS

LIST OF FIGURES

LIST OF EXHIBITS

LIST OF TABLES

ACKNOWLEDGEMENTS

I am grateful to the editors of several journals and the publishers of books in which earlier versions of some of these chapters first appeared for permission to make use of the material. Two of the studies were originally co-authored with PhD students at Rutgers University: one with Rajneesh Narula, now Assistant Professor of International Business at the University of Limburg in Maastricht; and the other with Sarianna Lundan, now Lecturer in International Business at the University of Reading. I much appreciate the contribution of these scholars to the volume.

Most of the typing of this volume was undertaken by Mrs Phyllis Miller of the Faculty of Management at Rutgers University. As on previous occasions, I owe her a great debt of gratitude, not least for her helpful suggestions on stylistic improvements.

Acknowledgement is also due to the copyright holders for their permission to reprint the following contributions. Chapter 2 is a reprint of a chapter (of the same name) in *Globalization and Developing Countries*, edited by K. Hamdani and myself and published by the United Nations in April 1996. Chapter 3 is a largely unrevised reproduction of an article published in the *Journal of International Business Studies*, Vol. 26(3), 1995, pp. 461–93. Chapter 4 was first published as a chapter in *Strategies and Structural Interdependencies*, edited by Gavin Boyd and Alan Rugman, published by Edward Elgar in 1996. Chapter 5 is a revised version of an article of the same name, which first appeared in the *International Trade Journal*, Vol. IX(2), 1995, pp. 153–202. Chapter 6 is an updated and enlarged version of a chapter in an edited volume by Lorraine Eden, *Multinationals in North America*, published by the University of Calgary Press in 1994 (pp. 277–308); and Chapter 7 is a modified version of a chapter in a volume *The Dynamic Firm*, edited by A. D. Chandler, P. Hagström and O. Sölvell and published by the University of Stockholm Press in 1996.

Chapter 8 appeared as an article of the same name, first published in *Transnational Corporations* Vol. 3, February 1994, pp. 23–52. Chapter 9 is a largely unrevised reproduction of Chapter 1 in an edited volume by Rajneesh Narula and myself, *Foreign Investment and Governments*, published by Routledge in London and New York in 1996 (pp. 1–41). Chapter 10 is a slightly modified version of an article entitled 'Think again Professor Krugman: competitiveness does matter', which was first published in *The International Executive*, Vol. 37(4), July/August 1995, pp. 315–24; while Chapter 11 was initially published in *Transnational Corporations*, Vol. 5, Summer 1996.

Chapter 12 is a largely unrevised reproduction of a chapter of the same name published in an edited volume by D. Encarnation and M. Mason entitled *Does Ownership Matter?*, Oxford University Press, 1994, pp. 59–96; while Chapter 13, which was co-authored with Sarianna Lundan, is due to be published as an article in *International Trade Journal* early in 1997. The contents of Chapter 14, which have not previously been published, were the subject of the 1996 Tore Browaldh Lecture delivered by myself at the University of Göteborg in April 1996.

John H. Dunning
Rutgers & Reading Universities

1

INTRODUCTION

Some personal reminiscences

THE 1960s: THE EFFECTS OF FDI

This is the sixth volume of my readings that Routledge (and previous publishers now part of the Routledge family)[1] has published. The contents of each very much reflect both the contemporary state of international business activities in the world economy and the evolution of my own thinking – and those of my colleagues – about the determinants and effects of foreign direct investment (FDI) and the multinational enterprise (MNE).[2]

The first book of readings, *Studies in International Investment*, appeared in 1970. Essentially, it updated and expanded a series of articles originally published in the 1960s, with the emphasis directed to the impact of FDI on both investing and host countries. Little attention was given to the determinants or institutional aspects of FDI, although it was clearly recognized even then that the study of international direct investment straddled the borders of international economics and the theory of the firm (Dunning 1970: 11). Shades of later theoretical discussion were also contained in such statements as 'FDI is only likely to occur when there is an imperfect market in the dissemination of knowledge and, where it is not profitable, to exploit the foreign markets in question by alternative means' (Dunning 1970: 10). At the time of writing (early 1969), my only exposure to Stephen Hymer's thesis (Hymer 1960) had been via his supervisor's series of essays on *American Business Abroad* (Kindleberger 1969), and it was not until later in that year, when *Studies in International Investment* was already in press, that I became fully familiar with Hymer's work.[3]

There were two main themes addressed in *Studies in International Investment*. Both, in rather different ways, were an extension of my earlier work on US FDI in the United Kingdom (Dunning 1958). The first was to look at the consequences of UK *outward* direct investment (which in the 1960s was growing faster than inward investment). This interest was stimulated by my participation in a study, commissioned by the British government[4] and conducted by Brian Reddaway and a team of Cambridge economists, on the effects of UK direct investment on domestic income and the balance of payments. In particular, I was interested in the role played by UK firms in fashioning the growth of the US economy – a subject which had not been addressed by scholars since before the First World War.[5]

The second theme was to give further attention to the nature of the competitive advantages of foreign manufacturing affiliates, cf. indigenous producers, and the consequences of those advantages for productivity, profitability, market and growth shares. There were separate chapters in *Studies in International Investment* both on the comparative efficiency of UK affiliates in the United States and Canada, and of US affiliates in the United Kingdom.

Turning to the first theme, it was most certainly the case that the main interest of home governments in FDI in the 1960s was its impact on the balance of payments and on domestic employment, and studies were commissioned in both the United States and the United Kingdom to assess this impact.[6] Understandably, economists tried to steer discussion to the wider consequences of FDI – particularly as it affected the productivity and restructuring of domestic economic activity, and part of the contribution of *Studies in International Investment* was to the debate on the nature of these costs and benefits. In particular, a good deal of emphasis was given to the differences between the social and private returns of outbound MNE activity, and also between the incremental and organic theories of FDI (see e.g. Dunning 1970: 124–5).

In anticipation of some of the contemporary discussion on globalization and industrial competitiveness, studies also emphasized the importance of FDI in upgrading the competitiveness of the investing firms. To quote directly from Chapter 4:

> Both in Europe and North America, UK firms have benefited from the access to knowledge of new products, techniques, materials and managerial methods which might not otherwise be obtained, and in the US from operating in a more competitive environment than that to which they are usually accustomed.
>
> (p. 125)[7]

It was during the 1960s that the United Kingdom began to rebuild its pre-war reputation as a pre-eminent capital exporter;[8] although, unlike the interwar years, the greater part of the new capital flows took the form of direct, rather than portfolio, investment. While traditional Commonwealth markets continued to attract the bulk of such investment, an increasing proportion of manufacturing and service activities by UK MNEs was beginning to be directed to the United States and Continental Europe.[9] In *Studies in International Investment* and other of my writings around this time,[10] I examined the reasons for, and consequences of, this geographical restructuring, and, in particular, why UK firms investing in the United

States and Canada were not performing as well as their US and Canadian counterparts investing in the United Kingdom. This I attributed largely to the inadequacies and lack of motivation of British management, although the UK economic climate at the time – and particularly the tax regime – did little to encourage innovation or entrepreneurship.

The subject of the comparative efficiency of US subsidiaries in the United Kingdom and their indigenous competitors continued to fascinate both UK academic researchers and politicians throughout the 1960s; and the final part of *Studies in International Investment* reproduced the results of some research undertaken by the author and a colleague at Southampton University for the (UK) National Economic Development Council (NEDC). This study confirmed the distinctive competencies or ownership-specific (O) advantages of US subsidiaries (as documented in my 1958 study (Dunning 1958), and that these tended to be concentrated in sectors in which US firms did relatively well in export markets. While, at the time, I ascribed most of the poorer performance of UK firms to managerial weaknesses, in retrospect, I probably underestimated the benefits accruing to US firms from their internalization and co-ordination of cross-border markets – particularly in intangible assets.

THE 1970s: THE DETERMINANTS OF MNE ACTIVITY

While my writings in the 1960s were mainly related to the economics of UK inward and outward direct investment, in the 1970s they took on a wider geographical perspective. I also became more interested in the institution of the multinational enterprise *per se*. This was partly due to my appointment as UK representative to the 'Group of Eminent Persons' set up in 1972 by the UN Economic and Social Council to examine the role of MNEs in economic development; partly a consequence of my acquaintance with Raymond Vernon and with Stephen Hymer's writings; and partly as a result of discussions with my own colleagues at the University of Reading.[11]

The outcome of this direction of my thinking, and also of the refocusing of the interest of both practitioners and governments towards the social and economic consequences of the growing significance of multinational (or transnational) activity,[12] was displayed in a series of articles and chapters in books written in the 1970s, which were reproduced as a set of readings in *International Production and the Multinational Enterprise* in 1981.

The volume was divided into three main parts. The first identified and described my own approach to understanding the determinants of international production – which I defined as production financed by FDI and undertaken by MNEs. This, I called the eclectic theory (later renamed paradigm) of international production. The word eclectic was deliberately chosen because of my attempt to integrate a variety of strands of thinking about the ownership, location and organizational form of cross-border value-added activities.[13] Until the early 1970s, most theorizing about the determinants of production financed by FDI had been partial in that it sought to explain a *particular* type or aspect of MNE activity. The eclectic paradigm (like its near neighbour, the internalization paradigm) offers an analytical framework by which the growth, industrial pattern, geographical disposition and form of *all* types and aspects of international business activity might be explained.

I like to believe that the eclectic paradigm has been one of the most powerful paradigms for explaining not only the foreign value-added activities of firms, but also the interaction between these activities and other forms of cross-border transactions, notably interfirm collaborative agreements and arm's length trade. At the same time, I have always acknowledged that the operational robustness of the eclectic paradigm is limited. This is partly because of the large number of possible OLI variables that may influence FDI, and partly because their value is likely to be dependent on contextual variables, such as those which are specific to countries, types of activities and the strategies of individual firms.

Hence, while FDI by Korean MNEs in the French consumer electronics sector can be examined within the same analytical framework as that of US-advertising MNEs in the Philippines, or that of the Chinese MNEs in the Australian copper mining industry, the precise nature of the OLI variables and their value (as, for example, identified and evaluated in a multiple regression equation) may be very different. This, I attempted to illustrate in an early empirical test of the eclectic paradigm, using data on the sales of US affiliates in seven countries and fifteen sectors in 1966 and 1970.[14] Both country- and sector-specific characteristics were shown to influence these activities strongly and their significance, relative to those of indigenous firms, independently of the value of the OLI variables tested in a series of multiple regression equations.

The second part of our 1981 collection of readings examined a number of specific consequences of the activities of MNEs which might be attributable to their foreignness or degree of multinationality. Such issues as the contribution of FDI to indigenous capital formation, and its impact on market structure, regional economic development and domestic macro-economic policies, were some of the themes being critically explored by analysts in the 1970s, along with the alternative policies towards FDI which might be adopted by host governments.

These latter issues were discussed in the third part of our volume, although, at the time, my own belief, that governments needed to get their own economic and political houses in order before they could appraise the true costs and benefits of either inbound or outbound MNE activity, was not generally upheld by policy makers, in either developed or developing countries.

INTRODUCTION

THE 1980s: THE ECLECTIC PARADIGM AND COMPETITIVENESS ISSUES

The 1970s, then, saw most of my research interests directed to explaining the determinants of international production and of how they impinged upon different aspects of economic analysis. Indeed, parallel to the sequence of readings now being described, I also convened a number of conferences which attempted to review the state of scholarly thinking on FDI and the MNE.

The first of these conferences was held at Reading in May 1970 under the title 'The Multinational Enterprise'. At this conference, different aspects of this (relatively new) phenomenon were analysed by the leading scholars of the day, including Bob Aliber, Jack Behrman, David Lea, Keith Pavitt, Edith Penrose, Stephen Hymer and Paul Streeten. Many of the issues which have since commanded critical attention by both academic researchers and policy makers were first aired at this conference.[15] The edited volume of the conference proceedings, which was published in 1971 (Dunning 1971), was shortly followed by another, namely *Readings in International Investment* (Dunning 1972), in the Penguin Modern Economics Series, the purpose of which was to reproduce and comment upon some of the most influential articles on both direct and portfolio foreign investment (but not the MNE) published over the past half century.[16]

The second conference I arranged was held at Bellagio, Northern Italy, in September 1972 and, on this occasion, my objective was more focused. It was no less than to explore the implications of the increasing significance of FDI and MNE activity for received economic theory. The resulting volume, *Economic Analysis and the Multinational Enterprise*, was published in 1974.

Looking back over the past quarter century since the contributions to this volume were first written, one can see that some have stood the test of time much better than others. For example, Max Corden's analysis of how international trade theory needed to be modified in the light of the cross-border mobility of factors of production implicit in FDI still remains as relevant today as it did in the 1970s, as, indeed, does George Bort's treatment of long-run capital movements, Guy Stevens' analysis of the determinants of investment and Charles Kindleberger's discussion of how FDI affects integration theory.[17] By contrast, in his evaluation of how the theory of the firm might be affected by the territorial expansion of its boundaries, Tom Horst made no mention of the theory of internalization, nor, indeed, of Edith Penrose's earlier work on the theory of the growth of the firm (Penrose 1959); while neither Raymond Vernon nor Richard Caves fully took on board the implications of the cross-border co-ordination of intrafirm value-added activities for the theories of location and industrial organization.[18]

Other essays in *Economic Analysis and the Multinational Enterprise* tended to reflect – and understandably so – the economic, technological and political environment of the early 1970s. Thus, Edward Mansfield's essay on technology and the MNE predates the writings of Richard Nelson and Stanley Winter and those of the Sussex economists,[19] which have done so much to advance our understanding of the evolution of technological change, not to mention the catalytic technological advances which have occurred over the last two decades. Similarly, Paul Streeten's appraisal of the contribution of FDI to economic development strongly echoed the political ideology of most developing countries in the early 1970s, and, in particular, their desire for economic independence and to obtain the maximum share of the economic rents arising from MNE activities in their midst.

Early in the 1980s, I sensed a marked change in the role of, and the attitude towards, FDI and MNEs. Partly, this change coincided with the election of Ronald Reagan as President of the United States and Margaret Thatcher as Prime Minister of the United Kingdom, and culminated at the end of the decade with the opening up of China and the demise of the Communist economic system in Central and Eastern Europe. Partly, too, a new generation of generic innovations – not least in transborder communications – was further extending the boundaries of firms, and facilitating a variety of cross-border interfirm alliances and networking arrangements.

Taken collectively, these events demanded a major restructuring of economic activity in both developed and developing countries. They also forced economists to give much greater attention to the determinants and dynamics of economic change – and especially of innovation – as a vehicle for upgrading the efficiency of indigenous resources and capabilities and for the reallocation of their use. During the 1980s, there was increasing evidence that the MNE was a critical contributor to this upgrading and restructuring process.[20] This being so, in 1983, I organized another conference at Bellagio at which the participants considered the extent and the ways in which MNEs were aiding or inhibiting economic restructuring and the upgrading of natural and created assets in a group of both developed and developing countries. The results of the conference were published in 1985 in a volume entitled *Multinational Enterprises, Economic Structure and Competitiveness*. Without exception, the authors of the ten country case studies[21] acknowledged the importance – and the increasing importance – of FDI in the restructuring process and in affecting the quality of domestic resources and competencies. Once again, much emphasis was given to the role of governments in providing the 'right' economic environment for FDI; to the size, industrial composition and stage of development of the investing and recipient countries; and to the rationale for FDI. But for the most part, the authors were very positive in their views on the contribution of MNEs to the productivity and growth of the participating countries – a conclusion which predated, by a decade or more, that of the OECD (1994) and UNCTAD (1995) in more detailed studies on MNEs and competitiveness.[22]

The growing technological intensity of FDI and the competitiveness of firms and countries was, indeed, the main thrust of several of my own writings in the early 1980s – and some of these were brought together in 1988 with the publication of my third book of readings, entitled *Multinationals, Technology and Competitiveness*. As it turned out, this became a companion volume to a more theoretically oriented book of readings which was published at the same time, entitled *Explaining International Production*. As well as an increasing volume of applied and policy-oriented research on the characteristics and effects of MNEs, the 1980s were also a period during which the mainstream economic theory of FDI and MNE activity was being refined and advanced. In this volume I presented a modified version of my original paper on the eclectic paradigm – in which I acknowledged that a firm might gain the ownership-(O-)specific advantages necessary for it to engage in FDI as a direct consequence of it internalizing cross-border intermediate product markets, that is, its O advantages might follow its territorial expansion rather than precede it. I also accepted that, as firms increase their degrees of multinationality,[23] the economic gains arising from the common governance of interrelated activities were likely to become relatively more important to those which arise from their privileged access to specific assets.[24]

As well as responding to some of the earlier criticisms to the eclectic theory (now renamed paradigm,) *Explaining International Production* also offered various applications of it. Many of these reflected the direction of my research interests towards embracing a number of unfamiliar areas of MNE activity. Were, for example, the determinants of FDI in primary and secondary activities equally applicable to FDI in the service sectors? To what extent were the kind of explanations of the growth of fully or majority-owned foreign ventures applicable to the no less impressive growth of minority investments or non-equity collaborative agreements? What determined the relationship between trade and FDI; and how, and for what reasons, might this relationship change over time? How far were theories of MNE activity, initially crafted to explain the territorial expansion of US and European firms, applicable to explaining the most recent rise in FDI by Japanese firms? And, what have been the effects of the post-war movement towards regional economic integration on the extent, pattern and geographical origin of MNE activity within the integrated areas?

One other feature of scholarly research on international business issues in the 1980s, which I tried to emphasize in *Explaining International Production*, and which has since become a major subject of research in its own right, was its growing interdisciplinary character. While there was nothing new about this feature, scholars were then increasingly accepting that, to understand properly the phenomena of MNE, a purely unidisciplinary approach – be it from economics, organizational theory, marketing, finance or business strategy – was inadequate to capture the richness of both the determinants and effects of MNE activity.[25] In *Explaining International Production* I tried to give voice to some of these issues, and to suggest some new avenues for cross-disciplinary alliances in research and teaching.

THE EARLY 1990s: GOVERNMENTS AND GLOBALIZATION

If the two sets of readings published in 1988 focused on general paradigms of international business, and their application to a series of world economic events then unfolding, my next set of readings, *Globalization of Business*, published five years later, took as its central theme the advent of the globalizing economy, and the impact of an ever-widening range of cross-border business activities on the competitiveness and growth of individual industries, nation states and regions, and on the world economy.

Undoubtedly, the single most important socio-institutional event of the late 1980s was the renaissance of the market system as the dominant form of economic organization. This was most dramatically demonstrated by the events in Mainland China, and in Eastern and Central Europe in the late 1980s. However, in both developed and developing countries, there has been, over the last decade, a remarkable renewal of faith in the market as a creator and allocator of natural and created assets, and a no less widespread disillusionment in the ability of governments to advance the economic welfare of their constituents.

In the light of the high rates of growth and relatively small government expenditures of most East Asian countries, other nations, including those zealously pursuing policies of self-reliance in the 1970s, began, in the later 1980s, to reconfigure their domestic economic strategies to meet the needs of the international market-place. And, although for a variety of reasons – not least the rise of unemployment and the escalating costs of social welfare programmes – the proportion of government expenditure to gross national product (GNP) has remained consistently higher in North America and Western Europe than in most of Asia, there is little doubt that the economic responsibilities of the state are now seen more as an overseer and fine tuner of the economic system, as a facilitator of efficient and dynamic markets, as an encourager of entrepreneurship, as an institution builder, and as a manager of conflict between its constituents arising from economic change or development, than as a controller of, or participator in, free markets.[26] But, while in the early 1990s, the emphasis was placed on reducing the role of government as a direct controller and allocator of resources, in the later 1990s it is becoming increasingly recognized that to fulfil properly their market enabling functions, governments need to be *strong*.[27] Rather unfortunately, in the past 'strength' has been equated by 'spending power'. This is not the case in the age of alliance capitalism, which is the subject of our present readings.

But, to return to *Globalization of Business*, four other features of the international business economy were beginning to manifest themselves in the late 1980s. The first was the increasingly significant role of FDI in the world economy, coupled with the emergence of MNEs from developing – and particularly East Asian – countries. By 1993, the value of the inward stock of FDI, expressed as a proportion of the gross domestic product of host countries, had risen to 8.7 per cent from 7.2 per cent in 1988 and 4.7 per cent in 1980. For the first time, in 1989, the sales of the foreign affiliates of MNEs exceeded the value of world trade, while, throughout the 1980s, the growth of FDI flows outpaced that of world trade (UNCTAD 1994).

No less significant than these data, however, was the trend towards more integrated international production (UNCTAD 1993). This trend was especially marked in those regions of the world which were liberalizing their macro-organizational policies – and particularly those towards trade and FDI. Increasingly, MNEs were pursuing regional and/or global strategies towards their sourcing, financing, production and marketing operations, and even in the case of their innovatory strategies, the proportion of research and development (R&D) located outside the home countries of MNEs, and patents arising from their foreign subsidiaries, increased considerably in the 1980s (Dunning 1993a). At the same time, MNEs were becoming increasingly conscious of the need to adapt both their procurement requirements and their product and marketing strategies to the unique factor endowments and consumer tastes of the countries in which they operated. Achieving a successful balance between such integrating imperatives as a global product mandate and common labour standards, and the advantages of recognizing the specific needs and aspirations of suppliers, labour unions and customers, is, indeed, one of the core competencies which distinguishes successful from unsuccessful MNEs in the 1990s (Bartlett and Ghoshal 1989).

In addition to the increasing pace of integrated MNE activity in the later 1980s, the *raison d'être* for such investment underwent a subtle change. Although the greater part of FDI – and particularly that directed to developing countries – continued to be of the traditional market-seeking, resource-seeking and efficiency-seeking variety, an increasing proportion of cross-border mergers and acquisitions (M&As) was being undertaken to *acquire* new competitive, or ownership-specific, advantages, rather than to exploit existing advantages. Elsewhere, I have described such M&As as strategic asset-acquiring FDIs,[28] primarily because they are part and parcel of a regional or global strategy of the investing firms to protect or advance their overall competitive positions. Owing, *inter alia*, to the pressures to reduce costs, to take advantage of scale economies, to penetrate new markets, and/or to innovate new products and processes more speedily –

pressures which have been intensified by the demands of the resuscitated international market-place – firms, especially those producing technology-intensive and branded goods in oligopolistic industries, have been bought out, merged or concluded non-equity alliances with their competitors, suppliers or customers. Such FDI – sometimes for aggressive and sometimes for defensive reasons – has caused scholars to reappraise some of their cherished notions on the determinants of FDI.

Closely allied to this second feature of the economic environment of the 1980s, and very much in consequence of it, has been the blurring of the boundaries of firms – including MNEs – as non-equity strategic alliances and interfirm networks become a more important form of business organization. At one time, the jurisdictional borders of firms were clearly determined by their ownership of resources. While, *de jure*, this may still be the case, *de facto*, firms are increasingly using a plurality of collaborative arrangements to advance their competitiveness. We shall take up this issue in more detail in Chapter 4 of this volume.

The fourth feature of the late 1980s, which has also continued into the 1990s, is the more welcoming stance of most host governments to inbound FDI – as compared with that adopted a decade earlier. Again, this is partly a reflection of their renewed faith in the market system, and partly the increasing need of firms from individual nation states – especially small countries – to tap into the world's supply of created assets, so as to maintain and improve the usage and competitiveness of their indigenous resources (including human resources). The implications of each of these events, which some writers (e.g. Lipsey 1997) assert would not have been possible without the far-reaching technological changes[29] of the previous decade, are discussed in some detail in *Globalization of Business*. As in earlier readings, and in the current volume, each of the chapters were first published as papers in professional journals or chapters in edited volumes. However, perhaps more than in previous monographs, our discussions in *Globalization of Business* were centred on the impact of the changing global economic environment on the extent, ownership and organization of cross-border transactions, and how the increasing mobility of firm-specific intangible assets was affecting the functions and organization policies of national governments. Among the more specific topics dealt with in the volume were a comparative analysis of the dynamics of Japanese FDI in Europe, the emergence of FDI in Eastern and Central Europe, and the continuing expansion of MNE activity in the service sector.

Globalization of Business also attempted to take on board two of the most frequent criticisms directed towards the eclectic paradigm. The first is that it fails to accommodate firm-specific *strategic* variables in its configuration of O-specific advantages. The second is that, even where this is done, it is unrealistic to offer any meaningful *general* explanation of international production because of the substantial differences in the strategic response by individual firms to any commonly agreed set of variables which influence that behaviour. In *Globalization of Business*, we argued that part of the difficulty of reconciling our own approach with that of the business strategist lay in the fact that the eclectic paradigm was initially couched in static, or comparative static, terms, while almost, by definition, strategic decision taking implies a time dimension. We followed this thesis through in two of the essays – but we would be the first to accept that our thoughts, at the time, were very exploratory, and that the debate between international economists and business strategists has hardly yet begun.[30]

A consideration of the *process* by which the growth and pattern of international production interfaces with development and structural change has been one of the main thrusts of my research interests over the last five years or so. However, unlike some scholars – and particularly those from Finland and Sweden – I have preferred to look at meso- or macro-economic aspects of FDI, rather than the internalization process of firms themselves. Some of my initial thoughts on the relationship between a country's international direct investment position and its stage of development – what may be termed a developmental application of the eclectic paradigm – were set out in a paper I wrote for *Weltwirtschaftliches Archiv* in 1981 (Dunning 1981b). Since that time, the concept of the investment development path (IDP), which explores the relationship between a country's inward and outward direct investment over time, has been modified and extended in several ways.[31]

In December 1994, together with Rajneesh Narula, an ex-PhD student of mine from Rutgers University, I convened a workshop in Rotterdam, at which the dynamics of the international direct investment position of some six industrialized and five industrializing countries was explored.[32] An edited volume of the proceedings of the workshop was published in January 1996 (Dunning and Narula 1996). Each of the contributors to the volume was asked to pay special attention to the role of FDI in fashioning the IDP path of developing countries and the restructuring process of developed countries.

In a concluding chapter to this volume, Sanjaya Lall (1996), while endorsing the main tenets of the IDP, emphasized the role of government, and particularly host government policies, in influencing the direction and shape of a country's IDP. In doing so, apart from the traditional leaders in FDI (e.g. the United Kingdom, Sweden and the United States), which have for years adopted largely neutral policies towards inbound MNE activity, Lall identified three groups of countries, which pursued respectively:

1. Passive open-door policies to FDI and to local technological development.
2. Pro-active policies to attract and guide FDI to activities that most benefit local development.

3 Selective policies towards using FDI as one of a number of possible ways to gain access to foreign 'created assets', and to promote the development of indigenous competitive capabilities.

Lall went on to argue that these strategies may have different affects both on the O advantages of foreign-owned and indigenous firms and on the L advantages of the immobile created assets of the countries concerned; and, indeed, on the very process of restructuring and upgrading these latter assets. Thus, passive policies can attract FDI to exploit existing locational advantages like domestic markets, natural resources or low-cost labour. They will yield certain externalities and growth benefits but, in the absence of specific measures to overcome market failures in the host country, they will not lead to a maximization of the benefits that MNEs have to offer. Pro-active FDI strategies, if accompanied by appropriate measures to provide the skills, technological backup and infrastructure that a modern industrializing economy needs, can have much greater benefits on development and locational advantages. By choosing to depend on FDI, however, they may not lead to the full development of indigenous capabilities. Finally, a selective strategy of choosing different modes of asset transfer, and combining it with efforts to develop the capabilities and entrepreneurship of local enterprises, can lead to larger long-term benefits accessing, and utilizing, foreign-owned assets.

Drawing upon the country case studies contained in the volume, Lall concluded that examples of each of these strategies were to be found in most developed countries, although most contained mixtures of different strategic elements. Currently, Spain and Mexico veer towards a passive strategy. Taiwan has elements of pro-active strategy, with a selective nationalist strategy thrown in. The best example of a pro-active FDI strategy is, however, that adopted by the Singaporean government, and which has used a battery of policy interventions to ensure that inbound FDI meets its development objectives. Japan is the best example of a selective nationalist strategy. Another good case is Korea, which has promoted its hand-picked local firms to giant conglomerate size and forced them into high-technology industries with a minimal reliance on FDI. In the process, it has developed the deepest and broadest base of technological capabilities anywhere in the developing world and has the largest investments in R&D (Lall 1996: 440–1).

The inclusion of such considerations (drawn from the current literature on industrial policy and development economics) can enrich the IDP analysis, taking it beyond the purely deterministic framework that links changes only to levels of income. In turn, the IDP approach has many insights that can help the development analyst (like the present author) and lead to a better understanding of the process of participation of developing countries in international production.

INTRODUCTION

THE MID-1990s: ALLIANCE CAPITALISM AND MNE ACTIVITY

Because of the increasingly important role being played by Third World outward direct investors, and the changing character of intra-Triad MNE activity, I have reproduced the introductory chapter of *Foreign Direct Investment and Governments* in the current selection of readings. I have also included a paper first published in *Transnational Corporations* in February 1994, which seeks to offer a contemporary exposition of the role FDI might (and does) play in upgrading the productivity of resources and capabilities of both home and host countries. It will be observed that much of the attention of this chapter – and, indeed, of other parts of the book – is given to the issue of competitiveness both of firms and countries, as this is now one of the most widely discussed aspects of international business.

While the concept of firm-specific competitiveness is generally widely accepted and understood, that of country-specific competitiveness is not. This is primarily because most international economists believe that in an open market economy, the main benefit of cross-border transactions is to restructure the allocation of country-specific resources and capabilities, and that they are essentially complementary, rather than substitutable, to each other. However, where assets are mobile across national boundaries, and where 'X' inefficiency exists in the deployment of immobile domestic resources and capabilities, FDI and other modes of cross-border entrepreneurial and asset transference may help to raise the productivity of domestic resources and, by their 'spillover' effects, improve the competitiveness of indigenous firms in global markets. In so doing, they may help realign the structure of value-added activity in both home and host countries. The role of national governments in affecting the competitiveness of the resources and capabilities within their jurisdiction also differs – both in its form and effectiveness – between countries. There are two readings in this present volume which focus on the interactions between the competitiveness of firms and countries and that of globalization.

However, the main thrust of this volume, as suggested by its name, *Alliance Capitalism and Global Business*, is the implication of contemporary trends in the capitalist system for international business activity, and particularly for the growing number of MNEs which are pursuing integrated transborder production, financial sourcing, technology and marketing strategies. In this book we suggest that, for a variety of reasons, it is not too much to assert that, in the last decade, the trajectory of capitalism in the world economy has evolved from that best described as *hierarchical* capitalism to that better described as *alliance* capitalism; and that, while still maintaining many of the characteristics of the dominant form of capitalism of the twentieth century, the distinctive features of its twenty-first century successor will be the extent to which, *in order to achieve their respective economic and social objectives while meeting the dictates of the domestic and international market-place, the main constituents, or stakeholders, in the wealth-creating process will need to co-operate more explicitly with each other.*

The thesis that *co-operation* and *competition* are complementary, as well as substitute, organizational forms in the wealth-creating process is explored at some length here, and particularly in the next three chapters. To the best of our knowledge, the term alliance capitalism was first used by Michael Gerlach (1992) to explain the social organization of Japanese business, and especially that of the *keiretsu* system of interfirm linkages. Two years earlier, Michael Best had coined the expression the 'new' competition to distinguish a micro-management system of flexible production, continuous product improvement, interfirm partnerships, networks of related activities and heterarchical organizational structures, with the 'old' competition, characterized by a mass production system of manufacturing, a Taylorist work organization, management hierarchies, large integrated firms and arm's length interfirm relationships (Best 1990).

In the last five years, other nomenclatures to describe the changes taking place in both the micro- and macro-organization of business activity have been coined. 'Co-operative', 'relational', 'collective' and 'stakeholder' capitalism are among these. All seek to convey a similar message: that is, that both along the value-added chain and across value-added chains, firms are increasingly replacing arm's length agreements with other firms by some kind of co-operative arrangements, which involves a time-related commitment of resources and capabilities. As Chapter 2 will show, the participating firms regard these agreements as necessary to protect and complement their core competitive advantages, and, in situations where they outsource activities previously undertaken internally, treat these as an integral part of their own value-adding activities.

However, alliance capitalism means much more than an increased volume and intensity of interfirm collaborative arrangements. The 'new' competition of the twenty-first century is also requiring the refashioning of relationships between *workers* and *management*. In Toyotaism, no longer is labour treated – or should be treated – as a cog in the wheel or as a passive factor of production to be used as management decrees. In an innovation-led production system, labour is valued as much as a source of knowledge and ideas, as for its physical or mental properties. Such a system also aids the functional integration of tasks, and more explicitly socializes the organization of work. *Inter alia*, this makes for a closer synthesis and interactive learning between workers engaged at different stages of the value-added process, for example between scientists and engineers in R&D laboratories and technicians and operators on the factory floor, or between fashion designers, sales personnel and distribution agents.

The growing integration between the innovatory and production tasks of firms, the disaggregation of the value chain, the miniaturization of key components and the increasing importance of networks and alliances in knowledge sharing and joint development is having enormous implications for the ecosystems and organizational structures of firms. Increasingly, the way in which a firm manages its assets and combines these with the complementary assets offered by the system of which it is part, is becoming as important a competitive advantage as the possession of the assets themselves. This is why the flexible production system has been called 'organcentric' in contrast to the 'technocentric' or 'machinocentric' production system of the Fordist era, and why the 'hierarchical' enterprise is being replaced by the 'alliance' enterprise, and by 'enterprise networks' (Sydow 1992).

Alliance capitalism also implies a more co-operative relationship between *firms* and *governments*. Certainly, in most Western economies, and for most of the period of hierarchical capitalism, that is from around the 1870s to the 1980s, the relationship between firms and governments was adversarial and confrontational (as, indeed, it was between firms and labour unions). In the case of MNEs, and host governments, this reached its peak in the 1970s, when, in that decade, there were more nationalizations and expropriations, and more new constraints, regulations and performance requirements imposed on MNEs or their subsidiaries than in any other decade before and since (UNCTAD 1993). By contrast, the early 1990s have seen a sweeping away of most of the earlier restrictions on the activities of MNEs, and these have been replaced by an array of incentives of one kind or another (UNCTAD 1995).

The main reason for the *volte face* of many governments towards FDI has been a growing awareness, not just of the technological and other benefits which such investment may bring to a country, but of the growing competition between governments for income-generating assets. The last decade or more has seen the emergence or renaissance of several market-based economies and the accelerated growth of others. But, more often than not, the domestic savings, technological capabilities and human resources of these nations have been insufficient to fuel the investment necessary for sustained development. Hence, foreign capital, technology and human capabilities have come to play a pivotal role. But, these resources are not in infinite supply, and countries have increasingly found themselves in competition with each other for FDI and other forms of foreign assets. Whatever tensions over national objectives, negotiation procedures, operational strategies and rent sharing between governments and MNEs still remain, in the context of the globalizing economy and the need to utilize better and upgrade the quality of domestic resources, the former currently see the latter as much as contributors towards, and less as inhibitors of, the attainment of their economic goals.

However, the advent of alliance capitalism has even broader implications for the economic role of national governments. In other writings, including *Globalization of Business* (1993b), I have suggested that the globalizing economy is requiring governments not only to reappraise their domestic macro-organizational policies[33] – which, in general, were initially implemented on the basis that resources and capabilities within their jurisdiction were locationally bound – but that, with the possible exception of trade policy, the belief that their own policies had no effect on those of foreign governments or vice versa. In a globalizing, increasingly interdependent world, this assumption is no longer valid; *de facto*, in a wide variety of ways, from the offering of very specific incentives to foreign investments to the provision of transportation infrastructure and educational opportunities, governments do influence the decisions of MNEs of where to place their (relatively) footloose movements.

There are, of course, appropriate and inappropriate ways for the state to intervene in a market-based economy. The former comprises those actions which will facilitate the long-term efficiency of the market system; reduce, or compensate, for market failure; and minimize intersocietal conflicts inherent in economic change and development. The latter is to create or add to structural distortions in resource allocation, such as that which occurred in the interwar years when governments – and particularly those of developed nations – pursued a wide range of nationalistic 'beggar my neighbour' policies. It was to combat such self-defeating behaviour that the General Agreement on Tariffs and Trade (GATT) was initiated in 1946. But, for the last half century, GATT – which is a multilateral form of alliance capitalism – although generally successful in establishing and maintaining the rules of the game for trade, has not affected (nor, it must be admitted, for most of this period has had the need to affect) the behaviour of governments in non-trade, yet trade-related, activities.

However, increasingly, as we have already seen, production financed by FDI and undertaken by MNEs has replaced trade as the main form of international transaction. So far, although by means of a variety of domestic macro-organizational policies, national governments have steered FDI to (or away from) the boundaries at the expense of (or to the benefit of) other countries, with the possible exception of fiscal incentives, non-trade distortions have been kept to the minimum. But, there are signs that they are growing, and for trade-related agreements between governments to be extended to a variety of non-trade areas. These issues are currently on the agenda of the World Trade Organization (WTO) and the Organization for European Co-operation and Development (OECD).

There are, of course, many other forms of intergovernmental co-operative regimes than those just mentioned. They range from regional economic unions, for example the European Union, through a gamut of free trade areas, for example NAFTA and APEC, to a range of informal bilateral agreements or multilateral institutions, such as the UN and its various agencies. In addition, there are a host of issues of sector-specific international agencies embracing such diverse areas as defence, property rights, the environment, the exploration of the sea bed, nuclear power, drugs and crime. Several of these institutions date back many years, but such 'clubs' have escalated as the advances in transportation and telecommunications technology have shrunk the costs of traversing space (Eden and Hampson 1990). And each new supranational regime, and every deepening of the activities of existing regimes, is just another example of alliance capitalism at work.

Alliance capitalism is then a generic expression which epitomizes a deep structural interdependence between corporations, governments, workers, consumers, shareholders and, indeed, all stakeholders – in the wealth-creating activities of society. As we shall be describing later in this chapter, it also has several spatial implications. Few technically sophisticated products of the late 1990s can be produced without the collaboration of the producing firms and their suppliers and industrial customers. We give just two examples. Aircraft manufacturers, such as Boeing and McDonnell Douglas, need to conclude alliances not only with their competitors to reap the maximum possible synergistic economies, and to speed up (and share the costs of) research and development, but also with their suppliers (particularly engine suppliers) on the function, design and manufacture of their products, and with their industrial consumers, that is the airlines, on performance, cabin design and amenity requirements. Pharmaceutical manufacturers are now increasingly turning to biotechnology R&D specialists to help them with their product development programmes, while they need to maintain close contact with their consumers, for example the medical profession, pharmacists and the government, over the cost-effectiveness of prescriptions (Whittaker and Bower 1994). They, too, like the aircraft manufacturers, are being compelled to engage in intraregional or cross-border alliances, and/or M&As,[34] to spread the huge and escalating costs of both R&D and marketing – not to mention accelerating the chances of a major innovatory breakthrough.

Most of the readings in this volume speak to this common theme. The volume starts (in Chapter 2) by placing alliance capitalism in the context of the globalizing economy, and of how and why this particular socio-institutional framework has evolved out of hierarchical capitalism. It also explores some of the consequences of alliance capitalism for the domestic policies of national governments.

Chapter 3 discusses the implications of alliance capitalism for our theorizing about the determinants of MNE activity; while Chapter 4 argues that contemporary economic and technological developments are obliging economists, organizational scholars and political scientists to look more carefully at the frontiers of firms, markets and nation states. Both chapters take my own particular approach to explaining international production, first enunciated twenty years ago, an important step further by incorporating the effects of interfirm transactions – other than those of a purely 'off the shelf' kind – into any evaluation of the OLI variables determining that production. Such transactions may vary in their extent and character from an informal, yet very specific, bilateral subcontracting arrangement, to a multiplicity of interrelated transactions undertaken within a web, or cluster, of related firms. However, while the twenty-first century will most surely increase the diversity of cross-border transactions, it is likely that, at the same time, such exchanges will be closely allied to each other, and will be particularly affected by the strategic direction and leadership of large MNEs,[35] which frequently possess the core competencies without which the web or cluster could not function efficiently. Because of this, we believe such business networks need to be embodied into the mainstream paradigms of international production.

Chapter 4 extends the argument of Chapter 3 by analysing some of the consequences of globalization for the economic jurisdiction of firms, markets and nation states. It suggests that the kind of organizational pluralism just described blurs the boundaries of three main kinds of economic governance, and inevitably leads to new organizational relationships. In particular, as in other chapters in this volume, we make use of Albert Hirschman's concept of 'voice' and 'exit' responses to a 'less than first best' economic or political situation (Hirschman 1970). Take, for example, market failure. Much of the received Anglo-Saxon literature tends to assume that firms respond to the presence of imperfect product markets by an exit strategy, that is by internalizing these markets. That the economic territory of the internalizing firm is extended by such a strategy, there can be no doubt. But, an alternative reaction to internalization is a voice strategy, in which the transacting parties seek to negotiate, or co-operate, with each other to reduce the market imperfections (e.g. such as those to do with incomplete information, uncertainties or opportunism). *De facto*, such a strategy also extends the jurisdiction – or at least the economic influence – of the participating firms, and, by so doing, causes the *de jure* boundaries to become more porous.

Chapter 4 offers similar examples to illustrate the growing interdependence of markets, which, *inter alia*, reflects the increasing importance of externalities in many contemporary exchanges, and also that of policy formation by national governments over an increasing sphere of activities.[36] It also suggests that an increasing preference for voice strategies by both private and public institutions to the forces of globalization is, itself, promoting further structural integration between firms, markets and nation states, and, hence, of alliance capitalism itself.

Parts III and IV of this volume look more specifically at some regional and spatial dimensions of globalization. Chapter 5 contains a criticism of the traditional trade theory in explaining most contemporary international economic transactions of goods and services, and especially intrafirm and intraindustry transactions. This chapter approaches the deficiencies of trade theory primarily from the perspective of the theory of FDI and MNE activity. A complementary, and for the most part, more rigorous, attempt to explain MNE activity, using the tools of the international economist, is to be found in the writings of such scholars as Helpman and Krugman (1985), Markusen and Venables (1995) and Markusen (1995).

Chapter 6 reproduces some thoughts about the similarities and differences between regional economic integration in North America and Western Europe – especially in so far as it has affected the level pattern and ownership of MNE activity in those regions. In particular, it uses both the theory of economic integration and the theory of international production to explain the growth of both intra- and extraregional FDI, the changing market orientation of such FDI – noticeably from that directed to supplying national markets to that aimed at supplying regional markets – and its interface with trade and other forms of cross-border transactions.

Alongside regional integration, which has been – and continues to be – one of the most powerful forces making for the structural interdependence of the participating countries and firms, there has been a renewed interest in the geography of *intra*national distribution of economic activity. In the last decade or so, three groups of scholars have sought to explain why certain types of economic activity tend to congregate in some provinces, districts or cities rather than in others, and what determines the organizational structure of, and linkages between, firms which site their activities in close proximity to each other. The first group are economists, such as Paul Krugman (1991), who have attempted to apply the techniques of international economics and location theory to understanding the spatial distribution of economic activity within a country. The second are economic geographers, such as Allen Scott (1994), Ann Markusen (1994) and Annalee Saxenian (1994), whose primary interest is to explain the changing industrial structure of regions and business districts and the different types of spatial interactions which might exist between firms. The third group are made up of industrial sociologists, such as Bennett Harrison (1994), who are principally concerned with the social organization of industrial and business districts. Each group of scholars, however, can trace its intellectual heritage to Alfred Marshall (1920), who first introduced the concept of agglomerative economies to explain both the geography of intranational production, and the importance of proximity as a factor fostering the efficiency of interrelated activities.

Throughout the world, there is evidence of the growing importance of spatial 'stickiness' and of regional clusters of related economic activities. Sometimes, the interface is between firms selling similar products, for example as in the textile industry in Prato, Northern Italy, and the Swiss watch industry. Sometimes it is between firms using similar inputs, for example the Scotch whisky industry and science parks. Sometimes it is between producers supplying goods or services jointly required by customers, for example as in the City of London; and sometimes it is between flagship firms and their network of suppliers, for example Toyota City in Japan and Boeing in the Seattle region of the United States. Storper and Harrison (1991) have characterized regional clusters according to the extent to which specialization of related activities is possible, the size of individual production units, the degree of connection among the units and the governance structure within the system. All such relationships represent a form of alliance capitalism but with an added twist: that is, the activities need to be concentrated within a localized community to reduce distance-related transaction costs.

Chapter 7 reviews the current state of scholarly thinking on the reasons for the changes now occurring in the inter- and intranational division of labour. In doing so, it pays particular attention to the spatial implications of four features of the globalizing economy of the late 1980s and 1990s. The first is the role of 'created' (cf. 'natural') assets in the production process – including those which are distance related[37] – and especially that of accumulated knowledge, learning experiences and organizational competence.[38] The second is the growing mobility of these former assets, and particularly those which are ownership or firm specific. The third is the growing importance of the co-ordination and transaction (cf. production) functions of firms; and the fourth is the increasing influence of governments in the intercountry distribution of economic activity, via their effect on the quality and price of immobile assets within their jurisdiction.

Each of these features is affecting the spatial allocation and organization of economic activity. Thus, both in their production and their usage, created assets display different locational needs than do natural assets. The transacting and co-ordinating functions of firms are more critically dependent on an efficient network of transport and communications facilities than are those requiring location-bound resources. The influence of governments on labour quality and costs (through their educational and vocational training programmes), on revenue- or cost-related incentives and disincentives, on environmental regulation, on research and development, on competition, on entrepreneurship, on trade and FDI policy, and on the renewal of decaying urban areas, may directly or indirectly affect the geography of resource allocation. Chapter 7 also pays some attention to the growing role being played by subnational governments (e.g. of states, business districts, cities, etc.) in affecting the spatial distribution of economic activity; of why and how this has occurred; and of its implications for the organization of national governments.

THE MID-1990s: REVISITING COMPETITIVENESS

Part III consists of some articles I published in the early 1990s on the subject of competitiveness and, especially, on the ways in which FDI and the activities of MNEs might affect the productivity of a country's location-bound resources, and the performance of its firms in global markets.

Chapter 8, which is based on a paper I presented, in 1993, at a conference in Beijing on 'Transnational Corporations and the Economic Development of China', surveys some current thinking about the contribution of MNE activity to the economic prosperity of host nations. In particular, it examines the reasons for the changing attitudes of both national governments and firms to FDI; relates the possible contribution of different types of FDI to the upgrading and restructuring of resources and capabilities of recipient countries; and rehearses, in the light of the characteristics of the globalizing economy of the early 1990s, the necessary macro-economic and macro-organizational policies which governments need to pursue if they are to maximize the benefits of inbound FDI. In discussing these latter policies, the chapter reconsiders the notion of 'competing' governments, first put forward in the late eighteenth century (Brennan and Buchanan 1985).

Chapter 9 pays more attention to the dynamics of structural adjustment brought about by the interaction of inward and outward FDI and government policy at different stages of a country's investment development path (IDP). I have already alluded to this concept in this introduction. Here I would emphasize that the novel feature of this chapter is that it gives considerably more attention to the later stages of the IDP path than did its original version, and it does so in the context of the growing significance of strategic asset-acquiring FDI, the emergence of alliance capitalism and the changing policies of governments, not only towards FDI *per se*, but towards the deployment and upgrading of indigenous resources in general.

In Chapters 10 and 11, I tackle the issue of competitiveness head-on. In Chapter 10 I take issue with Paul Krugman on his apparent denigration of the concept of country competitiveness. I write 'apparent' because I suspect that, once Krugman and I are settled on what we are both talking about, there is little disagreement between us. We are certainly both of one mind that competitiveness is a much abused word, and, at the end of the day, what matters to a country's economic prosperity is the productivity of its indigenous resources and capabilities, the ways in which its own firms and foreign affiliates organize these and any others they can draw upon from outside its national boundaries.[39] I suspect that where the difference of emphasis between Krugman and myself lies is on the usefulness of making comparison on the GNP per head – and its sectoral composition – between countries, and most noticeably, between countries in which the structure of natural and created assets is very different. For reasons stated in Chapter 10,

I believe such benchmarking exercises can be very useful in identifying reasons why the productivity of the location-bound resources and the more mobile intangible assets of domestic firms may be less than optimal; and to national and provincial governments, in the framing of their macro-economic and organizational policies, which, in a globalizing economy, are becoming increasingly interdependent of each other.[40]

In Chapter 12, I return to controversial ground in considering the competitive advantages of firms. Here I am specifically interested in assessing the extent to which firms perceive that they derive competitive advantages of one kind or another as a direct result of the activities of their foreign affiliates and/or from the non-equity collaborative arrangements they enjoy with foreign firms. For some time, I have been uncomfortable with the emphasis placed by some scholars – notably Michael Porter (1990) – on the quantity, quality and composition of domestic resources and capabilities as the critical determinant of the competitiveness of firms, and particularly of those from smaller industrial countries. In 1994, I conducted a survey of some of the world's largest 500 industrial firms to try to gain the insights of senior business executives on this issue. As the chapter reveals, one of the most unambiguous (and not entirely unexpected) results of the survey was that the value of gaining access to foreign 'diamonds' of competitive advantage (Porter 1990, Rugman 1993) increases quite remarkably according to the degree of multinationality of the respondent firms. Two other clear findings of our study were: first, that the extent to which FDI or cross-border alliance formation supplements a home-based competitive advantage varies according to the nature of that advantage; and second, that, over recent years, the value derived from access to foreign 'diamonds' of competitive advantage has become relatively more important.

THE MID-1990s: JAPANESE FDI

Since the early 1980s, I have been interested in the similarities and contrasts between Japanese and Western-style FDI. My interest in this subject was initially stimulated by Kiyoshi Kojima's emphasis on the *differences* between the determinants and the economic effects of the two kinds of investment (see e.g. Kojima 1978, 1990). I have never been completely persuaded by the overwhelming emphasis given by Kojima to the distinctive domestic backgrounds of Japanese and US MNEs, although, of course, I accept that they do exist and, in some cases, may be important determinants of FDI. But, in general, I have preferred Hal Mason's explanation for the differences in the FDI patterns of Japanese and US firms in the 1970s: that, at that time, Japan was at a much earlier stage in her IDP than the United States (Mason 1980).[41] And Kojima must surely acknowledge that in the globalizing economy of the 1990s, both the geographical and industrial patterns of Japanese and US MNEs are converging, although, for obvious economic, cultural and other reasons, firms from widely separated continents tend to invest in their own hinterlands, rather than in distant regions (UNCTC 1991).

My first book on Japanese FDI in the UK appeared in 1986 (Dunning 1986a). This used my own analytical framework to explain the structure and growth of the first generation of post-war Japanese affiliates in UK manufacturing industry, and also to identify some of the distinctive effects of their presence on UK suppliers, and on UK labour–management relationships. This was followed by a series of research papers. The first examined the similarities and differences between the decision-taking structures of US and Japanese manufacturing affiliates in the United Kingdom (Dunning 1986b); part of this work was republished in *Explaining International Production*. The second compared and contrasted the pattern, growth and governance structures of Japanese MNEs in Europe and the United States (Gittleman and Dunning 1992); this was later reprinted in *Globalization of Business*. In the last three years, I have published three other papers, two of which make up Chapters 12 and 13 of this set of readings. The one I have chosen not to reproduce is a lengthy analysis of why FDI in Japan has been so low over the last three or so decades.[42] However, part of the argument set out in this paper is contained in a later contribution jointly authored with Sarianna Lundan of Rutgers University, which is republished as Chapter 12. In this paper, we observe that, in 1970, the per capita stock of inbound direct investment in the United States was considerably less than its counterpart in Japan in 1990. Yet, at the time, no one asked the question 'Why is FDI in the United States so low?' as they do now of FDI in Japan. Since 1970, as is well known, the United States has become the leading recipient of inbound FDI, and the ratio of its outward/inward direct capital stock has fallen from 4.92 in 1973 to 1.25 in 1993.[43] Chapter 12 speculates a little as to whether or not Japan will follow the US IDP in the late 1990s, and, if not, why not.

Chapter 13 returns to a now familiar theme of Japanese FDI in Europe – first explored by myself in the late 1980s (Dunning and Cantwell 1992) – but uses received economic theory to explain why the industrial composition of US and Japanese MNE activity in the early 1990s was quite different. In particular, the chapter suggests that several of the early theories of FDI (e.g. the product cycle theory, the intangible assets thesis, and the follow my leader hypothesis) offer useful partial explanations for the recent growth of Japanese-owned firms in Europe, but that the most general explanation of the unique sectoral distribution of those firms, compared with that of their US counterparts, is based on the different competitive (O-specific) advantages of the two groups of firms, and their different reactions to the locational (L) advantages offered by Europe as a production base. In particular, the chapter shows that, in the late 1980s, the O-specific advantages of Japanese MNEs were relatively stronger in the fabricating than in the processing and manufacturing sectors, but that, apart from the greater impact of selective non-tariff barriers (e.g. import quotas) on Japanese exports, relative to US exports – especially of fabricated products – there are no locational variables which unambiguously explain the differences in the sectoral composition of the FDI of Japanese and US firms. The chapter concludes by setting out some unresolved questions, and looks into some of the factors likely to influence the future penetration of European markets by the two groups of investors.

THE PARADOXES OF GLOBALIZATION

This introduction has offered a brief review of the origin and contents of five of my previous readings, and a more detailed account of the contents of the present volume. The reader may, perhaps, have noticed an evolution in my own research interests from the subject of FDI – and particularly that of US and UK origin – to the broader subject of globalization, which embraces more pluralistic forms of cross-border transactions, and which has much wider economic and social implications for firms, governments and individuals.

In the last two or three years, I have been increasingly struck with the paradoxes of globalization and alliance capitalism, and, in the final chapter of this volume, I have sought to identify and analyse the reasons for some of the more significant of these and how they affect the composition and form of international business activity. This chapter, which is written as a prelude to the events of the next decade or longer, suggests that we may be moving into an *age of paradoxes*, which will supplant what the eminent historian Eric Hobsbawn (1994)[44] has described as the *age of extremes* of the twentieth century. It also asserts that the way in which the paradoxes are recognized and managed will determine the success or failure of globalization as an economic entity. Like many objects, events and conditions of life, globalization is a neutral phenomenon of itself; it is neither good nor bad. But, how we as human beings, both individually and collectively, affect, and are affected by, globalization is not neutral in its effects; and perhaps more than most phenomena of recent years, the ways in which we fashion and use the instruments of globalization, namely technology, institutions and market forces, and how we manage the consequences, are likely to determine critically the future prosperity of our global village. It is to be hoped we will use our power of choice courageously and wisely.

NOTES

1 Namely, Allen and Unwin and Unwin Hyman.
2 Also called the transnational enterprise or corporation. We use the terms interchangeably with each other.

3 In a slightly revised version of the Introduction to this book, published two years later (Dunning 1972), I acknowledged Hymer's contribution to the theory of FDI.
4 More particularly, the Board of Trade.
5 With the possible exception of Cleona Lewis (1938).
6 See especially those of Hufbauer and Adler (1968) and Reddaway *et al.* (1968).
7 In 1964, according to the Reddaway *et al.* study (1968: 322), 89 per cent of the UK capital in US manufacturing industry was in subsidiaries which were recorded to yield a significant feedback of knowledge. The corresponding percentage for West Germany was 74 per cent, Australia 68 per cent and for Canada 48 per cent.
8 From being a net creditor of $21.6 billion, the United Kingdom emerged from the Second World War owing as much as it was owed.
9 In the early 1960s, we estimated that the UK FDI stake in the United States was $2,450 million, 76.7 per cent of the corresponding US FDI stake in the United Kingdom (Dunning 1961).
10 See especially Dunning (1961) and Dunning and Rowan (1965).
11 Particularly with Mark Casson and Peter Buckley. During the 1970s and early 1980s, H. Peter Gray, Robert Hawkins, Seev Hirsch, Stephen Magee, Richard Moxon, Teretumo Ozawa, Alan Rugman and David Teece all spent some time as Visiting Research Fellows in the Department of Economics.
12 Expressed, for example, in the writings of Jacques Servan-Schreiber (1968) with respect to the growth of US FDI in Europe, and several scholars about the impact of MNE activity on economic development (e.g. as summarized in UN 1973 and 1974).
13 Also known as the ownership (O), location (L) and internalization (I) paradigm of MNE activity. (Internalization embraces the organizational form by which firms replace external market transactions by vertically or horizontally integrating the activities giving rise to these transactions.)
14 Originally published in Dunning (1980).
15 For example, those relating to the transfer of technology, industrial relations, less developed countries and multilateral policies towards MNEs.
16 Among the best-known contributors were Ragnar Nurske, Brinley Thomas, Harry Johnson, Paul Streeten, Donald McDougall, Ivor Pearce and David Rowan.
17 Indeed, of all the authors writing in our volume, Kindleberger was, perhaps, the most prophetic and his analysis is directly pertinent to issues now being discussed on the role of the nation state in a globalizing economy. See also Part II of this volume.
18 Though each subsequently did so in their later writings.
19 See especially Nelson and Winter (1982) and Dosi *et al.* (1988).
20 Especially with respect to the creation, transfer and discrimination of all forms of knowledge and information.
21 Namely, the United Kingdom, the United States, France, Germany, Sweden, Canada, India, Singapore, Korea and Japan.
22 At the same time, the contributors to the 1985 volume well acknowledged that FDI might bring with it less beneficial or unwelcome consequences. Some of these are set out in Chapter 8.
23 As measured, for example, by the proportion of world-wide sales or employment accounted for by the foreign affiliates of MNEs.
24 In one 1988 set of readings, we called the former type of O advantages, transaction cost (Ot) advantages, and the latter type asset-possessing (Oa) advantages. See Dunning (1988a: 42).

25 Such acknowledgement grew in the 1980s, and culminated with a conference on 'Perspectives in International Business' organized by Brian Toyne and Douglas Nigh at the University of Carolina in May 1993. The conference proceedings have since been published (Toyne and Nigh 1996).

26 For a recent discussion of the contemporary role of the state, see Chang and Rowthorn (1995).

27 Or, in the words of one scholar, 'a free market requires a strong state' (Gamble 1987).

28 See, for example, Chapter 3 of Dunning (1993a).

29 Both in the introduction of new products and processes and in the creation, processing and dissemination of knowledge, and the movement of people across national boundaries.

30 In *Globalization of Business*, I suggested a framework for a dynamic theory of international production by which the ownership (O) advantages of firms in time $t + 1$ were functions of their O advantages and the location (L) advantages of countries in which they operated (or might operate) in time t, and the strategic response of firms to these advantages (via, for example, the organization of their own assets and those acquired through non-ownership routes) over the time $t \rightarrow t + 1$. I also suggested that not only could the strategic related characteristics of firms be incorporated into the eclectic paradigm (e.g. as 'dynamic' O advantages or disadvantages), but that in many cases, it was possible to generalize about the kind of firms likely to engage in particular OLI strategies which affected the extent and character of their future O advantages.

31 At the same time, other explanations of the role of FDI in the industrialization of countries have been put forward. Among those which are specially persuasive is Terutomo Ozawa's 'stages of development' paradigm, as, for example, is described by him in Ozawa (1992) and Ozawa (1996).

32 Namely, the United Kingdom, the United States, Sweden, Japan, New Zealand and Spain; and Mexico, Taiwan, Indonesia, India and China.

33 For example, policies which affect the structure and long-term development of indigenous resources and capabilities, rather than the level and stability of economic activity, namely macro-economic policies.

34 Recent M&As have made Glaxo-Welcome the largest United Kingdom manufacturing pharmaceutical company in the United Kingdom; while Smith Kline Beecham, which is, itself, the result of several M&As in the last decade, is now the largest pharmaceutical MNE in the world.

35 And particularly of what Rugman and D'Cruz (1995) have referred to as 'flagship' firms and what Lorenzoni and Baden Fuller (1995) have termed 'central' firms or 'strategic centers'.

36 As set out earlier in Part 4 of *Globalization of Business.*

37 See Dunning (1993b: Chapter 13) and Storper and Scott (1995).

38 For a more recent examination of created and natural assets see Dunning and Narula (1996).

39 Of course productivity (or GNP per head) is not the only, nor necessarily the best, index we have of the economic and social welfare of the citizens of a country. Other indices include a human development index, as devised by the World Bank. For a recent critical analysis of the usual monetary measures of economic welfare, see Handy (1995) and Goldsmith (1994).

40 A view also shared by Hufbauer and Stephenson (1995).

41 Mason suggests that, for much of the nineteenth century, most outbound FDI of US companies was directed to resource-based activities in the rest of the American continent.

42 This paper was originally presented at a conference on 'Foreign Direct Investment in Japan' at the Wharton School, University of Pennsylvania, in October 1994, and later published in a volume edited by M. Yoshitomi and E. Graham; see Dunning (1996).
43 See Tables 2.3 and 2.4 in Chapter 2.
44 More particularly 1914–91. In his earlier writings, Hobsbawn referred to the period from 1789 to 1848 as the *age of revolution*, that from 1848 to 1875 as the *age of capital* and that from 1875 to 1914 as the *age of empire*.

REFERENCES

Bartlett, C. G. and Ghoshal, S. (1989) *Managing Across Borders: The Transnational Solution*, Boston: Harvard Business School Press.
Best, M. (1990) *The New Competition: Institutions of Restructuring*, Cambridge, MA: Harvard University Press.
Brennan, G. and Buchanan, J. M. (1985) *The Power to Tax*, Cambridge: Cambridge University Press.
Chang, H. J. and Rowthorn, R. (eds) (1995) *The Role of the State in Economic Change*, Oxford: Clarendon Press.
Dosi, G., Freeman, C., Nelson, R., Silverberg, G. and Soete, L. (eds) (1988) *Technical Change and Economic Theory*, London: Pinter.
Dunning, J. H. (1958) *American Investment in British Manufacturing Industry*, London: George Allen & Unwin, reprinted by Arno Press, New York.
——(1961) 'British investment in US industry', *Moorgate & Wall Street* Autumn: 5–23.
——(1970) *Studies in International Investment*, London: Allen & Unwin.
——(1971) *The Multinational Enterprise*, London: Allen & Unwin.
——(1972) *Readings in International Investment*, Harmondworth: Penguin Modern Economics Series.
——(1974) *Economic Analysis and the Multinational Enterprise*, London: Allen & Unwin.
——(1980) 'Toward an eclectic theory of international production: some empirical tests', *Journal of International Business Studies* 11(1), Spring/Summer: 9–31.
——(1981a) *International Production and the Multinational Enterprise*, London: Allen & Unwin.
——(1981b) 'Explaining the international direct investment position of countries: towards a dynamic or developmental approach', *Weltwirtschaftliches Archiv* 117: 30–64.
——(ed.) (1985) *Multinational Enterprises, Economic Structure and International Competitiveness*, Chichester and New York: John Wiley.
——(1986a) *Japanese Participation in British Industry*, London: Croom Helm.
——(1986b) *Decision-making Structure in US and Japanese Manufacturing Affiliates in the UK: Some Similarities and Contrasts*, Geneva: ILO, Working Paper No. 41.
——(1988a) *Explaining International Production*, London and Boston: Unwin Hyman.
——(1988b) *Multinationals, Technology and Competitiveness*, London: Unwin Hyman.
——(1993a) *Multinational Enterprises and the Global Economy*, Wokingham: Addison Wesley.
——(1993b) *Globalization of Business: The Challenge of the 1990s*, London and New York: Routledge.

——(1996) 'Explaining foreign direct investment in Japan: some theoretical insights', in M. Yoshitomi and E. Graham (eds) *Foreign Direct Investment in Japan*, pp. 8–63, London: Edward Elgar.

Dunning, J. H. and Cantwell, J. A. (1992) 'Japanese direct investment in Europe', in B. Burgenmeier and J. L. Mucchielli (eds) *Multinationals and Europe*, pp. 155–84, London and New York: Routledge.

Dunning, J. H. and Narula, R. (eds) (1996) *Foreign Direct Investment and Governments*, London and New York: Routledge.

Dunning, J. H. and Rowan, D. C. (1965) 'British direct investment in Europe', *Banco Nationale del Lavoro Quarterly Review* June: 3–32.

Eden, L. and Hampson, F.O. (1990) *Clubs are Trumps; Towards a Taxonomy of International Regimes*, Ottawa Center for International Trade and Investment Policies, Carleton University, C/TQS, 90–102.

Gamble, A. (1987) *The Free Market and the Strong State*, London and Basingstoke: Macmillan.

Gerlach, M. L. (1992) *Alliance Capitalism: The Social Organization of Japanese Business*, Oxford: Oxford University Press.

Gittleman, M. and Dunning, J. H. (1992) 'Japanese multinationals in Europe and the United States: some comparisons and contrasts', in M. W. Klein and P. J. J. Welfens (eds) *Multinationals in the New Europe and Global Trade*, pp. 237–64, Berlin and New York: Springer-Verlag.

Goldsmith, J. (1994) *The Trap*, London: Macmillan.

Handy, C. (1995) *The Empty Raincoat*, London: Arrow Business Books.

Harrison, B. (1994) *Lean and Mean*, New York: Basic Books.

Helpman, E. and Krugman, P. R. (1985) *Market Structure and Foreign Trade*, Cambridge, MA: MIT Press.

Hirschman, A. O. (1970) *Exit Voice and Loyalty*, Cambridge, MA: Harvard University Press.

Hobsbawn, E. (1994) *The Age of Extremes*, London: Abacus.

Hufbauer, G. C. and Adler, M. (1968) *U.S. Manufacturing Investment and the Balance of Payments*, Washington, DC: Treasury Department, Tax Policy Research Study No. 1.

Hufbauer, G. C. and Stephenson, S. (1995) 'Competitive advantages in the world economy', in H. Siebert (ed.) *Locational Competition in the World Economy*, pp. 45–63, Tubingen: Mohr.

Hymer, S. (1960) 'The International Operations of National Firms: A Study of Direct Investment', *PhD thesis*, MIT. Published by MIT Press (also published under same title in 1976).

Kindleberger, C. P. (1969) *American Business Abroad*, New Haven, CT: Yale University Press.

Kojima, K. (1978) *Direct Foreign Investment: A Japanese Model of Multinational Business Operations*, London: Croom Helm.

——(1990) *Japanese Direct Investment Abroad*, Tokyo: International Christian University, Social Science Research Institute, Monograph Series 1.

Krugman, P. (1991) *Geography and Trade*, Leuven: Leuven University Press, and Cambridge, MA: MIT Press.

Lall, S. (1996) 'Conclusions', in J. H. Dunning and R. Narula (eds) *Foreign Direct Investment and Governments*, London and New York: Routledge.

Lewis, C. (1938) *America's Stake in International Investment*, Washington, DC: Brookings Institution.

Lipsey, R. G. (1997) 'Technology, market failure and governments: an economist's perspective', in J. H. Dunning (ed.) *Governments, Globalization and International Business*, Oxford: Oxford University Press.

Lorenzoni, G. and Baden Fuller, C. (1995) 'Creating a strategic center to manage a web of partners', *California Management Review* 37(3): 146–63.
Markusen, A. R. (1994) 'Studying regions by studying firms', *Professional Geographer* 46: 477–90.
Markusen, J.R. (1995) 'The boundaries of multinational enterprises and the theory of international trade', *Journal of Economic Perspectives* 9(2): 169–89.
Markusen, J. R. and Venables, A. (1995) *Multinational Firms and the New Trade Theory*, Cambridge: NBER Working Paper No. 5036, February.
Marshall, A. (1920) *Principles of Economics* 8th Edition, London: Macmillan.
Mason, R. H. (1980) 'A comment on Professor Kojima's Japanese type versus American type of technology transfer', *Hitosubashi Journal of Economics* 20: 42–52.
Nelson, R. R. and Winter, S. G. (1982) *An Evolutionary Theory of Economic Change*, Cambridge, MA: Harvard University Press.
OECD (1994) *The Performance of Foreign Affiliates in the OECD Countries*, Paris: OECD.
Ozawa, T. (1992) 'Foreign direct investment and economic development', Transactional Corporation 1(1): 27–55.
——(1996) 'Japan: a flying-geese formation as a competitiveness strategy and the Japanese disease', in J. H. Dunning (ed.) *Governments, Globalization and International Business*, Oxford: Oxford University Press.
Penrose, E. T. (1959) *The Theory of the Growth of the Firm*, Oxford: Basil Blackwell.
Porter, M. E. (1990) *The Competitive Advantage of Nations*, New York: The Free Press.
Reddaway, N. B., Potter, S. T. and Taylor, C. T. (1968) *The Effects of UK Direct Investment Overseas*, Cambridge, MA: Cambridge University Press.
Rugman, A. M. (ed.) (1993) *Management International Review* Spring, 33: (2) (special edition on Michael Porter's *Diamond of Competitive Advantage*).
Rugman, A. M. and D'Cruz, J. R. (1995) *The Five Partners Business Model*, Toronto: University of Toronto (mimeo).
Saxenian, A. L. (1994) *Regional advantage: Culture and Competition in Silicon Valley and Route 128*, Cambridge, MA: Harvard University Press.
Scott, A. J. (1994) 'The geographic foundations of industrial performance', University of California, Los Angeles (mimeo).
Servan-Schreiber, J. J. (1968) *The American Challenge*, London: Hamish Hamilton.
Storper, M. and Harrison, B. (1991) 'Flexibility, hierarchy and regional development: the changing structure of industrial production systems and their forms of governance in the 1990s', *Research Policy* 20: 207–422.
Storper, M. and Scott, A. J. (1995) 'The wealth of regions', *Futures* 27: 505–26.
Sydow, J. (1992) 'Enterprise networks and co-determination: the case of the Federal Republic of Germany', in ILO (ed.) *Is the Single Firm Vanishing? Inter-enterprise Networks, Labour and Labour Institutions*, Geneva: ILO.
Toyne, B. and Nigh, D. (eds) (1996) *International Business: An Emerging Vision*, Columbia, SC: USC Press.
United Nations (1973) *Multinational Corporations and World Development*, New York: Department of Economic and Social Affairs.
——(1974) *The Impact of Multinational Corporations on Development and International Relations*, New York: Department of Economic and Social Affairs.

UNCTAD (1993) *World Investment Report 1993, Transnational Corporations and Integrated International Production*, New York and Geneva: UN.

——(1994) *World Investment Report 1994: Transnational Corporations, Employment and the Workplace*, New York and Geneva: UN.

——(1995) *World Investment Report, Transnational Corporations and Competitiveness*, New York and Geneva: UN.

UNCTC (1991) *World Investment Report 1991: The Triad in Foreign Direct Investment*, New York: UN.

Whittaker, E. and Bower, D. J. (1994) 'A shift to external alliances for product development in the pharmaceutical industry', *R&D Management* 24(3): 249–60.

Part I

ALLIANCE CAPITALISM

2

THE ADVENT OF ALLIANCE CAPITALISM

GLOBALIZATION, ITS MEANING AND THE REASONS FOR IT

In many respects, the globalizing economy of the 1990s is the latest stage in the enlargement of the spatial dimension of economic activity which dates back to pre-industrial times. Essentially, its speed and direction has been conditioned by advances in transport and communications technologies, and by the actions of governments in affecting the creation, management and disposition of physical and human assets. Yet, it is only in our lifetime that the role of trade, foreign direct investment and cross-border strategic alliances has become such a critical determinant of economic progress. And, it has only been in the last twenty years that the world economy has become so structurally interdependent that the use of the world *global*, as distinct from *international*, has become justifiable.

There have already been a plethora of books, articles and newspaper stories written on the nature and extent of globalization. In the last year or so, three volumes with the intriguing titles *Global Embrace*, *Global Dream* and *Global Paradox* have seen the light of day.[1] However, of the various definitions of globalization, my preference is for the one given by Anthony McGrew, who in a jointly edited book *Globalization and the Nation State*, published in 1992 (McGrew 1992), writes:

> Globalization refers to the multiplicity of linkages and interconnections between the states and societies which make up the present world system. It describes the process by which events, decisions, and activities in one part of the world come to have significant consequences for individuals and communities in quite distant parts of the globe. Globalization has two distinct phenomena: scope (or stretching) and intensity (or deepening). On the one hand, it defines a set of processes which embrace most of the globe or which operate worldwide; the concept therefore has a spatial connotation.... On the other hand it also implies an intensification of the levels of interaction, interconnectedness or *interdependence* between the states and societies which constitute the world community. Accordingly, alongside the stretching goes a deepening of global processes.
>
> (p. 23)

In short, then, economic globalization is a process towards the widening of the extent and form of cross-border transactions, and of the deepening of the economic interdependence between the actions of globalizing entities – be they private or public institutions or governments – located in one country and those of related or independent entities located in other countries.

The *shallowest* form of globalization – if that is not a misnomer for the term – is where an economic entity in one country engages in arm's length trade in a single product with another economic entity in one other country. The *deepest* form of globalization – and it is here we can most easily distinguish globalization from other forms of internationalization – is where an economic entity transacts with a large number of other economic entities throughout the world; where it does so across a network of value-added chains; where these exchanges are highly co-ordinated to serve the world-wide interests of the globalizing entity; and where they consist of a myriad of different kinds or forms of transactions.

Thus, a typical global *firm* will own or control subsidiaries, and engage in value-added business alliances and networks in each continent and in each major country. It will source its inputs of labour, capital, raw materials and intermediate products from wherever it is best to do so; it will engage in financial transactions independent of time and space; and it will sell its goods and services in each of the main markets of the world. Similarly a *country* which is fully open to the forces of globalization is likely to be geographically diversified in its financial, trading and investment relationships, and the value added associated with these relationships should constitute a significant part of its gross national product (GNP).

In practice, few firms – or for that matter – countries engage in either the *shallowest* or *deepest* forms of globalization. More important than situating entities on this continuum, however, is the almost universal trend by both firms and countries towards a more integrated cross-border organization of economic activity. As a consequence, the structure of the world economy is very different today than it was even a generation ago. We would, in particular, emphasize three features. First, the significance (and scope) of all kinds of cross-border transactions has greatly increased. For example, as a proportion of world GNP, such transactions have more than doubled since 1970. Second, the value of the foreign production of firms, that is, production financed by foreign direct investment (FDI), and that arising from cross-border strategic alliances – both of which are deeper forms of internationalization than that of arm's length trade – now considerably exceeds that of trade. And third, there are a variety of signs that the major institutional players are changing their ways of thinking and modes of operation, and are adopting a more systemic approach to their behaviour and activities.

It is, of course, the case that the pace and pattern of globalization has been very uneven among firms, sectors and countries. Moreover, while some markets, for example financial markets, are largely globalized, others, for example those for technology and most kinds of labour, still remain national or regional. Since many of the features of globalization just described are principally applicable to members of the Triad nations, some scholars have argued that the term regionalization better describes the current stage of development. This may well be so; certainly, intraregional production and transactions of all kinds in Europe, America and Asia have risen faster than interregional transactions. It is also true that certain parts of the world, notably sub-Saharan Africa, have been relatively unaffected. But, like ripples in a pond, regionalization may spread outwards, initially to the immediate hinterland of the developed countries, but then further as this hinterland generates its own momentum of growth. Neither should one overlook the surge of autonomous development within certain parts of the developing world – particularly in much of East Asia and parts of Latin America. Indeed, with growth rates in the advanced countries slipping, international transactions involving developing countries have risen faster in the last three years than those internal to the Triad countries.

The main causes of globalization are well known. We shall focus on just two. The first is the pressure on business enterprises – by consumers and competitors alike – continually to innovate new products and to upgrade the quality of existing goods and services. At the same time, the escalating costs of research and development (R&D), coupled with ever truncated product life cycles, are compelling corporations both to downsize the scope of their value-added activities, and to search for wider markets. Moreover, in order to exploit effectively and speedily their core competencies, firms are increasingly finding that they need to combine these competencies with those of other firms.

The second cause of globalization – which, in many respects is better described as a removal of an obstacle – is the renaissance of market-oriented policies pursued by national governments and regional authorities. In the last five years alone, more than thirty countries have abandoned central planning as the main mode of allocating scarce resources, while over eighty countries have liberalized their inward FDI policies. The privatization of state-owned enterprises, the liberalization and deregulation of markets – especially for services – and the removal of a bevy of structural distortions, have all worked to stimulate cross-border corporate integration, both within TNCs and between independent firms, or groups of firms.

Underlying and reinforcing these two explanations for globalization and fashioning its character, have been changes in the organization of economic activity. At a *micro* level, the changes are best exemplified by the introduction of a more flexible approach to production, together with a growing appreciation by firms of the need to form close and ongoing relationships with other firms to capture fully the benefits of their own competencies. At a *macro* level, they reflect the changing costs and benefits of alternative systems for allocating scarce resources, and the demands being made by globalization on national governments and supranational regimes. At an *international* level, and of particular relevance to developing countries, has been the replacement of non-conditional sources of finance by more fragile and 'quicksilver' sources of funding, for example portfolio investment. Together with the increasing participation of developing countries in regional integration schemes and the restructuring of the global financial system, this is making for a convergence of macro-economic and macro-organizational policies among national governments.

Since we are in the midst of these techno-economic and socio-institutional changes, it is premature to judge either their extent or their consequences for the world economy. But the clues we have been able so far to discern point to a very different path of economic development than the one we have lived through over the past twenty or thirty years.

With respect to the micro-organization of business activity, there are several forces at work which are leading firms to reappraise the benefits of the Fordist or mass production system, which has been the hallmark of hierarchical capitalism for most of the twentieth century (Ruigrok and Van Tulder 1995). First, improved living standards – particularly in the Triad nations – have caused consumers to reorient their spending habits. There is a greater expectancy of fault-free products, continuous product improvement, and new and innovative goods and services. At the same time, competitive pressures are demanding that firms re-examine their cost control procedures; this spans all areas of business, from inventories, to manning levels and to advertising budgets. Lean production has become the order of the day.

Second, the new technologies of the 1980s and 1990s, such as computer-aided design and manufacturing techniques, and the miniaturization of components, are not only enabling firms to exercise more rigorous quality control, but permitting them to make use of multi-purpose machinery and equipment.

Third, contemporary technological and organizational advances are demanding a much closer synthesis, and more interactive learning, between the innovatory and production functions of the firm. Indeed, in the words of two scholars (Kenney and Florida 1993: 303), 'the factory itself is becoming a research laboratory – a setting for both product and process innovation'. In this new environment, knowledge and intellectual labor are being mobilized on a collective basis, and the skills and ideas of shop-floor workers are being actively tapped to raise product quality and productivity. Such innovation-driven production both facilitates the functional integration of tasks and socializes the organization of production.

With respect to the macro level, two observations are in order. The first is that globalization is requiring national governments to reappraise their domestic macro-organizational policies, and, in doing so, to take a more systemic approach to the implementation of these policies. It is also demanding a reconsideration of the role of supranational regimes (e.g. WTO, IMF, OECD and the UN) as fashioners and sustainers of the ground rules for international transactions of one kind or another. The second is that, if individual nation states are to encompass fully the challenges of the global market-place, their governments need not only to appreciate the distinctive characteristics of the new international division of labour, but to take more constructive and co-ordinated action to help cross-border markets to work efficiently.

Neither of these propositions necessarily implies that there should be less government. Nor do they endorse the view that governments should intervene more in the decision-taking process of the wealth creators of society, namely business enterprises. But what they do mean is that governments should understand and accept that, as an organizational mechanism, markets are *not* a free good; they cost resources to set up, to operate and to maintain. They also mean that governments need to recognize that the efficiency of many markets – and particularly those supplying products for global customers – is not solely determined by the transactions of the buyers and sellers in those markets, but by a host of other factors, including the actions taken by other governments, over which they may have no immediate influence or control. They mean that national governments, like firms competing in the global market-place, need to re-examine their organizational structures and to concentrate on only those activities which they are comparatively best able to perform. And, they finally mean that, in times of disturbingly high structural unemployment, and as governments seek to attract the highest possible share of the world's 'quicksilver' resources of capital, technology and managerial skills to their territories, the role of supranational regimes may need to be re-examined if the playing field of the global competitive game is to be kept reasonably fair and level.

MODALITIES OF GLOBALIZATION

A distinctive feature of globalization is the impact on the modes of undertaking cross-border business activity. For most of modern industrial history, that is since around 1750, arm's length trade in goods, services and financial assets has been the main means of conducting international commerce. However, by 1914, FDI, which is the modality by which a package of resources and capabilities are transferred across national boundaries *within* the same firm, had already begun to assume some importance in linking national economies – particularly between the Metropolitan countries and their colonies, and between the North American and European economies. But it was not until after the Second World War that FDI really took off as a mechanism for delivering goods and services to foreign markets; and, it has only been since the 1980s that outbound activity by multinational enterprises (MNEs) has become a significant form of international economic activity by other than a handful of the advanced industrial economies. It has also only been during the last decade that the world – and particularly the industrialized world – has witnessed such an explosive growth in mergers and acquisitions (M&As) and co-operative cross-border arrangements (such as strategic alliances) between firms. Like FDI, such M&As and alliances are both a cause and a consequence of globalization.

Let us now present a few statistics which portray the growth of international transactions, and reveal that the modality of these transactions has moved from those making for *shallow* to those making for *deep* integration. First, we make reference to Table 2.1. The most noticeable feature of the contents of this table is that world trade, world investment and the number of non-equity technology transfers and/or cross-border associations have all increased at a faster rate than the world GNP since 1980.[2] A separate set of data, set out in Table 2.2, shows that, for the great majority of countries, the significance of both trade and FDI to their domestic economies has risen substantially over the last decade or more.

Next, let us consider the role of FDI and the role of MNEs in the globalizing economy. Some critical statistics of the level and geographical composition of outbound and inbound FDI stocks are set out in Tables 2.3 and 2.4. Table 2.5 makes some estimates of the role of US FDI as a means of servicing three leading industrial markets compared with that of exports and licensing; Table 2.6 presents some 'bullet' points about the main features of TNC activity; and Table 2.7 sets out the reasons for the fastest-growing form of FDI in the 1980s, by way of M&As.

In reviewing these data, we would like especially to emphasize seven points:

1 Inbound and outbound FDI stocks as a percentage of the GDP of virtually all countries have substantially increased over the last twenty-five years. Our own estimate for 1995 is that, for the world as a whole, this percentage was 9.7 per cent – and it is still rising. These data are, perhaps, the best indicator we have on the growth of deep cross-border economic integration.
2 Outbound FDI is still predominantly accounted for by the leading industrial countries, although such investment by some developing countries, noticeably Republic of Korea, Taiwan Province of China, is increasing quite rapidly.
3 The slowdown in FDI growth between 1990 and 1992 – and this has been largely reversed since then – was partly cyclical, and reflected the recession in the United States and Europe. It was also partly a reflection of a sharp cut-back in Japanese FDI, which, *inter alia*, was a reaction to the huge outflow of such FDI in the second part of the 1980s, and to a less dynamic domestic economy.

Table 2.1 Worldwide foreign direct investment and selected economic indicators, 1993, and growth rates for 1981–5, 1986–90 and 1991–3

Indicator	*Value at current prices, 1993 (billions of dollars)*	*Annual growth rate (%)*		
		1981–5[a]	*1986–90*[a]	*1991–3*[a]
FDI outflows	222	0.8	28.3	5.6
FDI outward stock	2,135	5.4	19.8	7.2
Sales of foreign affiliates of TNCs[b]	5,235[c]	1.3[d]	17.4	–2.6[c]
Current gross domestic product at factor cost	23,276	2.1	10.6	3.3
Gross domestic investment	5,351	0.7	9.9	3.2
Exports of goods and non-factor services	4,762	–0.1	14.3	3.5
Royalty and fees receipts	38	0.7	21.8	13
Strategic alliances[h] (number)	327[f]	258[g]	388[g]	297

Source: UNCTAD, Division on Transnational Corporations and Investment, based on International Monetary Fund, balance-of-payments tape, retrieved in June 1995; and unpublished data provided by the Organization for Economic Co-operation and Development Secretariat and the World Bank, International Economics Department

[a] Compounded growth rate estimates, based on a semi-logarithmic regression equation.

[b] Estimated by extrapolating the world-wide sales of foreign affiliates of TNCs from France, Germany, Italy, Japan and the United States on the basis of the relative importance of these countries in world-wide outward FDI stock. However, the data on sales of foreign affiliates for France are included only after 1988 because of unavailability of data prior to that. For Italy the sales data are available only for 1986, 1988, 1990 and 1992.

[c] 1992.

[d] 1982–5.

[e] 1991–2.

[f] Average per annum 1981–93.

[g] Average per annum.

[h] In high-technology sectors

Table 2.2 Two indicators of the extent to which a country is globally integrated (percentages)

	FDI to GDP ratio (stock) 1980 and 1993 Inward + outward Investment divided by GDP × 2				*Trade to GDP ratio 1980 and 1993 Exports + impo divided by GDP × 2*		
		1980	*1993*			*1980*	*1992*
1	Netherlands	18.3	35.8	1	Hong Kong	104.1	126.6
2	Belgium/Luxembourg	5.2	27.4	2	Singapore	206.9	123.4
3	Switzerland	18.1	27.1	3	Malaysia	44.9	62.7
4	Malaysia	13.5	24.4	4	Belgium/Luxembourg	58.0	54.1
5	United Kingdom	13.6	24.0	5	Ireland	55.2	50.4
6	Australia	4.9	20.1	6	Netherlands	42.8	44.9
7	Canada	14.4	17.9	7	Taiwan	n/a	35.3
8	Sweden	3.6	15.4	8	Thailand	23.5	29.7
9	Spain	2.8	13.7	9	Portugal	32.0	28.7
10	France	3.2	11.4	10	Hungary	n/a	28.6
11	Norway	1.2	11.4	11	Switzerland	32.5	27.3
12	Chile	1.7	10.6	12	Austria	27.3	26.6
13	Germany	5.5	9.1	13	Denmark	27.0	26.0
14	South Africa	13.4	8.3	14	Norway	30.9	24.9
15	Finland	1.2	8.2	15	Indonesia	23.4	24.2

Table 2.2 (cont)

	FDI to GDP ratio (stock) 1980 and 1993 Inward + outward Investment divided by GDP × 2				*Trade to GDP ratio 1980 and 1993 Exports + imports divided by GDP × 2*		
		1980	*1993*			*1980*	*1993*
16	United States	5.8	7.9	16	Chile	n.a.	24.0
17	Venezuela	1.3	7.4	17	Korea	34.2	23.9
18	Hungary	n/a	7.0	18	Canada	24.2	23.7
19	Italy	2.0	6.4	19	Germany	23.2	23.4
20	Thailand	1.5	5.9	20	New Zealand	23.3	22.9
21	Austria	2.6	4.8	21	Sweden	26.2	21.4
22	Japan	2.0	3.3	22	Venezuela	25.5	21.0
					Greece	22.0	21.0
				23	Finland	29.8	20.9
				24	United Kingdom	22.5	19.8
				25	France	18.9	17.8
				26	South Africa	30.1	17.6
				27	Pakistan	18.5	17.1
				28	Turkey	9.8	16.6
				29	Italy	22.5	15.0
				30	Australia	14.3	14.6
				31	Spain	13.8	14.3
				32	Mexico	10.4	11.5
				33	United States	9.1	8.3
				34	Japan	12.7	7.8

Sources: World Economic Forum and IMEDE (1993), World Bank (1994b) UNCTAD (1995).

Table 2.3 Stocks of outward foreign direct investment, by major home countries and regions, 1967–93 (billions of dollars)

Countries/regions	*1967*			*1973*			*1980*			*1993*		
	Value	*% of total*	*% of GDP*	*Value*	*% of total*	*% of GDP*	*Value*	*% of total*	*% of GDP*	*Value*	*% of total*	*% of GDP*
Developed market economies	**109.3**	**97.3**	**4.8**	**205.0**	**97.1**	**5.1**	**503.6**	**97.2**	**6.2**	**2,016.6**	**94.5**	**10.7**
United States	56.6	50.4	7.1	101.3	48.0	7.7	220.2	40.0	8.2	559.7	26.2	8.9
United Kingdom	15.8	14.1	14.5	27.5	13.0	9.1	79.2	14.8	15.2	253.2	11.9	26.9
Japan	1.5	1.3	0.9	10.3	4.9	2.5	19.6	6.6	3.4	259.8	12.2	6.2
Germany (FDR)	3.0	2.7	1.6	11.9	5.6	3.4	43.1	7.8	5.3	185.0	8.7	9.7
Switzerland	2.5	2.2	10.0	7.1	3.4	16.2	22.4	7.0	37.9	89.1	4.2	38.4
Netherlands	11.0	9.8	33.1	15.8	7.5	25.8	42.4	7.6	24.7	134.7	6.3	43.5
Canada	3.7	3.3	5.3	7.8	3.7	6.1	21.6	3.9	8.2	86.3	4.0	15.8
France	6.0	5.3	7.0	8.8	4.2	3.8	20.8	3.8	3.2	160.5	7.5	12.8
Italy	2.1	1.9	2.8	3.2	1.5	2.4	7.0	1.3	1.8	73.8	3.5	7.4
Sweden	1.7	1.5	5.7	3.0	1.4	6.1	7.2	1.3	5.8	44.6	2.1	24.0
Other[a]	5.4	4.8	0.8	20.0	9.5	1.7	15.4	3.2	1.9	169.9	8.0	8.8
Developing countries	**3.0**	**2.7**	**0.6**	**6.1**	**2.9**	**0.6**	**13.3**	**2.8**	**0.7**	**117.4**	**5.5**	**2.7**
Total	**112.3**	**100.0**	**4.0**	**211.1**	**100.0**	**4.2**	**516.9**	**100.0**	**4.9**	**2,134.6**	**100.0**	**9.0**

Sources: World Bank, *World Development Report*, various editions; UNCTAD, *World Investment Report*, various editions

a Australia, Austria, Belgium, Denmark, Finland, Greece, Ireland, New Zealand, Norway, Portugal, South Africa, Spain

Table 2.4 Stocks of inward foreign direct investment, by major host countries and regions, 1967–93 (billions of dollars)

Countries/regions	*1967*			*1973*			*1980*			*1993*		
	Value	*% of total*	*% of GDP*	*Value*	*% of total*	*% of GDP*	*Value*	*% of total*	*% of GDP*	*Value*	*% of total*	*% of GDP*
Developed Market Economies	**73.2**	**69.4**	3.2	**153.7**	**74.0**	**3.8**	**394.1**	**78.0**	**4.7**	**1,564.7**	**75.2**	**8.3**
Western Europe	31.4	29.8	4.2	79.9	38.4	5.6	211.6	42.0	4.8	883.5	42.5	12.2
United Kingdom	7.9	7.5	7.2	24.1	11.6	13.9	63.0	12.5	12.0	196.8	9.5	20.9
Germany	3.6	3.4	1.9	13.1	6.3	3.8	47.9	9.5	5.8	128.0	6.2	6.7
Switzerland	2.1	2.0	8.4	4.3	2.1	9.8	14.3	2.8	14.1	37.1	1.8	16.0
United States	9.9	9.3	1.2	20.6	9.9	1.6	83.0	16.4	3.2	445.3	21.4	7.1
Other[a]	31.9	30.2	4.2	53.2	25.6	4.2	99.5	19.7	6.5	251.9	12.1	4.7
Japan	0.6	0.6	0.3	1.6	0.8	0.4	3.3	0.7	0.2	16.9	0.8	0.4
Developing countries	**32.2**	30.6	**6.4**	**54.4**	**26.1**	**5.4**	**111.2**	22.0	**5.4**	**500.9**	**24.1**	**11.6**
Africa	5.6	5.3	9.0	10.2	4.9	8.7	13.1	2.6	4.1	50.2	2.4	14.5
Asia	8.3	7.8	3.9	15.3	7.4	3.6	35.8	7.1	5.0	279	13.4	11.0
Latin America and the Caribbean	18.5	17.5	15.8	28.9	13.9	12.3	62.3	12.3	8.4	167.6	8.1	12.2
Total	**105.5**	100.0	**3.8**	**208.1**	100.0	**4.1**	**505.3**	100.0	4.7	**2,079.5**	100.0	8.7

Source: As for Table 2.3
[a] Australia, Canada, Japan, New Zealand, South Africa, Algeria, Egypt, Tunisia, Morocco

4 For the reasons set out in Table 2.7, M&As were a major form of FDI in the 1980s, but less so in the early 1990s; 1994 and 1995 however, saw some resurgence in M&A activity.
5 FDI is strongly concentrated in technology-intensive, knowledge-intensive and growth-oriented manufacturing and service sectors. Much of the FDI by developing countries in other developing countries, however, is to seek out low-cost labour and natural resources.
6 There has been a marked increase in FDI activity in developing countries since 1990. Partly this reflects the robustness and renaissance of market-oriented policies of many developing countries, for example China and India, and partly the faster rate of growth of the leading inward investors (cf. that of the rest of the world). Of the FDI flows directed to developing countries, in the first half of the 1990s, China accounted for 28.2 per cent, the rest of South, East and South East Asia for 34.5 per cent[3] and Latin America and the Caribbean for 28.1 per cent.

Table 2.5 Alternative modalities of servicing Japanese, UK and German markets by US firms

	Japan			
	Affiliate sales	*Exports*	*Licensed sales*	*Total*
All industries (US$ billion)	49.7	42.8	20.9	113.4
(Per capita) (US$)	403.7	347.7	169.8	921.2
(% of total)	43.8	37.7	18.4	100.0
	UK			
	Affiliate sales	*Exports*	*Licensed sales*	*Total*
All industries (US$ billion)	125.3	20.8	3.2	149.3
(Per capita) (US$)	2,190.5	363.6	55.9	2,610.0
(% of total)	83.9	13.9	2.1	100.0
	Germany			
	Affiliate sales	*Exports*	*Licensed sales*	*Total*
All industries (US$ billion)	71.7	16.8	2.7	91.2
(Per capita) (US$)	1,156.5	271.0	43.5	1,471.0
(% of total)	78.6	18.4	3.0	100.0

Source: US Department of Commerce (1992a, b, 1993a, b), Weinberg (1993)
Notes: Affiliate sales represent sales of US manufacturing affiliates (excluding exports) in the three countries
Exports represent all exports to the three countries by all US firms (NB part of these may be included in affiliate sales)
Licensed sales represent royalties and fees paid by unaffiliated Japanese, UK or German firms to US firms multiplied by 20 (it being assumed that royalties and fees were calculated as 5% of gross sales)

Table 2.6 Multinational enterprises and the global economy, some facts 1993–4

- There were 38,000 Multinational enterprises (*MNEs*) (3,800 from developing countries) with more than 250,000 affiliates (101,000 in developing countries)
- FDI stock at the end of 1994 was $2.4 trillion. Of this amount, 66% was accounted for by France, Germany, Japan, the United Kingdom and the United States. Developing countries accounted for about 6.0% of the world-wide FDI
- The sales of foreign affiliates of MNEs in 1993 were estimated to be $5.2 trillion (compared with $4.8 trillion of world exports). The slowdown in outbound direct investment since 1990 has been mainly concentrated in the Triad countries and is primarily the result of the falling profits earned on past FDI, and the 'bursting of the Japanese bubble' of outbound FDI. In 1993 and 1994 there was, however, some recovery in FDI outflows from Japan
- China was the leading developing country recipient of FDI flows between 1991 and 1994. Asia received 60% of the total flows to developing countries and Latin America 30%
- The largest 1% of MNEs accounted for one-half of stock of FDI in 1993
- World-wide cross-border acquisitions accounted for 65% of FDI outflows between 1986 and 1990, for 35% in 1991 and for 55% in 1992 and 1993
- Of all FDI stock in 1993 75–80% was in sectors requiring above-average human skill, capital or technology intensity
- Of the FDI stock in 1993 55–60% was in the tertiary (service) sector compared with 40% a decade earlier. One of the major features of globalization is the growing tradeability of services (e.g. financial services). Frequently such services are owned by, or within the control of, MNEs
- FDI and strategic alliances are growing faster than other forms of international transactions
- Some four-fifths of the stock of inward investment at the end of 1993 was in developed countries, though between 1991 and 1993, developing countries accounted for nearly 30% of all new FDI. Provisional figures for 1994 suggest the figure could be as high as 40% and in low-wage sectors around two-thirds. (Central and Eastern Europe accounted for 3–4% of world-wide inflows of FDI between 1992 and 1994)
- Over the period 1989–93, FDI from privatization schemes amounted to over $7.5 billion, or 60% of the total FDI inflows to Central and Eastern Europe and $12.2 billion, or 8% of the total FDI inflows into developing countries

Source: Data derived from UNCTAD (1994, 1995)

7 The significance of both outbound and inbound FDI in the globalizing economy varies considerably between countries. Table 2.5, for example, shows that in 1989, the affiliates of US firms in Japan accounted for only 43.8 per cent of the foreign-related sales in Japan, compared with 83.9 per cent in the UK and 78.6 per cent in Germany.

Two other characteristics of the FDI of the last decade which are not demonstrated in the statistics just presented also need emphasizing. These are:

8 The orientation of the motivation for MNE activity has changed from that of seeking *markets* and *natural resources* to exploit better the existing

Table 2.7 The international business environment and mergers and acquisitions in the 1980s

Forces driving mergers and acquisitions	*Application to cross-border mergers and acquisitions*
Growing competition, globalization and favourable government policies	To achieve internationalization and geographical market diversification and to increase market share rapidly, firms prefer to engage in mergers and acquisitions as opposed to greenfield investment as a faster way to do so. Merger-friendly government policies encouraged the wave of mergers and acquisitions of the 1980s
Higher efficiency in the face of growing competition and globalization	To achieve scale economies and synergies in value-adding activities, firms build integrated international production networks aimed at improving efficiency of the firm as a whole. Mergers and acquisitions allow the speedy establishment of such networks
Access to technology and reduced costs of research and development	To gain access to new technology, share the risks and costs associated with technology development and reduce the time needed for product innovation, TNCs may acquire firms engaged in research and development or merge with such firms to access their technological capabilities and resources
Response to the Single Market programme of the European Community	The Single Market programme created competitive pressures, as well as opportunities for European Community and third-country firms for mergers and acquisitions aimed at rationalizing production and distribution of goods and services within the European Community and increasing market share
Availability of low-cost financing options available after the financial liberalization of the 1980s in many developed countries	To take advantage of the substantial growth in the availability of credit, innovations in corporate finance and the valuation of many companies below break-up values
New investment opportunities in developed countries during the boom period in the second half of the 1980s	To take advantage of favourable investment opportunities created by economic growth to expand into new markets or activities. Periods of economic growth are also associated with a greater availability of investible funds from corporate profits or loans to finance mergers and acquisitions

Source: UNCTAD (1994)

competitive advantages of the investing companies, to that of acquiring *created assets* perceived necessary to *sustain and augment existing competitive advantages.*

9 Firms, particularly MNEs, are becoming more pluralistic in their modes of capturing the benefits of globalization, and the way firms co-ordinate (i.e. integrate) their transborder activities is an amalgam of hierarchical and co-operative capitalism.

These two latter features of contemporary business activity, as well as those already identified – and especially the growth of strategic alliances – suggest that the role of FDI in the international market economy is in the process of important change. For most of the period of modern capitalism – whether FDI has been undertaken to obtain natural resources and labour, to secure or protect markets, or to promote a more cost-effective distribution of its foreign activities – the main *raison d'être* of FDI has been to exploit the core competencies of the investing corporations, and to do so by internalizing cross-border intermediate product markets. Spurred by local market opportunities, much of US direct investment in Europe in the 1960s and 1970s, and most of Japanese investment in Asia, Europe and the United States in the early 1980s, was of this kind. For the most part, too, this FDI was of a 'stand-alone' or discrete character, in the sense that its success was judged mainly by the ability of the investing companies to exploit their home-based competitive advantages and to co-ordinate related intrafirm (hierarchical) value activities across national boundaries.

Since around the mid-1980s, however, the same features which have fostered globalization – and of these, technological advances and the renaissance of the market system are, perhaps, the two most important – have also impacted on both the motives for FDI and on its role in the strategy of firms. Increasingly – and as reflected especially by the dramatic increases in intra-Triad M&As – firms have expanded their territorial horizons, not so much to exploit existing competitive advantages, but to protect or enhance these advantages and their global market positions by acquiring, or gaining access to, new resources and capabilities. In the late 1980s, there was hardly a day when the financial press did not report a new takeover of a US firm by a European firm, or vice versa, which was usually justified by the acquiring firm in terms of 'the need to strengthen our technological or product base *vis-à-vis* our global competitors'; or, 'to rationalize our cross-border production capabilities or to capture new scale or synergistic economies'; or, 'to better access unfamiliar markets and distribution networks'.

The critical feature of *strategic asset-seeking* FDI[4] is that the acquiring firm in a takeover, or both partners in the case of a merger, accept(s) that its (or their) internal, or stand-alone, resources and capabilities are insufficient to sustain its (or their) international competitiveness, and that it (or they) need(s) to draw upon resources and capabilities of *other* firms to achieve this goal. This is one of the characteristics of the emerging 'collective', 'relational' or 'alliance' capitalism of the 1990s. And, although, by internalizing the markets for these resources and capabilities, it would appear that global hierarchies are being strengthened, this is not always the case. This is because asset-acquiring investment is frequently accompanied by asset shedding as firms have sought to specialize in those activities which (they perceive) will best protect or advance their core competencies. Strategic asset-acquiring investment is, then, best regarded as an integral part of a restructuring of the resources and capabilities of firms, and as a response to globalization.

At the same time, it is becoming increasingly evident that FDI, while a necessary condition, is not always a sufficient condition for a successful global strategy. Indeed, FDI is not always the most efficient means of accessing foreign assets. Often, a firm does not want to acquire *all* the assets of a foreign firm, but only those which directly advance its competitive position. In such cases, the conclusion of interfirm alliances to achieve a specific objective may be preferable to FDI. These alliances may serve as alternatives to vertical integration, and sometimes to horizontal or lateral diversification.

Moreover, the aforementioned shedding of value-adding activities does not mean that firms now rely more on arm's length markets for the intermediate products they buy or sell. More often than not, the market imperfections which promoted the internalization in the first place still remain; indeed, the strategic need to maintain an influence over the quality and supply of inputs, or the processing of downstream activities, and the pace and direction of innovation in times of competitive pressures, is even greater (Quinn and Hilmer 1994). So, in addition to FDI, firms have been engaging in a myriad of bilateral or multilateral co-operative arrangements, in order to capture the economic benefits which a 'stand-alone' strategy cannot achieve.

In practice, it is extremely difficult to assess the role of strategic alliances as part of the internationalization process of firms – or, indeed, to value their outcome from the perspective either of the participants or of the countries involved. Yet, it is important that policy makers seeking to attract FDI (e.g. to upgrade the competitiveness of indigenous resources, or to assist their own firms in capturing global markets) should recognize that, in some cases, the objectives may just as well be reached by the formation of cross-border alliances. Indeed, research suggests that those countries whose governments have striven to provide the right environment for alliance formation (e.g. Japan, Republic of Korea and Taiwan Province of China) are often also those which do best in the global economy.

While there are many reasons why firms conclude alliances with other firms – and some of these are set out in Table 2.8 – the great majority of those concluded over the past decade have been for four main reasons. These are:

1. To acquire new product or process technologies and organizational competencies – and especially those perceived necessary to advance the core competence of the acquiring firm.
2. To spread the risk of high capital outlays, or reduce the time of product development.
3. To capture the economies of synergy or scale.
4. To gain access to new markets or distribution channels.

It should be observed that each of these motives runs parallel to strategic asset-acquiring FDI (see Table 2.7).

As might be supposed, cross-border alliances – like FDI – are concentrated in particular industrial sectors, and, in the main, these are similar to those in which FDI is concentrated (i.e. the dynamic technology- and information-intensive product and service sectors).

Of course, cross-border strategic alliances are not the only form of co-operative arrangements. These range from very specific technical service and subcontracting agreements, to less formal – but no less binding – modes of interfirm co-operation found in business or industrial districts, and also to *keiretsu*-type relationships. But, although the type of arrangements vary, all represent a kind of quasi-internalization of cross-border assets and should be considered as integral parts of the total portfolio of the firm's assets.

The evidence, then, suggests that asset-acquiring FDI and co-operative arrangements are critical features of the contemporary global economy and of alliance capitalism; and that, while the first is primarily a response by Western nations to the demands of the global market-place, the second is primarily a response by Eastern nations. But there is plenty of casual evidence to suggest that both forms of corporate restructuring are now spreading throughout the industrialized world – and throughout parts of the industrializing world as well.[5]

THE CONSEQUENCES OF GLOBALIZATION

We now turn to consider some of the likely consequences of globalization for economic development. In doing so, we shall argue that just as globalization is qualitatively different from previous stages of internationalization, so its effects on development are distinctive.

So far in this chapter, we have painted an optimistic view of globalization, and it is true that the structural transformation of the world now occurring does hold out great promise for the future. It is also the case that the political changes and technological advances of the last decade have provided a stronger basis for economic growth than at any other time since the mid-1940s. The world has the necessary resources, knowledge and experience. It has the technical means by which these assets can be transmitted

Table 2.8 Some reasons for firms to conclude cross-border strategic business alliances (NB these may be aggressive or defensive, they may be market facilitating or collusory, they may be between firms along a value chain or between value chains)

- To capture economies of synergy (e.g. by pooling of resources and capabilities, and by rationalization of production)
- To lower capital investment, to disperse or reduce fixed costs, to exploit scale and/or scope economies better, to lower unit costs by using comparative production advantages of each partner
- As a consequence of the convergence of technologies and interdependencies among innovation processes, to spread R&D costs, to gain speedy access to new technologies
- As a response by firms to growing competition, a shorter product cycle and a faster rate of technological obsolescence
- To obtain reciprocal benefits from the combined use of complementary assets, to exchange patents and territories
- To overcome government-mandated trade or investment barriers
- As a means of promoting joint R&D and design efforts with suppliers and/or customers
- To assist the entry process of small firms into high-risk entrepreneurial ventures, especially in emerging technology sectors
- To gain new knowledge about, or achieve quicker access to, markets and/or to spread marketing and distribution costs, to widen market sources
- To pre-empt or neutralize the strategy of competitors, or to advance monopoly power, as a defensive strategy to reduce competition
- To better secure contracts from foreign governments who favour local firms, to deal with local suppliers and/or labour unions better
- As an initial entry strategy in unfamiliar markets
- To reduce cross-border political risks

Source: Dunning (1993b: 250)

between countries. It has the economic systems, policies, institutions and structures capable of translating human and physical resources into the goods and services which people want. Moreover, at first sight, the 'organ-centric' production system, with its focus on smaller production runs, multi-purpose machinery, economies of scope, and relational networking, its renewed reliance on the 'putting out' of some value activities, and its greater respect for the individual in the workplace, appears to be particularly well suited to the needs and capabilities of developing countries, and to the linking of these with those of the flagship nations in the global economy.

Already, we see signs of the fruits of alliance capitalism in East Asia, where much of the expansion of cross-border activity has taken the form of networking by small and medium-sized firms. We also see a much greater willingness of the newly emerging TNCs from China, Republic of Korea, Mexico and Thailand to collaborate with local firms, than was earlier demonstrated by their US and European counterparts. To my mind, one of the great promises for development which ranks at least as highly as regional integration and intra-Southern Hemisphere trade and investment is the emergence of a new brand of capitalism, which blends the richness of the Confucian ethos of co-operation with that of the staunch individualistic culture of the West.

Unfortunately, however, there are downsides to globalization. There is, in John Naisbitt's words, 'a global paradox' (Naisbitt 1994).[6] The most immediate and visible consequences of the downside – which all countries of the world are currently experiencing – is the increase in structural unemployment brought about by competitive pressures, the implementation of new technologies and the introduction of more market-oriented systems of governance. Across the globe, for developed and developing countries alike, change is bringing economic hardship. It is transforming the lifestyles of people, and their expectancies of the future. Nowhere is this more clearly observed than in China and in Central and Eastern Europe, and in the dynamic, but internationally mobile, sectors of economic activity.

It has long been recognized that the invisible hand of the market is only acceptable if there is some way that the losers from market forces are compensated by the winners; this primarily means helping the losers to adjust to political and technological change. And, as we see it, the possible Achilles heel of globalization and alliance capitalism is that they could so easily become dysfunctional if they cannot accommodate the desires of ordinary men and women looking for and willing to work, and if they fail to equip individuals with the skills and talents necessary for the kind of jobs which are now being created.

This, indeed, is one of the most daunting challenges of the 1990s. For there can surely be little doubt that long-term unemployment is one of the most socially divisive and destabilizing forces of modern times. While an innovation-led, as opposed to a Fordist, production system offers more purposeful, responsible and rewarding job opportunities for those in work, it does not help reduce unemployment, at least not in the short run. This is because the new system requires a different mix of labour skills than the one it is replacing, and to match these needs, not only do labour markets need to be more flexible, but quite huge adjustment assistance and retraining programmes are needed.

More generally, if global economic interdependence offers the prospects of higher productivity and living standards, it also more closely links national economies to exogenous financial and other disturbances. The world economy of the 1990s is intrinsically more fragile and turbulent than that of thirty, forty or fifty years ago. No longer is it just the case that if the United States sneezes, the world catches a cold. Economic shocks originating in any one of the five or six leading economies are now electronically and instantaneously transmitted across the globe, with possibly devastating affects on nations which may have had nothing to do with the causes of the shocks. Even being part of a micro-network of value-adding activities can bring external costs, as well as external benefits, to the participating firms. This is why a more systemic approach to the management of macro-economic affairs, and a more educated understanding of the spatial implications of economic turbulences, needs to be high on the political agenda of national and regional governments in the next ten years.

We would make two further points. The first is that while the forces of globalization are leading to a convergence of the spending habits of the world's consumers, they are also exposing substantial differences in the way people think and behave. Indeed, not all countries welcome the effects of globalization, as they fear it may erode their traditional lifestyles. As we have observed, this leads to a global dilemma. On the one hand the universality of such goods as the motor car, the television set, hamburgers and jeans, and such services as tourism, sport and pop music, is leading to cultural convergence. On the other hand, most people want to remain loyal to their distinctive customs and institutions. The task of peacefully resolving this dilemma is, indeed, likely to tax the minds of both scholars and politicians well into the next century. How, for example, does one balance the advantages of sovereignty with those of interdependence, of homogeneity with diversity, of centralization with decentralization, of community with individualism and so on? There is, of course, nothing new in these perplexities, but globalization has put them in a new and starker perspective, and has given their resolution a new urgency.

There seems little doubt that the end of the cold war, and the growing pressures towards economic 'at-one-ness', are refocusing the attention of people towards cultural, ideological and religious issues, over which most of the wars in history have been fought. We also sense that the battle lines are being drawn not primarily between the haves and have-nots, but between groups of nations with different ways of looking at the world. The picture painted by Samuel Huntington (1993) on the future relationships between the major civilizations of the world is not an optimistic one. Our own feeling is that there is more in common among the ideologies and religions of these civilizations – at least what they preach about attitudes and conduct – than there are differences, and that a focus on these similarities, rather than on the differences, offers the best hope for global peace.

We have already referred to the dominant organizational system now evolving as that of alliance capitalism. This is because the unit of economic activity – the individual firm – in order to promote fully its own objectives, needs increasingly to be part of – that is, allied to – a network or web of related activities. We believe that this concept can be extended to a global level. From the time of the Roman Empire and beyond, history is littered with the debris of once all-powerful nations. For much of the nineteenth century, the United Kingdom really did rule the economic waves. The pound sterling was the business currency of the world and the principles of the craft system were practised by all industrial countries. The mantle of economic leadership passed to the United States around 1870, and the mass, or scale, production system became the symbol of its hegemony. But today there is no single dominant nation. Instead, as Fred Bergsten (1990) has observed, it is likely that the leadership of the world over the next century will have to be collectively shared by the European Community, Japan and the United States. Such an alliance of flagship nations, particularly if widened to embrace China – which, according to some sources, already has the second largest GNP in the world – will require all the bonding characteristics of interfirm and intercommunity collaborative schemes.

THE DEVELOPING ECONOMIES

What about the developing countries? How and where do they fit in to the future? What, indeed, does globalization mean for the trajectory of economic development? So far, in this chapter, we have paid little specific attention to the problems and needs of the developing world. This is partly because we believe the opportunities and challenges of globalization cut across the traditional North/South divide, and partly because, over the next twenty-five years, it is likely that many millions of the descendants of yesterday's impoverished generation will come to enjoy at least the basic creature comforts which the inhabitants of richer countries so easily take for granted.

That is in the future; and, notwithstanding the possibility that the East Asian miracle might spread westwards to India and northwards to China, and that more developing countries will be drawn into North–South regional integration schemes, we think there is little prospect that most of the poorer countries will derive much immediate benefit from the new global economic order. Indeed, the share of new FDI that went to the least developed nations in the early 1990s was only one-half that of the 1980s (UNCTAD 1994).

At the same time, the prospects for economic growth in the 1990s are considerably better than those actually achieved in the 'lost' decade of the 1980s. The World Bank has projected that, on average, the GDP growth rate of developing countries will be 4.7 per cent per annum between 1992 and 2002, and that even in the poorest countries – excluding India and China – the rate of growth will be 3.5 per cent (World Bank 1994a).

The World Bank offers four main reasons for its cautious optimism. The first is that the macro-economic and organizational reforms introduced in the 1980s are now starting to show results. The second is that internal supply-side sources of growth, that is domestic savings rates, incentives to invest and the emergence of a production system less dependent on the economies of scale, are expected to improve. The third is that commodity prices are predicted to stabilize in real terms – a sharp break from their twenty-year declining trend. And the fourth cause for optimism is the increased flow of capital now being directed to the Third World. Between 1989 and 1994, for example, developing countries attracted 26.7 per cent of the FDI flows compared with 20 per cent for most of the previous decade (UNCTAD 1995). Private portfolio flows rose even more dramatically – from $6 billion a year between 1982 and 1988 to $34 billion in 1992 (World Bank 1994a). In recent years, too, such investments have been supplemented by new financial instruments, that is debt–equity swaps and depository receipts, and also by the setting up of new financial institutions (e.g. the European Bank for Reconstruction and Development).

Overall, then, we sense that the portends for real growth in the developing world – taken as a whole – are probably better than they have been for many years. There is a huge untapped reservoir of young and energetic labour and an equally huge unmet set of consumer needs, waiting to be activated. The development of countries like Japan and Singapore, which lack the natural resources which were the foundation of nineteenth-century development, ought to provide good heart to even the poorest of countries. Increasingly, as we have seen, the key to economic prosperity in the twenty-first century lies in the ability of firms and countries to acquire and create new knowledge – and in the case of smaller developing nations, new markets.

To what extent is economic development currently being led by exogenous – mainly Triad-related – globalizing forces, and to what extent is it being endogenously induced? The answer to these questions will, obviously, vary from country to country, depending, for example, on the size and structure of the economy, its stage of development, and the government policies it pursues. However, even the larger and most prosperous developing countries now accept that, to paraphrase John Donne, 'no nation in this global age can afford to be an island'. The only question at issue is 'how far', 'with whom', 'in what way' and 'by what means' should developing countries engage in alliance capitalism?

We earlier suggested that the hierarchical production system was centrifugal as it decentralized the production of labour-intensive activities to low-wage countries. This resulted in a scale-related division of labour, with consequences broadly similar to those arising from the resource-based division of labour in the nineteenth century. While this system aided development, it was an uneven development. It encouraged interdependence, but it was asymmetrical. All too frequently, the foreign sector was not fully integrated into the host economy; as a result, the syndrome of the dual economy began to emerge.

In both kinds of international specialization, it was the smaller economies which usually benefited the most, although both in Latin America and East Asia, regional integration schemes did lead to some intraregional alliance capitalism. Most larger developing countries also had trading and investment links with the developed world, but, as the main objective of several of these economies – particularly in the 1970s – was to use these links as a means of advancing their own economic autonomy, there were few genuine cross-border alliances and only a limited transfer of organizational systems.

The advent of alliance capitalism, at a time when most developing nations are modifying their internal economic strategies to benefit better from economic interdependence, is encouraging such countries to play a more pro-active role in the globalizing economy. At the same time, the extent which alliance capitalism is primarily a phenomenon of the Triad nations is yet to be seen. Certainly, outside the apparel and footwear industries, the great majority of joint ventures and networks so far concluded have been between firms in the dynamic industrial or service sectors, and have involved at least one developed nation (Hagedoorn 1993). Moreover, the experience of smaller European nations, both within and outside the EC, suggests that their counterparts in the developing world may find it extremely difficult to create the sophisticated infrastructure which networks require.

History also suggests that the probable winners are likely to be those developing countries which can offer the best educational and communication infrastructures to foreign firms, and which are geographically close to the industrial heartland of the Triad. However, by the late 1990s, it may be expected that at least the larger and more prosperous developing countries will have built up their own internal networks, and that their firms will have established alliances with firms from developing countries in the same region. In so doing, they will take the first step towards developing-world-led globalization. Indeed, it is already occurring in the Chinese economic space of East Asia and in the Malaysian–Thailand axis. And, as more Latin American countries adopt outward-looking development strategies, it is likely to happen there too (World Bank 1994b). By contrast, because of ethnic, religious and cultural differences, the prospects for intraregional integration in Central Asia, the Middle East and much of sub-Saharan Africa seem less promising although some progress on this front is being made.

Although, as we have suggested, there are aspects of flexible production systems and interactive learning which favour the resources and capabilities of developing countries, and which may lead to a revitalization of the 'putting out' system of production, there are others, notably the increasing role played by costly created assets in the competitive process, and the need for a physically close and ongoing relationship between firms in dynamic sectors along the value chain,[7] which are centripetal in their effects. Because of this, it follows that, at least for the foreseeable future, and with the possible exception of China and India, developing countries are unlikely to be the flagships of global alliance capitalism. However, there are reasons to suppose that some at least could become hubs of regional alliance capitalism. Singapore is already bidding to be the leading financial and high-technology centre and cruise gateway, and Taipei the leading regional operations centre, of South East Asia. At the same time, US computer firms are increasingly favouring the Caribbean as a regional centre for their software facilities.

For the poorer developing countries, most of which are far removed from the critical nodes of growth, the impact of globalization and alliance capitalism is likely to be marginal – except in so far as they may benefit from a 'trickle-down' effect of some kinds of subcontracting.[8] This, however, should not be taken to mean that these countries will not benefit from other economic events in the 1990s, but rather that any such gains will be the outcome of internal economic and institutional reforms, and of the higher spending power of the faster-growing nations; and, in the case of resource-rich countries, the stabilization of commodity prices, the direction of resource-related innovation and the emergence of new sources of supply. But, in their attempts to upgrade their wealth-creating abilities, the least developed nations will most surely have to rely mainly on aid and loans from foreign governments and international institutions.[9] This is simply because their most pressing need is to improve their educational, legal and commercial infrastructures which, in the past at least, private investors have been unwilling to finance.

At the same time, with the introduction of more market-oriented macro-organizational policies, we would expect the threshold at which FDI becomes viable to fall. We would also like to think that such policies – and the kind of technological advances earlier described – will make it easier for both governments and firms from the poorer nations to explore the possibility of partnerships and cross-border alliances, and will promote more regional economic co-operation.

THE IMPLICATIONS OF GLOBALIZATION FOR NATIONAL GOVERNMENTS

Let us now consider the consequences of the emerging global economy and alliance capitalism for national governments.[10] The first and the most significant of these arises from the increasing ease with which competitive enhancing assets can move across national boundaries. This means that any actions governments might take which affect the competitiveness of these assets cannot be divorced from the actions taken by other governments. The theory of competing governments suggests that, in the last resort, a country's citizens can respond to high taxation – or any other unacceptable government policies – by 'voting with their feet' (Brennan and Buchanan 1985), that is by emigrating to another country. This idea can readily be extended to explain the locational choices of firms, as they may be affected by the tax and macro-organizational policies of national polities. No longer can governments assume that the firms, resources and capabilities presently located in their areas of jurisdiction are inextricably bound to those territories, nor that they are impotent to attract resources and capabilities now sited in other countries. Finally, there are suggestions that the actions of governments are becoming increasingly interdependent of each other. Governments – on behalf of their constituents, and like firms – may compete as oligopolists.[11]

Yet, while most large MNEs have responded to the demands of globalization and alliance capitalism by reconfiguring their organizational structures and decision-taking procedures, there is little evidence that governments have elected to do so. The result is that most are singularly ill equipped to deal with the consequences of globalization. Exceptions include some East Asian administrations, which are not only taking a more holistic approach to the organization of their tasks and functions, but are replacing a 'hub and spoke' hierarchical structure of governance by a 'spider's web' network structure, in order to encourage more fruitful interdepartmental exchanges of information and cross-fertilization of ideas.

We would suggest that the main reason for the reluctance of governments to embrace new structures of governance is the inflexibility and intransigence of established institutional regimes, and the opposition of powerful sectoral interests within the executive branch to changing the 'status quo'. It is, perhaps, no accident that the administrations with the least institutional impediments are those which are most successfully adapting to the needs of the global market-place. To this extent, developing nations could well have a comparative organizational advantage – particularly if their cultures are sympathetic to alliance capitalism.

The second consequence concerns the direct impact of government behaviour on the competitiveness of the firms located in their territories. This impact arises because many of the complementary assets needed by firms, to create and effectively exploit their core competencies, are, themselves, government owned or influenced. This suggests that the ability of governments and private firms to work together (e.g. with respect to innovatory activities, retraining, environmental protection and the promotion of interfirm alliances) might be a competitive advantage in its own right. Again, developing countries would do well to take note of this particular aspect of alliance capitalism as they seek to develop and capitalize on their unique strengths in a global economy.

The third implication of globalization and alliance capitalism is that it requires national governments to reappraise their role as overseers of economic activity. To the economist, the only justification for such a role is that the net benefits arising from it can be achieved at a lower real cost than any other form of organization, such as the market, individual hierarchies or networks of firms. It has long been recognized that, as well as being responsible for the defence of the realm, law and order, and the definition and enforcement of property rights, governments are particularly well equipped to supply – or to organize the supply of – some kinds of public and social goods, especially those whose benefits accrue as much to the community at large as to the producing institution.

Yet, there is nothing fixed or immutable about *which* organizational form is best suited to produce particular products. Yesterday's case for the public ownership of public utilities or transportation systems may no longer hold today. Technological developments, for example, have undermined most of the *raison d'être* for a government monopoly of mail and telephone services. New methods of monitoring and charging for the use of highways have better enabled private firms to supply these products, while the growth of interfirm networks offers an alternative to government funding of expensive capital projects.

However, it would be wrong to conclude that the renaissance of the market system should reduce the role of government to a minimalist one. It is yet another paradox of globalization and alliance capitalism that, to ensure its efficient functioning, there needs to be a closer co-operation between the public and private sectors. The underlying characteristics of most markets of the 1990s are very different than those of the craft or the scale production eras. There is more uncertainty attached to them. The specificity of assets has enormously increased. There is more information asymmetry between buyers and sellers. There are more opportunities for opportunism. Markets cost more to set up and monitor, and they generate more externalities than once they did. Underlying demand and supply conditions are continually changing, and an increasing number of products are taking on the form of 'public' goods. Moreover, globalization brings with it its own governance costs, such as those which arise from the structural integration of different cultures and institutional regimes. At the same time, the market system is *par excellence* an example of a social good, and it is the government's responsibility to see that this system works to the interests of its constituents.

Too often, we would argue, governments, hierarchies and markets are considered as substitutes for each other. This is a false dichotomy. Today's economy requires a pluralism of organizational modes, each working in tandem with the other – each supporting the other. Too often taxation is regarded as a necessary evil, rather than a price which has to be paid for the supply of competitiveness-enhancing public or social goods and services. Too often, too, governments are perceived as regulatory and controlling agencies, rather than as facilitators of markets, and as suppliers or stimulators of the appropriate learning systems and mind sets for the upgrading of human and physical assets.

To some extent the problem is one of reforming opinions and attitudes towards the role of governments. There is need for a new vocabulary to promote the image of government as a public good rather than as a necessary evil. We need a 'perestroika' of government. We need to recognize that, just as 'Fordism' is an outdated method of organizing work, so the kind of government interventionism appropriate to a 'Fordist' environment is outdated. And, just like the emerging managerial structure of twenty-first-century firms, we need governments to be lean, flexible and anticipatory of change. The new paradigm of government should eschew such negative or emotive sounding words such as 'command', 'intervention', 'regulation', and replace them with words such as 'empower', 'steer', 'co-operative', 'co-ordination' and 'systemic'. Taxation should not be regarded as a burden or a discouragement to work and enterprise, but as an investment in the upgrading of human resources (e.g. by education and training), and a social responsibility to care for the aged, sick and unemployed. Moreover, not only must governments recognize the need for a much more integrated and holistic system of organizing their responsibilities, but it is necessary for all those affected by governments – and particularly ordinary tax payers – to take a more positive view of the benefits which only the former can produce.

It is beyond the scope of this chapter to suggest how the organization of governments should change to accommodate the kind of remoulding we have articulated. But, this issue is now very much being considered in the literature. Douglas Hague has, in a book with the intriguing title *Transforming the Dinosaurs* (Hague 1993), identified four ways in which institutions – be they public or private – can re-engineer themselves, namely by coercion, contagion, coaching and learning. While the latter three are usually more acceptable agents of change than the first, in practice, such change usually has to wait until some kind of crisis coerces action. While Hague's remarks are primarily addressed to the UK situation, they would strike a chord of sympathy with the business leaders of Japan who, in April 1995, made a powerful plea for a radical redesign of the central administrative structure of the Japanese government. Among other things, they argued for a greater degree of co-ordination between the different ministries and agencies of the executive, and for a flattening of the pyramidal system of decision taking. Unless this is done – and done efficiently – then, according to the Keidaren, Japan's economic future may be put at risk.

We do not wish to imply that actions taken by national governments to overcome or reduce market failure are costless, or that such actions are necessarily the most cost-effective way of achieving that objective.[12] At the same time, it is possible to identify the kind of situations which favour government intervention of one kind or another. Figure 2.1, which is derived and adapted from Robert Wade's evaluation of the role played by national administrations in fostering the economic development of Japan, Taiwan Province of China and Republic of Korea (Wade 1988), sets out some of these situations, and the ways in which they may help reduce the transaction costs of governance. While the data are fairly self-explanatory, and provide a set of guidelines for governmental intervention, they have not yet been subject to rigorous scrutiny by scholars. The globalizing economy

Exhibit 2.1 Some examples of situations in which governments might successfully contain their own organizational costs

Intervention or form of government intervention	**Consequences for the reduction of government-related transaction costs**
• The containment of interventionist policies to activities severely hampered by market failures	• Reduces effectiveness of rent-seeking special-interest groups
• A holistic approach to the co-ordination of complementary policies and in- and institutional mechanisms	• Increases work effort of public agents • Makes policy trade-offs easier to identify and solve • Clarifies the tasks of policy makers and reduces problem of bounded rationality
• An ethos of consensus and co-operation between private and public policy makers, e.g. with respect to mutually beneficial goals and the means by which goals can best be achieved	• Reduces likelihood of suboptimization of decision taking • Captures economies of scope in governance and increases intra-organizational information flows and learning
• The recruitment of the most talented and well motivated individuals for public sector employment, e.g. by offering competitive working conditions and encouraging initiative and entrepreneurship	• Reduces transaction costs of interaction between representatives of private and public sector • Increases knowledge of public decision takers
• The insulation of the policy making process from the strongest (and most undesirable) pressure groups	• Reduces chance of uninformed or biased media coverage in forcing governments into ill-advised or hasty decision
• The presence of a national ethos or mentality of the need to be competitive and create wealth. Partly, this embraces a 'commutarian' culture and partly one which encourages personal initiative, entrepreneurship scientific specialization and competition	• Likely to inhibit the pursuance of suboptimal goals and to reduce bounded rationality and opportunism and use of inefficient production technologies • Reduces the effectiveness of rent seeking by special-interest groups, and relieves the policy making process from the pressure of day-to-day politics
• The absence of strong sectoral interest groups, e.g. farmers and left-wing labour groups, which might press for interventionist measures by governments other than those which are market facilitating	• Favours co-ordination of strategies and policies of public and priate organizations and reduces the suboptimization problem in the public sector • Reduces possibility of ideological conflicts and undue emphasis being placed on the redistribution of incomes as a (short-term) social good

Sources: Compiled from Wade (1988), Stiglitz (1989), Grestchmann (1911), Hämäläinen (1994)

may well enhance the need for such a scrutiny, as it increases the costs of misinformed or inappropriate government action.

In many respects, governments of developing countries are in a good position to meet the demands of the global economy. In almost all countries there is a history of strong interventionist governments, and also an ability to change trajectory speedily. In the last decade, there has been not only a marked realignment in macro-economic policies, but also a movement towards a less confrontational stance between governments and the business community. Some of the actions taken normally take several years to have any real effect. Others involve major institutional and attitudinal changes, which could take a generation or more to accomplish.

SUPRANATIONAL REGIMES

We conclude this chapter with a brief reference to the role of supranational forms of governance. Because of space limitations, we will do little more than acknowledge the role of privately sponsored international associations or consortia of firms.

There are two main reasons why supranational regimes may be necessary in a global economy. The first is that the unilateral behaviour of governments, which is geared to promoting the good of their own citizens, may not be globally welfare maximizing. This is because of the possible adverse affects (i.e. negative externalities) of this behaviour on the citizens of another nation. These might arise, for example, from the pursuance of geo-economic and rent-seeking strategies by one government, which might lead to retaliatory action by other governments. The 'beggar my neighbour' trade sanctions imposed by governments of industrial countries in the interwar years are a classic example of welfare-reducing policies, and it was precisely to deter this kind of behaviour that GATT was established in 1946 to draw up the 'rules of the game' for international trade. But, as we have seen, the globalization of the world economy has considerably widened the scope of competition and interdependence among governments. This has, consequently, enlarged the international playing arena, and has made it necessary for more rules to be established if geo-economic conflict is to be avoided and if the game is to be played fairly and to the benefit of all (Luttwack 1993).

The second reason why supranational regimes may be needed is that there are some cross-border market failures which cannot be fully compensated for, or surmounted, either by the actions of hierarchies or by national governments. The presence of international politico-market failure is most dramatically seen in the fields of satellite communications, the exploration of the sea bed, the protection of the ozone layer, environmental pollution and military security. In each of these instances, supra- or intergovernmental action may be necessary either to reduce the co-ordinating and transaction costs of such activities, or to capture the extraterritorial benefits of intercountry networking. The twenty-first century seems certain to witness a growing number of these international public and social goods, each of which will require pluralist governance structures if they are to work for the global good.[13]

It is perhaps worth remembering that intergovernmental co-operation on non-economic matters dates back many years. Agreements on technical standards, weights and measures, and meteorological systems were all first concluded in the last century. However, the idea that supranational regimes may be an appropriate mean of governing *economic* activity is relatively new, and is still very controversial. However, two things should be considered. The first is that it is becoming increasingly difficult to distinguish between what is and is not an economic activity. For example, each of the examples of politico-market failures we have just described affect, in some way or another, the infrastructure of modern economic activity. The second is that the emergence of the global economy, alliance capitalism and the widening competing interface between governments is forcing a reappraisal of our attitudes towards the role of transnational economic regimes.

There are essentially two ways of implementing supranational governance. The first is by the subordination of the sovereignty of nationhood to some kind of supranational authority. One form of such subordination is a merger of nation states – which carried to its extreme, leads to world government. While all the evidence seems to point to the disintegration, rather than the integration, of nation states, we are also witnessing – and here there are some interesting parallels with what is happening in the corporate world – the growth of intercountry alliances, or networks. These are usually set up to achieve a specific objective, but they all address problems, challenges and opportunities which can only be effectively dealt with at a supranational level.

In the economics arena, however, supranational control is likely to be primarily exercised at a functional or issue level. In spite of the protracted and tortuous GATT negotiations establishing the World Trade Organization (WTO), there is a lot of room for grafting on other issues to the agenda of the new organization. The indirect ways in which national governments can, for good or bad, affect trade and FDI are growing all the time. Besides the most obvious of below-cost competition measures (i.e. dumping), price competition, industrial, environmental and social policy can all be used as instruments for tilting the level of the playing fields. Perhaps the WTO (we say newly established, although it was first recommended nearly fifty years ago) will provide the institutional framework for this.[14]

Alongside the strengthening of global governance systems – particularly at an issue level – regional governance systems are also becoming more important. It is much more likely that national governments will be prepared to surrender parts of their economic jurisdiction to a supranational authority made up of nations with similar institutional, cultural and ideological backgrounds to their own, than to one which comprises nations which are widely different in these respects.

At the same time, there is nothing to prevent representatives of regional schemes from getting together to discuss issues of extraregional interest. This, in fact, is what the G7 is mainly about, and it has had a good deal of success in the past. While it would anticipated that regional integration – of one form or another – is likely to be an increasingly preferred way of supranational governance, particularly where the harmonization of national policies is desired, we can foresee a whole set of new alliances among nations being established in the next few years, and these could pose new problems for the co-ordination of governance itself. Again, we think there are lessons to be learned from the success and failures of inter-*firm* networking.

The other main (and complementary) avenue to supranational governance[15] is, in many respects, more in the spirit of alliance capitalism, in that its success rests less on mandates and regulations and more on the sharing of ideas, co-operation, trust, reciprocity and forbearance among its participants. The aim of this form of polity is to co-ordinate the actions of national governments in their response to cross-border market failure. Attempts to achieve this objective usually originate in the debating chambers of the United Nations and its various agencies, the OECD, the European Community, ASEAN and similar institutions. But the influence of such bodies should not be taken lightly, particularly as it affects developing countries. We certainly do not see these institutions playing a less important role as globalization proceeds. Indeed, we are reasonably sanguine that, with the ending of the cold war, and with at least some harmonization of economic policies among governments in tackling the remaining, but no less serious, problems facing the nations of the world, a spirit of fusion, rather than fission, in the ideas expressed and decisions reached will prevail.

CONCLUSIONS

To sum up, then, globalization is requiring the adoption of a new form of capitalism – which we have called alliance capitalism – if it is to be successful in promoting economic welfare and sustainable development. The distinctive feature of alliance capitalism is that its success depends upon the harmonious interaction between the wealth-creating constituents in society and those of governments. Co-operation and competition go side by side; they are opposite sides of the coin of economic progress.

Where it has been permitted and where it has been in response to market forces, we believe that FDI – like trade – has had a generally positive affect on both economic growth and the international division of labour. As subsequent chapters in this volume will show, the relationship between trade, FDI and cross-border co-operative ventures is ambivalent. In some cases (e.g. in response to barriers to trade) FDI may be a substitute for trade; in others (e.g. in most natural-resource-based and efficiency-seeking investment) it is likely to be trade enhancing. For the most part, and until recently, FDI and co-operative arrangements have been regarded as substitutes for each other, with the latter often being regarded as a second-best alternative to FDI.

In today's globalizing economy, however, and with the emergence of alliance capitalism, they are becoming more complementary and supportive of each other. This new trend is particularly being demonstrated in the activities of the large MNEs in the industrialized countries; and governments do well to recognize this fact in the formation of their policies towards trade, foreign investment and competition – which, all too often, are conceived and implemented in isolation of each other. FDI is one of the deepest forms of structural integration between countries. Not only are the resources and capabilities of one country transferred to that of another, but their use – as well as that of the complementary assets of the recipient country – is controlled, or influenced, by the transferring firms. Thus, the motives for FDI, and the conditions under which it is undertaken, are, through the 'embedded' factor, likely to determine its impact.

We have also argued that the transition from hierarchical to alliance capitalism has very considerable implications for sustainable development. On balance, we believe these implications to be welfare enhancing, although the extent and form of the benefits is likely to differ between sectors and countries. At the same time, we have argued that it is desirable for developing countries to try to create their own networks of value-added and interactive learning activities, and to do so in a way which promotes their own comparative dynamic advantage. We are somewhat less optimistic that, in the near future, the most impoverished nations, and particularly those which are most distant from the hubs of economic power, will gain much from globalization *per se*, although the secondary, or spillover, effects of other economic and political events may be more positive.

We have further asserted that, in the formation of their macro-economic and organizational strategies, national governments are being forced to interact more closely with each other. Sometimes, this interaction takes the form of competition,[16] and sometimes of voluntary or involuntary co-operation. At the same time, the globalizing economy is demanding a re-examination of the scope and authority of supranational economic regimes, both to minimize the regional or global welfare-reducing actions by national governments, and to encourage the harmonization of these actions whenever they can help reduce the costs of organizing cross-border production and transactions. We have finally suggested that emerging economies may well have a comparative advantage in the implementation of domestic economic policies in the globalizing economy, *inter alia*, because they are not faced with the same institutional rigidities which face the older industrialized nations.

NOTES

1 The respective authors of these books were Henry Wendt (1993), R. J. Barnett and John Cavanagh (1994) and John Naisbitt (1994).

2 Measured in SDRs, these growth rates would have been rather different; in particular, the FDI growth rates in the 1980s would have been lower, and those since 1990 higher.

3 India's realized annual inward FDI increased from $113 million in 1991 to $959 million in 1994. It is estimated that total inflows for 1995 would amount to $1.7 billion (UNCTAD 1995).

4 Which is the fourth type of FDI, along with *market-seeking, resource-seeking* and *efficiency-seeking* FDI.

5 The exception is that strategic asset-acquiring FDI is still very limited in Japan – not so much by legal restrictions as by less tangible entry barriers (e.g. to do with business customs and practices, and *keiretsu* relations in Japan).

6 A concept further explored in Chapter 14 of this volume.

7 The increasing need for close proximity would appear to run counter to the reduction in transaction and co-ordinating costs arising from telecommunication advances. Yet, the example of the City of London is instructive. While many of the routine banking, financial and insurance operations have been decentralized, a network of the core and innovating activities remains firmly embedded in the square mile. This is because the perceived gains from face-to-face contact between the constituents of the network are greater than ever. As manufacturing firms – at least in dynamic sectors – upgrade their R&D and skilled labour, they become more closely interdependent in their informational and technological needs; and as trust and forbearance become a more important component of transactions, then, at least at the top end of the value chain and in the early stages of their production cycles, the need for close physical proximity increases rather than diminishes. This need was recognized nearly thirty years ago by Raymond Vernon (1966). The idea of the factory as a research laboratory also suggests closer physical linkages between R&D and production activities (Kenney and Florida 1993), another facet of alliance capitalism.

8 For example, in the garment and footwear industries, although the first-tier suppliers of flagship MNEs are usually located in the more advanced developing countries (e.g. Hong Kong and Singapore) these suppliers may, themselves, 'put out' the more labour-intensive production processes to small firms and artisans as far afield as Bangladesh, Sri Lanka and Nigeria.

9 Sometimes this funding may help to support outbound FDI by other developing or developed countries to the poorer developing countries (e.g. investment by Chinese firms in parts of Indo-China and by Canadian firms in Central Africa).

10 This subject is more fully explored in Dunning (1997).

11 This is particularly the case as between governments of countries of a similar size, economic structure and stage of development.

12 Among the possible failures of direct government intervention to overcome successfully the deficiencies of the market, one might mention the rent-seeking activities of powerful pressure groups; the magnification of market failures (e.g. with respect to the supply of environmental or social products) by the news media or other politically motivated interests; the inability of governments to

attract the best talents (due, *inter alia*, to ineffective incentive systems); the lack of commercial expertise and bounded rationality of public decision takers; the pursuance of non-economic (especially ideological) goals by politicians; the inadequacy of market-related performance indicators which may lead to the establishment of suboptimal standards (e.g. with respect to budgets, investment and control of information flows); the high-time discount (or short-termism) of political decision takers; the lack of market pressures to minimize X inefficiency, especially in the case of public monopolies; uncertainties and ambiguities inherent in the provision of goods and services, which are in the domain of governments (e.g. defence equipment, educational and health services); and the lack of a co-ordinated system of governance (cf. with that in case of private hierarchies); and the difficulty of adjusting policies and institutional structures to meet quickly the needs of technological and economic change. For a more detailed examination of these and other factors which might lead to excessive or inappropriate governmental intervention or the suboptimal provision of public goods and services, see for example Wolf (1988), Grestchmann (1991), Stiglitz (1989) Hämäläinen (1994) and Chang (1994).

13 For a more detailed examination of international regimes and politico-market failure, see Eden and Hampson (1990).

14 Since this chapter was written the OECD has announced its intention to conclude a multilateral investment agreement (MIA) which, *inter alia*, will set high standards for governments in their treatment of MNEs, and in their macro-organizational policies which are likely to affect the costs and benefits of FDI. For further details see Witherell (1995).

15 In this chapter, we do not intend to deal with the issue of bilateral governance.

16 As described, for example, by Ostrom (1971), quoted in McKenzie and Lee (1991).

REFERENCES

Barnett, R. J. and Cavanagh, J. (1994) *Global Dreams*, New York: Simon & Schuster.

Bergsten, C. F. (1990) 'The world economy after the cold war', *Foreign Affairs* 69: 96–112.

Brennan, G. and Buchanan, J. M. (1985) *The Power to Tax*, Cambridge: Cambridge University Press.

Chang H. J. (1994) *The Political Economy of Industrial Policy*, London and Basingstoke: Macmillan.

Dunning, J.H. (ed.) (1997) *Government, Globalization and International Business*, Oxford: Oxford University Press.

Eden, L. and Hampson, F. O. (1990) *Clubs are Trumps: Towards a Taxonomy of International Regimes*, Ottawa Center for International Trade and Investment Policy Studies, Carleton University Working Paper 90–02.

Grestchmann, K. (1991) 'Analyzing the public sector: the received view in economics and its shortcomings', in Franz-Xaver Kaufman (ed.), *The Public Sector: Challenge for Coordination and Learning*, Berlin: Water de Gruyter.

Hagedoorn, J. (1993) 'Strategic technology alliances and modes of cooperation in high technology industries', in G. Grabher (ed.), *The Embedded Firm*, London: Routledge.

Hague, D. C. (1993) *Transforming the Dinosaurs*, London: Demos.

Hämäläinen, T. J. (1994) *The Evolving Role of Government in Economic Organization*, Newark, NJ: Rutgers University (mimeo).

Huntington, S. (1993) 'The clash of civilizations', *Foreign Affairs* 72, Summer: 22–49.

Kenney, M. and Florida, R. (1993) *Beyond Mass Production*, Oxford and New York: Oxford University Press.

Luttwack, E. N. (1993) 'The coming global war for economic power', *The International Economy* September/October: 18–21, 64–7.

McGrew, A. G. (1992) 'Conceptualizing global politics', in A. G. McGrew, and P. G. Lewis (eds) *Global Politics: Globalization and the Nation State*, pp. 83–117, Cambridge: Polity Press.

McKenzie, R. and Lee, D. (1991) *Quicksilver Capital: How the Rapid Movement of Wealth has Changed the World*, New York: The Free Press.

Naisbitt, J. (1994) *Global Paradox: The Bigger the World Economy, the More Political its Smallest Players*, New York: William Morrow.

Ostrom, V. (1971) *The Political Theory of the Compound Republic: A Reconstruction of the Logical Foundation of American Democracy as Presented by the Federation*, Blacksburg, Va.: Centre for the Study of Public Choice.

Quinn, J. B. and Hilmer, F. G. (1994) 'Strategic outsourcing', *Sloan Management Review* 35, Summer: 43–55.

Ruigrok, W. and Van Tulder, R. (1995) *The Logic of International Restructuring*, London and New York: Routledge.

Stiglitz, J. (1989) *The Economic Role of the State*, Oxford: Basil Blackwell.

United Nations (1986) *United Nations Statistical Year Book 1983–1994*, New York: UN.

UNCTAD (1994) *World Investment Report 1994: Transnational Corporations, Employment and the Workplace*, New York and Geneva: UN.

——(1995) *World Investment Report 1995: Transational Corporations and Competitiveness*, New York and Geneva: UN.

United States Department of Commerce (1992a) *US Direct Investment Abroad: 1989 Benchmark Survey Final Results*, Washington, DC: Department of Commerce Bureau of Economic Analysis.

——(1992b) *US Direct Investment Abroad: Operation of US Parent Companies and Their Affiliates, Preliminary 1990 Estimates*, Washington, DC: Department of Commerce Bureau of Economic Analysis.

——(1993a) 'US direct investment abroad 1990–1992', *Survey of Current Business* July: 97–120.

——(1993b) *Survey of Current Business*, August, September and October editions.

Vernon, R. (1966) 'International investment and international trade in the product cycle', *Quarterly Journal of Economics* 80: 190–207.

Wade, R. (1988) 'The role of government in overcoming market failure in Taiwan, Republic of Korea and Japan' in H. Hughes, (ed.), *Achieving Industrialization in East Asia*, Cambridge: Cambridge University Press.

Wendt, H. (1993) *Global Embrace*, New York: Harper Business.

Witherell, W. H. (1995) 'The OECD Multinational Agreement on Investment', *Transnational Corporations* 4 August.

Wolf, C. J. (1988) *Markets and Governments*, Cambridge, MA: MIT Press.

World Bank (1993) *The East Asian Miracle*, Oxford: Oxford University Press.

——(1994a) *Global Economic Prospects and the Developing Countries*, Washington, DC: The World Bank.

——(1994b) *World Development Report 1994*, Oxford: Oxford University Press.

World Economic Forum and IMEDE (1993) *World Competitiveness Report 1993*, Geneva and Lausanne: World Economic Forum and IMEDE.

3

REAPPRAISING THE ECLECTIC PARADIGM IN AN AGE OF ALLIANCE CAPITALISM

INTRODUCTION

Over the last decade or so, a number of events have occurred that, viewed collectively, suggest that the world economy may be entering a new phase of market-based capitalism – or, at least, changing its trajectory of the past century. These events recognize no geographical boundaries, and they range from changes in the way in which individual firms organize their production and transactions, to a reconfiguration of location-specific assets and the globalization of many kinds of economic activity.

The pre-eminent driving force behind these events has been a series of systemic technological and political changes, of which a new generation of telecommunication advances and the demise of central planning in Eastern Europe and the renaissance of the market economy in China are, perhaps, the most dramatic. But no less far reaching has been the economic rejuvenation of Japan and the emergence of several new industrial powers – especially from East Asia – whose approach to market-based capitalism – both at a socio-institutional and a techno-economic level (Freeman and Perez 1988, Ruigrok and Van Tulder 1995) – is very different from that long practised by Western nations.

The interrelated and cumulative effects of these phenomena have compelled scholars to re-examine some of their cherished concepts about market-based capitalism, and to do so in two major respects. The first is the growing acceptance that, by themselves, competitive market forces do not necessarily ensure an optimum innovation-led growth path in a dynamic and uncertain world. This is partly because technology is an endogenous variable – not an exogenous one as assumed in the received literature – and partly because the pressures of frequent and unpredictable technological and political changes do not permit a Pareto-optimal allocation of resources (Pigou 1932). With the acceleration of technological change, and a growing emphasis on institutional learning and continuous product improvement, both the concepts and the policy prescriptions of our forefathers are becoming less relevant each day.

The second revered concept that is now under scrutiny is that the resources and competencies of wealth-creating institutions are largely independent of each other, and that individual enterprises are best able to advance their economic objectives, and those of society, by competition, rather than by co-operation. Unlike the first idea, this concept has only been severely challenged over the last decade, although, for more than a century, scholars have acknowledged that the behaviour of firms may be influenced by the actions of their competitors (Cournot 1851), while Marshall (1920) was one of the first economists to recognize that the spatial clustering or agglomeration of firms with related interests might yield agglomerative economies and an industrial atmosphere, external to the individual firms, but internal to the cluster.

It is the purpose of this chapter to consider some of the implications of the changes now taking place in the global market-place for our understanding of the determinants of multinational enterprise (MNE) activity, and especially the eclectic paradigm of international production.[1] The main thrust of our argument is that, although the autonomous firm will continue to be the main unit of analysis for understanding the extent and pattern of foreign-owned production, the OLI configuration determining transborder activities is being increasingly affected by the collaborative production and transactional arrangements between firms, and that these need to be more systematically incorporated into the eclectic paradigm. But, prior to subjecting this idea to closer examination, we briefly outline the underlying assumptions of the extant theory of MNE activity in the mid-1980s.

HIERARCHICAL CAPITALISM

For most of the present century, the deployment of resources and capabilities in market-oriented economies has been shaped by a micro-organizational system known as Fordism and a macro-institutional system known as hierarchical capitalism.[2] The essential characteristic of both these systems is that the governance of production and transactions is determined by the relative costs and benefits of using markets and firms as alternative organizational modes. In conditions of perfect competition, where exchange and co-ordination costs are zero and where there are no externalities of production or consumption, all transactions will be determined by market forces. Business entities will buy their inputs at arm's length prices from independent firms and households, and sell their outputs at arm's length prices to independent purchasers.

In practice, such a governance structure has rarely existed; to some degree, all markets contain some impurities. Such impurities are of two kinds. The first is structural market failure, which arises from the actions of participants in or outside the market to distort the conditions of demand or supply. The second is endemic or natural market failure, where either, given the conditions of supply and demand, the market qua market is unable to organize transactions in an optimal way, *or* it is difficult to predict the behaviour of the participants. Such endemic market failure essentially reflects the presence of uncertainty, externalities, and the inability of producers to capture fully increasing returns to scale in conditions of infinite demand elasticity. It also accepts that bounded rationality, information asymmetries and opportunism are more realistic principles governing economic conduct (Williamson 1985, 1993) than perfect cognition and profit- or utility-maximizing behaviour on the part of the transactors in the market.

It is partly to avoid or circumvent such market imperfections, and partly to recoup the gains of a unified governance of interrelated activities, that single-activity firms choose to internalize intermediate product markets and, in so doing, become diversified firms. To co-ordinate these different activities, the administrative system takes on the guise of a hierarchy, and as Chandler (1962, 1990) has well demonstrated, as US firms internalized more markets in the last quarter of the nineteenth century, so hierarchical capitalism came to replace 'arm's length' capitalism.

Throughout most of the present century, as economic activity has become increasingly specialized and more complex, and as technological advances and political forces have created more endemic market imperfections, the role of large hierarchies, relative to that of markets, as an organizational modality has intensified. At the firm level, the fully integrated production facilities of enterprises such as the Ford Motor Company[3] in the 1960s epitomized the *raison d'être* for, and the extreme form of, hierarchical capitalism; hence the coining of the term 'Fordism'. At a sectoral level, the proportion of output from most industrial countries supplied by vertically integrated or horizontally diversified firms rose throughout most of the twentieth century.[4] Until the late 1970s, scholars usually considered co-operative modes of organizing economic activity as *alternatives* to hierarchies or markets, rather than as part and parcel of a micro-organizational *system*, in which interfirm and intrafirm transactions complement each other. This, in part, reflected the fact that, in the main, economists viewed the boundary of a firm as the point at which its owners relinquished *de jure* control over resource harnessing and usage, and, to a large extent, this boundary was thought to be coincident with a loss of majority equity ownership. It is not surprising, then, that, for the most part, minority joint ventures were regarded as a second-best alternative to full ownership. At the same time, most contractual arrangements were considered as market transactions – even in situations in which there was some element of a continuing and information-sharing relationship between the parties to the exchange.

We would mention two other important features of twentieth-century hierarchical capitalism. The first is that it implicitly assumes that the prosperity of firms depends exclusively on the way in which their managements internally organize the resources and capabilities at their disposal. These include the purchased inputs from other firms and the marketing and distribution of outputs. Admittedly, the behaviour of such firms might be affected by the strategies of other firms, for example oligopolistic competitors, monopolistic suppliers, large customers, and labour unions. But, with these exceptions, in hierarchical capitalism, the external transactions of firms are assumed to be *exogenous*, rather than *endogenous*, to their portfolio of assets and skills, and to the way in which these assets and skills are combined with each other to create further value-added advantages.

The second characteristic of hierarchical capitalism is that firms primarily react to endemic and structural market failure by adopting 'exit' rather than 'voice'-type strategies. Hirschman (1970) first introduced this concept of exit and voice to explain the responses of firms and nation states to threats to their economic sovereignty. He postulated two such responses: 'exit' to a better alternative, and 'voice', which he defined as any attempt at all to change, rather than escape from, an objectionable state of affairs (p. 30). Borrowing from Hirschman's terminology, we might identify two reactions of firms to the presence of market failure. These are: (i) to 'exit', where the response is to replace the market by internal administrative fiat, and (ii) to 'voice', where the response is to work with the market (in this case the buyers of its products or the sellers of its purchases) to reduce or eliminate market failure.

Our reading of the *raison d'être* for hierarchical capitalism, particularly its US brand, is that it was (and still is) an 'exit' reaction to market failure.[5] To a limited extent, 'voice' strategies are evident in joint equity ventures and contractual agreements, and in compensatory institutional instruments (e.g. futures and insurance markets). But, in general, collaborative production, marketing or innovatory projects or problem solving are eschewed. Contract disputes are usually resolved by litigation procedures rather than by propitiating attempts to remove the cause of the disputes. Competition and adversarial relations, rather than co-operation and synergistic affinities, are the hallmarks of hierarchical capitalism, and this is evident in the conduct of both interfirm and intrafirm co-ordination procedures and transactions. Hierarchical capitalism rarely interprets the roles of firms and governments as being complementary to each other (World Bank 1991).

It is beyond the scope of this chapter either to trace the factors that led to hierarchical capitalism and the scale system of production, or to describe its characteristics in any detail. (The reader is invited to consult Oman (1994) and Ruigrok and Van Tulder (1995) on these matters.) Suffice to mention that, between the mid-1870s and the early 1970s, a series of technological, organizational and financial events occurred that helped reduce the transaction and co-ordination costs of multi-activity hierarchies relative to those of arm's length intermediate product markets. Moreover, in contrast to the craft system of production which preceded it, the main impact of the mass production system was felt in the fabricating or assembling, rather than in the processing, sectors. And, it was in the former sectors where – in order to co-ordinate better the stages of production, to reduce the risks of supply irregularities, and to ensure quality control over downstream operations – firms began to internalize intermediate product markets and to engage in vertical integration and horizontal diversification in order to capture the economies of scope and scale.

We have already asserted that mainstream economic and organizational theorists paid only scant attention to this phenomenon until the post-war period,[6] and that much of the credit for such work as was done must go to scholars interested in the explanation of the growth of MNEs.[7] In the 1950s, both Edith Penrose (1956) and Maurice Bye (1958) sought to explain the extension of a firm's territorial boundaries in terms of the perceived gains to be derived from vertical and horizontal integration. Later, Penrose formulated a more general theory of the growth of firms (Penrose 1959), but her penetrating insights into the advantages of internalized markets (although she never used this term)[8] had to wait many years before they were adequately acknowledged.[9]

Since the mid-1970s, there has been a plethora of academic papers and monographs that have tried to interpret the existence and growth of MNEs in terms of the benefits that such firms are perceived to derive from internalizing cross-border intermediate product markets.[10] Although several scholars have considered co-operative arrangements as alternatives to fully owned affiliates, and as forms of quasi- internalization,[11] for the most part, they have been accommodated in a market/hierarchies transaction costs model, with such arrangements being perceived as a point on a continuum between arm's length markets and complete hierarchies.

The eclectic paradigm, first put forward by the present author at a Nobel Symposium in 1976, is different from internalization theory[12] in that it treats the competitive (so called O-specific) advantages of MNEs, apart from those which arise from the act of cross-border internalization, as *endogenous* rather than as *exogenous* variables. This means that the paradigm is not just concerned with answering the question of why firms engage in FDI, in preference to other modes of cross-border transactions. It is also concerned with why these firms possess unique resources and competencies – relative to their competitors of other nationalities – and why they choose to use at least some of these advantages jointly with a portfolio of foreign-based immobile assets.

At the same time, as so far enunciated, the eclectic paradigm is embedded within a socio-institutional framework of hierarchical capitalism, which, as stated earlier, presumes that the wealth-creating and efficiency-enhancing properties of an MNE are contained within the jurisdiction of its ownership. Thus, using the OLI nomenclature, except where they are acquired by M&As, the O advantages of firms are presumed to be created and organized quite independently of their dealings with other firms; the L advantages of countries are assumed to reflect the scope and character of their unconnected immobile assets, and the way in which hierarchies and markets determine their use; and the propensity of firms to internalize intermediate product markets is based primarily on the presumption that most kinds of market failure[13] faced by firms are generally regarded by them as immutable (i.e. exogenous). Currently, the eclectic paradigm only peripherally embraces the ways in which the participation of firms in collaborative arrangements, or in networks of economic activity, affect the configuration of the OLI variables facing firms at a given moment of time, or on how this configuration may change over time. Partly (one suspects) this is because the value of such arrangements is difficult to quantify; and partly because interfirm transactions have been perceived to be of only marginal significance in the techno-economic production system of Fordism and in the socio-institutional paradigm of hierarchical capitalism.

ALLIANCE CAPITALISM

As suggested in the introduction, a series of events over the last two decades has led several scholars to suggest that the world is moving to embrace a new trajectory of market capitalism. This has been variously described as alliance, relational, collective, associate and the 'new' capitalism.[14] A critical feature of this new trajectory – which is essentially the outcome of a series of landmark technological advances and of the globalization of many kinds of value-added activity – is that it portrays the organization of production and transactions as involving both co-operation and competition between the leading wealth-creating agents.[15] This view is in marked contrast to that which has dominated the thinking of economists since Adam Smith, whereby collaboration among firms is viewed as a symptom of *structural* market failure,[16] rather than as a means of reducing *endemic* market failure. And, it would be a bold scholar who would argue that most agreements concluded between firms over the last hundred years have been aimed at facilitating rather than inhibiting competition.

But our reading of the literature suggests that, both the *raison d'être* for concluding interfirm alliances, and their consequences for economic welfare, have significantly changed over the last two decades. We would at least hypothesize that a powerful contemporary motive for concluding such arrangements is to reduce the transaction and co-ordinating costs of arm's length market transactions, and to leverage the assets, skills and experiences of partner firms. Another motive is to create or extend hierarchical control, which may also prompt firms to engage in M&As. However, co-operative arrangements differ from M&As in three respects. First, the former usually involve only a part – and sometimes a minor part – of the collaborating firms' activities. Second, they may entail no change in the ownership structure of the participating firms; and third, whereas the hierarchical solution implies an 'exiting' by firms from the dictates of the market-place, the alliance solution implies a 'voice' strategy of working within these dictates to maximize the benefits of the joint internalization of interrelated activities.

The choice between a hierarchical and alliance modality as a means of lessening arm's length market failure clearly depends on their respective costs and benefits. The literature on the rationale for joint ventures and non-equity transactions – *vis-à-vis* markets and hierarchies – is extensive and well known, and will not be repeated here.[17] It is, however, generally accepted that the choice rests on a trade-off between the perceived benefits of sharing risks and capital outlays on the one hand, and the costs of a loss of control associated with a reduced (or no) ownership on the other. Partly, the outcome will be influenced by the success of the 'voice' strategy between the participants, as illustrated, for example, by the exchange of information, the division of managerial and financial responsibility, and the distribution of profits. But, in the main, most scholars view the choice as being determined by the most cost-effective way of organizing a portfolio of resources and capabilities.

Another reason for collaborative arrangements, however, has less to do with reducing the co-ordinating and transaction costs of alternative organizational modalities, and more to do with protecting existing – or gaining new – proprietary, or O-specific, advantages. Co-operative alliances have a parallel with strategic asset-acquiring FDI: according to several researchers, over the past decade, the principal incentives for alliance formation have been to lower transaction costs, develop new skills and overcome or create barriers to entry in national or international markets.[18] Sometimes, these alliances take the form of shared ownership, that is, the merging of firms, or the setting up of greenfield joint ventures. But, since the early 1980s, the great majority of interfirm associations have tended to be less formal in structure and more specific in scope and purpose. According to research undertaken at MERIT (Hagedoorn 1993a), the goal of most strategic alliances has been to gain access to new and complementary technologies, to speed up innovatory or learning processes and to upgrade the efficiency of particular activities – for example, research and development (R&D), marketing and distribution, manufacturing methods, etc. – rather than to enhance the overall prosperity of the participating firms.

It is perhaps worth rehearsing some of the reasons for the spectacular growth of competitiveness-enhancing alliances since 1980. Essentially, these reduce to the impact that technological advances and the globalization of the market economy have had on the organization of economic activity. The consequences of the former – a supply-side phenomenon – have been fivefold: first, to raise the fixed – and particularly the learning and innovatory – costs of a wide range of manufacturing and service activities; second, to increase the interdependence between distinctive technologies that may need to be used jointly to supply a particular product;[19] third, to enhance the significance of multi-purpose, or core, technologies, such as robotization, informatics and biotechnology; fourth, to truncate – and sometimes dramatically so[20] – the product life cycle of a particular product; and fifth, which is partly a consequence of the other four characteristics and partly a result of the changing needs of consumers, to focus on the upgrading of core competencies of firms, and on the way these are organized, as a means of improving global competitive advantage.

One of the main consequences of the globalization of economic activity described earlier has been to force firms to be more dynamically competitive. This is particularly the case for firms from advanced industrial countries, and it is demonstrated in two main ways: first, a more determined effort to raise the efficiency with which they produce their existing products, and second, by the successful innovation of new products and the upgrading of assets and skills throughout their value chains.

This combination of global supply and demand pressures on competitiveness has caused firms – and particularly large hierarchies – to reconsider both the scope and organization of their value-added activities. In particular, the 1980s and early 1990s have seen three major responses. First, there has been a fairly general movement by firms towards the shedding or disinternalization of activities both along and between value chains, and towards the specialization on those activities that require resources and capabilities in which firms already have (or can acquire) a perceived competitive advantage. This is a *concentrate on critical competency response*. At the same time, because of the interdependence of technological advances (e.g. computer-aided design and manufacturing techniques), firms find that they need to assure access to the products over which they have now relinquished control. Firms may also wish to exercise some influence over the quality and price of these products, and over the innovation of new products. This means that disinternalization is frequently replaced, not by arm's length transactions, but by controlled interfirm co-operative arrangements. Such agreements are particularly noticeable between firms and their subcontractors in the more technologically advanced and information-intensive sectors (Hagedoorn 1993b).[21]

Second, because of competitive pressures, the huge and rising costs of R&D and speedier rates of obsolescence, firms – particularly in high-technology sectors – have been increasingly induced to engage in cross-border alliances. Freeman and Hagedoorn (1992) traced 4,192 of these alliances between 1980 and 1989. They found that 42 per cent were organized through R&D pacts; that 90 per cent were between companies from the Triad; and that 63 per cent were formed during the second half of the 1980s. The majority of the alliances involved large firms competing as oligopolies in global markets.[22] The need, on the one hand, for operational participation and, on the other, for complementarity, shared learning and an encapsulation of the innovation time span has combined to make the 'voice' strategy of co-operative ventures a particularly suitable mode for sustaining and advancing competitive advantage.[23] At the same time, to be successful, an *asset-seeking alliance response* does have implications for governance structures, a point we will take up later in this chapter.

The third response of firms to recent events has been to try to widen the markets for their core products, so as to benefit fully from the economies of scale. This is, itself, a cost-reducing strategy. It serves to explain much of market-seeking and strategic asset-acquiring FDI – especially between firms servicing the largest industrial markets – as well as those of minority-owned foreign joint ventures and non-equity arrangements that are intended to gain speedy entry into unchartered and unfamiliar territories. Thus, of the 4,192 alliances identified by Freeman and Hagedoorn, 32 per cent were geared towards improving access to markets. As might be expected, such alliances were particularly numerous among firms with Japanese partners. Such a 'voice' strategy might be termed a *market-positioning alliance response*.

Each of the three responses identified has widened the sphere of influence of the firms participating in external partnerships. Such actions have also caused a heightened degree of dependence on firm partners for their own prosperity. Thus, the resources and capabilities of companies such as Philips, IBM and Toyota – each of which has several hundred interfirm alliances – cannot be considered in isolation. Gomes-Casseres and Leonard-Barton (1994) have identified some eighty recently established learning, supply and positioning partnerships in the personal digital assistants (PDA) sector alone.[24] One must also consider the impact that these alliances have had on their internally generated O-specific advantages. The design and performance of the next generation of automobiles, microchips and computers critically depend not only on the advances in innovatory and manufacturing capabilities of the leading assembling companies, but also on the way these capabilities interact with those of their suppliers. Boeing's competitive advantages in producing the next breed of large passenger aircraft are likely to rest as much on the interaction it has with its suppliers and its customers (e.g. the airlines) as it does on its own technological and commercial strengths. Siemens – a leading producer of mainframe computers – relies heavily on cutting-edge technology supplied by Fujitsu. In its venture to explore the sea bed, Kennecott's mining consortium brings together a large number of firms supplying very different, but interrelated, technologies from many different sectors. Lorenzoni and Baden Fuller (1995) give several examples of organizations which view their subcontractors as partners in innovation and skill development.[25]

Of course, interfirm co-operation is not a new phenomenon. What is, perhaps, new is its relative significance as an organizational form, whereby the success of the firms involved is being increasingly judged by each party's ability to generate innovation-led growth; by the range, depth and closeness of the interaction between themselves and their alliance or networking parties; and by the effect that such alliances are having upon overall industrial performance. It is the combination of these factors, taken together with the twin forces of the disinternalization of hierarchical activities and the impressive growth of M&As to gain access to complementary assets,[26] which leads us to suggest – along with Gerlach (1992) – that the term *alliance* capitalism might be a more appropriate description of the features of innovation-led capitalism now spreading through the globalizing economy, than the term *hierarchical* capitalism.

A distinctive feature of alliance capitalism is its governance structure. Within a hierarchy, decisions rest on a pyramid of delegated authority. In establishing and strengthening relationships with other firms, customers and labour unions, success is usually judged by the extent to which the hierarchy is able to obtain its inputs at the least possible cost, and to sell its output at the most profitable price. Relationships between firms and within firms are normally defined by a written contract.

In alliance capitalism, decisions are more likely to rest on a consensus of agreement between the participating parties, and there is rarely any formal structure of authority. Such an agreement is based upon a commitment, on the part of each party, to advance the interests of the alliance, and upon mutual trust, reciprocity and forebearance between the partners. In the modern factory practising flexible manufacturing or Toyota-like production methods, labour is not thought of as a cog in the wheel, as it is in traditional Fordism, but as a partner in the wealth-producing process. Suppliers are not just expected to produce goods to agreed specifications, but to work actively with the purchasing firms to upgrade continually the quality and/or lower the price of their outputs. Even within the hierarchical firm, technological and organizational imperatives are requiring each function, activity or stage of production to be closely integrated with the other. Thus, for example, the purchasing and R&D departments may be expected to work with the manufacturing departments on the design and development of new products and production methods. The personnel, finance and production departments each need to be involved in the introduction of new working procedures and incentive arrangements. At the same time, industrial customers and large wholesale and retail outlets may be expected to play an increasingly significant role in determining the direction and pattern of product improvement.

The growing significance of interfirm co-operative transaction arrangements would suggest that 'voice', relative to 'exit', strategies are becoming more cost-effective. This, of course, could be due either to the 'push' factor of the increasing net costs of hierarchical control, or to the 'pull' factor of the reduced costs of alliances. It is likely that both factors have been at work in recent years, but it can surely be no accident that the thrust towards alliance capitalism first originated in Japan, whose culture, like that of many other Eastern nations, especially values such qualities as teamwork, trust, consensus, shared responsibility, loyalty and commitment, which are the essential ingredients of any successful partnership. These qualities – together with the recognition that, by improving quality control throughout the value chain and cutting inventories to the minimum – enabled Japanese producers, particularly in the fabricating sectors, to break into their competitors' markets, and to adopt the production strategies and working practices that conformed to the resource and institutional advantages of their home countries. Indeed, most researchers are agreed that the two most significant competitive advantages of Japanese firms that evolved during the post-war period were, first, the way they restructured their production and intrafirm transactions, and second, the way they managed and organized their vertical and horizontal relationships with other firms.[27]

Before considering the implications of the new trajectory of market-based capitalism for our theorizing about MNE activity, we would mention three other trends in economic organization that are also favouring more, rather than less, interfirm co-operation. The first concerns the renewed importance of small and medium-sized firms in the global economy.[28] This has led some commentators, notably Naisbitt (1994), to assert that yesterday's commercial behemoths are tomorrow's dinosaurs. The reasoning behind this assertion that 'small is beautiful' is that modern production methods, accelerating technological advances, more demanding consumers and the growing importance of services are all eroding the advantages of large plants based on a continuous, scale-friendly and relatively inflexible production system.

While accepting that there is some evidence for this contention (e.g. much of the growth in employment now taking place in the advanced industrial countries is in small to medium-sized firms) we, like Harrison (1994), are not convinced that the strategic influence of large firms is diminishing. We would prefer to suggest that any restructuring of the activity of large firms reflects their preferences for replacing hierarchical with alliance relationships, and that an increasing number of small firms are, in fact, part of *keiretsu*-like networks, which, more often than not, are dominated by large, lead or flagship firms (D'Cruz and Rugman 1992, 1993, Rugman and D'Cruz 1995) or as Lorenzoni and Baden Fuller (1995) put it, 'strategic centers'. Many small firms, too, are either spin-offs of large firms, or owe their prosperity to the fact that the latter are frequently their main clients and suppliers of critical assets. The kinds of example one has in mind are the hundreds of second- or third-tier suppliers to the large Japanese automobile companies;[29] the intricate web of horizontal relationships between the various associated companies of the Japanese 'soga shosa'; the extensive outsourcing of both hardware and software development by the Japanese video game producer Nintendo; the network of knitwear firms in the Modena region of Northern Italy; the many hundreds of Asian subcontractors to the giant footwear and apparel firms (e.g. Nike and Benetton).[30] The competitive advantages of the firms in these and similar groups are closely dependent on the exchange of skills, learning experiences, knowledge and finance between the firms in the network, and on the example and lead given by the flagship firms.

The second trend is related to the first. It is the growth of spatial clusters of economic activities that offer external or agglomerative economies to firms located within the cluster. This trend is explored in more detail in Chapter 7 of this volume. The idea, of course, is not new. Marshall paid much attention to it in his study of UK industry in the early twentieth century (Marshall 1920). Recently, it has been given a new lease of life by Porter (1990), who considers the presence of related industries as one of the four key determinants of a country's competitive assets, and by Krugman (1991) who believes that such economies largely explain the geographical specialization of value-added activities. While the evidence on the subnational spatial concentration of particular activities is still fragmentary, what information we have (including that documented in a new book by Kenichi Ohmae 1995) such as it is, suggests that, in the technology and information-intensive sectors, not only are MNEs creating multiple strategic centres for specialized activities, but such clusters are becoming an increasingly important component of competitiveness (Enright 1994). The form and extent of the clusters may differ.[31] Sometimes, they relate to a range of pre-competitive innovatory activities (e.g. science parks); sometimes to very specific sectors (e.g. auto assemblers and component suppliers);[32] and sometimes to entrepreneurial or start-up firms and co-operative research organizations (e.g. SEMITECH). Sometimes the local networks are contained in a very small geographical area (e.g. financial districts in London and New York); sometimes they spread over a whole region (e.g. the cluster of textile firms in north Italy).

The third trend is the growth of industrial networks. Interfirm alliances can range from being simple dyadic relationships to being part of complex, and often overlapping, networks consisting of tens, if not hundreds, of firms. The literature on industrial networks is extensive;[33] but, up to now, the subject has been mainly approached from a marketing or an organizational, rather than from an economic, perspective. This is, perhaps, one reason why internalization theory and the eclectic paradigm of international production have sometimes been portrayed as alternative approaches to network analysis. But to the economist, a network is simply a web of interdependent dyadic relationships. One must admit, this makes theorizing about the behaviour of the participants very difficult, but no more so than theorizing about the behaviour of oligopolists. It is also true that the economist is primarily concerned with the firm as a unit of analysis, but this in no way should inhibit him (or her) from considering the implications for the firm when it is a part of a network of related firms.

What is clear, however, is that, as networks of alliances become more important, the composition and behaviour of the group of firms becomes a more important determinant of the foreign production of the individual firms comprising the network. Nowhere is this more clearly seen than in the role played by the *keiretsu* in influencing both the competitive advantages of its member firms, and in the way in which these advantages are created, upgraded and used.

REAPPRAISING THE ECLECTIC PARADIGM

We now turn to consider the implications of alliance capitalism for our theorizing about the determinants of MNE activity, and, more particularly, for the eclectic paradigm. In brief, the implications are threefold. First, the concept of the competitive, or O-specific, advantages of firms, as traditionally perceived, needs to be broadened to take *explicit* account of the costs and benefits derived from interfirm relationships and transactions (both at home and abroad), and particularly those that arise from strategic alliances and networks. Second, the concept of location (or L) advantages of countries (as traditionally perceived) needs to give more weight to the following factors: (i) the territorial embeddedness of interdependent immobile assets in particular geographical areas;[34] (ii) the increasing need for the spatial integration of complex and rapidly changing economic activities; (iii) the conditions under which interfirm competitive-enhancing alliances may flourish; and (iv) the role of national and regional authorities in influencing the extent and structure of localized centres of excellence.

Third, the idea that firms internalize intermediate product markets, primarily to reduce the transaction and co-ordination costs associated with them, needs to be widened to encompass other – and, more particularly, dynamic and competitiveness-enhancing – goals, the attainment of which may be affected by micro-governance structures. The incorporation of external alliances into the theory of internalization presents no real problems, other than semantic ones. Either one treats a non-equity alliance as an extension of intrafirm transactions, and accepts that the theory is concerned less with a *de jure* concept of hierarchical control and ownership, and more with the *de facto* ways in which interdependent tangible and intangible assets are harnessed and leveraged, or one treats the interfirm alliance as a distinctive organizational mode, and more specifically one which is complementary to, rather than a substitute for, a hierarchy. Partly, of course, the choice will depend on the unit of analysis being used. Is it the alliance or the network, *per se*, in which case the idea of 'group internalization' may be a relevant one? Or, is the unit of analysis the individual enterprises that comprise the alliance or network? For our purposes, we shall take the individual enterprise as the unit of analysis.[35]

Let us now be more specific about the modifications that alliance capitalism seems to require of the eclectic paradigm. We consider each of its components in turn. On the left-hand side of Table 3.1, we set out some of the more important OLI variables that scholars traditionally have hypothesized to influence the level and structure of MNE activity. Research has shown that the composition and significance of these determinants will differ according to the value of four contextual variables: (i) the kind of MNE activity being considered (*market*, *resource*, *efficiency* or *strategic asset seeking*, (ii) the portfolio of location-bound assets of the countries from which the FDI originates, and in which it is concentrated, (iii) the technological and other attributes of the sectors in which it is being directed, and (iv) the specific characteristics (including the production, innovatory and ownership strategies) of the firms undertaking the investment.

The variables identified in Table 3.1 are more than a checklist. They are chosen because a trilogy of extant economic and behavioural theories – namely, *the theory of industrial organization and market entry*, *the theory of location*[36] and *the theory of the firm*[37] – suggests that they offer robust explanations of the ownership structure of firms, the location of their activities, and the ways in which they govern the deployment of resources and capabilities within their control or influence. However, until very recently, none of these theories have paid much attention to the role of co-operative agreements in influencing MNE activity.

On the right-hand side of Table 3.1, we identify some additional OLI variables which we believe, in the evolving era of alliance capitalism, need to be incorporated into our theorizing about MNE activity. The table shows that not all of the OLI variables listed require modification. Thus, of the Oa-specific variables, we would not expect the formation of strategic partnerships to influence greatly the internal work processes of the participating firms, although technological advances, and the need for continuous product improvement, are likely to demand a closer interaction between related value-adding activities, and may well enhance the contribution of shop-floor labour to raising process productivity. Nor would we expect the proprietary rights of brand ownership, favoured access to suppliers, or the financial control procedures of firms to be much affected by co-operative agreements.

By contrast, Oa advantages stemming from a firm's ability to create and organize new knowledge, to maintain and upgrade product quality, to seek out and forge productive linkages with suppliers and customers, especially – in unfamiliar markets – to externalize risk, to manage successfully a complex portfolio of core assets and value-creating disciplines, and to internalize the skills and learning experiences of other organizations, may be strongly influenced by some kinds of co-operative arrangements. Moreover,

Table 3.1 A reconfiguration of the eclectic paradigm of international production

1 Ownership-specific advantages (of enterprise of one nationality (or affiliates of same) over those of another)	
Hierarchical-related advantages	*Alliance or network-related advantages*
(a) Property right and/or intangible asset advantages (Oa) Product innovations, production management, organizational and marketing systems, innovatory capacity, non-codifiable knowledge: 'bank' of human capital experience; marketing, finance, know-how, etc.	(a) *Vertical alliances* (i) Backward access to R&D, design engineering and training facilities of suppliers. Regular input by them on problem solving and product innovation on the consequences of projected new production processes for component design and manufacturing. New insights into, and monitoring of, developments in materials, and how they might impact on existing products and production processes
(b) Advantages of common governance, i.e. of organizing Oa with complementary assets (Ot)	(ii) Forward access to industrial customers, new markets, marketing techniques and distribution channels, particularly in unfamiliar locations or where products need to be adapted to meet local supply capabilities and markets. Advice by customers on product design and performance. Help in strategic market positioning
(i) Those that branch plants of established enterprises may enjoy over *de novo* firms. Those due mainly to size, product diversity and learning experiences of enterprise, e.g. economies of scope and specialization. Exclusive or favoured access to inputs, e.g. labour, natural resources, finance, information. Ability to obtain inputs on favoured terms (due, for example, to size or monopsonistic influence). Ability of parent company to conclude productive and co-operative interfirm relationships, e.g. as between Japanese auto assemblers and their suppliers. Exclusive or favoured access to product markets. Access to resources of parent company at marginal cost. Synergistic economies (not only in production, but in purchasing, marketing, finance, etc., arrangements)	(b) *Horizontal alliances* Access to complementary technologies and innovatory capacity. Access to additional capabilities to capture benefits of technology fusion, and to identify new uses for related technologies. Encapsulation of learning and development times. Such interfirm interaction often generates its own knowledge feedback mechanisms and path dependencies
(ii) Which specifically arise because of multinationality. Multinationality enhances operational flexibility by offering wider opportunities for arbitraging, production shifting and global sourcing of inputs. More favoured access to and/or better knowledge about international markets, e.g. for information, finance, labour, etc. Ability to take advantage of geographic differences in factor endowments, government intervention, markets, etc. Ability to diversify or reduce risks, e.g. in different currency areas, and creation of options and/or political and cultural scenarios. Ability to learn from societal differences in organizational and managerial processes and systems. Balancing economies of integration with ability to respond to	(c) *Networks* (i) of similar firms: Reduced transaction and co-ordination costs arising from better dissemination and interpretation of knowledge and information, and from mutual support and co-operation between members of network. Improved knowledge about process and product development and markets. Multiple, yet complementary, inputs into innovatory developments and exploitation of new markets. Access to embedded knowledge of members of networks. Opportunities to develop 'niche' R&D strategies, shared learning and training experiences, e.g. as in the case of co-operative research associations. Networks may also help promote uniform product standards and other collective advantages.

Table (3.1) (cont)

Hierarchical-related advantages	*Alliance or network-related advantages*
difference in country-specific needs and advantages	ledge-based institutions, e.g. universities, co-operative R&D establishments etc.
(ii) business districts: As per (i) plus spatial agglomerative economies, e.g. labour market pooling. Access to clusters of specialized intermediate inputs, technological spillovers, and linkages with know	*3 Location-specific variables (these may favour home or host countries)* *Hierarchical-related advantages* Spatial distribution of natural and created resource endowments and markets

2 Internalization incentive advantages (i.e. to circumvent or exploit market failure)

Hierarchical-related advantages	*Alliance or network-related advantages*
Avoidance of search and negotiating costs To avoid costs of moral hazard, information asymmetries and adverse selection, and to protect reputation of internalizing firm To avoid costs of broken contracts and ensuing litigation Buyer uncertainty (about nature and value of inputs (e.g. technology) being sold) When market does not permit price discrimination Need of seller to protect quality of intermediate or final products	While, in some cases, time-limited interfirm co-operative relationships may be a substitute for FDI, in others they may add to the I incentive advantages of the participating hierarchies, R&D alliances and networking which may help strengthen the overall competitiveness of the participating firms. Moreover, the growing structural integration of the world economy is requiring firms to go outside their immediate boundaries to capture the complex realities of know-how trading and knowledge exchange in innovation, particularly where intangible assets are tacit and need speedily to adapt competitive-enhancing strategies to structural change
To capture economies of interdependent activities (see (b) above) To compensate for failure or absence of future markets To avoid or exploit government intervention (e.g. quotas, tariffs, price controls, tax differences, etc.) To control supplies and conditions of sale of inputs (including technology) To control market outlets (including those which might be used by competitors) To be able to engage in practices, e.g. cross-subsidization, predatory pricing, leads and lags, transfer pricing, etc., as a competitive (or anti-competitive) strategy	Alliances or network-related advantages are those which prompt a 'voice' rather than an 'exit' response to market failure; they also allow many of the advantages of internalization without the inflexibility, bureaucratic or risk-related costs associated with it. Such quasi-internalization is likely to be most successful in cultures in which trust, forbearance, reciprocity and consensus politics are at a premium. It suggests that firms are more appropriately likened to archipelagos linked by causeways rather than self-contained 'islands' of conscious power. At the same time, flagship or lead MNEs, by orchestrating the use of mobile O advantages and immobile advantages, enhance their role as arbitragers of complementary cross-border value-added activities

Table 3.1 (cont)

Hierarchical-related advantages	*Alliance or network-related advantages*
Input prices, quality and productivity, e.g. labour, energy, materials, components, semi-finished goods International transport and communication costs Investment incentives and disincentives (including performance requirements etc.) Artificial barriers (e.g. import controls) to trade in goods Societal and infrastructure provisions (commercial, legal, educational, transport and communication) Cross-country ideological, language, cultural, business, political, etc., differences Economies of centralization of R&D production and marketing Economic systems and policies of governments: the institutional framework for resource creation and allocation	The L-specific advantages of alliance formations arise essentially from the presence of a portfolio of immobile local complementary assets, which, when organized within a framework of alliances and networks, produce a stimulating and productive industrial atmosphere. The extent and type of business districts, industrial or science parks and the external economies they offer participating firms are examples of these advantages which, over time, may allow foreign affiliates and cross-border alliances and network relationships better to tap into, and exploit, the comparative technological and organizational advantages of host countries. Localized networks may help reduce the information asymmetries and likelihood of opportunism in spatially linked markets. They may also create local institutional thickness, and foster interfirm learning economies and social embeddedness. Note that globalization, while heightening the mobility of some O-specific advantages, is also increasing some distance-related transaction costs, and leaning to more 'sticky' places (Markusen 1994)

each of these advantages may better enable a firm both to engage in transborder activities and to seek out appropriate agreements to strengthen and consolidate its competitive competencies.

The literature identifies two groups of competitive Ot advantages arising from the way in which a firm combines its own resources and capabilities with those of other firms. The first are those which a firm gains from being a multi-activity enterprise, independently of where these activities are located. Such economies of common governance may enable an established firm of one nationality to penetrate a foreign market more easily than a single-activity competitor of the same or of another nationality. The second type of Ot advantage arises as a direct consequence of foreign production.[38] The impact of alliance capitalism is to offer an additional avenue for firms to acquire and build up both types of advantages – and, normally, to do so with less financial outlay and risk than hierarchical capitalism might involve.[39]

It is, however, the second kind of Ot advantage that is the quintessence of both the multi-activity and the multinational firm. The implication is, then, that any decline in hierarchical activity reflects a diminution in the net benefits of internalized markets, which may lead to a *concentrate on core competency strategy*. It is also implied that other ways of obtaining the advantages are becoming more attractive (e.g. as a result of a reduction of other kinds of market failure). In our present context, the switch in organizational form is a reflection of a shift in the techno-economic system of production. As we have already argued, this tends to favour a 'voice', rather than an 'exit', response to the inability of markets to cope with the externalities of interdependent activities in the first place.

It is too early to judge the extent to which the economies of synergy (and operational flexibility) are being realized in a more cost-effective way by external partnerships, rather than by hierarchical control. In any event, as we have already stated, many – indeed, perhaps, the majority of – strategic business alliances identified by scholars should not be regarded as substitutes for FDI, as they are directed to achieving very specific purposes.

Turning next to the internalization advantages (I) of MNE activities, it is perhaps here where the co-operative interaction between Japanese firms is most clearly demonstrated as a viable alternative to the full ownership and control favoured by US firms. Here, too, it is not so much that interfirm agreements add to the internalization incentives of firms. It is rather that they may help to achieve the same objective more effectively, or spread the capital and other risks of the participating firms. In other words, interfirm agreements may provide additional avenues for circumventing or lessening market failure where the FDI route is an impractical option.

Clearly, the impact of alliance capitalism on the organization of economic activity will vary according to the type of market failure being considered; it is also likely to be highly industry and country specific. Institutional structures, learning paths, the extent of social and territorial embeddedness, cultural values, and national systems of education and innovation are likely to play an especially important role. In some countries, such as Japan, there is less incentive by firms to internalize markets in order to avoid the costs of broken contracts, or to ensure the quality of subcontracted products. The reason is simply because these types of market failure are minimized by the 'voice' strategies of buyers and sellers, which are built upon mutual interest, trust and forbearance. The *keiretsu* network of interfirm competitive interaction – sometimes between firms in the same sector and sometimes across sectors – is perhaps one of the most frequently quoted alternatives to hierarchical internalization. Although there is frequently some minority cross-ownership among the networking firms, the relationship is built upon objectives, values and strategies that negate the need for the internalization of some kinds of market failure. At the same time, the extent and pattern of *keiretsu* ties is likely to vary between industrial sectors. It is, for example, most pronounced in the fabricating sectors (where the number and degree of complexity of transactions are the most numerous) and the least pronounced in the processing sectors. And, as chapter 13 will illustrate in more detail, it is a fact that Japanese FDI in Europe – relative to its US counterpart – is concentrated in those sectors in which interfirm, rather than intrafirm, transactions are the preferred modality of counteracting market failure in Japan.

While it would be inappropriate to generalize from this example, it is nevertheless the case that – again due to the adoption of new and flexible production techniques – American firms in the auto and consumer electronic sectors are disinternalizing parts of their value chains. At the same time, they are reducing the number of major suppliers and delegating more design and innovatory functions to them.[40] Moreover, Japanese-owned auto assemblers in the United States are replicating or modifying the *keiretsu*-type relationships of their parent companies as more Japanese suppliers have been setting up subsidiaries, or engaging in co-operative agreements with US firms to supply components to the assemblers (Banjerji and Sambharya 1996).

Most certainly, a 'voice' response to market failure is raising the profile of strategic partnerships in the organizational strategies of MNEs. Nevertheless, it is the case that some kinds of benefits of cross-border value-added activity can only be effectively realized through a full hierarchical control over such operations. Examples include situations in which path dependency, learning experience and the global control over financial assets and key technologies and competencies bring their own O-specific advantages, which, because of possible conflicts of interest, would not be realizable from interfirm agreements. Such agreements, then, would probably be confined to very specific areas of a firm's value-added activities, and, noticeably, those that are outside its core competencies need specialized proficiencies or require to be closely monitored for quality control, and are too costly to produce internally (Quinn and Hilmer 1994). But, to achieve and sustain many of the most valuable O-specific advantages of multinational operations, hierarchical control probably will remain the principal mode of internationalization, and this applies as much to the Japanese as it does to US- and European-based MNEs.

We finally consider how the advent of alliance capitalism is affecting the location-specific variables influencing international production. We have already indicated that the received literature generally assumes these variables to be exogenous to individual firms, at least at a given moment of time, although, over time, such firms may affect the L advantages of particular countries or regions.

There are essentially two main ways in which alliance capitalism may affect, or be affected by, the presence and structure of immobile assets. The first is that it may introduce new L-specific variables, or modify the value of those traditionally considered by location theory. The second is that the response of firms to economic geography may be different because of the impact that external alliances may have upon their competitive strengths and global strategies.

Let us first deal with the first type of effect. Chief among the L variables affecting MNE activity – and that surveys have revealed have become more significant in the past decade – is the availability of resources and capabilities that investing firms believe are necessary both to upgrade and make best use of their core O-specific advantages. In some cases, these complementary assets, or the rights to their use, can be bought on the open market (e.g. power supplies and transport and communication facilities), but, in others, and noticeably in regimes of rapid technological progress (Teece 1992), the 'continuous handshake' of an alliance relationship rather than the 'invisible hand' of the market is favoured (Gerlach 1992). Since frequently FDI requires the establishment of several of these bilateral relationships, it follows that the positioning of a constellation of related partners becomes a prime locational factor. Where part or all of the constellations are sited in close proximity to each other, then additional benefits may arise. These include not only the static agglomerative economies earlier identified, but also the dynamic externalities associated with the gathering and dissemination of information, and the cross-fertilization of ideas and learning experiences.

The attention given by governments of host countries – or of regions in host countries – to the building of a critical mass of interrelated activities, which is consistent with the perceived dynamic comparative advantage of their location-bound assets, and to the use of FDI in order to create or upgrade core competences to advance this goal, is just one illustration of the growing benefits to be derived from interfirm linkages.[41] These serve as an L-pull factor. Casual empiricism, both past and present, provides ample examples of how the presence of spatially related business networks attract new investors, and recent evidence unearthed by Wheeler and Mody (1992), Harrison (1994), Lazerson (1993), Herrigel (1994), Audretsch and Feldman (1994) and Enright (1994) confirms these impressions. It also reveals that an innovation-driven industrial economy, which seeks to be fully integrated into world markets, needs to focus more attention on the development of clusters of interfirm linkages, of intelligent regions and of local institutional thickness (Amin and Thrift 1994).

A later chapter in this volume will give attention to some of the paradoxes of the emerging globalized economy. One of these relates to the apparent contradiction between the truncation of geographical space, for example in the financial services industries, brought about by advances in telecommunications and information technologies, and the growth of new local or regional economic districts, made up of economic activities which need to be in close propinquity of each other. We believe that the key to this paradox lies in the changing significance of different kinds of distance-related transaction and co-ordination costs. While recent innovations and organizational changes have enhanced the cross-border mobility of many kinds of goods, services and assets, they have also led to new rounds of specialization and 'stickiness' in economic activity, such that 'vast areas of substantively complex, irregular, uncertain and extremely time dependent transactions have been created' (Storper and Scott 1995: 508). These transactions are not only unstructured and highly sensitive to distance; they also confer substantial interactive learning benefits on the participating firms. Examples of such closely knit economic clusters of activity are given in Chapters 1 and 14 and in Enright (1994), Markusen (1994) and Storper and Scott (1995).

The new trajectory of capitalism has other implications for the locational requirements of MNE investors. Some of these are set out in Table 3.1. As a generalization, while traditional production-related variables generally are unaffected or becoming less important, those to do with minimizing transaction and co-ordination costs of markets or the dysfunctioning of hierarchies, those specific to being part of a group or cluster of related activities, and those that help protect or upgrade the global competitiveness of the investing firm, are becoming more important.[42]

Turning now to the second type of effect that alliance capitalism has on L advantages, we ask the following question: how far, and in what ways, are the responses of MNEs to the L advantages of countries themselves changing because of the growing pluralism of corporate organizations? The answer is that such pluralism allows firms more flexibility in their locational strategies, and that the immobile assets of countries will affect not only the extent and pattern of foreign participation, but also its organizational form. Thus, on the one hand, the opportunities for networking in a specific country may increase FDI. This is particularly the case when an MNE acquires a firm that is already part of a network. On the other hand, networking may also reduce FDI, as it may allow a foreign firm to acquire the complementary assets it needs without making an equity stake.

Of the two scenarios, the one which is more likely to occur will, of course, depend on a host of industry-, firm- and country-specific circumstances. But, our point will have been made if it is accepted that the hypotheses of scholars about the responses of firms to at least some L-specific variables may need to be modified in the light of the growing significance of non-equity-based co-operative arrangements, and of networks of firms with related interests. We also believe that the ways in which MNEs choose to leverage and use a portfolio of interrelated location-bound assets, with those of their own O-specific advantages and the complementary competencies of external partners, are, themselves, becoming an increasingly important competitive advantage of such firms.

CONCLUSIONS

This chapter has suggested that the socio-institutional structure of market-based capitalism is undergoing change. The catalyst is a new wave of multi-purpose generic technological advances and the demands of knowledge-based production, which are compelling more co-operation among economic agents. Though part of that co-operation is 'bought' by firms through M&A activity, the growing significance of interfirm partnering and of networking is demanding a re-examination of traditional approaches to our understanding of the extent and form of international business activity.

Our discussion has concentrated on only one of these approaches, namely the eclectic paradigm of international production, and has suggested that its explanatory framework needs to be modified in three main ways. First, the role of innovation in sustaining and upgrading the competitive advantages of firms and countries needs to be better recognized. It also needs to be more explicitly acknowledged that firms may engage in FDI and in cross-border alliances in order to acquire or learn about foreign technology and markets, as well as to exploit their existing competitive advantages. *Inter alia*, this suggests a strengthening of its analytical underpinnings to encompass a theory of innovation – as, for example, propounded by Nelson and Winter (1982) and Cantwell (1989, 1994) – that identifies and evaluates the role of technological accumulation and learning as O-specific advantages of firms, and the role of national education and innovation policies affecting the L advantages of countries.

Second, the paradigm needs to recognize better that a 'voice' strategy for reducing some kinds of market failure – and particularly those to do with opportunism and information impactness by participants in the market – is a viable alternative to an 'exit' strategy of hierarchical capitalism, and that, like hierarchies, strategic partnerships are intended to reduce endemic market failure, and may help to advance innovatory competitiveness rather than inhibit it. Among other things, this suggests that theories of interfirm co-operation or collective competition, which tend to address issues of static efficiency (Buckley 1993), need to be widened to incorporate questions of dynamic efficiency, for example market positioning.

Third, the eclectic paradigm needs to acknowledge that the traditional assumption that the capabilities of the individual firm are limited to its ownership boundaries (and that, outside these boundaries, factors influencing the firm's competitiveness are exogenous to it) is no longer acceptable whenever the quality of a firm's efficiency-related decisions is significantly influenced by the collaborative agreements it has with other firms. The concept of decision taking has implications that go well beyond explaining FDI and international production; indeed, it calls into question some of the fundamental underpinnings of the theory of industrial organization.

Much of the thrust of this chapter has been concerned with suggesting how these three evolving concepts – innovation-led growth, a 'voice' reaction to market failure, and co-operation as a competitiveness-enhancing measure – affect the OLI configuration facing firms engaging, or wishing to engage, in cross-border transactions. In doing so, it has thrown up a number of casual hypotheses as to the kinds of O-specific advantages that are most likely to be affected by interfirm alliances and networks, and about how the opportunities to engage in such alliances or networks may affect, and be affected by, the portfolio of interrelated location-specific assets. The analysis has also sought to identify some of the implications of the gathering pace of innovation-led production, and of alliance capitalism, for the organization of economic activity. In doing so, it has suggested that the internalization paradigm still remains a powerful tool of analysis, as long as it is widened to incorporate strategic asset-acquiring FDI and the dynamic learning activities of firms, and to take account more explicitly of the conditions under which a 'voice' strategy of interfirm co-operation may be a preferable option to an 'exit' strategy for reducing the transaction and co-ordination costs of arm's length markets, and building interactive learning-based competitiveness.[43]

There has been some exploratory empirical testing, using both field and case study data, of the impact of alliances and networks on the performance of locational and organizational strategies of participating firms. Studies by Gomes-Casseres (1994, 1995) on the global computer and electronics industries; by Gomes-Casseres and Leonard-Barton (1994) on the multimedia sector; by Mowery (1988) on the commercial aircraft industry; by Brooks *et al.* (1993) on the container transport industry; by Shan and Hamilton (1991) and Whittaker and Bower (1994) on the pharmaceutical industry; by Peng (1993) on the role of network and alliance strategies in assisting the transition from a collectivist to a market-based economy; by Helper (1993) on the 'exit' and 'voice' sourcing strategies of the leading auto assemblers; by Enright (1993, 1994), Glaismeier (1988), Henderson (1994), Lazerson (1993), Piore and Sabel (1984), Saxenian (1994) and Scott (1993) on the rationale for regional clusters and specialized industrial districts in Europe and the United States; and multiple case studies by a number of authors on the roles of *keiretsu*-based transactions and relational contracting as alternatives to hierarchies (e.g. Lincoln 1990) are just a few examples.

But much more remains to be done. Indeed, it is possible that the basic contention of this chapter – if not this whole volume – that innovation-led production systems and co-operative interfirm agreements are emerging as the dominant form of market-based capitalism, is incorrect. At the same time, it would be difficult to deny that important changes – and, for the most part, irreversible technological changes – are afoot in the global economy, and that these changes are requiring international business scholars to re-examine at least some of the concepts and theories that have dominated the field for the last two decades or more.

NOTES

1 As set out, most recently, in Dunning (1993a: Chapter 4).

2 See, for example, Dunning (1994a) and Gerlach (1992) for a more extensive analysis of this proposition.

3 Especially at River Rouge (USA), where its empire included ore and coal mines, 70,000 acres of timberland, saw mills, blast furnaces, glass works, ore and coal barges, and a railway (Williamson 1985).

4 As, for example, is shown by data published in the US Census of Manufacturers and the UK Census of Production (various issues).

5 For full details, see Chandler (1962) and Dunning (1994a).

6 At the time it was published (1937), Coase's article on 'The nature of the firm' was treated as an 'aberration' by his fellow economists (Williamson 1993). As Coase himself acknowledged (1993), in the 1980s there was more discussion of his ideas than during the whole of the preceding forty years.

7 I do not know for sure which particular scholar first used the concept of market failure to explain the existence and growth of the MNE. I first came across the concept of internalization in the early 1970s in a chapter by John McManus entitled, 'The theory of the multinational firm', in an edited volume by Pacquet (McManus 1972).

8 It is also of some interest that Penrose did not cite Coase in any of her work.

9 There were, I think, two reasons for this. The first was that mainstream micro-economists were strongly influenced (one might almost say hidebound) by the static equilibrium models of Chamberlin (1933) and Robinson (1933); and the second was that Penrose had not formalized her theory in a manner acceptable to her colleagues.

10 Among the most frequently quoted scholars are Buckley and Casson, Hennart, Rugman and Teece. A summary of the views of the internalization school are contained in Dunning (1993a). See also Rugman (1981), Hennart (1982), Buckley and Casson (1985) and Casson (1987).

11 See, for example, the contributions to Buckley's edited volume (1993).

12 Elsewhere (Dunning 1993b), we have suggested paradigm is a more appropriate term to apply to explain the reactions of firms to cross-border market failure.

13 Exceptions include structural market failure deliberately engineered by firms and the extent to which they may be able to influence the content and degree of market failure, for example by lobbying for particular government action, and by the setting up of compensating institutions, for example insurance and future markets, to reduce risk.

14 See especially Best (1990), Gerlach (1992), Lazonick (1991, 1992), Michalet (1991), Dunning (1994a) and Ruigrok and Van Tulder (1995).

15 Here, we think it appropriate to make the point that the expression *alliance capitalism* should be perceived partly as a socio-cultural phenomenon and partly as a techno-organizational one. The former suggests a change in the ethos and perspective towards the organization of capitalism and, in particular, towards the relationships between the participating institutions and individuals. The latter embraces the formal structure of the organization of economic activity, including the management of resource allocation and growth. Alliance capitalism is an

eclectic (*sic*) concept. It suggests both co-operation and competition *between* institutions (including public institutions) and between interested parties *within* institutions. *De facto*, it is also leading to a flattening out of the organizational structure of decision taking of business enterprises, with a pyramidal chain of command being increasingly replaced by a more heterarchical interplay between the main participants in decision taking. Finally, we would emphasize that we are not suggesting that alliance capitalism means the demise of hierarchies, but rather that the rationale and functions of hierarchies require a reappraisal in the socio-economic climate of the global market-place now emerging.

16 In the words of Adam Smith (1776) 'people of the same trade seldom meet together, even for merriment and diversion, but the conversation ends in a conspiracy against the public, or in some contrivance to raise prices'.

17 See especially Buckley and Casson (1988), Contractor and Lorange (1988), Kogut (1988), Hennart (1988, 1989) and Hagedoorn (1993a, b).

18 The facts are documented in various publications, for example Freeman and Hagedoorn (1992), Hagedoorn (1990, 1993a, b), Gomes-Casseres (1993) and UNCTAD (1993, 1994).

19 Some examples are set out in Dunning (1993a: 605ff): 'Optoelectronics, for example, is a marriage of electronics and optics and is yielding important commercial products such as optical fibre communication systems [Kodama 1992]. The latest generation of large commercial aircraft, for example, requires the combined skills of metallurgy, aeronautical engineering and aero-electronics. Current medical advances often need the technological resources of pharmacology, biotechnology, laser technology, and genetic engineering for their successful commercialization. The design and construction of chemical plants involves innovatory inputs from chemical, engineering and materials sectors. New telecommunication devices embrace the latest advances in carbon materials, fibre optics, computer technology, and electronic engineering. Modern industrial building techniques need to draw upon the combined expertise of engineering, materials and production technologies. In its venture to explore the sea-bed, Kennecott's consortium brings together a large number of technical disciplines and firms from many different industrial sectors [Contractor and Lorange 1988]. Since both the consumption and the production of most core technologies usually yield externalities of one kind or another, it follows that one or the other of the firms involved may be prompted to recoup these benefits by integrating the separate activities, particularly those which draw upon the same generic technology.'

20 Examples include the rapid obsolescence of successive generations of computers and the information-carrying power of microchips.

21 One particularly good example is the pharmaceutical industry, where the large drug companies are increasingly disinternalizing the most novel and risky types of biotechnology innovations to small specialist firms. In the words of two British researchers (Whittaker and Bower 1994): 'The large pharmaceutical companies no longer view themselves as the primary innovators in the industry.... The biotechnology companies take on the role of supplier of innovatory activity.' The authors go on to illustrate the symbiotic supplier/buyer relationship that is developing between the two groups of firms. 'The large drug company needs technologically novel products to market and the biotechnology company needs finance, sometimes some ancillary technical expertise in later-stage process development and formulation, skill in handling regulatory agreements and marketing forces' (p. 258). However, it should be pointed out that in the last two years there have been some significant acquisitions of biotechnology companies by pharmaceutical MNEs.

22 For example, of the alliances identified by Freeman and Hagedoorn, 76.3 per cent were accounted for by twenty-one MNEs, each of whom had concluded 100 or more alliances.
23 At the same time, MNEs have increased the R&D intensity of their foreign operations, and have set up technological listening posts in the leading innovating countries.
24 The authors assert that such alliances result from the fusion of technologies from computer communications and consumer electronics; and that because no single firm had (or has) the internal capabilities or the time needed to produce a PDA, it was necessary to form a cluster of 'matching' alliances.
25 In their words, 'Competitive success requires the integration of multiple capabilities (e.g., innovation, productivity, quality, responsiveness to customers) across internal and external organizational boundaries' (p. 151).
26 Not to mention to preclude competition from gaining such assets.
27 See, for example, several chapters in an edited volume by Encarnation and Mason (1994).
28 As shown by a variety of indices.
29 See, for example, Banjerji and Sambharya (1996).
30 For further illustrations, see Hamel (1991), Harrison (1994), Stopford (1995), Whittaker and Bower (1994) and Lorenzoni and Baden Fuller (1995).
31 For an interesting discussion of the differing nature of business districts both in the United States and in other countries, see Markusen *et al.* (1991).
32 It is estimated that 70 per cent of all Toyota's suppliers are within 100 miles (160 km) of Toyota's main assembling complex in Tokyo.
33 See, particularly, Forsgren and Johanson (1991), Håkansson and Johanson (1993), Johanson and Mattsson (1987, 1994) and Johanson and Vahlne (1977).
34 In the words of Amin and Thrift (1994), and in the context of the globalizing economy, 'centers of geographical agglomeration are centers of representation, interaction and innovation within global production filieres'. It is their 'unique ability to act as a pole of excellence and to offer to the wide collectivity a well consolidated network of contacts, knowledge, structures and institutions underwriting individual entrepreneurship which makes a center a magnet for economic activity' (p. 13)
35 For an examination of the alliance as a unit of analysis, see Gomes-Casseres (1994).
36 Where country-specific characteristics are regarded as endogenous variables, then the theory of international economics becomes relevant. This is the position of Kojima (1978, 1990), who is one of the leading exponents of a trade-related theory of MNE activity.
37 In particular, the transaction cost theories of Coase and Williamson. The resource-based theory of the firm (Wernerfelt 1984, Barney 1991, Peteraf 1993) is much broader and, in many respects, closer in lineage to industrial organization theory, as it is concerned with explaining the origin of a firm's sustainable competitive advantages in terms of resource heterogeneity, limits to competition and imperfect resource immobility.
38 It is these latter advantages that internalization economists claim *follow* from foreign-owned production, rather than *precede* it; although, of course, once established, these advantages may place the MNE in a more favoured position for sequential investment.
39 Of course, in some instances (e.g. jointly funded R&D projects), the resulting economic rents may also have to be shared.

40 Stopford (1995), drawing upon the World Automotive Components supplement published by the *Financial Times* on 12 July 1994, gives several examples of this phenomenon.

41 As is amply realized by the national governments of foreign investment agencies in their attempts to attract foreign firms to locate in their territories.

42 We accept that it may be difficult to separate the specific effect of alliance capitalism from the other forces influencing the L advantage of countries. This, indeed, is a fertile area for empirical research.

43 According to Storper (1994) those firms, sectors, regions and nations that are able to learn faster and more efficiently become competitive because knowledge is scarce and, therefore, cannot be imitated by new entrants or transferred by codified and formal channels to other firms, regions or nations.

REFERENCES

Amin, A. and Thrift, N. (eds) (1994) *Globalization, Institutions and Regional Development in Europe*, Oxford: Oxford University Press.

Audretsch, D. B. and Feldman, M. P. (1994) 'External economies and spatial clustering', in P. R. Krugman and A. Venables (eds) *The Location of Economic Activity: New theories and evidence*, London: Center of Economic Policy Research (CPER).

Banjerji, K. and Sambharya, R. B. (1994) *Vertical keiretsu and international market entry: The case of the Japanese automobile industry, Journal of International Business Studies* 27(1): 89-114.

Barney, J. B. (1991) 'Firm resources and sustained competitive advantage', *Journal of Management* 17: 99–120.

Best, M, (1990) *The New Competition: Institutions of Restructuring*, Cambridge, MA: Harvard University Press.

Brooks, M. R., Blunder, R. G. and Bidgood, C. I. (1993) 'Strategic alliances in the global container transport industry', in R. Culpan (ed.) *Multinational Strategic Alliances*, pp. 221–50, New York and London: The Haworth Press.

Buckley, P. J. (ed.) (1993) *Cooperative Forms of TNC Activity*, UNCTC Library on Transnational Corporations, Vol. 13, London and New York: Routledge.

Buckley, P. J. and Casson, M. C. (1985) *The Economic Theory of the Multinational Enterprise*, London: Macmillan.

——(1988) 'A theory of cooperation in international business', in F. J. Contractor and P. Lorange (eds) *Cooperative Strategies in International Business*, pp. 31–53, Lexington, MA: D. C. Heath.

Bye, M. (1958) 'Self-financed multiterritorial units and their time horizon', *International Economic Papers* 8: 147–78.

Cantwell, J. A. (1989) *Technological Innovation and Multinational Corporations*, Oxford: Basil Blackwell.

——(ed.) (1994) *Transnational Corporations and Innovatory Activities*, United Nations Library on Transnational Corporations, Vol. 17, London: Routledge.

Casson, M. C. (1987) *The Firm and the Market*, Oxford: Basil Blackwell.

Chamberlin, E. (1933) *The Theory of Monopolistic Competition*, Boston: Harvard University Press.

Chandler, A. D. Jr (1962) *Strategy and Structure*, Boston: Harvard University Press.

——(1990) *Scale and Scope: The Dynamics of Industrial Capitalism*, Cambridge, MA: Harvard University Press.

Coase, R. H. (1937) 'The nature of the firm', *Economica* 4, November: 386–405.

——(1988) *The Firm, the Market and the Law*, Chicago and London: University of Chicago Press.
——(1993) 'The nature of the firm: meaning and influence', in O. E. Williamson and S. G. Winter (eds) *The Nature of the Firm*, pp. 34–74, New York and Oxford: Oxford University Press.
Contractor, F, J. and Lorange, P. (1988) *Cooperative Strategies in International Business*, Lexington, MA: D. C. Heath.
Cournot, A. A. (1851) *Researches into Mathematical Principles of the Theory of Wealth*, trans. N. T. Bacon, New York: Macmillan.
D'Cruz, J. R. and Rugman, A. M. (1992) 'Business networks for International Business', *Business Quarterly* 54, Spring: 101–7.
——(1993) Business networks for global competitiveness, *Business Quarterly* 57, Summer: 93–8.
Dunning, J. H. (1993a) *Multinational Enterprises and the Global Economy*, Wokingham Addison Wesley.
——(1993b) *Globalization of Business*, London and New York: Routledge.
——(1994a) *Globalization, Economic Restructuring and Development*, The Prebisch Lecture for 1994, Geneva: UNCTAD.
——(1994b) 'The strategy of Japanese and US manufacturing investment in Europe', in M. Mason and D. Encarnation (eds) *Does Ownership Matter? Japanese Multinationals in Europe*, pp. 59–86, Oxford: Clarendon Press.
Encarnation, D. and Mason, M. (eds) (1994) *Does Ownership Matter? Japanese Multinationals in Europe*, Oxford: Clarendon Press.
Enright, M. J. (1993) 'Organization and coordination in geographically concentrated industries', in D. Raff and N. Lamoreaux (eds) *Coordination and Information: Historical Perspectives on the Organization of Enterprise*, pp. 103–146, Chicago: Chicago University Press.
——(1994) 'Regional clusters and firm strategy', Paper presented to Prince Bertil Symposium on *The dynamic firm: The role of regions, technology, strategy and organization*, Stockholm, June.
Forsgren, M. and Johanson, J. (eds) (1991) *Managing Networks in International Business*, Philadelphia: Gordon & Breach.
Freeman, C. and Hagedoorn, J. (1992) *Globalization of technology*, Maastricht Research Institute on Innovation and Technology (MERIT), Maastricht: Working Paper 92.013.
Freeman, C. and Perez, C. (1988) 'Structural crises of adjustment, business cycles, and investment behavior', in G. Dosi, C. Freeman, R. Nelson, G. Silverberg and L. Soete (eds) *Technical Change and Economic Theory*, London: Pinter.
Gerlach, M. L. (1992) *Alliance Capitalism: The Social Organization of Japanese Business*, Oxford: Oxford University Press.
Glaismeier, A. (1988) 'Factors governing the development of high tech industry agglomeratives: a tale of three cities', *Regional Studies* 22: 287.
Gomes-Casseres, B. (1993) 'Computers, alliances and industry evolution', in D. B. Yoffie (ed.) *Beyond Free Trade: Firms, Governments and Global Competition*, pp. 62–74, Boston: Harvard Business School Press.
——(1994) 'Group versus group: How alliance networks compete', *Harvard Business Review* July–August.
——(1995) *Collective Competition: International Alliances in High Technology*, Boston: Harvard University Press.
Gomes-Casseres, B. and Leonard-Barton, D. (1994) *Alliance Clusters in Multimedia: Safety Net or Entanglement?*, Boston: Harvard Business School (mimeo).

Hagedoorn, J. (1990) 'Organizational modes of inter-firm cooperation and technology transfer', *Technovation* 10(1): 17–30.

——(1993a) 'Understanding the rationale of strategic technology partnering: interorganizational modes of cooperation and sectoral differences', *Strategic Management Journal* 14: 371–85.

——(1993b) 'Strategic technology alliances and modes of cooperation in high technology industries', in G. Grabher (ed.) *The Embedded Firm*, pp. 116–37, London: Routledge.

Håkansson, H. and Johanson, J. (1993) 'The network as a governance structure', in G. Grabher (ed.) *The Embedded Firm*, pp. 35–51, London: Routledge.

Hamel, G. (1991) 'Competition for competence and inter-partner learning with international strategic alliances', *Strategic Management Journal* 12: 82–103.

Harrison, B. (1994) *Lean and Mean: The Changing Landscape of Power in the Age of Flexibility*, New York: Basic Books.

Helper, S. (1993) 'An exit-voice analysis of supplier relations: the case of the US automobile industry', in G. Grabher (ed.) *The Embedded Firm*, pp. 141–60, London: Routledge.

Henderson, V. (1994) 'Externalities and industrial development', in P. Krugman and A. Venables (eds) *The Location of Economic Activity: New Theories and Evidence*, London: Centre of Economic Policy Research (CPER).

Hennart, J. F. (1982) *A Theory of the Multinational Enterprise*, Ann Arbor, MI: University of Michigan Press.

——(1988) 'A transaction costs theory of equity joint ventures', *Strategic Management Journal* 9: 361–74.

——(1989) 'Can the new forms of investment substitute for the old forms? A transaction costs perspective', *Journal of International Business Studies* XX: 211–33.

Herrigel, G. B. (1994) 'Power and the redefinition of industrial districts: the case of Baden Württemberg', in G. Grabher (ed.) *The Embedded Firm*, pp. 227–52, London: Routledge.

Hirschman, A. O. (1970) *Exit Voice and Loyalty*, Cambridge, MA: Harvard University Press.

Johanson, J. and Mattsson, L. G. (1987) 'Internationalization in industrial systems – network approach', in H. Hood and J. E. Vahlne (eds) *Strategies in Global Competition*, Chichester and New York: John Wiley.

——(1994) 'The markets-as-networks tradition in Sweden', in G. Laurent, G. L. Lilien and B. Pras (eds) *Research Traditions in Marketing*, pp. 321–46, Dordrecht and Boston: Kluwer.

Johanson, J. and Vahlne, J. E. (1977) 'The internationalization process of the firm – a model of knowledge development and increasing foreign market commitments', *Journal of International Business Studies* 8, Spring/Summer: 23–32.

Kodama, F. (1992) 'Japan's unique capability to innovate: technology, fusion and its international implications', in T. S., Arrison, C. F. Bergsten and M. Harris (eds) *Japan's Growing Technological Capability: Implications for the US Economy*, Washington, DC: National Academy Press.

Kogut, B. (1988) 'Joint ventures: theoretical and empirical perspectives', *Strategic Management Journal* 9(4): 319–22.

Kojima, K. (1978) *Direct Foreign Investment: A Japanese Model of Multinational Business Operations*, London: Croom Helm.

——(1990) *Japanese Direct Investment Abroad*, Mitaka, Tokyo: International Christian University, Social Science Research Institute Monograph Series 1

Krugman, P. R. (1991) *Geography and Trade*, Leuven: Leuven University Press and Cambridge, MA: MIT Press.

Lazerson, M. (1993) 'Factory or putting out? Knitting networks in Modena', in G. Grabher (ed.) *The Embedded Firm*, London: Routledge.
Lazonick, W. (1991) *Business Organization and the Myth of the Market Economy*, Cambridge: Cambridge University Press.
——(1992) 'Business organization and competitive advantage: capitalist transformation in the twentieth century', in G. Dosi, R. Giannetti and P. A. Toninelli (eds) *Technology and Enterprise in a Historical Perspective*, pp.119–63, Oxford: Clarendon Press.
Lincoln, J. (1990) 'Japanese organization and organizational theory', *Research and Organizational Behavior* 12: 255–94.
Lorenzoni, G. and Baden Fuller, C. (1995) 'Creating a strategic center to manage a web of partners', *California Management Review* 37(3): 146–63.
Markusen, A. (1994) *Sticky Places in Slippery Spaces: The Political Economy of Post-War Fast Growth Regions*, New Brunswick Center for Urban Policy Research, Rutgers University Working Paper No. 79.
Markusen, A., Hall, P., Deitrick, S. and Campbell, S. (1991) *The Rise of the Gunbelt: The Military Remapping of Industrial America*, New York and Oxford: Oxford University Press.
Marshall, A. (1920) *Principles of Economies*, London: Macmillan.
McManus, J. C. (1972) 'The theory of the multinational firm', in G. Paquet (ed.) *The Multinational Firm and the Nation State*, Toronto: Collier Macmillan.
Michalet, C. A. (1991) 'Strategic partnerships and the changing international process', in L. K. Mytelka (ed.) *Strategic Partnerships: States, Firms and International Competition*, London: Pinter.
Mowery, D. C. (1988) *International Collaborative Ventures in US Manufacturing*, Cambridge, MA: Ballinger.
Naisbitt, J. (1994) *Global Paradox: The Bigger the World Economy, the More Political its Smallest Players*, New York: William Morrow.
Nelson, R. R. and Winter, S. G. (1982) *An Evolutionary Theory of Economic Change*, Cambridge, MA: Harvard University Press.
Ohmae, K. (1995) *The End of the Nation State: The Rise of Regional Economies*, London: Harper Collins.
Oman, C. (1994) *Globalization and Regionalization: The Challenge for Developing Countries*, Paris: OECD Development Centre.
Peng, M. W. (1993) *Blurring Boundaries: The Growth of the Firm in Planned Economies in Transition*, Washington Center for International Business Education and Research, University of Washington (mimeo).
Penrose, E. T. (1956) 'Foreign investment and growth of the firm', *Economic Journal* 60: 220–35.
——(1959) *The Theory of the Growth of the Firm*, Oxford: Basil Blackwell.
Peteraf, M. (1993) 'The cornerstones of competitive advantage: a resource based view', *Strategic Management Journal* 14: 179–91.
Pigou, A. C. (1932) *The Economics of Welfare*, 4th Edition, London: Macmillan.
Piore, M. J. and Sabel, C. F. (1984) *The Second Industrial Divide: Possibilities for prosperity*, New York: Basic Books.
Porter, M. (1990) *The Competitive Advantage of Nations*, New York: The Free Press.
Quinn, J. B. and Hilmer, F. G. (1994) 'Strategic outsourcing', *Sloan Management Review* Summer: 43–55.
Robinson, J. (1933) *The Economics of Imperfect Competition*, London: Macmillan.
Ruigrok, W. and Van Tulder, R. (1995) *The Logic of International Restructuring*, London and New York: Routledge.

Rugman, A. M. (1981) *Inside the Multinationals: The Economics of Internal Markets*, London: Croom Helm.
Rugman, A. M. and D'Cruz, J. R. (1995) *The Five Partners Business Network Model*, Toronto: University of Toronto (mimeo).
Saxenian, A. L. (1994) *Regional Advantage: Culture and competition in Silicon Valley and Route 128*, Cambridge, MA: Harvard University Press.
Scott, A. J. (1993) *Technologies: High-technology industry and regional development in Southern California*, Berkeley and Los Angeles: University of California Press.
Shan, W. and Hamilton, W. (1991) 'Country-specific advantage and international cooperation', *Strategic Management Journal* 12(6): 419–32.
Smith, A. (1776) *An Inquiry into the Nature and Clauses of the Wealth of Nations*, Vol. 1 (1947 edition published by Dent, London).
Stopford, J. M. (1995) 'Competing globally for resources', *Transnational Corporations*4(2): 34-57.
Storper, M. (1944) *Institutions of a Learning Economy*, Los Angeles School of Public Policy and Social Research, UCLA.
Storper, M. and Scott, A. J. (1995) 'The wealth of regions', *Futures* 27(5): 505–26.
Teece, D. J. (1992) 'Competition, cooperation and innovation', *Journal of Economic Behavior and Organization* 18: 1–25.
UNCTAD (1993) *World Investment Report 1993: Transnational Corporations and Integrated International Production*, New York and Geneva: UN.
—— *World Investment Report 1994: Transnational Corporations, Employment and the Workplace*, New York and Geneva: UN.
Wernerfelt, B. (1984) 'A resource-based view of the firm', *Strategic Management Journal* 5(2): 171–80.
Wheeler, K. and Mody, A. (1992) 'International investment and location decisions: the case of US firms', *Journal of International Economics* 33: 57–76.
Whittaker, E. and Bower, D. Jane (1994) 'A shift to external alliances for product development in the pharmaceutical industry', *R&D Management* 24(3): 249–60.
Williamson, O. E. (1985) *The Economic Institutions of Capitalism*, New York: The Free Press.
——(1993) 'The logic of economic organization', in O. E. Williamson and S. E. Winter (eds) *The Nature of the Firm*, New York and Oxford: Oxford University Press.
World Bank (1991) *The World Development Report*, New York and Oxford: Oxford University Press.

4

RECONFIGURING THE BOUNDARIES OF INTERNATIONAL BUSINESS ACTIVITY

INTRODUCTION

Once upon a time, there was the firm, and the boundaries of its economic jurisdiction were clearly demarcated by its ownership. There were few intrafirm transactions, and all interfirm transactions were conducted between independent parties at arm's length prices. This is no longer the case. Once upon a time, there were identifiable and autonomous markets, the confines of which were unambiguously delineated by the particular assets, goods and services being traded, and by the parties to the exchange. This is no longer the case. Once upon a time, there were nation states, whose political domain largely corresponded with their economic domains, and whose governments produced largely independent macro-economic and macro-organizational policies.[1] This is no longer the case.

As Chapter 2 has described, the globalizing economy of the current decade is the outcome of a succession of radical technological and political changes, the lineage of which can be traced back to the industrial revolution of the late eighteenth century. At this former time, the boundaries of firms, markets and governments were easily recognizable and, for the most part, impermeable. Over the past two centuries, the extent and nature of economic activity has become increasingly specialized, complex and porous. At the same time, its spatial dimension has widened from the subnational to the national, and then to the regional, international and global.

Such changes have had widespread implications for both the macro- and micro-organization of resource allocation. The single-activity, autonomous firm is now the exception rather than the rule. Most contemporary firms are multi-activity, and are often part of a web of interfirm co-operative alliances. Markets are increasingly interdependent, rather than independent, of each other; and the consequences of market-related transactions frequently affect institutions and individuals other than those who are the direct participants in the markets. As assets have become increasingly mobile, or 'quicksilver' across national boundaries, so the dichotomy between economic and political space has widened; and in the framing of their economic strategies, which affect the competitiveness and profitability of business activities within their jurisdiction, governments need to be increasingly aware of the strategies of the governments of other countries, which offer a comparable portfolio of location-specific assets.

This chapter has two main tasks. The first is to identify the extent and character of the changes which have taken place in each of the three main organizational entities which govern the deployment of resources in a capitalist economy, and particularly those which arise from the globalization of business activity. The second is to look more specifically at the role of government as initiator, overseer and arbitrator of the economic system which determines the contribution and effectiveness of these entities.

THE DOMAIN OF THE FIRM

At one time, the formal or jurisdictional confines of the firm were assumed to be discrete and coincident with its ownership. Such confines related both to the scope of the value-added activities of the firm – be they process or product based – and to the geographical space in which it operated. Implicit in this assumption was that ownership conferred full sovereignty over decision taking. Without such ownership[2] the firm was presumed to have no legitimacy or authority. All transactions within the firm, whatever their spatial dimensions, were presumed to be the responsibility of the owners of the company – although in practice, this responsibility was devolved to the board of directors and executive management. All transactions between firms were assumed to be off the shelf, and conducted at arm's length prices. Little attention was given to co-operative agreements involving a continuing relationship between economic agents or an exchange (or sharing) of resources, experience, information or advice.

Over the years, the formal boundaries of the firm have steadily extended as a result of the internalization of intermediate product markets and the territorial extension of its activities. The contemporary multinational enterprise (MNE) is both the owner and orchestrator of a complex portfolio of interrelated assets, located in two or more countries. In some instances, these internal markets are closely integrated, and the parent company enjoys advantages of common governance and diversification of risk. In others, the MNE is better regarded as a multi-domestic company in which the foreign subsidiaries operate more or less independently of each other (Porter 1986). Over the last thirty years, and particularly as the range and extent of international production has increased, and as regional integration has facilitated the cross-border specialization of economic activity, an increasing number of MNEs have begun to embrace globally integrated strategies (UNCTAD 1993).

At the same time, the range and character of the *informal* boundaries of the firm have also been reconfigured. Like that of intrafirm activities, the recent growth of interfirm agreements has also been in response to the increasing costs of arm's length transactions, but, unlike internalization, this response is better described as a *voice* rather than *exit* strategy.[3] We shall take this point up further in a later section of this chapter.

The net result of the growth of both inter- and intrafirm activities is that the boundaries of the firm have become more porous. Badaracco (1991), quoted in Dicken (1994), has attempted to draw a new map of the firm which 'displays no sharp dividing line separating the inside of the firm from the outside'. Because of this, traditional analytical concepts are found wanting in a number of respects. First – and this is well known but deserves repeating here – the traditional, that is, neo-classical, theory of the firm focused on its role as a *production* unit rather than a *transacting* and *co-ordinating* unit. However appropriate this emphasis may have been when firms engaged in one or a few activities, and served only limited markets, it is no longer the case today. As several economists (notably Douglass North 1990) have shown, as society becomes more complex, the transaction and co-ordinating costs of economic activity become more important.[4] This is not only because of the increasing costs of acquiring information to measure the multiple dimensions of what is being exchanged, but also because of those associated with enforcing contracts and making credible commitments across time and space, necessary to realize the potential of technological and organizational advances.

About a half century ago, there was debate among economists as to the supply-side limits of the size of the firm producing in perfectly competitive conditions.[5] The consensus of opinion, at that time, was that the constraints to a firm's size were not its rising (marginal) production costs, but were the increasing difficulties faced by managers of co-ordinating resources, capabilities and markets, for example rising transaction and co-ordinating costs. Although the debate was mainly conducted within the context of equilibrium analysis and firms were assumed to engage in only one activity, it is not difficult to argue that the more diverse the activities of a firm, the higher these latter costs are likely to be, and thus the profit-maximizing level of output will be less.

This analysis suggests that the *de facto* boundaries of the firm will be limited by its production and organizational competency, and by the size and geographical composition of the market. It follows, then, that any upgrading of the former, or extension of the latter, variables will enable the boundaries of the firm to be pushed out. And, indeed, history is replete with examples of the increased size of firms being brought about by changes in both exogenous variables (e.g. larger markets, falling transport costs, lower raw material costs) and endogenous variables (e.g. an improvement in labour or managerial productivity), while, from a dynamic perspective, the extent to which the boundaries are pushed out rests on the ability of firms to innovate new, or upgrade the quality of existing, products.

There is, however, another sense in which the boundaries of the firm are being reconfigured. This concerns the extent to which a firm is engaging in informal (i.e. non-ownership) linkages with other firms which have an impact on their ability to sustain or enlarge their economic activities. Here we may introduce the concept of 'soft' boundaries as influencing both the organizational limits and the size and scope of production. Although the *de jure* boundaries of a firm may require little reconfiguration, as long as it has a 51 per cent equity interest in any joint venture, it may, nevertheless, be the case that the minority partners – particularly if they are large institutional investors[6] – will have something to contribute to the efficiency of the majority partner. This may be no less so in minority-owned ventures, and, indeed, in non-equity alliances, for example subcontracting, research and development (R&D) agreements and management contracts. Of course not all such agreements require a recasting of even the 'soft' boundaries of the firm. The key question is the extent to which such agreements, or, indeed, organizational arrangements associated with them, may affect the production and organizational activities of firms, for example by offering advice, providing additional inputs or markets or by making possible economies in the common governance,[7] which in their absence would not have occurred.

There are, of course, a plurality of organizational modes by which the 'soft' boundaries of firms may be widened. These include vertical and horizontal alliances formed to accomplish very specific objectives (e.g. access to new technology, management skills, learning and organizational capacity, markets, etc.), as well as more general alliances intended to share risks, accelerate the innovatory process and strengthen the overall competitiveness of the participating firms. These may variously affect a firm's performance. Thus a firm may lower its input prices or improve the quality of its end products by forming appropriate alliances with its suppliers. New markets may be tapped by franchising and other agreements with foreign distributors. A firm may best benefit from technological advances and their speedy application by jointly sharing R&D programmes with one or other of its competitors. It may gain the economies of intranational geographical clustering if it allies itself in space with related firms (Porter 1990, Feldman 1994).

In the previous two chapters, we have suggested that the world may be entering into a new phase of capitalism, namely *alliance capitalism*, and that if firms are to benefit most from innovation-led production, the upgrading of consumer demand and the imperatives of globalization, they may need to engage in a network of co-operative agreements with other firms. This reflects the fact that economic activity is becoming more interdependent, and that to exploit their core assets effectively, firms have to combine these with the core assets of other firms – or of public authorities. However, rather than enlarge their hierarchical influence, they prefer to establish co-operative relationships with other firms, that is extend their 'soft' boundaries. By so doing, they are able to improve and make better use of their own competencies, which, in turn, will help them sustain or push out further their market boundaries.

All these developments, then, point not only to the need for more flexible and readily changeable boundaries of firms, but to the fact that the very nature of these boundaries should be re-evaluated. So while a reduction in the scope of a firm's ownership may reduce its 'hard' boundaries, if such disinternalization is replaced by an increase in interfirm co-operative agreements this may widen its 'soft' boundaries.

It is also quite clear that the nature and porosity of a firm's boundaries is both *industry* and *country* and sometimes *firm* – or even *activity* – specific. The porosity of the domain of firms would appear to be most marked in the information and technology intensity, manufacturing and service sectors (notably in the biotechnology, computer, telecommunications and financial services industries) and in countries, e.g. Japan and Korea, whose industrial culture seems to favour interfirm co-operation as much as intrafirm hierarchies. Moreover, such boundaries tend to be even 'softer' when firms go abroad, particularly where, *inter alia*, owing to ideological and political differences, there are substantial intercountry risks and uncertainties, and where the opportunities for synergistic economies are the most pronounced.

THE BOUNDARIES OF MARKETS

The neo-classical notion of a market is that it is an autonomous organizational entity in which the consequences of the transactions concluded are confined to the participants of the market, and are independent of those in other markets, that is there are no intermarket spillovers or externalities. It is also an implicit assumption of neo-classical economics that the costs of establishing and sustaining markets – be they factor or product markets – are minimal. Indeed, no real consideration is given at all to endemic or 'natural' market failure – it being presumed that any inability of markets to perform effectively is due to the distorting behaviour of one or other of the participants of the market, or to extramarket forces (e.g. the intervention of the governments).

However, as North (1990) and others have demonstrated, as societies become more sophisticated, not only are markets likely to be less perfect (i.e. in a Pareto-optimality sense), but any imperfection is reflected in the increasing transaction and co-ordination costs of using this organizational mechanism. Such endemic failures have been well addressed in the literature (see e.g. Wolf 1988). In short, they reduce to the presence of uncertainties, economies of scale and externalities, and the increasing public good characteristics of intermediate and final products, which contain a high ingredient of *created* (as opposed to *natural*) assets.

In this chapter, as we are primarily interested in the boundaries rather than the character of markets, we shall be most concerned with those properties which affect these boundaries. Essentially, these reduce to the externalities, or spillover effects, of market transactions, which lead to the interdependence between transactions and encourage the co-ordination of them. Such interdependence is of three kinds. First, some products need to be jointly demanded with others if they are to give the purchaser full satisfaction. In this case, the demand for one product is contingent upon the other being available at an acceptable price; in other words, the markets for the two goods are linked. Second, some products need to be jointly supplied if their combined worth (e.g. productivity) is to be optimized. This is especially true of intangible assets, for example different kinds of information. Increasingly, as the demands of both industrial and final consumers become more sophisticated, several interrelated technologies may be needed to produce a given product. Again, the markets for these intermediate products are linked.

Third, there are the extramarket consequences of particular market transactions. The concept of external diseconomies, and the distinction between the private and social costs of producing a product, particularly where viewed in an environmental context, dates back to the time of A. C. Pigou and Alfred Marshall. The notion of the extramarket benefits of activities is perhaps more recent, and is currently best captured in those which arise from an increase in the created assets of firms – and especially of innovatory capacity and accumulation of human skills and experience. It is, for example, generally accepted that the social returns of R&D expenditure exceed the private returns,[8] which, *inter alia*, suggests that the private market for R&D cannot perform in a socially optimal fashion. The issue of apportioning the benefits of an investment no less applies to the upgrading of human capital, and to much transportation and communications infrastructure. The problem arises because the firms investing in these activities do not necessarily capture all the benefits from them, or, if they do, the benefits are spread over an unacceptably long period of time.[9]

In some cases of course, firms may (and do) respond to the kind of market failures just described by internalizing the extramarket benefits. This is most vividly demonstrated in the economies of common governance of interrelated activities. Indeed, much of the rationale for the diversified firm and for international business operations rests on the benefits perceived to arise from the economies of scale and scope. Such gains, it should be noted, arise as much from the reduction of transaction and co-ordination costs as from production economies. It surely follows, then, that if such costs play a more important role in economic activity, increasing attention should be given to organizational issues!

A later section of this chapter will deal with the implications of the reconfiguration of the domain of markets. Here we wish to emphasize that this reconfiguration may take a variety of forms depending on the nature of the markets. In some instances, the reconfiguration may be to strengthen the influence of arm's length markets. In others, the nature of the market may be affected with arm's length transactions being replaced by relational transactions between the parties to the exchange, or between these parties and others affected by it. Much will depend on the relative transaction costs of alternative market arrangements, and these will clearly vary over time and space. The fact that there are unique externalities of international business activities – associated *inter alia* with producing or transacting in countries with different languages, ideologies, institutions and organizational structures – suggests that the international business scholar needs to consider the impact of globalization on the domain of markets very seriously indeed; for it is in those sectors which are most internationalized, where the boundaries of product and factor markets are becoming most porous. Examples include telecommunications, computers, biochemicals, robotics and financial services.

NATION STATES

In considering the spatial frontiers of MNE activity we shall distinguish between economic and political space.[10] Economic space comprises the geographical area in which production and transactions are undertaken by economic agents whose centre of governance, or residence, is within a particular country. Political space refers to the geographical area comprising the jurisdictional responsibility of a particular sovereign legislature. In the case of a national or federal government, this is usually coincident with a single country, although it may extend to its foreign possessions.

While, over the past two centuries or more, economic space has continually widened, from the subnational to the national and, then, to the regional and international level, the main unit of political sovereignty has remained the nation state – even though, as we shall see, in their policies and strategies, national governments are increasingly having to take account of the widening of economic and other space. In a closed economy, political and economic territory are the same and easily identifiable. The boundaries of a nation state or a country represent the extent of the jurisdiction of authority and the legitimacy of its governing policy, for example the national and federal government. Once, however, the economic agents of a country engage in international commerce, political and economic sovereignty may no longer be equated. For example, once a country's firms begin trading goods and services, although the political jurisdiction of its government remains the same, its economic sovereignty is reduced to the extent that it is dependent upon foreign buyers and sellers for part of its prosperity. As a country engages in deeper forms of integration, for example foreign direct investment (FDI), then not only are the boundaries of its firms and consumers widened, but so also are its geographical sources of wealth.[11]

Most scholars (e.g. McGrew and Lewis 1992) tend to think of the boundaries of nation states as being determined by the extent to which they are politically or economically independent or interdependent of each other. The opposite end of the spectrum of autonomy and self-sufficiency is one in which one country is merged with another. In between the two extremes are various stages and kinds of interdependence. The thesis we are suggesting is that the globalization of the world economy is leading to a watershed in, or a radical reshifting of, the *effective* boundary lines of a country, which we may define as the point at which, as a result of its association with other countries, there is no further effect on its *social* domestic production and transaction functions.

If the *extent* of interdependence influences the effective boundaries of nation states, the *form* of interdependence affects the degree and character of its porosity. Thus, for example, a regional free trade area impinges on the boundaries in a softer fashion than a customs union, and this, in its turn, less so than a monetary union. The deeper the integration between nations, the more widespread the implications for sovereignty of the participating nations.

The last twenty years have seen a number of trends, each of which is requiring scholars to reappraise the significance of national boundaries. The first is the increasing mobility of firm-specific assets between countries, one consequence of which is that (some) countries are becoming more like regions within a country.[12] This increased mobility has been especially revealed in the rapid growth of both intra- and interfirm cross-border alliances, which, in turn, has been aided and abetted by (i) advances in transport and communications technology and (ii) the reduction of barriers to the movement of goods, assets and people brought about by regional integration.

The ability of firms to 'vote with their feet' is one thing. The extent to which they are willing to do so is another. Here a different but related aspect of the changing character of national boundaries is manifesting itself. That is, that national governments, by their various actions (or non-actions), are increasingly influencing the competitiveness of location-bound resources and capabilities within their jurisdiction, in a way which determines the disposition of mobile resources and capabilities between countries. At one time, as we have seen, such government action was confined to influencing patterns of trade. Today, it extends to influencing the production and transaction costs of domestic resources, and the wealth-creating opportunities of its firms and people. No longer, then, are government (or country-specific) policies independent of each other. Governments, like firms, may, and do, act as oligopolists; in consequence, their spatial horizons are different than they used to be. They are broader in the sense that, by their organization policies, they may encourage or inhibit the flow of foreign assets to its borders; yet, they are narrower in the sense that other governments may affect the competitiveness of their own assets and sometimes cause domestic firms to relocate or restructure their activities outside their home countries.[13]

There is nothing new with the idea that governments may both co-operate and compete with each other, and that the balance of such interaction may be both country and time specific.[14] However, with the convergence of economic structure among at least the major industrial nations, and the widening of economic space, there has come a burgeoning of both quasi-public institutions and intragovernmental agencies. In most cases, these have been activity or issue specific, but occasionally – especially in the area of macro-economic policies – they have been more general. The geographical scope of the arrangements has also varied. In some cases it has been bilateral; in others it has been multilateral. Of the supranational arrangements, some, for example as agreed in the UN or UNCTAD, have been informal and non-binding; others, for example environmental and standards legislation in the European Union (EU), have been more binding. The point we wish to stress is that alliance capitalism is leading to more *inter*governmental intervention and, in an increasing number of cases, this intervention is taking the form of co-operation. But, at the end of the day, governments often compete with each other for the mobile created assets of firms and, as for example is demonstrated by the policies of member countries of the European Community and/or individual States in the United States, they have considerable leeway to do so.

By promoting the structural integration of nation states, the globalizing economy is restructuring the effective boundaries of both economic and political space. While some scholars have gone as far as to suggest that this may lead to the demise of nation states, the majority point to a change in its functions. Thus, while the EU is leading to a reduced role in some of the functions of the governments of the participating nations (cf. those of the States in the United States with those of the federal government), the macro-organizational actions of such national administrations – in influencing the production and transaction costs of economic activity in their midst – are becoming more important.

At the same time, such policies are being increasingly affected by those of other governments, who are seeking to upgrade the competitiveness of their own resources and capabilities. It is in this sense, and for this reason, that the spatial boundaries of nation states, and indeed the significance of the location-specific advantages of countries, need to be reconfigured.

THE RESPONSE OF INSTITUTIONS TO THE RECONFIGURATION OF BOUNDARIES

The previous sections have hypothesized that the boundaries of the main organizational forms used to allocate resources and capabilities in a capitalist economy are undergoing a radical shift as the global economy moves from a socio-institutional paradigm of *hierarchical* capitalism to one of *alliance* capitalism. Such a transformation, which is still in its early stages, is causing the relationships between firms, between markets and between nation states (or, more particularly, the governing bodies of nation states) to be changed in such a way that the boundaries are becoming blurred, and co-operation among firms is becoming as much a feature of capitalism as competition between them.

It is also worth mentioning that the boundaries between different organizational forms are also being reconfigured. Thus as nation states upgrade the issue of competitiveness on their national agenda, and firms (including MNEs) and governments evolve more co-operative and less adversarial relationships,[15] the interaction between governments and markets is also changing. While much government intervention has long been criticized by economists as market distorting – except where it is designed to inhibit or regulate anti-competitive behaviour by one or other of the participants in the market – it is being increasingly recognized that in a knowledge-based globalizing economy, governments may play an important *market-facilitating* role. This they may do both by ensuring the supply of the public goods which private firms perceive to be too costly or risky to provide, and by assisting the readjustment of markets to technological change, wherever the social net benefits of such assistance are believed to be higher than the private net benefits.[16]

Finally, the interaction between firms and markets is changing. As its name implies, *hierarchical* capitalism emphasizes the importance of large vertically integrated and horizontally diversified firms in the organization of economic activity. But as we have already indicated, recent years have seen a growth of interfirm co-operative agreements, which, in effect, represent a 'voice' reaction of the participants in the intermediate product markets to reduce the imperfections of those markets, rather than an 'exit' strategy of replacing the market by administrative fiat.

More generally, we have argued in this chapter that the globalizing economy is changing the costs and benefits of alternative modes of organizing economic activity, as well as affecting the systemic role of government as the organizational overlord of such activity. The responses to these changing costs and benefits by the various organizational forms are essentially fivefold. First, if the costs of supplying the product, asset or factor service in question are increased (or lowered) independently of the organizational mode, then the appropriate response may be to produce or transact less (more), that is shift the organization supply curve to the left (right). Clearly this response will be highly sector specific, but as the transaction and co-ordination costs of economic activity rise, one may assume that a change in these will have a more pronounced effect on the level and structure of such activity than once it did.

The second response is to replace one organizational mechanism with another. Thus, the growth of hierarchies in the late nineteenth century represented a replacement of (i.e. exit from) arm's length markets, while the nationalization of private firms by the post-war socialist governments of the United Kingdom represented a replacement of the private by the public sector. The third response is to seek to reduce the deficiencies of an imperfect organizational mode rather than to replace it. So, rather than exiting from the costs of inefficient governments, by deregulating or privatizing markets, a 'voice' strategy would try to make the actions of governments more cost effective. Rather than acquire subcontractors who fail to meet quality standards or adhere to delivery dates, the contracting firms might prefer to reduce such transaction costs by establishing closer and more productive working relations with such contractors. Similarly, governments, by reducing micro-economic uncertainties, removing market-inhibiting practices and lowering trade barriers, for example discriminatory purchasing procedures, might help lower the transaction and co-ordination costs of both hierarchies and arm's length markets.

The fourth solution is for governments or some other extramarket institutions (e.g. groups of firms) to counteract the intrinsic deficiencies of the market by offering producers and consumers inducements to behave as if a 'first-best' market existed. Examples include the provision of tax concessions and subsidies to increase the private benefits of R&D and training to the level of their social benefits; improving information about the export opportunities for small firms; setting up investment guarantee schemes to protect outbound MNEs against political risks; making certain that patent legislation and procedures properly reflect the needs of innovators; assisting the market in its provision of risk capital – especially for projects which are likely to generate social benefits and are long term in their gestation; and ensuring, directly or indirectly, that the hassle costs of doing business (e.g. industrial disputes, inadequate transport and communication facilities and time-consuming bureaucratic controls) are kept to the minimum.

It is not difficult to think of many other examples of endemic market shortcomings, but most reduce to the presence of X inefficiency of one kind or another. But, there is another aspect of market failure which economists frequently neglect, mainly because they like to assume human beings behave in a consistent and rational manner and are only interested in the pursuance of wealth. Organizational theorists question this, and talk about the bounded rationality and opportunistic behaviour of producers and consumers, and about the *Homo psychologicus* of cognitive psychology as compared with the *Homo economicus* of economics.

It is too unrealistic to extend this idea of psychological man (or woman) to the mentality or culture of wealth-creating activities by countries and corporations? Even the most cursory glance at the ways in which the Arab countries and the Germans conduct their daily business; or the attitudes of the Japanese and Nigerians to interfirm relationship and contractual obligations; or the ethos of work and leisure of the Taiwanese and Greeks; or the perceived responsibilities and duties of workers, business managers and governments of the Koreans, Chileans and Russians; or the cross-border operational and organizational strategies of Nissan and Toyota or Motorola and Texas Instruments, reveals wide differences in the culture or mentality of wealth-creating behaviour. The globalizing economy is affording a new importance to concepts such as trust, forbearance and reciprocity, and to informal, rather than formal, organizational forms in affecting national competitiveness and, hence, the disposition of resources and capabilities.

The extent to which the culture of wealth-creating behaviour is an intrinsic characteristic of a country or a corporation or can be shaped by exposure to other cultures, by decree or economic pressure, or by a reorientation of personal or business values, is debatable. But, there can be little doubt that the forces of globalization are compelling firms and governments to review their respective roles in influencing mental attitudes towards wealth-creating activities. Whether we like it or not, the trade-offs between these and other activities, such as leisure pursuits, are changing; and, whether we like it or not, to a large extent, they are being set by countries which place the highest value on competitiveness. The grasshopper's attitude to life is fine as long as the grasshopper does not aspire to the living standards of the ant. The trouble is that most of us want to retain our lifestyles of work and leisure, but also enjoy all the material benefits of our economically more successful neighbours.

The fifth response, and one which is particularly germane to international business activity, is for supranational organization arrangements either to complement or replace national organizational arrangements. The argument here is that rather than an 'exit'[17] or 'voice' response to the costs of organizational failure by national institutions, the best solution would be for some agreement to be undertaken at an international level. The establishment of a range of early post-war supranational regimes (e.g. GATT, World Bank, IMF, etc.) was a recognition that national regulatory agencies were sometimes inadequate to optimize the international allocation of resources. With the spread of cross-border hierarchies and the globalization of an increasing number of markets, the areas for supranational intervention seem to be expanding.[18] In particular, the current debate over the widening of the terms of reference of the WTO to embrace competition policy, labour standards, etc., and the growing pressure for a multilateral investment regime, is a recognition of the inability of national organizational modes to provide a first-best solution to minimizing the production and transaction costs of economic activity in a world in which national borders are porous to the movement of resources and capabilities. At the same time, there has so far been little systematic research on the costs and benefits of supranational governance, and we have no clear indication of the conditions under which the fifth response to organizational failure is the optimal one.[19]

THE SYSTEMIC ROLE OF GOVERNMENT

A review of the writings of past scholars on the appropriate role of governments in a market-based economy reveals that little attention has been given to the role of government as a creator and overseer of economic organization as opposed to a participator in the system (Dunning 1997). Apart from the institutional school of economists,[20] most scholars have either assumed that the setting up and management costs of a market-based system of resource allocation are zero minimal or have ignored these costs altogether. At the time of Adam Smith, when most products were simple and natural resource based, the degree of division of labour was limited, and when most markets were subnational, this neglect was perhaps understandable – although it is perhaps worth observing that in the contemporary world economy, the costs of setting up even a rudimentary market system in a poor developing country are far from negligible. In today's structurally integrated world economy, and particularly in the Triad of advanced industrial economies, such an assumption is quite inappropriate, and it is becoming even less so as the components of the market system are becoming more complex and interdependent of each other.

Even accepting the almost intractable problems of both identifying the first-best system (which is likely to be both country and time specific) and the static and dynamic costs of supervising that system, it is none the less the case that, with the noticeable exceptions of Stiglitz (1989), Wade (1988) and Chang (1994), most mainstream economists, while implicitly acknowledging this role of government,[21] pay only lip service to it. Yet as Amsden *et al.* (1994) vividly demonstrate, the failure of the East European economies to embrace successfully and speedily a market-based capitalism is at least partly due to the gross underestimation by Western economists of the institutionally related costs of setting up the system. Wade (1988) shows that there have been no such illusions among East Asian economists, who from the early post-war period have recognized the critical role of the state to fund most of the setting up costs of the market system, and those associated with its efficient maintenance. The market system is *par excellence* a public good, and so it is reasonable that governments, on behalf of their constituents who benefit from it, should bear at least some of the costs of it. This, indeed, is the unique and special macro-organizational role of government, and it is the reconfiguration of this role, as much as its role as a participatory organizational entity, which the globalizing economy is currently demanding.

The precise character of the systemic and market-facilitating role of government is still a matter of debate, but, gradually with the increasing interaction between the particular macro-organizational strategies of national governments (e.g. competition, innovation, environmental, educational policies), it is rising on the agenda of both these governments and supranational regimes. Except in East Asia, the idea that governments may beneficially co-ordinate (some of) their organizational arrangements in the same way they co-ordinate (some of) their macro-economic policies has not yet gained much credence, but this may well be forced on them in the emerging era of *alliance* capitalism.[22]

SOME CONCLUDING REMARKS

The aim of this chapter has been to argue that the boundaries of the main organizational entities in a capitalist economy are undergoing radical change as market-based capitalism is moving from being *hierarchical* to *alliance* in character, and as production and markets are becoming increasingly globalized. It has described the extent and form of these boundary changes in respect of firms, markets and governments (acting on behalf of the constituents for which they are responsible).

The chapter has four main conclusions. First, not only are the boundaries of each of the organizational forms becoming more porous and interdependent of each other, but there is a growing complementarity between them. Such interdependence is demanding a reappraisal of the cost-effectiveness of the alternative forms.

Second, the globalization of economic activity is requiring a re-evaluation of the optimal way in which the three main organizational entities, namely firms, markets and governments, respond to changes in the costs of organizing resource allocation.

Third, not only is globalization causing the systemic role of national governments to become more important, but it is compelling them to give more attention to how their policies might be integrated or harmonized with those of other governments, either formally through customs unions or other regional integration schemes, or by the participation in supranational regimes and arrangements.

The fourth conclusion is that scholars interested in the determinants and consequences of international business activity need to modify their paradigms and theories to encompass the implications of *alliance* capitalism for the boundaries of economic activity. This, indeed, was the subject of the previous chapter. In particular, we saw that the concept of the competitive or ownership advantages of firms needs to be widened to take account of the benefits to be derived from interfirm alliances and networking, while that of the locational advantages of countries needs to give more attention to the consequences of the mobility of firm-specific assets and the role of governments in the ways in which such assets may be combined with those which are locationally immobile within their areas of jurisdiction. More generally, scholars need to give more careful attention to the alternative responses to organizational failure, and particularly those directed to trying to overcome, rather than exiting from, those failures.

The consequences of international business activity may also need re-examination as a result of the growing interdependence between firms, markets and nation states. The internal transfer of technology by an MNE to its subsidiary, which has few spillover effects and the results of which only affect the recipient country, is one thing; such a transfer between two independent firms, the success of which depends on complementary technologies being available, and the output of which has social as well as private consequences, is quite another. By the same token, the competition for created assets by national governments may, if it leads to the establishment or strengthening of supranational institutions which may constrain that behaviour, affect the cross-border alliance-related strategies of MNEs, while a harmonization of national technical and environmental standards may have no less important consequences for the kinds of value-added activities (as well as their externalities) which MNEs and other firms undertake in particular countries.

It may be this chapter has exaggerated the distinctive nature and consequences of alliance capitalism and the reconfiguration of the frontiers of international business activity. Only time will tell whether this is so or not.

NOTES

1 By macro-organization we mean the organization of a country's resources and capabilities, undertaken by governments on behalf of their constituents; and by micro-organization we mean the organization of a firm's or an individual's resources and capabilities.
2 Or at least 51 per cent of the (voting) equity stock.
3 See Chapter 3 for further details.
4 When the spatially specific transaction costs are added to the North model, then the significance of these costs further increases.
5 See particularly Knight (1921), Sraffa (1926), Kaldor (1934) and Robinson (1934).
6 An example is the influence exerted by the German and Japanese banks on the German and Japanese systems of corporate governance (Prowse 1995).
7 Albeit perhaps for a limited time period.
8 One estimate is that the average social returns to R&D exceed those appropriated by the innovating firms by 50–100 per cent (Aaron and Schultze 1992).
9 Implicit in these kinds of externalities is the 'free rider' issue – which, of course, can work either to the advantage *or* disadvantage of firms, depending on whether they, or their competitors, are enjoying the 'free ride'.

10 There are, of course, other kinds of space (e.g. cultural and ideological space) but for the purposes of this chapter we shall consider these only as they affect economic and political space.

11 This may lead to a divergence between gross national product (GNP) and gross domestic product (GDP). GNP is the output produced by the residents of a country including the income earned on foreign assets. It is equal to GDP plus income earned in foreign countries by its own residents (including subsidiaries of its firms) less income accrued to foreign residents on assets they own within their domestic territory. See Dunning (1988: Chapter 4).

12 Compare, for example, countries in the European Union with those of states in the United States.

13 For another, but complementary, view on the economic jurisdiction of national governments, see Helm (1989).

14 We appreciate that in classical and neo-classical economics the concept of competing governments had no place. But in the late twentieth-century globalizing economy, in which national competitiveness is innovation driven, where many assets are mobile across national boundaries, and where there is substantial unemployment, this particular tenet of neo-classical economics no longer holds true.

15 Although the form and extent of the co-operation varies markedly between countries. Compare, for example, the various forms of government/firm interaction in East Asian countries with those in the United States.

16 The subject of the optimal 'social' investment in dynamic public goods is one which has so far received only scant attention in the literature.

17 Paralleling an 'exit' response to rising costs, one could also consider an entry response to rising benefits of a particular organizational form.

18 No less are such institutions proliferating in a variety of non-economic fields, for example the environment, technical standards, defence, health and crime-related issues, etc. See Eden and Hampson (1990).

19 It is hoped that some current research by David Vines (of Oxford University) and David Currie (of the London Business School) will help shed light on these issues. For a brief description of this research, see Currie and Vines (1992).

20 For succinct accounts of the evolution and contemporary views of this school see North (1990) and Dunning (1996).

21 See for example Friedman (1962), Wolf (1988).

22 For an excellent analysis of recent changes in the macro-organizational policies published by East Asian and Latin American governments, especially towards innovation, trade, industrial development and competitiveness, see Bradford (1994a, b).

REFERENCES

Aaron, H. J., and Schultze, C. L. (1992) *Setting Domestic Priorities: What Can Government Do?*, Washington, DC: The Brookings Institution.

Amsden, A., Kochanowicz, J. and Taylor, L. (1994) *The Market Meets its Match: Restructuring the Economies of Eastern Europe*, Cambridge, MA, and London: Harvard University Press.

Badaracco, J. L. Jnr (1991) 'The boundaries of the firm', in A. Etzioni and P. R. Lawrence (eds) *Socio-Economics: Towards a New Synthesis*, Armonk, NJ: Sharpe.

Bradford, C. I. (1994a) *The New Paradigm of Systemic Competitiveness: Toward More Integrated Policies in Latin America*, Paris: OECD.

——(1994b) *From Trade-Driven Growth to Growth-Driven Trade: Reappraising the East Asian Development Experience*, Paris: OECD.

Chang, H. J. (1994) *The Political Economy of Industrial Policy*, New York: St Martin's Press.

Currie, D. and Vines, D. (1992) 'A global economic policy agenda for the 1990s: is there a special British role?', *International Affairs* 68(4): 585–602.

Dicken, P. (1994) 'Global local tensions: firms and states in a global space-economy', *Economic Geography* 70(2): 101–28.

Dunning, J. H. (1988) *Multinationals, Technology and Competitiveness*, London and Boston: Unwin Hyman.

——(1997) 'Governments and the macro-organization of economic activity: an historical and spatial perspective', in J. H. Dunning (ed.) *Governments, Globalization and International Business*, Oxford: Oxford University Press.

Eden, L. and Hampson, F. O. (1990) *Clubs are Trumps; Towards a Taxonomy of International Regimes*, Ottawa Center for International Trade and Investment Policies, Carleton University, C/TQS, 90–102.

Feldman, M. P. (1994) *The Geography of Innovation*, Dordrecht: Kluwer.

Friedman, M., (1962) *Capitalism and Freedom*, Chicago and London: University of Chicago Press.

Helm, D. (ed.) (1989) *The Economic Borders of the State*, Oxford: Oxford University Press.

Kaldor, N. (1934) 'The equilibrium of the firm', *Economic Journal* 44: 70–1.

Knight, F. H. (1921) *Risk, Uncertainty and Profit*, Boston and New York: Houghton Mifflin.

McGrew, A. G. and Lewis, P. G. (eds) (1992) *Global Politics: Globalization and the Nation State*, Cambridge: Polity Press.

North, D. (1990) *Institutions, Institutional Change and Economic Performance*, Cambridge: Cambridge University Press.

Porter, M. (1986) *Competition in Global Industries*, Boston: Harvard University Press.

Porter, M. E. (1990) *The Competitive Advantage of Nations*, New York: The Free Press.

Prowse, S. D. (1995) *Financial Markets, Institutions and Instruments*, Oxford: Basil Blackwell.

Robinson, E. A. G. (1934) 'The problem of management and the size of firms', *Economic Journal* 44: 240–54.

Sraffa, P. (1926) 'The laws of return under competitive conditions', *Economic Journal* 36: 535–50.

Stiglitz, J. (1989) *The Economic Role of the State*, Oxford: Basil Blackwell.

UNCTAD (1993) *World Investment Report 1993, Transnational Corporations and Integrated International Production*, New York and Geneva: UN.

Wade, R. (1988) 'The role of government in overcoming market failure in Taiwan, Republic of Korea and Japan', in H. Hughes (ed.) *Achieving Industrialization in East Asia*, Cambridge: Cambridge University Press.

Wolf, M. (1988) *Markets or Governments*, Cambridge, MA: MIT Press.

Part II

TRADE, INTEGRATION AND LOCATIONAL ISSUES

5

WHAT'S WRONG – AND RIGHT – WITH TRADE THEORY?

INTRODUCTION

What distinguishes international from intranational economic transactions? How much and to what extent do national boundaries matter? Is the globalizing economy eroding such boundaries? Why do we need – if indeed we do need – a separate theory of cross-border trade and direct investment of firms? What is the justification for international economics, or for that matter international business,[1] as a distinct area of study?

Economics is, if nothing else, a pragmatic social science. Its primary purpose is, or should be, to explain, in the most rigorous way possible, the way in which scarce resources are allocated between alternative uses, and to suggest ways and means of improving this allocation. Some of our braver – but not necessarily wiser – colleagues also engage in predicting future economic events. But, for most of us, we are content to be judged on our ability to explain the real world as it is. The late nineteenth-century economist could hardly have anticipated the supersonic aircraft, the microchip or laser surgery, much less the geopolitical and cultural scenario of the late twentieth century. The happenings of the last century – or even the last two decades – surely confirm that economists must be prepared to modify their paradigms, theories or models to meet the needs of the time.

In some areas of economics, creditable progress has been made – particularly in development theory, macro-economics and industrial economics – but in other areas, such changes have been minimal. Relative to the demands placed on economists by changes in the world economic environment, international economics – especially international micro-economics – must take the 'booby' prize, with the possible exception of work on the new theory of trade[2] and foreign direct investment (FDI) (Helpman 1984, Helpman and Krugman 1985, Krugman 1990, 1991, Markusen 1995, Markusen and Venables 1995, Dunning 1988b, 1993a, Froot 1993) to which we shall return later. For example, it was not until the 1950s that trade theorists gave any attention at all to technology, market imperfections and differential consumer tastes.

Why is it then, that, apart from some advances in model building, the textbooks on international trade are more or less the same as they were thirty or forty years ago? Is it because economists believe that the old paradigms – particularly when modified to embrace new variables – are still a good – if not the best – explanation of today's cross-border transactions? Is it that they are well aware of the deficiencies of orthodox theory, but do not know how to remedy them? Is it because the real world poses analytically awkward challenges to traditional modes of thought? Or, is it because the *distinctive* features of international economics as a subject for study no longer merit the attention of economists, because there are more exciting research opportunities?

We believe that each of these explanations has some truth in it. But, we wish to suggest another, and look at this in some detail in the chapter.[3] This is that the nature and character of international transactions have so much changed in recent years (and, indeed, are continuing to do so in the 1990s) that the traditional intellectual apparatus of the international economist is, by itself, no longer adequate to explain real-world phenomena, and that only by drawing upon the tools of other branches of economics – notably industrial, institutional and techno-growth economics – can contemporary cross-border flows of goods, services and assets be properly understood. But, with few exceptions, intradisciplinary alliances between economists are rare. A cursory look at journals on, for example, international, business and regional economics reveals little spreading of the interest of trade scholars beyond the narrow confines of their subject. The writings of Ray Vernon, Charles Kindleberger, Richard Caves, Giovanni Dosi, Luc Soete, and most recently Paul Krugman and James Markusen stand out as beacons in an otherwise dimly lit territory. Others, notably Michael Porter, have been critical of traditional theoretical constructs, but have offered only limited guidance as to what should replace them. As to trade-related topics, that of international direct investment is particularly interesting, not only in its own right, but because it acts as an intellectual bridge between mainstream trade theory as it is and how it ought to be in explaining what is really going on in the world economy.

We find it astonishing that in a global economy in which the value of production financed by FDI (i.e. the sales of the foreign subsidiaries of multinational enterprises (MNEs)) exceeds that of trade; where the great bulk of trade (nobody knows the exact figure – it is thought to be between 60 and 70 per cent) is directly or indirectly connected to FDI; where upwards of one-half of trade is either within the same organizational entity (i.e. intrafirm trade) or between parties which engage in some kind of medium- to long-term co-operative relationship (e.g. subcontracting, strategic alliances).

WHY HAS INTERNATIONAL ECONOMICS NOT KEPT UP WITH THE TIMES?

Several reasons might be adduced for the apparent lack of attention given by orthodox trade theorists to non-traditional cross-border transactions. These include a lack of knowledge or understanding about their importance, and the belief that such 'connected' transactions[4] can be satisfactorily explained by arm's length trade theory; that is, connectedness *per se* is perceived to be of only marginal importance in explaining trade.

The latter reason is worthy of particular attention. At the end of the day, its validity must rest on whether or not it is supported by the facts. Here, as shown by a wealth of empirical studies, the evidence is mixed. Some kinds of trade (i.e. those in natural-resource-intensive products between resource-poor and resource-rich countries) are well explained by Heckscher–Ohlin (H–O) factor endowment models; others (i.e. most intraindustry trade between advanced industrial nations in sophisticated high-technology products) need a quite different kind of explanation. Most of the efforts of trade theorists in the last thirty years, under various guises (i.e. neo-factor, neo-technology, 'neo-neo'-technology,[5] monopolistic competition, scale, product cycle, product differentiation theories, etc.), have been directed to resolving these issues, and especially to explain trade among countries with similar economic structures.

While it is generally recognized that it is difficult – if not impossible – to construct satisfactorily a single comprehensive *theory* – as opposed to paradigm – of international trade, none the less each of the newer (i.e. post-1950) theories – with a couple of exceptions – has made use of the analytical tools of the international economist. By contrast, advances in the theory of FDI have primarily stemmed from the work, and made use of the tools, of industrial economics and the theory of the firm. Why the difference in approach?

In a chapter of a book co-authored with George Norman several years ago (Dunning and Norman 1985), reprinted in Dunning (1988a), we set out a 3 × 3 matrix. This matrix has been modified for this chapter and is presented as Figure 5.1. It depicts nine different kinds of international economic transactions. Each kind is distinguished by two criteria. The first is the degree of similarity between the goods and services imported and exported by a country. This is presumed to vary along a continuum from zero to complete substitutability. Second, each transaction is classified by its organizational mode. This, also, is assumed to vary along a continuum from that of an intrafirm (or hierarchical) transaction through a variety of co-operative arrangements to arm's length trading.[6] The top left-hand cell of the matrix – characterized by trade between independent parties in completely different products – essentially depicts Ricardian or H–O trade. Diagonally opposite, the bottom right-hand cell – characterized by

Composition of transactions		Spot Markets	Inter-firm Alliances and Networks	Hierarchies
Inter-industry	Assets	Arm's length transactions Different assets traded Portfolio investments	Licensing, management contracts, strategic alliances, etc. between 'relational' firms	Internalized intermediate product markets
Inter-industry	Products	Neo-technology and neo-factor trade	Product or process specialization between 'relational' firms and within networks	Intrafirm trade
Inter/intra-industry	Assets	Some cross-hauling of similar assets	As above	Vertical and horizontal FDI to reduce transaction and/or co-ordination costs of markets
Inter/intra-industry	Products	Trade in similar products	As above	Intrafirm trade
Intra-industry	Assets	Cross-hauling of similar assets	Cross-hauling of closely similar assets between firms or within networks	Intrafirm trade and horizontal FDI
Intra-industry	Products	n/a — Oligopolies trading in similar products	Cross-hauling of similar products between firms or within networks	Intrafirm trade among MNE oligopolies

(Column heading: ORGANIZATION OF TRANSACTIONS; row heading: COMPOSITION OF TRANSACTIONS)

n/a = not applicable

Figure 5.1 The evolution of international transactions of assets and products

Note: Broadly speaking the evolution has proceeded from left to right and diagonally downwards, though in the last decade, there has been some movement from the bottom right-hand corner to the bottom middle section of the matrix

intrafirm transactions in substitutable products – essentially represents trade in knowledge-intensive products internalized by MNEs (i.e. that associated with FDI). The rest of the matrix into which other forms of cross-border transactions can be fitted, embraces different combinations of organizational modes and kinds of products traded. The matrix attempts to illustrate the assertion that any paradigm – let alone theory – of trade must embrace both a *theory of organization* and a *theory of the location of economic activity*.

In our analysis of the evolution of trade patterns, George Norman and I suggested that for much of the nineteenth and early twentieth century, trade was of a type depicted by the top left-hand section of the matrix. Since the Second World War, it has increasingly been of an intraindustry, intrafirm character, as best illustrated by the bottom right-hand sections of the matrix. In turn, these trade types reflect the kinds of micro-techno-economic and macro-socio-institutional systems operating at the time. Nineteenth-century trade was mainly conducted within the discipline of the gold standard, with relatively little direct government intervention in economic affairs, and by firms producing under the craft or batch systems of production. For most of the present century, the techno-economic system has been dominated by scale or Fordist production, while relative to market forces, governments and hierarchies have played a more important organizational role in influencing the level and pattern of trade. As this century draws to a close, we are entering into a new trajectory, or age, in capitalism, which at the micro-organizational level has been referred to as flexible, or post-Fordism, value-adding activity; and at a macro-institutional level we refer to as alliance (rather than hierarchical) capitalism. For reasons which shall be explained later, this latest era of capitalism is likely to shift the dominant pattern of trade to the left of the bottom right-hand corner of the matrix.

The feature about most received trade theory is that, at best, it considers as neutral and, at worst, it ignores altogether the co-ordination and relational costs and benefits associated with the *production* and *consumption* of tradable products, and those associated with the *transactions* of those products, as relevant explanatory variables of the amount and pattern of trade. While more recent theories, notably strategic trade models and Krugman's foray into geography (Krugman 1991), have incorporated some of the analytical tools of industrial and locational economics,[7] none adequately embrace either the organizational or institutional characteristics of demand and supply, or those associated with alternative modes of exchange.[8] The assumption continues to be made that the entities engaging in trade are single-activity firms, and that there is no incentive for these firms *not* to use the market as an exchange mechanism. In neo-classical theory, at least, each trading firm is presumed to be operating on its optimum production function;[9] and because it supplies only one product, and produces on one point of the value chain, it is also presumed to engage in no intermediate transactions. Issues of interfirm alliances or the clustering of firms to gain agglomerative economies are disregarded altogether.

But, an even greater criticism of trade theory is that the act of exchanging goods and services in the open market is assumed to be costless.[10] When one thinks about this, it is an incredible assumption. It implies that buyers and sellers have full and symmetrical information both about each other's motives and capabilities, and about the characteristics and quality of the goods and services being transacted. Each party to any exchange is presumed to behave towards the other with complete honesty and transparency, and there is a complete absence of opportunism. H–O theory also explicitly assumes zero spatial costs, but we suspect that even had these been included, no attention would have been paid to such transaction costs as failed delivery dates.

Micro-economists from Ronald Coase (1937) onwards have been well versed in these concepts; but, is it not odd that the transaction cost paradigm has been used primarily to explain the growth of multi-activity and multinational firms rather than the level and pattern of international trade? Are we, then, to assume that the size and character of transactional costs makes no difference to the amount of a good or service traded? In practice, we know this is not true. Indeed, is it arguable that one of the most powerful facilitators of the cross-border division of labour (and hence trade) is a reduction in transaction costs brought about by the establishment of an acceptable legal and commercial system and by the reduction of cross-border psychic and physical distance? And what is the function of such institutions as GATT and the newly formed World Trade Organization (WTO) if it is not to reduce market failure in products traded across national borders?

In short, both neo-classical and much of modern trade theory gives short shrift to the firm as an organizing unit. The location of economic activity, and hence trade arising from it, is assumed to be entirely dependent on location-bound, country-specific characteristics, although some attention is given by Helpman and Krugman (1985) and Markusen (1995) to the distinction between firm-level and plant-level scale economies, and on the distribution of intrafirm value-added activities, for example headquarters, services and subsequent production processes.[11] The doctrine of comparative advantage – that each country should allocate its resources to the production of goods which require inputs for which it is comparatively well endowed, and trade these for goods and services which require resources in which it is relatively poorly endowed – follows quite logically from the assumptions underlying the theory which, it should be noted, are essentially *normative*, rather than *positive*, in character. According to H–O logic, the comparative advantage of a country is entirely determined by the *allocative* efficiency of its value-added activities. Questions relating to *technical* or *scale* efficiency or to the competitive advantage of firms are regarded as predetermined or irrelevant! And, only comparatively recently has the ability of a country to adjust its pattern of resources and capabilities to changing demand and supply conditions been embraced by trade theorists.

Once, however, one accepts that there are different modalities of organizing economic activity, and that each of these involves costs and benefits, it is no longer acceptable to assume that the market is necessarily the most beneficial way of organizing resources. In particular, the role of other organizing agents (e.g. hierarchies, networks, consumer groups and governments) may legitimately be considered. Sometimes, these roles, and/or their outcomes, may conflict with those of markets; sometimes they are complementary to them, or provide the infrastructure for markets to operate effectively. This does not mean that non-market forms of organization (e.g. hierarchies, networks or governments) will necessarily be more cost effective than markets; this may or may not be the case. Moreover, over time, the net benefits of alternative organizational modes may change. But what it does mean is that, in order for markets to perform effectively at a future date, for example $t + 1$, $t + 2$, etc., some extramarket supporting or enabling mechanism might be required in time t. Hence, for example, before the market can work even moderately well in China or Russia, an efficient legal, institutional, financial and commercial infrastructure – not to mention a market culture – needs to be established, which, unaided, private enterprise system may be unable to achieve. As a conclusion to this part of our chapter and as an introduction to what follows, it may be useful to compare and contrast three different scenarios assumed by economists in their attempts to explain international transactions. These are set out in Table 5.1.

The first scenario contains the assumptions underlying the traditional theories of trade put forward up to around 1950, while those marked with an asterisk (*) are also assumed by post-1950 trade theories. The second scenario contains the assumptions which scholars versed in FDI theory have used to explain both the foreign value-added activities of MNEs and the trade of these enterprises.

The third scenario looks to the future. It sets out the kind of real-world situations which several analysts believe will condition the pattern of future international transactions. We have already described this scenario as one of 'alliance' capitalism – to contrast it with the scenario of 'hierarchical' capitalism, which typified the economies of the Western world in much of the twentieth century.

It may be inferred from Table 5.1 that each of these scenarios requires very different explanations for the extent and pattern of international transactions. But do they? There are three aspects of the changing world environment that we believe have not been given the attention they deserve by traditional trade economists. The three aspects are:

Table 5.1 Alternative scenarios for theorizing about determinants of trade in goods and services

Scenario I Neo-classical trade (NCT) theory 1950	*Scenario II Modern trade theory plus direct investment (DI) theory 1950–90*	*Scenario III Emerging theory of international transactions in the age of alliance capitalism 1990*
* No unique competitive (O) advantages of firms	• Unique competitive (O) advantages of individual firms	• As for DI theory, plus those advantages external to individual firms, but as influenced and/or co-ordinated by those firms
* Immobility of natural resources	• Mobility of created assets	• Less mobility of created assets because of increasing significance of agglomerative (i.e. clustering) economies
• Allocation of economic activity mainly based on allocation of natural resources and finance capital	• Allocation of economic activity based on disposition of natural and created assets	• Allocation of economic activity as for DI theory, but also influenced by economies of subnational agglomeration, e.g. business districts
* Government activity largely ignored; supranational regimes considered superfluous	• Government activity viewed as an asset (or liability!). Role of supranational regimes acknowledged	• As for DI theory, but also as embracing cross-border alliances and interfirm networking
* Single-activity firms	• Multi-activity firms	• More concentration on 'core' competences of individual firms, but growing significance of multi-activity networks
• Transactions mainly of an inter-industry character	• Transactions mainly of an intraindustry character	• As for DI theory
* All transactions conducted between independent firms	• Transactions conducted between related firms or within multinational hierarchies	• As for DI theory, but more focus on intranetwork activities
* No endemic market failure, hence zero transaction costs	• Endemic market failure overcome by hierarchical internalization	• Endemic market failure reduced (or overcome) by interfirm co-operation (quasi-integration)
* No attention given to co-ordinating costs and benefits of related activities	• Gains and costs from co-ordinating cross-border activities specifically acknowledged	• As for DI theory, but greater plurality of organizational forms for co-ordinating economic activity
• Perfect competition	• Imperfect competition	• As for DI theory, but fewer imperfections in intermediate product markets involving co-operation among firms

1 The significance of micro-organizational costs and benefits.
2 The growing mobility of firm-specific assets.
3 The role of national governments in the macro-organization of economic activity.

THE RELEVANCE OF MICRO-ORGANIZATIONAL COSTS AND BENEFITS

What is the main organizational task of firms? Surely, it is to co-ordinate the use of separate – including those bought from other firms – inputs in such a way that, when taken together, they maximize the value added of the output they help to create. That is to say, although firms create value through production, in order to best achieve this goal, managers need effectively to co-ordinate the contributions of various inputs into the production and marketing process.

Indeed, one of the earliest conceptions of the firm was that it is a co-ordinated unit of decision taking. Yet, only in the last twenty years or so has the co-ordinating role of the firm been explicitly considered – and this largely from an intra- rather than an interfirm perspective. It is true that neo-classical economists have always accepted that there are alternative ways of utilizing available factor inputs, but basically this is presumed to rest on the quality and costs of the inputs, rather than on the costs of co-ordination *per se*. Most economics textbooks pay only passing attention to the organizing function of firms. Implicitly, they are presumed to buy their inputs at arm's length on the open market, and that even when they have some choice over the conditions of purchase, the costs of search and negotiation surrounding these choices are assumed to be zero. Although when it comes to international trade, textbooks switch their focus of interest from the firm to the country, implicitly at least the same assumptions about co-ordinating costs apply.

Consider for a moment what has occurred in the nature of transborder production and transactions over the past two decades. We would point to three features which have especially affected the organizing principles of resource allocation. The first is the rising co-ordinating costs of an increasingly complex division of labour. This is partly a reflection of the nature of the products produced and partly that of the underlying demand and supply conditions. Thus, more specialization of economic activity tends to raise a firm's co-ordination costs, by increasing the number and specificity of tasks and of information links. It may also raise transaction costs, as the likelihood of information asymmetry and opportunistic behaviour increases. Second, specialization may yield benefits from the common governance of activities which require similar inputs or which yield economies of scope. Third, the outcome of decisions associated with various kinds of value activities has increasingly affected economic entities beyond the participants involved in any particular transaction.

Each of these factors – by raising the costs of using arm's length markets and/or using the benefits of other (notably intra- or interfirm) co-ordinating mechanisms – has resulted in the co-ordination of value-added activities, which were previously undertaken separately and independently. Except in the factor and final goods markets, and for much of the twentieth century, hierarchical transactions have gradually assumed greater importance. In the last decade or so, as markets have become increasingly liberalized and deregulated, and as firms have downsized the range of their activities, various interfirm and governmental arrangements, including networks, have replaced some intrafirm hierarchies, although, other than in the primary goods sector, pure arm's length transactions of intermediate products remain the exception rather than the rule.

The greater costs of using arm's length markets have then changed both the structure of firms and the relationships between them. This has not only affected patterns of trade or exchange within countries, but also between countries. Indeed, international transactions are likely to incur their own specific co-ordination and transaction costs. Some of these reflect a lack of information about, or unfamiliarity with, foreign markets, or uncertainty about institutions, organizational structures, business customs and actions of foreign governments. To be sure, trade economists have embraced, and have examined the effect of, structural market failure (e.g. that brought about by the imposition of import barriers), apart from the presence of scale and some aspects of vertical integration on trade patterns. However, they have largely ignored the role of *endemic* market failure, in so far as it has affected both the underlying demand and supply conditions under which tradable goods and resources are produced, and the costs and benefits of alternative forms of organizing their cross-border exchange.[12]

How then does the presence of endemic market failure affect our theorizing about trade patterns? It is, we suggest, possible to consider five possible responses by traders to the incorporation of such variables as bounded rationality, increasing returns to scale, externalities and uncertainties into the 'terms' of trading. The first is simply to cease trading. Thus, an unaccountably high risk of non-, or late, delivery, or the unreliable quality of intermediate products, may result in the buyer ceasing to trade in those products. Whether no trade is better than second- or third-best trade is a moot point!

The second response to cross-border market failure is to try to reduce market failure. This Hirschman 'voice'-type strategy (Hirschman 1970) is usually accomplished by an exchange of views and information between buyers and sellers; by each seeking to establish and maintain a climate of trust, forbearance and commitment; and, in the case of interfirm transactions, by the parties to the exchange working together to reduce transaction and co-ordination costs, and to upgrade the quality and/or lower the cost of the intermediate products. Sometimes, such transaction costs can be best reduced by establishing formal contractual relationships (a kind of half-way house between arm's length trade and hierarchies), and sometimes by establishing less formal but none the less binding ties between the trading parties, for example of a *keiretsu* kind. The initial costs of creating such relationships may be quite high, particularly where the trading cultures of the parties are different, or when there is information asymmetry about the quality of products. However, over time, these may be expected to fall as a congenial working ethos is built up and as this ethos spreads to competitors and other suppliers alike.

As we have already indicated, the main market-facilitating or sustaining costs considered in the trade literature are those to do with the removal of *structural* market distortions, for example trade barriers and monopoly power. And yet, not only throughout history have the costs of *endemic* market failure acted as impediments to trade (and some of these have fallen as a result of telecommunication advances) but others (and especially those to do with asymmetries in knowledge) have risen sharply as economic activity has become more complex and multi-faceted.

The third reaction to market failure is for firms to try to reduce the costs of arm's length transactions by internalizing international product markets. Vertical and horizontal intrafirm trade then replaces interfirm trade. The subject of intrafirm (as opposed to intraindustry) trade is a very under-researched topic. While a great deal has been written on *why* firms may wish to internalize cross-border markets,[13] much less attention has been given to the ways and extent to which the level and pattern of hierarchical trade differs from arm's length trade, or, indeed, if and when the former is more efficiency enhancing than the latter. In some cases, intrafirm trade may be structurally distorting, as, for example, when firms seek to exploit or extend their monopoly power (à la Hymer 1960). But in others, where hierarchical trade replaces trade previously conducted under conditions of endemic market failure, it may improve economic welfare. And while it is possible to identify situations when the second hypothesis is likely to be more plausible than the first, virtually no attention has been paid to whether or not a hierarchical internalization of market failure is the most cost-effective way of responding to that failure.

The fourth possible response to market failure is for some kind of non-market agency (e.g. government) to step in to try to simulate a perfect or near-perfect market, or to encourage the participants in the market to behave in a way which has similar results to those which would have been brought about by a perfect market. Finally, traders may accept the transaction or co-ordinating costs associated with arm's length markets, on the basis that any alternative organizational mode of exchange would be less cost efficient.

It is worth observing that each of these reactions will vary according to both the nature of the goods or services being traded and the participants involved in the trade. Less directly, but no less importantly, it will depend on the techno-economic characteristics of production and the socio-institutional framework of the macro-economic system. Thus, while a scale production system and hierarchical capitalism tended to encourage the third type of response to endemic market failure, the advent of flexible production and alliance capitalism is leading to a greater emphasis on the formation of interfirm co-operative relationships and networks. This is partly because it is perceived that at least some of the benefits of internalized markets can be captured by non-equity alliances, and partly because, in recent years, the Japanese experience has shown that a 'voice' rather than an 'exit' approach to market failure (i.e. an attempt to reduce, rather than bypass, arm's length transaction costs) may be a more cost-effective response. In so far as this kind of reaction is taking root, some of the assumptions of neo-classical theory about the characteristics of markets are becoming *more*, rather than *less*, apposite than they once were.

In their explanation of why firms engage in intrafirm trade, scholars versed in direct investment theory usually focus on two kinds of cross-border transactions. The first is that of intangible assets which essentially comprise both the rationale and ingredients of FDI; and the second is the intermediate or finished (but not final) products traded between commonly owned affiliates located in different countries. In both cases, the relative significance of intra-, (compare interfirm), trade is likely to vary according to *what* is being traded and with *whom* the trade is being conducted. It follows, then, that the effect of cross-border market failure on the international division of labour will be, to some extent at least, country and activity (or industry) specific. But, even if a relatively few markets are imperfect, the substitution of hierarchical for arm's length trade may, none the less, affect the *comparative* advantages of the constituent countries – and hence an explanation of *which* countries trade in *which* goods.

Let us illustrate what we mean. Assume a Swiss MNE discovers a cost-effective cure for AIDS, and that it alone has the right to produce the drug. Assume too that the firm's only option for selling the drug to a foreign market is to export it from a home production base. In choosing to export, not only is its own competitive advantage affected, but so is the structure of the revealed comparative advantage of Switzerland (i.e. it increases in pharmaceuticals and decreases in other products). Suppose next it is discovered that it is possible to manufacture the drug more cheaply in another country, say in Brazil. However, suppose that the Swiss firm is not prepared to sell the knowledge about the drug (i.e. the intangible asset) to a Brazilian firm at either arm's length prices – because it fears opportunism on the part of the buyer – or through an interfirm co-operative agreement – because it is not able to gain the economies of co-ordination between its Brazilian activities and those of the rest of its organization,[14] or because it cannot ensure cross-effective quality control of the Brazilian product. In this instance, the locational advantages of Brazil – and the consequential restructuring of the comparative advantage of both Brazilian and Swiss location-bound resources[15] – is outweighed by endemic market failure. In seeking ways to reduce such failure, let us finally assume the Swiss firm decides to set up, or acquire, a subsidiary in Brazil in the expectation that, by so doing, it can capture both the gains of a Brazilian location and those of minimizing its co-ordination and transaction costs.

The kind of scenario just outlined will cause trade in pharmaceutical products between Switzerland and Brazil (and possibly elsewhere in the world) to be different than that which would have occurred had cross-border exchanges been limited to arm's length transactions. Exactly how much and in what way will depend on the nature and extent of the market failure. Similarly, the structure of hierarchically related trade described in our example would, itself, be different than that which might have arisen had the drug (produced by the Swiss subsidiary in Brazil) been supplied by a Brazilian firm which was part of a co-operative network of activities in which both it and the Swiss firm were members. Again, the critical issue is how significant are such organizational modes as compared with other possible determinants in explaining international trade in the AIDS-curing drug?

In short, any paradigm of intercountry patterns of trade and direct investment needs to embrace both the co-ordinating costs and benefits of engaging in multiple activities – or the same activity – in more than one country, and it must embrace the transaction-related costs of the alternative routes of organizing trade. Such costs and benefits will be partly country specific; indeed, we shall argue later in this chapter that the capability of a country to organize its production and exchange efficiently may be considered as a competitive advantage in its own right. Hence, countries with a well-ordered system of markets, and those whose institutions are appropriate to optimizing production and cross-border exchanges, are likely to be in a better position to supply products which are transaction cost intensive, or to engage in interrelated activities which yield high externalities and/or co-ordinating benefits. Costs and benefits will also be partly sector specific; hence, the trading patterns of countries which specialize in the kind of activities and exchanges which are transaction and/or co-ordinating cost intensive are likely to be more affected than those which do not, by the incorporation of such costs.

THE GROWING MOBILITY OF FIRM-SPECIFIC ASSETS

Among the assumptions, or presumptions, of extant trade theory, perhaps the two least appropriate to the reality of the global economy of the 1990s are, first, that resources consist of location-bound natural assets – notably land and unskilled labour – and, second, that these assets are equally available to all firms to acquire and utilize in their production processes. In the 1990s, not only are most assets 'created' from natural resources[16] – information, knowledge capital, innovatory and organizational capacity, experience, and institutional infrastructure are examples – but a significant proportion of these assets are, at least at a particular point in time, the proprietary right of particular firms; that is, not equally available to all producing entities. Moreover, unlike natural assets, many created assets are intangible. These include such location-bound assets as the culture of a country and the economic policies of its government.[17]

The growing importance of *created*, relative to *natural*, assets in the explanation of the competitive and comparative advantages of countries is impelling economists to rethink some of their cherished notions about the determinants of trade. For example, since at least some created assets are footloose across national boundaries, it follows that a country's comparative advantage in a global economy is as much determined by the structure of inbound and outbound direct investment as by that of trade. To some extent, the mobility of assets was embraced in an extension to H–O theory introduced by Mundell (1957), when he argued that the movement of (finance) capital could be assumed to substitute for the movement of goods. The question arises as to whether this idea can be extended to other forms of assets – and especially those which are the privileged possession of particular firms.

The idea that a firm might possess, or have access to, unique assets denied to its competitors, is fundamentally alien to traditional trade theory, which asserts that the competitive advantage of any particular country is entirely dependent on the way in which its indigenous resources are allocated among different uses. The theory argues that to optimize this advantage, these resources should be distributed to sectors in which the country – relative to other countries – has a *comparative* advantage. That the firm is treated as a 'black box' naturally follows from the presumption that trade is (or should be) conducted under perfectly competitive conditions. This, in turn, negates the possibility of structural market distortions, and/or of differentiated or dynamic products (Gray 1994). Yet, it is these latter products, rather than the more standardized goods and services with which H–O theory is concerned, which make up much of world trade, and especially intraindustry trade between the Triad nations. And, it is precisely these products which are likely to be 'created asset' intensive in their production; whose locational needs are likely to be 'footloose'; and which are produced under conditions of endemic market failure.

In short, trade and investment patterns of dynamic products are as much likely to be determined by the structure and distribution of *firm-specific created assets* as they are by that of *country-specific natural assets*. We shall address the role of these former assets in affecting the pattern of trade and investment in the next section. For the moment, we would observe that, *de facto*, even in the most market-oriented economies, the role of non-market institutions (e.g. governments and supranational agencies such as GATT) can critically affect how, and in what way, endemic market failure may be overcome, and hence our thinking about the determinants of trade.

But, even accepting the fact that firm-specific advantages do exist, what difference does this make to our theorizing about trade patterns? The previous section dealt with issues surrounding the governance of firms and markets;[18] and, in particular, how the presence of co-ordination and transaction costs might affect the structure and ownership of international activity. In this section, we shall be primarily concerned with the way in which the distribution of the ownership of assets among firms may impact on the geography of their creation and usage.

Here, apart from some foraging by Helpman and Krugman (1985) and Markusen (1984, 1995), we are largely in uncharted territory – and there are several separate questions we might wish to explore. We shall attempt to examine only two, and in doing so will adopt a step-by-step approach in our reasoning. The first question is, in what way does the principle of comparative advantage need to be modified to take account of the existence of firm-specific advantages? Let us concentrate on just two of such advantages:[19] the privileged possession of a specific piece of technology, say a chemical formula protected by patent; and a branded product which is perceived by consumers to be uniquely different from that of its nearest substitute. Although both advantages confer at least a degree of temporary monopoly power to the firm possessing them, both may also help upgrade product quality and/or widen consumer choice, and hence advance economic welfare. However, without knowledge of the utility functions of consumers, it is impossible to say whether the social benefits of this situation are more or less than those resulting from perfect competition, since the latter is simply not equipped to deal with variables other than price and quantity.

Now, to some extent, post-H–O–S trade theories implicitly take account of these firm-specific characteristics, but each assumes that their origin stems from the resources and markets *exogenous* to the firms but endogenous to their home countries. Thus, US firms in the computer industry may have an advantage over UK firms, simply because the United States offers a more supportive technological infrastructure and economic environment than does the United Kingdom. Michael Porter (1990) would appear to support this hypothesis, although his interpretation of the term economic environment goes well beyond that of most trade economists.[20] However, in today's globalizing economy, this proposition is less persuasive than it used to be for two reasons. The first is that firms – and especially MNEs with significant foreign operations – may, directly or indirectly, derive some of their competitive advantages from tapping into the created assets and markets of other countries. And second, the business literature suggests that firms develop their own particular trajectories of technological, managerial and marketing capabilities and experiences, which are as much fashioned by their own strategic objectives and organizational cultures, as they are by the location-bound characteristics of their home countries. This is particularly likely to be the case in the more dynamic sectors of industry, and where competition between firms is oligopolistic.[21] In such cases, then, one needs a separate theory of business strategy to explain fully why countries trade with each other.

The second step in the reasoning is to allow for the mobility of intangible assets. This is precisely what Ray Vernon and his colleagues did in their exposition and empirical testing of the product cycle,[22] which is now explicitly acknowledged by FDI theory. Indeed, it is generally accepted that MNEs are the main vehicles for transferring non-financial assets across national boundaries, and that, in so doing, they affect both the competitive advantages of firms in the exporting and importing countries, and the comparative advantages of location-bound resources in both home and host countries.

Taking this analysis to its logical extreme, if all assets were completely mobile across national boundaries, a critical conclusion of the neo-classical trade theory, namely that all countries can benefit from engaging in trade, would fall to the ground. This is because, in response to market forces, assets may choose an 'exit' rather than a 'voice' strategy, by moving rather than being utilized (or reallocated) within a country. History is, indeed, replete with examples of the *absolute* decline of nation states, which – in theory, at any rate – is inconsistent with the principle of comparative advantage. It follows, then, that countries whose current comparative advantages rest largely in their possession of mobile-created, firm-specific assets are likely to be more vulnerable to exogenous economic forces than those whose advantages rest on the possession of immobile country-specific assets. At the same time, as the experience of the Japanese and Singaporean economies has shown, the opportunities of countries dependent on created assets to upgrade and restructure their comparative advantages are just as, if not more, promising than those reliant on their natural resources.

Of course, in practice, not only are some resources completely location bound (e.g. land and (most) buildings), but most (e.g. labour, R&D laboratories and culturally sensitive intangible assets) are only partially mobile. Hence, the principle of comparative advantage may still hold good – particularly when it incorporates firms and non-market (e.g. government) related variables, and is viewed from a dynamic, rather than a static, perspective. Yet, while it is difficult to fault the proposition that, viewed from a *country's* perspective, its resources and capabilities should concentrate on producing goods and services which the international market-place deems it is comparatively best suited to produce, this should not be taken to mean that it is necessarily in the best interests of the *owners* of those resources and capabilities to deploy those assets in any one specific location.[23] This, to our mind – and this is especially true in a situation of global structural unemployment – is why the notion of countries competing with one another is not quite the mindless obsession Krugman (1990) claims it to be.[24]

THE ROLE OF NATIONAL GOVERNMENTS IN THE MACRO-ORGANIZATION OF ECONOMIC ACTIVITY

Up to this point, we have been primarily concerned with two main organizing entities of the structure of economic activity, namely firms and markets. We now turn to consider a third, that is national governments and supranational economic regimes. Once again, we shall argue that the globalization of economic activity is requiring a reappraisal of the role of non-market institutions as both pro-active and reactive players in the determination of the pattern and distribution of international activity. To give more focus to our argument, we shall give specific consideration to the role of national governments and supranational agencies as fashioners of the economic environment for cross-border transactions. Elsewhere,[25] we have examined the consequences of government actions on the competitiveness of firms and countries. Here, we shall confine our attention to their impact on the received theories of trade and FDI.

For the last two centuries, the main body of international economics has taken as axiomatic that the level and pattern of cross-border trade is best left to free market forces. On efficiency grounds, government interaction is thought legitimate in only two cases. The first is that, in order to promote a country's dynamic comparative advantage, it might be necessary to protect potentially competitive, but fledgling, firms and industries from their more robust foreign competitors. For the last two centuries, such protection has been widely practised by many governments; indeed, the 'infant industry' argument is often used to justify the resuscitation of well-established firms and industries. The second rationale for government intervention is to counter anti-competitive or other forms of structurally distorting behaviour practised by one or other of the participants in the market – including foreign governments. Although not expressed in these terms, neo-classical economists accept this rationale of government intervention – as long as it is directed to facilitating the workings of the free market, *and* as long as such intervention is cost effective. Of course, it is also recognized that governments might intervene to achieve goals other than that of economic efficiency, but an examination of these is normally considered outside the purview of the economist.

At the same time, it is a fact that, in the pursuance of their macroeconomic and macro-organizational policies, governments *do* strongly influence trade patterns. It is our contention not only that the globalizing economy is requiring national administrations to take a more active stance as the guardian of the well-being of their constituents, but that their willingness and ability to do this efficiently should, itself, be perceived as a public good in its own right.

Our justification for this last statement is basically an extension of the argument of the previous two sections. There it was asserted that the way in which each firm organizes its value-added activities is as much a factor in influencing its trading capabilities as is its ability to innovate new products or production processes.[26] In this section, we shall argue that the way in which governments organize the resources, capabilities and markets within their jurisdiction – and this includes the extent to which they are prepared to delegate this responsibility to private hierarchies, groups of firms or markets – is a critical determinant of the pattern of international transactions.

At first sight, it might be supposed that globalization – driven by technological imperatives and facilitated by market-supporting economic policies – is fashioning a scenario more in accord with the tenets of neoclassical trade theory than those which it replaced. And, it is difficult to deny that, by and large, the structural impediments to many kinds of international transactions in the 1990s are less than those in the 1970s, while advances in telecommunications and informatics are dramatically reducing the costs of physical and psychic distance. At the same time, as we have already observed, there are suggestions that, as the techno-institutional fabric of society becomes more complex and interwoven, various forms of endemic market impurities – such as those associated with asset specificity, information impactness and bounded rationality – increase, and that, at the very least, governments have the responsibility to their constituents for ensuring that the cost of these impurities is minimized.[27]

Earlier in this chapter, we distinguished between *natural* and *created* assets, and between assets which would normally be supplied by the private sector in response to, or in anticipation of, market signals, and those which take the form of public goods – which, because of their high fixed and low variable costs, or the uncertainties associated with their supply, are more likely to be produced, or at least financed by, the public sector. Secondary school education and pre-competitive R&D are two examples. To exploit their full value, many of these assets (e.g. roads and airports) require to be used jointly with privately owned assets; and it is the way firms co-ordinate the use of both sets of assets – and any other assets which they may acquire – which will determine their competitiveness in global markets. Indeed, it is the quality of complementary assets available to firms – and the way in which they are packaged – which is a major element of the co-ordinating and transaction costs earlier described (Teece 1992).

Another aspect of globalization which requires a response by governments is the increasing ease with which assets are able to move across national boundaries. Firms, like people, can 'vote with their feet.'[28] *Inter alia*, this is demonstrated by the sharp increase in all kinds of MNE activity and in interfirm co-operative arrangements (UNCTAD 1993). At the same time, there are strong suggestions that the kinds of international transactions which have grown the most rapidly in the last decade are those which are determined less by the availability, price and quality of location-bound natural assets and more by those of location-bound *created* assets – the production of which governments, directly or indirectly, influence a great deal. Each of these latter assets, together with a culture which favours entrepreneurship, innovation, wealth creation and the acquisition of new markets, helps to lower the transaction or hassle costs of economic activity, and furnishes firms with the ability and the motivation to organize efficiently their value-adding activities.

How might the actions of governments be incorporated into traditional trade theories? One possibility is to treat government as an additional location-bound factor of production. However, apart from the difficulty of identifying and measuring either its input or output, there is little reason to suppose that more government leads to better macro-organizational management or lower production and transaction costs.[29] At the same time, there is reason to suppose that the *quality* of government action is an important element in determining both the competitiveness of firms and the comparative advantage of countries. Indeed, just as organizational competence is an essential prerequisite for corporate competitiveness, so it is a critical precondition for successful government intervention. *Inter alia*, this means governments should know *when* to intervene, *how much* to intervene and in *what ways* they should intervene. The most noticeable feature of the economic success of East Asian nations like Hong Kong, Singapore, Japan, Taiwan and Korea, is not the extent or form of government intervention – this has differed considerably between these nations – but the fact that, in each case, the visible hand of government has been aimed at facilitating the invisible hand of markets and promoting the dynamic comparative advantage of their resources and capabilities. Although it cannot be denied that such government action was (and still is, to some extent) sometimes market distorting, the main thrust of such intervention has been to aid the structural adjustment of indigenous resources and capabilities, and of consumer needs, and to facilitate its firms to behave in a way that is consistent with long-term market needs.

All this is not to ignore the strategic role of governments in helping to ensure that their own firms, *vis-à-vis* their competitors, are not penalized in international markets; nor, indeed, to ignore the deliberate aggressive actions of national administrations to capture the maximum economic rent from the activities of their firms outside their boundaries and from foreign firms within their national boundaries. Like it or not, such actions are increasing – and not only through measures directly targeted to influencing trade and investment patterns, but also by a gamut of other measures – notably industrial, environmental, competition and tax policies – which indirectly affect both the ability and motivation of their own firms and resources to be competitive in world markets. Sometimes such measures are market facilitating, and sometimes market distorting. One thing is certain, however: in the global economy of the 1990s, the concept of commercial policy needs to embrace all actions by governments which impact on the organization of economic activity, and hence on the structure of a country's comparative advantage.

But, to what extent does the incorporation of the actions of governments – and particularly those to do with macro-organizational policy – improve the predictions of traditional trade theory? This is essentially an empirical question which can, at least, be partially answered by reference to history. Here, the answer is a mixed one. There have been times (e.g. the late nineteenth century and the 1960s) when the market-facilitating role of governments has probably outweighed its market-distorting impact, and in these years, such intervention has helped improve trade patterns. On other occasions (e.g. the interwar years, and during the 1970s) when import-substituting policies on the part of governments were at their zenith, the reverse has been the case.

In the global economy of the 1990s, we venture to suggest that the power and responsibility of national governments to exercise each of these functions has intensified, and this, in spite of the growth of international economic regimes (e.g. GATT) and regional economic blocs (e.g. the EC). This is because of the growing role of government-influenced co-ordination and transaction costs in affecting trade and investment, and particularly that of an intraindustry character. Those governments which, by their macro-organizational policies, can successfully lower these costs – or exploit the benefits of agglomerative and other forms of market externalities – are those most likely to induce trade patterns which are consistent with dynamic comparative advantage. By the same token, however, the power of national governments to distort structurally the cross-border allocation of resources has also risen.

In spite of fears about the emergence of regional fortresses or blocks, we believe that the pressures of globalization are disciplining national governments to adopt policies that are more, rather than less, conducive to optimizing trade patterns. These pressures are essentially twofold. The first is the outcome of the widespread liberalization and deregulation of markets, and the privatization of state assets over the past decade.[30] The second – which is still largely in its infancy – is the recognition of the need for the strengthening of multilateral and supranational mechanisms which sets the rules of the game for national government actions.

Already, in the area of macro-economic policy, the G7 have played a major (though admittedly not always successful) role in discouraging 'beggar my neighbour' exchange rate policies by national governments which might have negative externalities for the rest of the world, and in encouraging monetary and fiscal policies which might promote positive externalities. And, of course, the IMF, in its monetary and financial strategies, and GATT, in its trade strategies, are designed to minimize the global disbenefits and maximize the global benefits of world trade, and of a stable monetary and financial regime.[31]

However, increasingly, the adequacy and scope of these institutions in a global economy are being questioned. This is because of the growing externalities of an increasing range of national government policies, which do not come within the purview of existing multinational regimes. Indeed, most of the macro-organizational policies – including, incidentally, FDI policies – currently implemented by national administrations are subject to no supranational governance at all.[32]

It is the concern that, as national macro-*economic* policies become more circumscribed, national macro-*organizational* policies may be increasingly deployed by governments to promote domestic economic interests, which have negative externalities for the rest of the world – and thus promote a vicious circle of retaliatory actions on the part of other governments. This is leading both economists and politicians to urge for a widening of the rubric of existing supranational regimes, and/or the creation of new regimes to embrace such issues as competition, FDI, technology and environmental policies. Unless this is done, it is feared that the gains from the renaissance of market economy will be negated by the rent-seeking activities of national governments. By contrast, if supranational regimes[33] – both public and private – are successful in reducing endemic market failure, they may help to promote, rather than inhibit, an efficient international allocation of resources, and thus uphold, rather than support, the principle of comparative advantage – as modified to take account of the actions of non-market institutions.

We believe that Michael Porter (1990) is wrong when he argues that the principle of comparative advantage is no longer useful in explaining the pattern of international trade. What, however, does need to be reconsidered is the composition of the location-bound factor endowments of a country, and their relevance in determining the competitiveness of a country's firms.[34] Richard Lipsey (1991), for example, has suggested that a country's culture might be considered as an input into economic activity, and that countries differ in the ability and willingness to supply culturally intensive products.[35] Likewise, it is possible to think of the macro-economic and organizational actions of governments as a location-bound variable which affects not only the competitiveness of all economic activity, but different activities to a greater or lesser degree. Thus, government actions which lower the transaction and co-ordinating costs of production and exchange would particularly favour those activities in which these costs were relatively the most important, and thus would affect the *comparative* as well as the competitive advantage of firms and countries. The actions of supranational, or multilateral, regimes may be evaluated in a similar way.

It is, indeed, a paradox that, as the world economy becomes more integrated, the role of non-market supranational institutions in facilitating the efficient operation of cross-border markets may become increasingly important. Moreover, paraphrasing Albert Hirschman (1970), as and when 'market exit' hierarchies are replaced by 'market voice' interfirm relationships, these, too – depending on the nature and content of the relationships – might be more in tune with the dictates of competitive markets than with those they replace.

At the same time, the increasing mobility of assets between countries, and the almost permanent disequilibrium in the use and allocation of resources between countries in an innovation-led global economy, considerably reduces the plausibility of the assumptions underpinning much of traditional trade theory. Just as within a country, there is no assurance that a particular county or region will fully share in the prosperity of the rest of the country – and that it may be to the advantage of the country as a whole, if resources move out of that region to other regions – so in a world of 'quicksilver' assets, the principle of absolute, rather than comparative, advantage becomes a reality. To this extent, and in the presence of the underutilization of resources in a country, the idea of countries (or governments of countries) competing with each other for resources and markets does make sense – particularly where the industrial structure of the countries is very similar. Taken to its extreme, if all resources were completely mobile, much of the rationale for trade theory as a separate branch of economics would disappear. However, as long as there is at least *one* completely location-bound resource, and/or there is some component of immobility in that or other resources, there is some justification for studying intercountry transactions of goods and services.

While the operationalization of the actions of national governments – not to mention supranational or multilateral regimes – may tax the minds of scholars, there can surely be no doubt that, in the last thirty years – both in respect of a particular country over time and between countries at a given time – these actions have varied a great deal – as has the competitiveness and trading patterns of nations. Surely, it should not be beyond the collective wisdom of international economists – perhaps with a little help from their colleagues in industrial economics and choice theory – to devise a measure which relates a particular type, or types, of government action to economic success, and to the promotion of a particular kind of trading advantage. We repeat, it is *not* primarily the question of the level of government expenditure or the amount of intervention which is at issue, but the willingness and ability of the government to superintend efficiently the organization of economic activity – including that in which it is, itself, directly engaged.

CONCLUSIONS

Let us now pull the threads of this chapter together. We have suggested that what's wrong is the failure of trade theory to address techno-economic micro- and macro-organizational issues, and particularly, the effect on trade of co-ordinating resources and transacting across exchanges by alternative modalities. In particular, we have asserted that the globalizing of the world economy is affecting the pattern of trade in three main ways. First, the increasing mobility of assets is widening the options of firms in their engagement in international commerce. In particular, FDI and strategic alliances have replaced trade as the main form of international transaction. The second is the declining significance of arm's length transactions, relative to those conducted between related parties.[36] The third is the increasing role of national governments and supranational regimes in the management of trade, and in influencing the disbursement of 'quicksilver' assets and the competitiveness of locationally immobile resources and capabilities.

At the same time, we have argued that, *de facto*, technological, political and economic changes of the past two decades which have virtually destroyed the credibility of any theory which assumes that firms are 'black boxes' and that governments play no role in affecting trade and investment, have led to a restructuring of economic activity which, in general, has been more in keeping with the extant tenets of the neo-factor and scale theories of trade, than that which it replaced. This is because the internalization of arm's length markets by hierarchies, the growth of strategic alliances, and the macro-organizational strategies of governments have not only been the response to the pressures of global competition, but often helped promote allocative and dynamic competitiveness. Even if, to some observers, this is a hypothetical, rather than proven, statement, it suggests that, far from being dead and buried, there is a good deal of life left in traditional trade paradigms, which aver that, given a chance and over time, market forces do work.

We would not want to press our argument too far, or to deny that there are some firm- or government-specific patterns of behaviour which run counter to the principles of neo-classical economics. Examples include strategies to promote rent seeking or to gain or exploit an oligopolistic or monopolistic position. But, our reading of the forces now making for globalization is that they are making such strategies more difficult to achieve – except, perhaps, at a regional level. For the moment, we would aver that many of the propositions of received trade theory are being upheld by the very organizational forces which they tend to neglect.

NOTES

1 However, for the purposes of this chapter, we shall be concentrating on international economic issues.
2 And especially the attention given to increasing returns as a determinant of trade.
3 This in no way denies the need for further theoretical extension of both traditional and newer trade models as, for example, set out by Bensel and Elmslie (1992) and Krugman (1990).
4 We use the adjective 'connected' to embrace transactions other than those conducted at arm's length. They include all intrafirm trade and trade between separately owned entities which arise from contractual agreements.
5 See especially the work of Dosi *et al.* (1990), which links technological accumulation theories of growth to those of dynamic comparative advantage.
6 We accept that the idea of a continuum of transactional relationships may fail to capture the complex realities of exchange, and in the words of Walter Powell (1990) is 'too quiescent and mechanical'. However, for the purposes of this chapter, I find it useful to delineate the main organizational routes for conducting trade.
7 Notably models of oligopolistic competition. For a review of these theories, see Krugman (1986).
8 The nearest, perhaps, is Markusen's recent attempts to examine the relationship between the boundaries of MNEs and the modern theories of trade (Markusen 1995).
9 It is unclear in more recent trade theories whether or not firms are presumed to be producing with zero X inefficiency!
10 These costs should embrace any and all costs which can be traced to a particular transaction, including those incurred before or after the transaction takes place.
11 According to Markusen (1995: 175), MNEs are 'exporters of the services of firm-specific assets'. Earlier models constructed by Helpman (1984) and Markusen (1984) separated the headquarters or firm-level activity such as R&D from the rest of the production process of firms. In both models, the MNE headquarter's activity is modelled as a joint input such that adding additional plants (at home or abroad) does not reduce the value of the input to existing plants. Later work by Brainard (1993) and Horstman and Markusen (1992) demonstrated that MNEs are supported in equilibrium wherever firm-specific fixed costs and spatial barriers are large relative to plant-level economies. The researchers also showed that MNEs are more likely to exist in equilibrium when the trading countries are large and when they have similar factor endowments. This view is generally supported by the voluminous empirical evidence on FDI and MNE activity (Dunning 1993a).
12 Again, the work of Markusen is an exception, and in one of his most recent papers (Markusen 1995) he explicitly considers such market imperfections as information asymmetry, the 'free rider' problem, buyer uncertainty and moral hazard in his analysis.
13 For a recent review of the literature, see Dunning (1993a) and Gray (1993).
14 These might include economies of risk diversification, marketing synergies, common sourcing, standardization of financial and accounting techniques, the feedback of know-how, and the easy transfer of learning and experience.
15 And, indeed, of other trading partners of both countries.
16 For a discussion of the role of technology in international trade, see Vernon (1966, 1970).

17 Which, in some instances, may be a liability rather than an asset! See Dunning (1994).
18 This is especially true of firms from smaller nations, whose growth and prosperity largely rests on the foreign operations of the MNEs.
19 For a discussion of the gains arising from access to HQ administrative, managerial and administrative services, see Helpman and Krugman (1985) and Markusen (1984, 1995).
20 See also later sections of this chapter.
21 For a further exposition of the role of the firm in explaining trade in dynamic goods, see Gray (1994).
22 See especially Vernon (1966) and Wells (1972).
23 Hence, as shown by Dunning (1988b), in the case of the United Kingdom, and Lipsey and Kravis (1987), in the case of the United States, it is quite possible for *firms* of a particular nationality to improve their international competitiveness as a result of their foreign value-adding activities while, at the same time, the competitiveness of the location-bound resources of their home countries might be declining.
24 See also Chapter 10 of this volume.
25 See especially Dunning (1993b, 1994) and Chapters 1, 7, 8, 9 and 14 of this volume.
26 For a more general exposition of the importance of organizational advantages in affecting the competitiveness and growth of firms, see Chandler (1962, 1990).
27 As, for example, identified in Dunning (1993b, 1994).
28 An expression first coined by public choice theorists to illustrate that, in the last resort, individuals can respond to an unacceptably high tax burden by emigrating. Similarly, if the net tax burden imposed on firms by the government of one country is higher than that imposed by another, this might result in a relocation of production away from the first to the second country (Gray 1994).
29 Indeed, quite the reverse. In a study carried out for the IMF, Ostry (1993) found little evidence that even selective interventionism by East Asian governments was positively correlated with superior growth performance. Instead, high domestic savings and investment ratios, an emphasis on the upgrading of human capital, flexible labour markets and an unrestricted access to foreign resources, capabilities and markets are among the shared factors in the success of Asian economies.
30 Again, neo-classical economics, with its concentration on economic man (or woman), dismisses the idea that the work ethic and the culture of competitiveness may differ in their desire to upgrade the choice and quality of goods and services available – particularly if this means harder or less congenial work or the sacrifice of leisure.
31 For a discussion of the external consequences of domestic economic policies on global economic welfare, see Eden and Hampson (1990) and Currie and Vines (1992).
32 Apart, that is, from those promised by national authorities which are part of a regional customs union or community. For a review of the ways in which supranational institutions may promote the convergence of national innovation, competition and financial market regulation, see Ostry (1991).
33 In addition to the more obvious supranational institutions, there are a host of other private, or semi-public, multilateral agencies or clubs, for example the World Intellectual Property Organization (WIPO) and the International Organization for Standardization (ISO). Depending upon their *raison d'être* and their power or influence over their members, each of these can either simulate efficient markets, or as in the case of many cartels (OPEC), structurally distort markets.

34 A similar view is held by Adrian Wood (1993), who argues for a re-examination of the H–O thesis in terms of factor endowments which are both immobile and (in the short run at least) non-reproducible. In his model of North/South trade, Wood excludes financial capital, but includes knowledge embodied in people and social infrastructure.

35 In other words, anything other than a 'perfect' culture for competitiveness could be considered a cost. This cost could vary from zero to one which was so high that no production, trade or investment was economically feasible.

36 We might also mention that FDI and trade are becoming increasingly complementary to, rather than substitutable for, each other (UNCTAD 1996).

REFERENCES

Bensel, T. and Elmslie, B. T. (1992) 'Rethinking international trade theory: a methodological appraisal', *Weltwirtschaftliches Archiv* 128 Heft 2: 249–65.

Brainard, S. L. (1993) 'A simple theory of multinational corporations and trade with a trade-off between proximity and concentration', Cambridge, MA: NBER Working Paper No. 4269, February.

Chandler, A. D. Jr (1962) *Strategy and Structure: The History of American Industrial Enterprise*, Cambridge, MA: MIT Press.

——(1990) *Scale and Scope: The Dynamics of Industrial Capitalism*, Cambridge, MA: Harvard University Press.

Coase, R. H. (1937) 'The nature of the firm', *Economica* (New Series) 4, November: 386–405.

Currie, D. A. and Vines, D. (1992) 'A global economic policy agenda for the 1900s: is there a special British role?', *International Affairs* 68(4): 585–602.

Dosi, G., Pavitt, K. and Soete, L. (1990) *Technical Change and International Trade*, New York: Harvester Wheatsheaf.

Dunning, J. H. (1988a) *Multinationals, Technology and Competitiveness*, London: Unwin Hyman.

——(1988b) *Explaining International Production*, London and Boston: Unwin Hyman.

——(1993a) *Multinational Enterprises and the Global Economy*, Workingham, England, and Reading, MA: Addison Wesley.

——(1993b) *Globalization of Business: The Challenge of the 1990s*, London and New York: Routledge.

——(1994) *Globalization: The Challenge for National Economic Regimes*, Dublin: The Economic and Social Research Council.

Dunning, J. H. and Norman, G. (1985) 'Explaining intra-industry international production', in A. Erdilek (ed.) *Multinationals as Mutual Invaders*, London: Croom Helm.

Eden, L. and Hampson, F. O. (1990) *Clubs are Trumps: Towards a Taxonomy of International Regimes*, Ottawa Center for International Trade and Investment Policies, Carleton University, C/TQS, 90–102.

Froot, K. A. (ed.) (1993) *Foreign Direct Investment*, Chicago and London: University of Chicago Press.

Gray, H. P. (ed.) (1993) *Transnational Corporations and International Trade and Payments, UN Library on Transnational Corporations*, Vol. 8, London and New York: Routledge.

——(1994) *A Firm Level Theory of International Trade in Dynamic Goods*, Newark, NJ: Rutgers University (mimeo).

Helpman, E. (1984) 'A simple theory of trade with multinational corporations', *Journal of Political Economy* 92: 451–71.

Helpman, E. and Krugman, P. R. (1985) *Market Structure and Foreign Trade*, Cambridge, MA: MIT Press.

Hirschman, A. (1970) *Exit Voice and Loyalty*, Cambridge, MA: Harvard University Press.

Horstman, I. and Markusen, J. R. (1992) 'Endogenous market structures in international trade', *Journal of International Economics* 32: 109–29.

Hymer, S. (1960) 'The international operation of national firms: a study of direct investment', *PhD Dissertation*, MIT (published by MIT Press in 1976).

Krugman, P. (ed.) (1986) *Strategic Trade Policy and the New International Economics*, Cambridge, MA: MIT Press.

——(1990) *Rethinking International Trade*, Cambridge, MA: MIT Press.

——(1991) *Geography and Trade*, Cambridge, MA: MIT Press.

Lipsey, R. (1991) *Economic Growth: Science and Technology and Institutional Change in the Global Economy*, Toronto: Canadian Institute for Advanced Research, CIAR Publication No. 4, June.

Lipsey, R. and Kravis, I. B. (1987) 'The competitiveness and comparative advantage of US multinationals 1957–1984', *Banca Nazionale del Lavoro Quarterly Review* 16, June: 147–65.

Markusen, J. R. (1984) 'Multinationals, multi-plant economics, and the gains from trade', *Journal of International Economics* 16: 205–26.

——(1995) 'The boundaries of multinational enterprises and the theory of international trade', *Journal of Economic Perspectives* 9 (2): 169–89.

Markusen, J. R. and Venables, A. (1995) *Multinational Firms and the New Trade Theory*, Cambridge: NBER Working Paper No. 5036, February.

Mundell, R. (1957) 'International trade and factor mobility', *American Economic Review* 47: 321–35.

Ostry, S. (1991) 'Beyond the border: the new international policy arena', in *Strategic Policies in a Global Economy*, Paris: OECD International Futures Program.

Ostry, J. (1993) 'Selective government interventions and economic growth: a survey of the Asian experience and its applicability to New Zealand', Paper on Policy Analysis and Assessment, Washington: IMF.

Porter, M. (1990) *The Competitive Advantage of Nations*, New York: The Free Press.

Powell, W. W. (1990) 'Neither market nor hierarchy: network forms of organization', in B. M. Staw and L. M. Cummings (eds) *Research in Organizational Behavior* Vol. 12, Greenwich, CT: JAI Press, pp. 295–316.

Teece, D. J. (1992) 'Competition, cooperation and innovation', *Journal of Economic Behavior and Organization* 7: 1–25.

UNCTAD (1993) *World Investment Report 1993: Towards an Integrated Production System*, New York and Geneva: UN.

UNCTAD (1996) *World Investment Report 1996: Transnational Corporations, Trade and International Production*, New York and Geneva:UN.

Vernon, R. (1966) 'International investment and international trade in the product cycle', *Quarterly Journal of Economics* 80: 190–207.

——(1970) *The Technology Factor in International Trade*, New York: Columbia University Press.

Wells, L. T. (ed.) (1972) *The Product Life Cycle and International Trade*, Cambridge, MA: Harvard University Press.

Wood, A. (1993) *Give Heckscher and Ohlin a Chance*, Sussex: Institute of Development Studies, Chance, Sussex (mimeo).

6

MNE ACTIVITY

Comparing the NAFTA and the European Community

INTRODUCTION

The purpose of this chapter is to review the effects of regional integration on the organization and structure of multinational enterprise (MNE) activity into and out of the European Community (EC)* and to compare and contrast these effects with those which might be expected to arise from a NAFTA. The first part of this chapter briefly outlines the similarities and differences between the kinds of economic integration forged by the two trading blocs. The second part theorizes on the likely consequences for foreign direct investment (FDI) arising from these interdependencies. The third part considers the role played by the changing regulatory environment in the EC for the intra-EC organization of MNE activity. The fourth part examines the evidence of the consequences of Mark I and Mark II European integration for the level, composition and organization of both EC- and non-EC-owned MNE operations. Finally, with this evidence in mind, the fifth part speculates on the possible effects of a NAFTA both within the free trade area and between the participating countries and the rest of the world.

FORMS OF ECONOMIC INTERDEPENDENCE

The considerable literature on regional economic integration identifies a spectrum of economic interaction between sovereign nation states which varies from complete isolation at the one extreme to complete political and economic union at the other. In between, the stages of economic interaction may be grouped, first, according to the degree of formality of the regime governing the behaviour of the member countries and, second, according to the areas of decision making over which national sovereignty is replaced, in whole or in part by regional sovereignty.

Table 6.1 summarizes some of the characteristics of the member states comprising the EC and the NAFTA in the post-war era, while Table 6.2 compares and contrasts some of the features of the NAFTA with those of

Table 6.1 Characteristics of member states in the EC and the NAFTA

EC	*NAFTA*
• Fifteen (at first six, later nine, ten and twelve) member states; no dominant country until 1992 Countries broadly comparable in economic structure (apart from Ireland) until the accession of Southern European countries in 1980s Central core of EC now industrial Rhineland, but distance between main industrial areas in leading EC countries tolerable Exchange rate instability, notwithstanding introduction of exchange rate mechanism (ERM)	• Three member states, dominated in population and GNP by the United States The economic asymmetry between the United States and Canada and Mexico is much greater than (economic) distances between core and periphery Land mass nine times greater than the EC Greater income differences between poorest and richest country Externally greater stability in exchange rates, at least in past 5–10 years
• A mixture of widely different languages, history, legal and political systems Long history of inter-European strife Clear distinction between Anglophile and Francophile cultures, work ethic and attitudes toward authority Broadly comparable population paths	• Fewer non-economic differences between Canada and the United States (although some noticeable intracountry regional differences) Ethnic and cultural differences greater between the main body of the United States and Mexico, but less pronounced in the border territories Noticeably higher rate of population growth of Mexico, the United States and Canada
• Broadly similar economic systems, but degrees of control exercised on trade and FDI vary considerably. Also system and role of government perceived to be very different in France and Italy, cf. (e.g.) UK and Germany	• Extensive government intervention in Mexico until mid-1980s Canada and United States have pursued largely liberal trade and FDI policies since early 1980s Canadian and US tariffs generally lower than their Mexican equivalents
• Both inter- and intra-MNE activity were initially largely confined to market-seeking (import-substituting) activities prior to formation of the EC. There were few intra-European special trading arrangements, except in particular products, e.g. steel • FDI in the 1950s was strongly concentrated in the larger industrialized countries, with the UK receiving the bulk of non-EC investment Within the EC, the UK was (and is) the leading outward foreign direct investor	• Owing to the special trading relationships, e.g. between the United States and Mexico and the United States and Canada, there was more efficiency-seeking FDI, particularly between the United States and Mexico, although in the 1960s and 1970s tariff barriers led to much defensive market seeking, e.g. US FDI in Canadian manufacturing industry There is more natural resource-based FDI in each of these countries than in Europe: in Canada and Mexico, largely by US or UK firms; in the United States, mainly by European MNEs

the EC in 1993.[1] As the tables show, the NAFTA (like the earlier Canada–US Free Trade Agreement) embraces some attributes of both a free trade area and a customs union. In many respects it is a less intensive or shallower form of integration than either the post-1957 (Mark I) EC (which comprised a customs union, but one in which there remained substantial intra-EC non-tariff barriers), or post-1992 (Mark II) EC integration (which is intended to remove all obstacles to the intra-EC movement of people, capital, goods and services). At the same time, the NAFTA does embrace several issues, for example with respect to government procurement, technical barriers to trade, and values of origin and dispute settlements not addressed by EC Mark I integration. Over the current decade – as spelled out by the Maastricht Treaty – it is the intention of (most of) the EC to move towards more complete monetary and fiscal union, including the formation of a European Central Bank, but such (Mark III) EC integration will not be considered in this study, as the issues it involves are of little relevance to the NAFTA partners.

SOME THEORETICAL ISSUES

The interface between MNE activity and regional integration juxtaposes the theory of economic integration, the newer theories of international trade, and the theory of international production. In brief, regional integration affects the level and composition of economic activity of the participating countries through its impact on both the locational decisions of firms and their ownership and organization structures. In the absence of transborder FDI, the issue becomes solely one of the location of production, and of trade patterns arising from such production.

As the literature suggests, integration – whether shallow or deep – may cause a relocation of activity through the diversion or creation of trade, both within the integrated area and between the member countries and the rest of the world. Thus, a lowering of tariffs by reducing the costs of transfer of goods and services from country A to country B is likely to redirect value-added activity from the previously protected country to the exporting country. At the same time, restructuring the natural resource or created asset advantages of the two nations may give rise to new opportunities for trade, economies of scale and specialization, and hence raise the level and/or change the composition of economic activity in both of them. Depending on the extent to which the external tariff between the integrated countries and the rest of the world is higher or lower than that prior to integration, there may be a diversion or creation of extra-integrated area trade. Depending on the size and economic strengths and weaknesses of the participating countries, and their respective responses to integration, the geographical concentration of value-added activities within the region may be intensified or lessened, and intraregional economic relationships may be more or less stabilized.[2]

Economists also find it helpful to distinguish between the *primary* or *initial* effects of integration and the *secondary* or *consequential* effects. The former embrace the immediate consequences of integration for the costs of supplying goods and services from various locations. Take, for example, the removal of tariff barriers, and some non-tariff barriers as a result of Mark I EC integration in 1958 and the conclusion of the Canada–US Free Trade Agreement in 1989. The primary consequence of this kind of integration is to increase the competitiveness of goods exported from (say) France to (say) Italy or from Canada to the United States, relative to those produced by domestic firms in Italy and the United States. Clearly, the extent to which exports will increase will depend on the relative importance of the transfer costs saved, any effect the extra sales of the exporting companies may have on their production costs, and the elasticity of demand for the final products traded. As far as firms from countries outside the integrated market are concerned, the locational effects will depend upon the value of the common external tariff and/or the level and structure of non-tariff barriers relative to those previously imposed by individual countries, although, like the companies producing within the integrated area, they, too, should benefit from the removal of intracountry trade barriers.[3]

To some degree, the primary or initial effects of integration – whatever its form – will be country, sector and firm specific. Certainly, the income and employment consequences from Mark I EC integration have not been equally spread among the six founding member states, any more than those of the NAFTA are likely to be symmetrically distributed between the United States, Canada and Mexico. Economic theory suggests that the countries most likely to gain from freer trade are those whose pre-integration tariff barriers most impeded the efficient allocation of their domestic resources. Also, in so far as small countries are likely to be more trade intensive than large countries, it might be supposed that they will especially benefit from integration – particularly if the supply and demand elasticities for their traded products are high. At the same time large countries which are sheltered from foreign imports may find that the additional competitive import competition may help raise the technical efficiency and widen the marketing networks of their domestic firms.

Clearly, too, the impact of the elimination of tariff barriers will vary according to how important they are in relation to the total costs of supply. In part this will depend on country-specific characteristics, such as the pre-integration tariff levels and the economic or psychic distance involved between the trading partners.[4] Product-specific factors are also likely to influence the effects of regional integration inasmuch as the level and relative significance of tariff reductions and the response of consumer demand and producer supply will vary according to the nature of the goods and services supplied.

Finally, the locational consequences of an economic integration are likely to be firm specific. Consider, for example, the removal of *non*-tariff barriers consequent upon Mark II EC integration (i.e. EC 92). The elimination of border controls, which represent a fixed cost to firms, is likely to benefit small (relative to large) firms. The cessation of favoured treatment in the

Table 6.2 The European Community (as of 1993) and NAFTA: some comparisons and contrasts

1 Trade and production (a) Informal co-operation	*European Community*	*NAFTA*
(b) Complementation agreements		
(c) Removal of tariff barriers	• All intra-EC barriers eliminated. Common external tariff adopted	• All to be eliminated or phased out over five, ten or fifteen years. Special provisions for agricultural products, energy and basic petrochemicals. No common external tariff, e.g. Mexico will be allowed to maintain relatively high tariff levels on imports from the rest of the world
(d) Removal of non-tariff barriers	• Most to be removed by the end of the 1990s	• Some degree of liberalization is occurring, e.g. with respect to safeguarding government procurement. The elimination of NTBs, e.g. technical standards, trucking and port service, may take longer to achieve. Immediate goal is national treatment and intra-NAFTA compatibility in standard-related measures. Sets up a new regime in intellectual property
(e) Rules of origin	• The question of what constitutes an 'EC-made' good (i.e. a good with a substantial EC content) is still a matter of controversy, but the EC is gradually establishing the rules of the game	• Involves preferential tariff treatment for goods considered to be North American. Local content percentages beginning to be identified, e.g. in automotive products. Within NAFTA, rules of origin are replacing intra-North American tariffs and NTBs
(f) Services	• Inter-EC regulations on trade and rights of establishment to be largely eliminated. Principle of mutual reciprocity established	• Principle of equal treatment to be established. Gradual liberalization of financial services up to 2000

Table 6.2 (cont)

1 Trade and production (a) Informal co-operation	*European Community*	*NAFTA*
(g) Dispute settlements	• Harmonized by European Commission	• Trilateralizes the Canadian–FTA process
(h) Special provisions	• For agriculture and a limited number of strategically sensitive manufacturing and service sectors	• Economic co-ordination and transfers found in EC unlikely to be part of NAFTA. For example, each nation will operate separate agricultural programmes
2 Free movement of people	• Gradually being accomplished by the introduction of the EC passport and the harmonization of labour laws and employment conditions	• A truly liberal movement of labour is not part of NAFTA. *De facto*, there are likely to be many obstacles to the free movement of people, especially between Mexico and the United States. Treaty specifically allows for cross-border movement of business persons
3 Free movement of assets	• Largely activated. Most financial markets are already deregulated. There are currently few restrictions on the sourcing of capital or on currency movements. Concept (but not practice) of European Monetary Union is accepted by most of the twelve member states	• Free movement of currency. Expropriation of assets forbidden. Concept of national treatment established. Some control permitted of intra-NAFTA corporate acquisitions, e.g. by Mexican authorities
4 Monetary and fiscal union	• A goal (of most of the EC) yet to be achieved. Some fiscal harmonization is being achieved in the EC 92 programme	• Not immediately envisaged. Only a limited amount of fiscal harmonization is currently in operation (especially between Mexico and the United States and Mexico and Canada)
5 Social programmes	• Extensive social policies and fiscal transfer mechanisms; EC developing its own environment policies	• Little co-ordination of social programmes; no clear policy on the environment
6 Policies of nation states towards FDI	• Attempts to move towards harmonization, but a recent study of the OECD shows considerable latitude among member countries remains, e.g. towards liberalization of FDI in services	• No formal co-ordinative system envisaged
7 Political union	• Not currently envisaged	• Not currently envisaged

procurement policies by governments towards firms located in their own country will clearly not be welcomed by uncompetitive firms in that country. Firms which already have a network of value-added activities, or marketing contacts and distribution outlets within the integrated region, are particularly well placed to benefit from the harmonization of technical standards. MNEs, and particularly those that are already pursuing a polycentric or regiocentric organizational strategy, are among those most likely to gain (Chakravarthy and Perlmutter, 1985).

It is, however, the secondary effects of integration that are most likely to be most significant in the long-term for the regional allocation of economic activity. These arise mainly from the geographical and industrial restructuring of production and markets by firms within and outside the integrated area, and from the new opportunities for 'insider' firms to increase their technical and scale efficiencies by reducing their production and transaction costs. As observed by Eaton *et al.* (1994), economic integration may also be expected to spur innovation and technological progress, and to refashion organizational structures. Such effects are dynamic and are likely to be a major force in the restructuring and growth potential of the participating economies.

Such gains may be substantial. The European Commission has estimated that the completion of the internal market will raise the GNP of the EC by up to 6.5 per cent per annum (Cecchini *et al.* 1988). This is expected to be achieved by both an improvement in industrial productivity and a reduction in unemployment. On average, too, consumer prices are expected to fall by 6.0 per cent. About two-fifths of this reduction is expected to be brought about by the elimination of non-tariff barriers; another one-third from the better exploitation by firms of the economies of scale and scope; and the balance from a reduction in business inefficiencies and monopoly profits, arising from more intensive competition.

For the NAFTA, estimates of the economic effects indicate small gains for both the United States and Canada and larger gains for Mexico.[5] Estimates of the increase in real GDP for the United States range from 0.02 per cent to 0.50 per cent and for Canada they range from 0.1 per cent to 0.4 per cent. Real GDP in Mexico is estimated to increase by 0.1 per cent to 11.4 per cent. Similarly, real wages are estimated to increase by 0.1 per cent to 0.3 per cent in the United States and by 0.04 per cent to 0.05 per cent in Canada; in Mexico, real wages are estimated to increase by 0.7 per cent to 16.2 per cent.

There are other consequences of regional integration as well, which, although less quantifiable, may be no less important for the ownership and location of economic activity. Foremost among these are the policies adopted by the supervising body of the integrated region (compare those of the individual member countries) towards competition and restrictive practices, industrial relations and work practices, social affairs, the migration of labour, employment legislation, regional inequities, environmental protection, accounting and auditing procedures, deregulation or privatization of financial services, and towards trade and investment negotiations with non-member countries.

One further point: not only is regional economic integration likely to affect the distribution of economic activity within the region, but it will also affect the relationship between that and the rest of the world. Currently, the perceived effects of EC 92 are encouraging EC-owned firms to conclude alliances with Japanese and North American firms to protect or advance, not just their European, but their global, competitive positions. This is particularly the case in high-technology sectors where the fixed costs of innovation, production and marketing are becoming so huge that firms can only survive by capturing regional or global markets, or by sharing these costs with other firms. In the last resort, then, the firm-specific effects of regional integration must be evaluated in terms of the costs and benefits of the co-ordination of global economic activity and not just that which takes place within the integrated area.

In so far as the substantive difference between the content of post-1992 EC integration and NAFTA integration lies in the more comprehensive elimination of non-tariff barriers in the former scheme, the primary and secondary effects of the two forms might be expected to be different. Exactly *how* different, however, will depend on the economic structure of the participating regions and especially on the relative sensitivity of intraregional trade in goods and services to the removal of non-tariff barriers as compared will tariff barriers. Mark I EC integration, for example, had little impact on intra-EC trade in services, as most obstacles to such trade consisted of government-related non-tariff barriers rather than an *ad valorem* tariff or quantitative duties. It may then be reasonably expected that the benefits of the NAFTA will be similarly directed to tariff-sensitive activities.[6]

Before further considering NAFTA/EC differences which arise from geography, economic structure, political and culture-specific variables, rather than the content of integration, let us now consider the role played by MNEs in affecting the consequences of integration.

HOW MNEs MAY AFFECT INTEGRATION

Intraregional FDI

In the absence of MNE activity, the transaction of goods and services across national boundaries is confined to arm's length trade. FDI introduces a new mode of delivery and also affects the pattern of ownership of producing and trading firms. The distinctive feature of MNE activity is that it internalizes cross-border markets in intermediate products – notably producer services – and enables the economies of scale and scope to be better exploited. As a consequence, interfirm trade is partially replaced by intrafirm trade, while the common ownership of production brings with it more plant specialization, closer cross-border value-added linkages, and also restructures both the industrial and geographical composition of trade.

The literature distinguishes between four main kinds of MNE activity: *market seeking, resource seeking, efficiency seeking* and *strategic asset seeking* (Dunning 1993a). In the EC, most MNE activity is of the first, third and fourth sorts. In the NAFTA, especially in Canada there is more resource-seeking FDI, while strategic asset-seeking investment is mainly confined to Canadian MNE activity in the United States.

The effects of integration on each of these types of MNE activity are very different, as are the subsequent consequences of such activity on the location and ownership and organization of international production. It is also important to distinguish between the impact of integration on *intra*regional FDI and *extra*regional FDI. Inasmuch as defensive market-seeking investment is partially driven by tariff or non-tariff barriers, an elimination of these may be expected to lead to a substitution of intraregional investment by intraregional exports. By contrast, regional integration is likely to induce an increase in aggressive intraregional *market-seeking* and *efficiency-seeking* FDI. This is because reduction in *structurally distorting* market failure, coupled with the particular ability of MNEs to capitalize on *endemic* market failure,[7] are likely to promote a more efficient territorial and industrial allocation of economic activity.

The literature identifies two kinds of efficiency-seeking FDI. The first is designed to take advantage of differences in the geographical disposition of natural or created factor endowments. Much MNE activity in export-oriented manufacturing production in the Far East and in Mexico is of this kind. Sometimes this leads to the vertical specialization of particular *processes* along the value-added chain, and sometimes it leads to the horizontal specialization of products across value chains. Where such specialization reflects differences in natural resources or labour costs, it tends to be between countries at different stages of economic development, although there is a good deal of US direct investment in Canadian natural resources. Within the EC, there is some MNE specialization of resource-seeking MNE activity between the Southern European countries and the more industrialized nations.[8] While the geographical distribution of Japanese investment in high-skill and technology-intensive sectors suggests the availability and quality of critical created assets (e.g. R&D facilities), skilled labour and a supportive transport and communications infrastructure are the key determinants (Dunning 1993b).

Efficiency-seeking FDI may also lead to a restructuring of intraregional investment to better exploit the economies of scale and scope. It also helps promote Linder-type trade, based on cross-border differences in consumer tastes. Once again, MNEs (especially those already operating in the integrated region) are in a privileged position to co-ordinate the required division of labour in their various production units, the location of which will be determined both by the ease of market access and by the availability of the appropriate supply capabilities.[9]

In so far as competition among firms in the integrating countries switches from being national to regional – or even global,[10] it is likely that, in addition to the reorganization of intrafirm activities, some restructuring of product markets and some strategic regrouping of firms will occur. In the first two decades of the European Common Market, such efficiency-seeking FDI was limited by very high intercountry transaction costs, including legal, cultural and language barriers. Some, at least, of these obstacles will be removed as a result of EC 92 and, in anticipation of this, the number of mergers and strategic alliances between EC firms – especially EC MNEs – has increased sharply in the last five years or so.[11] Most of these associations fall under the category of strategic asset-seeking FDI, which is defined as investment prompted primarily by the need to acquire foreign assets to protect or advance a regional or global marketing position of the acquiring company (or merging companies), *vis- à-vis* that (those) of its competitors.

Much of this latter kind of MNE activity has been in high-technology or information-intensive sectors, and has been between firms in the larger and most advanced industrial countries. Although some such intra-North American FDI – especially by Canadian and Mexican firms seeking to align themselves with US companies – might be expected, the removal of non-tariff barriers would not likely be as significant an incentive for such investment as it is proving to be in the EC.

Finally, the extent to which intraregional MNE activity will increase as a result of integration will depend on the competitiveness of MNEs *vis-à-vis* uninational firms. In the EC, for example, the contribution of EC-owned subsidiaries to the output and trade of the Community has risen considerably over the past decade, especially in sectors which are technology and trade intensive. Data assembled and published by EUROSTAT and the UN Transnational Corporations and Management Division (TCMD)[12] confirm that FDI has been one of the main vehicles by which EC firms have gained from regional integration. As a result, their stake in EC output – particularly manufacturing output – has increased. Similarly, there is reason to suppose that home-based NAFTA MNEs will increase their share of the output of the three participating countries over the next decade or more.[13]

Extraregional FDI

The effect of regional integration on direct investment by corporations with headquarters outside the region (i.e. extraregional MNEs) will depend first on the extent, level and structure of the trade barriers between the region and the rest of the world; second, on the global competitive or ownership advantages of these MNEs *vis-à-vis* those originating from the region, or of unilateral firms; and third, on the extent to which regional integration *per se* is likely to favour extra- relative to intraregional, MNE activity.

Once again, the response of firms producing outside the integrated area (outsider firms) will essentially rest on two things: the extent to which outsider firms are treated differently by the regulating authorities, relative to firms producing inside the area (insider firms); and the ability of the former to reorganize or restructure their value-adding activities both within the integrated area and between the area and the rest of the world. The evidence from the EC strongly suggests that, prior to the late 1990s, US-owned firms were more successful in rationalizing their European activities to meet the challenges of the customs union than EC-owned firms (Cantwell 1992). This success may be due to the US firms' experience of operating multiple plants in their home countries; or because US firms have found it easier to exploit non-economic intra-EC market failures[14] than have their European counterparts; or because, being insiders, EC firms have tended to service other EC markets by way of exports more than have non-EC firms.

The completion of the internal market has given further impetus to non-EC firms to become insiders. Japanese and non-EC European MNEs have joined US firms in stepping up their direct investments in the EC to safeguard markets that might otherwise be lost to EC-based firms following the removal of such non-tariff barriers as discriminating procurement policies by national governments and the harmonization of technical standards.[15] The main thrust of Japanese FDI in the EC only dates back to the mid-1970s,[16] but from the start, Japanese firms have treated the EC (and, indeed, Western Europe as a whole) as a unified market and have organized their production, procurement and marketing strategies accordingly.

Indeed, in some sectors, notably motor vehicles, electronics, rubber tyres and investment banking, the organization of the European activities of Japanese MNEs is part of a long-term strategy directed towards increasing their penetration of global markets. So far, except, perhaps, in the auto industry, the Japanese have not viewed North American integration in quite the same way. This may be because the United States dominates its NAFTA partners as a production base in most of the sectors in which their MNEs have strong ownership advantages. At the same time, one might expect more Japanese investment in Mexico in the more labour-intensive component-supplying sectors in the 1990s.

Earlier in this chapter, we suggested that the consequences for regional integration are likely to vary between sectors and countries. Since the level and structure of MNE involvement is also sector and country specific, it follows that the effects of integration on FDI in, and between, the member countries will be highly selective. The removal of intra-EC tariff barriers in the 1960s, for example, led to the most dramatic increase in intra-EC trade in products that possessed four attributes. First, the tariffs to which they were previously subjected accounted for a relatively significant component of total costs; second, their price supply and demand elasticities were high; third, their production was subject to scale economies; and fourth, they were faced with relatively few non-tariff barriers. Such products included motor vehicles, most domestic electrical appliances, pharmaceuticals, office equipment, rubber tyres, some kinds of mass-produced machinery and industrial instruments. In most of these sectors, non-EC MNEs (of mostly US origin) not only had a significant investment stake prior to the formation of the EC, but have either maintained or increased that stake since the mid-1960s.[17]

The completion of the internal market is likely to affect a rather different group of sectors, as identified, for example, by Buiges *et al.* (1990). These are set out in Table 6.3, alongside the degree of MNE involvement in these sectors, and our estimate of the MNEs (by country of origin) most likely to gain following the removal of non-tariff barriers. As the table shows, the leading service sectors in countries in which there is a medium to high MNE involvement, together with some manufacturing industries which were relatively unaffected by Mark I integration, are among the most likely to be affected by EC 92. The table also suggests that while the Japanese MNEs may be among the main gainers in the electronics, office equipment and financial services sectors, European (especially EC) foreign investors are well poised to increase their market share of products in which MNE involvement is relatively low, and especially those that are dependent on public authorities for their procurement.

As has been argued elsewhere (Dunning 1988a), there are two contrasting views of the effects of Mark II integration on the ownership of economic activity. First, since the European-owned firms failed to take advantage of Mark I integration because of their relative inability to overcome intra-EC non-tariff barriers, the removal of these barriers will be particularly beneficial to them. Among the expected gainers are most services and manufactured products where the idiosyncratic requirements of customers are especially important, for example white goods and telecommunication equipment. It is further believed that, in the technologically more advanced countries, the completion of the internal market will help EC-owned firms to become more globally competitive.

The second and opposing view is that extraregional (especially Japanese) MNEs that currently enjoy substantial competitive advantages over their US and EC counterparts will build on these advantages, and that, even in those international sectors in which they do not currently possess such advantages (e.g. food processing, pharmaceuticals, etc.), they will seek to use their financial strength and marketing opportunism to acquire European-based rivals.

However, there is little doubt that Europe 1992 is providing a new catalyst to MNE activity. In contrast to the situation in the 1960s and

Table 6.3 Some sectors likely to be most affected by EC 92 and MNE involvement

	Impact		*Sector*	*MNE involvement*	*Likely gainers*
1	Reduction in protection	a	Financial services	High	Mixed
	Increased competition	b	Pharmaceuticals	High	E and US
		c	Telecommunication services	Medium	E
		d	Office machines	High	E and J
2	Shift from fragmented local to integrated EC-wide market	a	Wholesale Trade	Low	E
		b	Food processing	Medium	E and US
		c	Transport (trucking)	Low	E
3	Gain of technical economies of scale through sale of standardized goods and services	a	Electronic goods	High	J
		b	Packaging materials	Medium	E and US
		c	White and other consumer goods	Medium	E and J
4	Dependence on public procurement	a	Computer equipment and services	High	E and J
		b	Railway equipment	Low	E
		c	Telecommunication equipment	Medium	E and US
		d	Pharmaceuticals	High	E and US
5	Industries where the Single Market leads to import substitution (EC goods instead of imports)	a	Chemicals	Medium	E and US
		b	Electrical components	High	J
		c	Office equipment	High	J
		d	Motor vehicles	High	Mixed
6	Industrial where price differential exists between countries with different indirect taxation (e.g. VAT) levels	a	Motor vehicles	High	Mixed
		b	White and other consumer goods	Medium	E and J
		c	Wine and wine-based products	Low	E
7	Sectors benefiting from deregulation of markets	a	Financial and business service	Medium	Mixed
		b	Pharmaceuticals	High	E and US
		c	Telecommunications	Medium	E

Source: Author's estimates. Since this table was compiled, data published by the US Department of Commerce (1995) on the geographical distribution of US FDI give general support to these suggestions. US subsidiaries in Europe recorded the largest percentage increase in their sales since 1982 in financial business services, pharmaceuticals and food products. However, relative to Japanese and European firms, they have lost some ground in electrical and electronic goods and in motor vehicles, See also Economist Advisory Group (1996).
Note: E, European firms; J, Japanese-owned firms; US, US-owned firms

1970s, it is European and Japanese MNEs that are currently the most aggressive foreign investors, and the most prone to engage in cross-border asset restructuring. Between 1988 and 1993, the share of Japanese and intra-EC FDI in the EC was nearly three-fifths, compared with 38 per cent in the preceding five years. In the four years ending 31 December 1992, intra-European merger and corporate transactions averaged $67.2 billion compared with $32.8 billion over the previous four years (1985–88) (De Long *et al.*, 1996). Taking the six-year period as a whole, French and Italian companies had the greatest increases in their European transactions, even though about 58 per cent of all intra-European M&As have involved UK firms (Walter 1992).[18] From the early 1980s, the Japanese have treated Western Europe as a single market, but, most certainly, EC 92 is encouraging them to engage in more high-value activities – including some research and development – and to transfer their unique system of pyramidal and multi-layered networking to an EC environment (Dunning 1986, Ozawa 1991).

There is also some suggestion that EC 92 has led to an acceleration of intra-EC product and process specialization – and, with it, intra-EC trade.[19] Thus, new clusters of auto production are being developed around the Nissan assembly plant in North East England and around the Toyota plant in the Midlands. The Rhine Valley, on the other hand, is the favoured location of Japanese firms for high-precision mechanical and electrical engineering activities. To some extent, the emerging pattern of Japanese MNE activity in the EC is replicating that which has already occurred in the United States,[20] but the Japanese investors' vision of a 'Fortress Europe', together with their concern over the future level of voluntary export restraints (VERs) – not to mention the continued appreciation of the yen in relation to most EC currencies – is speeding up the transplant of downstream activities in sectors like autos and electronics. At the same time, several Japanese MNEs are hedging their bets by increasing their exports to EC markets from their offshore Asian subsidiaries, which are not currently subject to VERs by the EC.

THE REGULATORY FRAMEWORK

For many years the regulatory framework affecting both intraregional and extraregional FDI in the EC has been very different from that likely to be established by the NAFTA. A review of the 293 directives issued by the European Commission to eliminate most intra-EC non-tariff barriers suggests that relatively few are significant obstacles to intra-North American trade and commerce.[21] Exceptions include those which relate to the cross-border marketing of services and the public procurement of sensitive manufactured goods (e.g. defence equipment). Examples include the exports of Canadian telecommunication equipment to the United States and the setting up of US-owned insurance companies in Mexico.

Since the establishment of the EC, both national and community policy towards inbound MNE direct investment activity has gradually become more liberal. By December 1995, there were few remaining exchange controls on either extra- or intra-EC investment flows; restrictions on the raising of local finance by foreign affiliates are largely non-existent; many sectors previously denied to foreign investors have now been opened up – at least to EC MNEs[22] – while most EC countries have replaced fairly detailed and multi-faceted authorization procedures by simple notification or verification devices (OECD 1991).

At the same time, several EC countries still impose a variety of performance conditions on the subsidiaries of extra-EC MNEs. Often the adherence to these is the price extracted by host governments for tax concessions and other fiscal incentives offered to foreign investors. Two requirements are most widely imposed – even by the most liberal administrations: first, that over a stipulated period of time, a certain proportion of the output of a foreign subsidiary in an EC country will be actually produced in the EC (the local content requirement); and second (and this is linked to the first), that a foreign investor will, by some agreed date, undertake at least some of its higher-value activities in its European subsidiaries. Both these provisions – together with the encouragement of VERs – are particularly addressed to Japanese investors. Certainly, the most serious concern – and one which is echoed by some US authorities in respect of Japanese FDI and by some Canadian authorities in respect of US inward investment – is that Europe might become a low value-added base serving the higher-value activities of Japanese MNEs undertaken in their home country.

In contrast to most of its constituent countries, the European Commission does not have a policy towards either outbound or inbound FDI activity. Indeed, its philosophy, as revealed in various of its published reports, is that nationality of ownership does not matter as a factor influencing the efficiency of intra-EC resource organization and utilization.[23] But through its various economic and social programmes, as agreed by the member countries, there is no question that nationality can, and does, influence the level and structure of MNE activity.

There has already been considerable research on the impact of the first phase of European integration on both the volume and direction of MNE activity, and the ownership and organization of such activity.[24] Much less work has been done on the consequences of pre-1992 EC integration for the policies of individual member states towards inward or outward investment. In a recent study, the OECD (1991) identified European integration as one of the factors making for a more liberalized climate towards MNE activity, although it would seem that the main changes in policy have occurred only in the last quarter of the Community's existence (i.e. over the last eight years or so). However, although regional integration has dramatically changed the FDI policies of national governments, it has affected both the costs and benefits of different kinds of MNE activity, and the opportunity costs of those activities. This has forced national governments to be more competitive in their bidding for inbound investment, and to reshape their general economic strategies (Panic 1991, 1995).

The completion of the European internal market is likely to liberalize even further both marketing and production opportunities open to MNEs. Since EC directives and regulations have also led to a harmonization of many national policy instruments and measures which might otherwise have affected the locational decisions of firms, it follows that purely commercial considerations will be of even greater importance – particularly those concerning the underlying supply capabilities offered by individual countries, many of which are strongly government influenced (Porter 1990).

It is, then, the way in which countries respond to regional integration in their resource organization and utilization policies, as much as regional integration *per se*, that will determine their success or failure in both attracting new inward investment and providing the opportunities and incentives for competitive-enhancing outward investment.

However, there are other aspects of European integration which have affected the intra-EC distribution of MNE activity. One is the social programme of the European Commission which, in the 1960s and 1970s, helped shape the attitudes of foreign MNEs towards investing in the EC (Robinson 1983). Another is the current attempt by the Commission to help the poorer parts of the Community to develop their resource potential, and to assist the restructuring of other regions suffering from above-average unemployment. To promote these latter two objectives, the Community provides grants or loans, known as *fiscal transfers*, which are financed by the more prosperous member states.

Such fiscal transfers are, quite intentionally, discriminatory in their consequences. They may be deployed by the recipient countries in various ways, some of which affect their relative attractiveness to foreign investors. Structural adjustment funds, for example, may be used to upgrade the infrastructure of less prosperous economies in such a way as to redirect *efficiency-seeking* MNE activity away from the wealthier EC countries. Fiscal transfers might be used to assist domestic firms in the upgrading of their technological capabilities, which may in turn help to improve their competitiveness *vis-à-vis* other European firms in the markets in which they both compete.

Thus, by a number of means designed to help the poorer regions of the EC become more productive, the Commission has affected the level and geographical composition of both inward and outward direct investment. But other policies (such as those aimed at stimulating the innovatory capacity of EC-based firms in cutting-edge technologies) are more likely to favour the wealthier countries, as it is from these that MNEs in advanced technology sectors tend to originate. A study of the membership of government-funded research-based consortia and of the recipients of grants from the various EC-funded science and technology initiatives reveals that these are mainly located in the high-income EC nations (Mytelka and Delapierre 1987). Such subsidies, then, will enhance the ability of countries to be outward investors, and, by improving their domestic resource capabilities, make them more attractive to inward investors.

Generally, the completion of the internal market will affect the relative competitiveness of EC firms *vis-à- vis* non-EC firms, and the attractions of a European location for production by all kinds of firms. Because some of the main beneficiaries of the deeper integration are likely to be in the service sectors, one would expect an increase in *efficiency-seeking* and *strategic asset-seeking* MNE investment in the years to come. Also, through an increase in intra-European competition, one might also expect to see the emergence of a leaner and fitter group of European MNEs, better equipped than their predecessors to penetrate global markets.

At the same time, the future policy of the Community towards the importation of products from non-EC countries is not yet clear. The outcome will certainly affect the amount of EC *market-seeking* investment, particularly that of products currently subject to VERs. The future stance of the Community is intimately tied up with the progress of the WTO negotiations, but it is precisely this area of international economic activity which the Community – by virtue of *being* the EC – is most likely to influence.

At a micro-organizational level, the European Commission can and does affect the actions of both domestic and foreign-based MNEs through the provisions of the Rome Treaty. Foremost among these provisions is a wide range of regulations designed to reduce monopolistic practices and encourage competition in the Community.[25] Examples include those laid down in Article 85 of the Treaty, which is especially directed to advancing employment protection and worker participation; the harmonization of aids to inward investment (Articles 92–94 of the Treaty); and a variety of directives and rulings on environmental, safety and health matters. One particularly pertinent example of a regional ruling directly affecting inward investment is that made by the Commission in July 1991 about the local content of a 'European-made' car produced in the Community by Japanese-owned firms. Cars with the prescribed amount of local (EC-made) content can then be traded freely in the EC without any barriers. At the same time, the Community pegged the level of imports of Japanese cars at the 1990 level until 1998, when all quotas are to be abolished. It is by decrees or directive measures such as these that the EC may have a direct impact on the level and direction of MNE activity and on the policies of individual member states.

In summary, although the European Commission does not have a policy towards MNE activity *per se*, many of its macro-organizational actions affect, for better or worse, both the total amount of FDI in the EC and its distribution among the member states. Take, for example, environmental standards and regulations. If these are kept at too high a level, they will not only divert MNE activity to non-EC countries (because an EC location will become less competitive), but within the EC, they will redirect it from low-wage, low-productivity countries to high-wage, high-productivity countries. These latter countries are also those tending to have high tax rates and social expenditures along with more stringent environmental standards (Sweeney 1993). By contrast, a reduction in domestic content requirements, or of other non-tariff barriers, is likely to lead to more foreign investment in the EC – from which all EC countries should benefit, to a greater or lesser extent.

Stated simply, the EC can opt for two rather different mixes of policies. One is to force poorer EC members to adopt a social charter that would, for example, force the poorer members to adjust their wages, welfare and environmental standards closer to the levels of the higher-income members. This would tend to put the poorer countries at a distinct disadvantage and divert the flow of inbound direct investment from them to their wealthier neighbours. It would also have the probable effect of reducing the total amount of FDI in the EC. At the other extreme, the EC might choose to implement policies that may or may not keep investment from being diverted from high-income to low-income member states. The likely outcome of this strategy would be that high-income countries would unilaterally reduce their tax rates and/or lower their social transaction costs so as to make themselves more competitive with the rest of the EC – and, indeed, the rest of the world. In this event, the net result would be an increase in both domestic and foreign investment and a reduction in structural unemployment (Sweeney 1993).

Under the NAFTA, the Free Trade Commission is responsible for overseeing the entire Agreement. Cabinet-level officers from all three countries, supported by their officials, are responsible for its implementation and further elaboration. Ultimately, they will also manage all disputes. In addition to the Commission, the NAFTA establishes eight Committees and six Working Groups. Although the NAFTA establishes these administrative organizations and determines their specific functions, collectively they fall far short of an EC-type supranational body. The NAFTA dispute settlement provisions come closest to establishing such a body.

The NAFTA provides detailed mechanisms for the resolution of both state-to-state and investor–state disputes. The NAFTA provides for binding arbitration of investor–state disputes under the Investment Chapter, and, in the case of Panels, resolution of disputes on anti-dumping and countervailing duty matters. In the case of state-to-state disputes on all other matters, the NAFTA dispute resolution provisions are non-binding.

The NAFTA will have little authority to standardize or to harmonize national policy instruments in any meaningful way. For this reason integration of the NAFTA is likely to be much shallower than either Mark I or Mark II EC integration, and its effect on both intra- and extra-MNE activities will be confined largely to those arising from trade diversion, the creation effects of the removal of tariff barriers, and those stemming from the changing competitive positions of 'insider' and 'outsider' MNEs, *vis-à-vis* uninational firms.

EMPIRICAL RESEARCH ON THE EFFECT OF INTEGRATION ON MNE ACTIVITY

The Literature

Using some of the concepts introduced earlier, we now turn to a review of some empirical studies of the consequence of (regional) economic integration on FDI and MNE activity. Broadly speaking, these fall into three main groups. The first comprises those that attempt to examine the relationship between integration and the level and pattern of inward or outward direct investment. Several cross-sectional studies undertaken in the 1960s (as described in UNCTAD (1993a)) pointed to a structural shift of US outward direct investment towards EC countries in the decade or so after the formation of the Community. Later work showed that Ireland's accession to the EC led to a substantial increase in FDI from both the United States and other Community members to that country, while the United Kingdom's share of new US investment in the EC increased sharply in the years immediately before and after its accession. Shelbume (1991) has argued persuasively that the rate of growth in the GNP of both Spain and Portugal has been increased as a direct result of their accession to the EC in 1986; by contrast, the decade after accession was one of anaemic growth and increasing unemployment for Greece. Other data suggest that, in the 1960s, US firms were substituting EC production for exports from the United States (Dunning 1993b), while their share of EC production and exports relative to that of EC-owned firms also rose. Finally, according to EUROSTAT, the annual flow of intra-EEC FDI more than doubled between the announcement of EC 92 and the end of 1992. This was more than twice as fast as extra-EC FDI.

A second group of empirical studies has focused on the link between the discriminatory tariff effects of economic integration and the extent to which US investment in the EC is replaced by US exports to the EC. The findings from these studies are mixed, and often contradictory. This is due partly to the difficulty of researchers in separating the tariff from other variables which might affect US investment in the EC; partly to the different measures used by researchers to identify the tariff changes; and partly to the differences in the specifications of the models used. However, even those studies which seem to suggest that the level of tariffs is a statistically significant variable influencing US direct investment have acknowledged that much of the more important 'pulling in' was the growth of the EC market. Indeed, one economist (Goldberg 1972) has calculated that about 80 per cent of the new investment of US firms in the EC during the period 1958 to 1970 could be explained by the market growth and broadening hypothesis. Of course, part of this growth and broadening was, itself, due to removal of the intra-EC tariff barriers.

A third group of studies has sought to examine the factors affecting the distribution of US investment within the EC. Since 1958, the role of inbound direct investment (*vis-à-vis* domestic investment) in each of the member states has increased, most dramatically so in some of the smaller nations, like Belgium, the Netherlands and Ireland. It is these latter nations which have attracted the largest share of efficiency-seeking export-oriented FDI, with MNEs in the heavy chemicals and metal-using sectors especially favouring Belgium and the Netherlands; and those in food, drinks, textiles and light chemicals preferring an Irish location. Unfortunately, none of the relevant empirical studies has attempted to evaluate the extent to which the changing geographical disposition of FDI is due to economic integration *per se*.

In the last decade, the factors influencing the location of foreign affiliates in the EC have changed. Increasingly, it is the availability of educated and well-trained labour, technological capacity and a good transportation and communications network which have become the main driving force. Size of country is no longer an important demand-related variable; rather it is the country's geographical position in relation to the major industrial markets of the EC. Exceptions include FDI in natural-resource-based and more labour-intensive manufacturing and service activities. Here, the peripheral countries of the EC (e.g. Spain, Portugal, Ireland and Denmark), and the more outlying regions of the core industrialized countries, continue to attract both Japanese and US FDI. A classic example is the proportion – probably around one-third – of Japanese-owned manufacturing activity currently directed to the less prosperous countries (e.g. Spain) or regions (e.g. South Wales) of the European Community.

Research findings on the consequences of the completion of the internal market (IM) for intra-EC and extra-EC FDI are still limited (Economists Advisory Group 1996). But, from what evidence we have, it would seem that EC 92 has not only sped up the growth of all kinds of FDI, but that this growth has been most pronounced in high-value activities and directed to those sectors thought to be most sensitive to the removal of non-tariff barriers. Such FDI has, in general, been complementary to, rather than substitutable for, trade flows (Buiges and Jacquemin 1994)[26] most sensitive to the removal of non-tariff barriers. There has also been a modest geographical reorientation of new FDI from the core countries to the peripheral countries, notably Spain.

Econometric analysis (Pain and Lansburg 1996) also suggests there is some suggestion that both UK and German FDI in the EU since 1987 has risen more rapidly than it might have done in the absence of the IM; and that, for both countries, EC 92 has had a significantly greater impact on intra-EC FDI in services than in manufacturing. The data also reveal that the impact of the IM on the level of intra-EC FDI appears to have strengthened, rather than weakened, since the mid-1980s.

At the same time, when considered relative to determinants of other possible extra- and intra-EC FDI, for example liberalization of markets, agglomerative economies, market size and growth, exchange rates, real input costs, trade restrictions, etc., most studies agree that *direct* and unique affects of the IM have been generally quite small. For example, a study by UNCTAD (1993b) concluded that about 90 per cent of the variation of FDI into the EC over the period 1972–88 could be explained by the size of the region's GNP (in the previous year), the change in the level of GNP, the deviation of the exchange rate and the ratio of domestic investment to GNP.[27] The same study also estimated that an increase of 1 per cent in the level of GNP in one year coincided with an increase of over 4 per cent in the growth of FDI in the following year. One obvious problem of this kind is that many of the explanatory variables are interdependent of each other and it is difficult to isolate the specific contribution of any one variable. Thus, as we have stated earlier in this chapter, the original Cecchini report estimated the completion of the IM would raise the EC's GNP by up to 6.5 per cent per annum. Using this figure and applying the UNCTAD model to it, this would suggest that quite a substantial part of the increase in FDI since 1986 may be attributed to the IM, but *via* its effect on GNP.

Field Studies conducted on the factors influencing the location of FDI within the EC all point to the increasing role played by transaction costs of business activity; that is, those costs associated with market failure, especially those influenced by government policy, at both national and regional levels (Dunning 1993b). Such government policies (those being pursued by the Clinton administration, for example) are also likely to become more (rather than less) significant in influencing the location or relocation of MNE activity in the NAFTA and within particular NAFTA countries – notably the United States and Canada. At the same time, the much greater asymmetries and distances between the member countries might be expected to work towards rather more geographical concentration of FDI in the three NAFTA countries than in most of the twelve EC nations.

Let us now look at one or two examples from the experience of MNEs operating in the EC. Broadly speaking, the literature (Doz 1986, Cantwell 1992, Dunning 1993a) records three kinds of corporate response to European integration. First there are companies like SKF, 3M, Scott Paper, Philips of Eindhoven, and Toshiba and Nissan which have adopted a pattern of more intensive product (i.e. horizontal) specialization among their European plants. Sometimes, but not always, this rationalization has been accompanied by a pan-European marketing strategy. GM concentrates its Nova production in Spain; 3M produces scotch tape in its German factory and its 'Post-it' notes in its UK factory. Previously, these companies manufactured a fairly wide range of products in each country for sale mainly to consumers of that country.

Second, there are the MNEs which have chosen to focus their activities along a particular value-added chain, that is vertical specialization. The Ford Motor Company now concentrates its European production of engines in Valencia (Spain), gearboxes and differentials in Bordeaux (France), and the major body-processing components in Saarlouis and Valencia. Like Ford, IBM, while practising dual or multiple sourcing, concentrates its European output of different parts and components for its computers in one or more of its EC facilities. Though fairly diversified at their final stages of production, most non-European pharmaceutical MNEs tend to limit the production of their active ingredients, as well as their R&D activities, to a few EC locations, notably the United Kingdom, France, West Germany and Ireland.

Third, the pattern of intra-EC economic activity may be changed by the type of *inter*firm competition promoted by regional integration. Thus, the removal of restrictions on government procurement, and the encouragement of the harmonization of cross-border technical standards may open possibilities for more interfirm specialization of similar products. In the European (and indeed global) paint industry, for example, the German firm BASF specializes in automobile paints, and the UK firms Courtaulds and ICI specialize in marine, decorative and industrial paints.

It should be noted, however, that not all MNEs have adopted a strategy of product or process specialization as a result of regional integration. Those which have to meet the needs of idiosyncratic markets may find any benefits from economies of scale are outweighed by the reduced demand or additional costs of product or process adaptation. The excellent documentation of the white goods sector in the EC by Baden-Fuller and Stopford (1991) shows that, although there has been an increase in industrial concentration, there is little evidence of any trend towards the globalization of products or markets. The authors show that, even within Europe, there are significant differences in cross-border consumer tastes, distribution channels, production, promotion and development methods which, taken as a whole, seriously inhibit European MNEs from exploiting the benefits of regional integration.[28] Other examples of the need to take account of country-specific consumer tastes outweighing the advantages of production economies include carpets and some kinds of textiles. In these cases, integration is likely to make little difference to corporate strategies; neither will it do so where transport costs are an important component of the total costs of production, or where products are strongly location bound.

In several respects, the response of MNEs to economic integration in the EC can be expected to be repeated in the NAFTA. However, there is likely to be relatively more vertical rationalization of US–Mexico manufacturing FDI than US–Canadian manufacturing FDI, due primarily to more substantial differences in labour costs between the United States and Mexico. By contrast, defensive import-substituting investment by US firms in Canada will probably fall, while horizontal efficiency-seeking investment, particularly in Southern Ontario, is likely to increase. It is also probable that there will be more strategic asset-seeking investment by the large Canadian MNEs in the United States as they seek to build up their global competitive positions.

Earlier research by Doz (1986) and Doz and Prahalad (1987) also emphasized the importance of national governments in influencing the strategies of MNEs. Using the percentage of the sales of particular sectors to government (i.e. the degree of public procurement) as a proxy for government influence, Doz (1986) concluded that in sectors (military aircraft and electricity generating equipment, for example) where this ratio was the highest in the early 1980s, MNEs were most likely to adopt nationally responsive strategies. By contrast, in those sectors where the ratio of government purchases was the lowest (CTV tubes, agri-tractors and autos, for example), they tended to practise regionally or globally integrated strategies.

Since EC 92 will reduce barriers to government procurements, along with the privatization and deregulation of national markets, it is highly likely that there will be a further reappraisal of the organization of transnational activities, and especially of those MNEs currently pursuing nationally responsive strategies.

There are, of course, other factors which have discouraged cross-border corporate integration for many years. These include cross-border controls, differential technical standards and fiscal policies. Others are more 'natural' barriers, for example transport, costs and differences in buying cultures. While most of the former will disappear with EC 92, the latter may not. As a result, at least some MNEs will continue to adopt nationally, rather than regionally, oriented strategies. According to Doz and Prahalad (1987), a successful locational strategy is one that balances the global advantages of exploiting the advantages of the governance of related assets and proprietary knowledge, while continuing to recognize the importance of adapting its products and production methods to the specific needs of local markets. However, such a reorganization of activities is unlikely to be undertaken by MNEs in the NAFTA because many of the 1992 EC-type barriers either do not exist or are unaffected by the free trade agreement.

Finally, the US Department of Commerce regularly provides macro-statistical data on the extent to which product or process specialization is practised among US multinationals in the EC and LAFTA, and how this has changed over time. *Inter alia*, these reveal, first, that the proportion of sales of US manufacturing affiliates in the EC exported to other parts of Europe more than doubled between 1957 and 1993. Second, they show that the export propensity of US affiliates in the EC and, to a lesser extent, in the major LAFTA countries (e.g. Brazil and Mexico) is considerably greater than that in other parts of the world. However, as a result of the NAFTA it might be reasonable to expect an increase in trade between US firms and their affiliates north and south of the US border.

A Recent Field Survey

A recent survey of fifty-six of the largest US, European and Japanese MNEs, carried out by Tom Gladwin, Teretumo Ozawa and the present author for the United Nations in 1993, reveals a wide diversity of strategic responses by senior executives to EC 92. The full results of this survey will be published by UNCTAD but, in the following paragraphs and in Table 6.4, we highlight (with the permission of UNCTAD) some of our findings and the extent to which we believe they may have relevance to the strategic thinking of MNEs now producing or contemplating producing in the NAFTA.

- EC 92 will trigger an acceleration of market growth in the EC relative to that in other parts of the world. However, most non-EC-based MNEs anticipate playing only a limited role. We believe this conclusion can be generalized to apply equally to the NAFTA situation.
- EC 92 will intensify intra-European competition. Most MNEs plan to cope with this by pursuing product differentiating rather than cost-reducing strategies. We believe that this conclusion is more applicable in the case of US–Canada than US–Mexico trading and FDI relationships.
- EC 92 is inducing only a small percentage of MNEs to exploit scale and scope economies, or to rationalize their supplier networks, manufacturing and distribution systems, in order to reduce their production or transaction costs. We believe that a rather larger proportion of US and non-NAFTA MNEs may seek to invest in Mexico to exploit such advantages.
- EC 92 does and will continue to encourage a wave of corporate restructuring. However, this is unlikely to involve much backward integration.

Table 6.4 Perceived effects of EC 92 and NAFTA on MNE activity

EC	*NAFTA*
	Market growth
• 0 → +	• + → ++
Noticeably industry specific: service finns recorded + → ++, while most market growth is expected to come from pan-European customer-segmented growth, increased EC importance in strategic planning and expected growth in EC	Again, strongly industry and country specific. Growth prospects probably most favourable for FDI in trade-related activities in which member states enjoy a comparative advantage
	Competitive strategy
• 0 → ++	• 0 → +
Very marked in some sectors, with response of MNEs tending to favour a product differentiation rather than a low-cost strategy. Also more co-ordination of value chain activities among EC affiliates, particularly those of US origin. EC 92 effects most likely to be experienced by large and service-intensive firms	Most pronounced effect likely to be felt in certain regions in the United States and Canada and in sectors exposed to additional competitive pressures (e.g. the more mature, but labour-intensive, U.S. industrial sectors)
	Cost reduction
• +0 → +	• 0 → ++
EC 92 has induced a massive wave of corporate restructuring in the EC. Increased cross-border M&A activity envisaged as well as a streamlining of organizational structures. Effect most marked in intra-EC investment in services	More selective impact which directly arises from economies of specialization. Could be quite significant in case of market-oriented Mexican and/or Canadian firms wishing to penetrate the United States or Latin American countries
	Technological innovation
• 0– → ++	• 0– → +
Economic integration thought to aid MNE participation in high-cost R&D projects by enlarging markets and easing conditions for strategic alliances. But not all sectors (e.g. services) considered this effect to be of importance	Again, more likely to be selective in view of overwhelming predominance of the United States in innovating activities. But some technological clusters in the NAFTA may evolve (sometimes with support of MNEs) in Canada and Mexico, e.g. especially those in more (natural-)resource-intensive sectors
	Location of economic activity
• 0 → ++	• 0– → +
Most firms agreed that EC 92 would markedly affect the modality by which they serviced EC markets, and that there would be a shift in value-added activity towards the EC away from other regions	Possibly less significant, except around national border of the United States with Canada. But likely to encourage more clustering of economic activities within member states

Table 6.4 (cont)

EC	*NAFTA*
	Sourcing and trade
• + → ++	• − → +
One of most important perceived effects on MNE activity of EC 92. FDI generally thought likely to supplant some exports and increase (through intra-firm intermediate product trade) others. Effect on concentration and relocation of value-added activity is likely to be highly industry-specific, e.g. services thought less likely to be affected than telecommunications and consumer electronics	More vertical specialization of MNE activity likely to occur between Mexico and United States (and Canada); more horizontal specialization between Canada and the United States
	Future protectionism
• 0 → + + +	• 0 → +
Perceived by firms – especially those in strategic sectors or those in which intra-Triad competition is especially fierce – to be most important. In particular, auto, textile fibres, consumer electronics and banking MNEs (especially those of Japanese origin) are viewed as a major likely influence for their investment strategies. Concern over reciprocity arrangements was most generally voiced by Japanese firms, but also US MNEs in some strategically sensitive and service sectors. Generally, the fear of 'Fortress Europe' was regarded by non-EC firms as the single most potent force leading to more defensive-seeking FDI in EC. Insider/outsider distinction was less marked in reciprocity requirements of Japanese and US firms, rights of establishment in public procurement policy, and in the recognition of technical standards	Probably much less significant as impact of NAFTA *per se* on intra-Triad trade and investment is likely to be comparatively small. However, the exact effects are difficult to assess, as the proposed NAFTA agreement currently makes no immediate provision for a common external tariff and there are few reciprocity arrangements with extra-NAFTA nations.

Source: Study on effect of EC on the activities of MNEs scheduled to be published by UNCTAD and author's own speculations

We believe that there will be more intra-NAFTA vertical integration between US and Mexican firms, but that otherwise the pattern of industrial consolidations will be broadly similar.

- EC 92 is having a significant effect on reallocating the locus and focus of corporate R&D intended to serve the needs of a unified EC market. We believe a similar relocation of such activities will occur in the NAFTA.
- EC 92 is likely to attract FDI into the EC that will be export substituting, but little locational shifting (either inside or outside of the EC) is

anticipated given the declining importance of labour costs. Specifically, the completion of the internal market appears to be providing little incentive for market-seeking investments by developing nations. In the NAFTA, we expect rather more locational shifting to take place, thus reducing labour costs, although this is unlikely to be the main effect of the Agreement.

- EC 92 is likely to induce net trade creation for developing nation suppliers of primary goods but net trade diversion for developing nation suppliers of manufactured goods, with intra-EC trade rising in importance. We anticipate that the NAFTA will have only a marginally adverse affect on the primary exports of outsider developing countries, except, perhaps, in the case of Caribbean textiles.[29]
- EC 92, as it interacts with the liberalization of Central and Eastern European markets, is likely to result in a relocation of some export-oriented FDI from developing nations to such countries as Hungary, Poland and Czechoslovakia, especially in selected sectors such as automobiles, consumer electronics and chemicals. By contrast, these developments are likely to have only a peripheral effect on MNE activity in the NAFTA.
- EC 92 is perceived as providing the foundation for a 'Fortress Europe', especially by Japanese and developing nation enterprises which anticipate continuing discriminatory quotas, local content requirements, public procurement barriers and EC/member state subsidies to key industries. These concerns could well be paralleled by a 'Fortress North America'. Much will depend on the future of GATT and bilateral US–Japanese and US–EC trade negotiations.

CONCLUSIONS

There are both similarities and differences between the content of Mark I and Mark II EC integration and the NAFTA. The similarities are mostly shown in their expected effects on trade and FDI following the removal of tariff barriers, although the form, content and distribution of the effects will vary according to industry-, country- and firm-specific characteristics. In the case of the NAFTA, the failure to agree on a common external tariff with the rest of the world may also bring with it distinctive consequences.

The differences arise from the more extensive removal of non-tariff barriers between EC countries compared with those currently envisaged by the NAFTA countries, and from the greater attention paid by the former area to social issues, and the intraregional distribution of costs and benefits. The experience of European integration suggests that the four kinds of FDI and MNE activity described in the text are affected differently by the removal of tariff barriers and other obstacles to the freedom of movement of assets, goods and people. Setting aside the important differences in the size, geography and economic structure of the countries comprising the NAFTA and the EC (and in particular the greater asymmetry in the economic relationship between the United States and its northern neighbour than that between any pair of countries in the EC), the consequences for FDI are likely to be similar, and follow the predictions set out earlier in this study. But, as in the case of the EC, the distribution of FDI between the member countries of the NAFTA is likely to be uneven, with the greatest gains being recorded by those countries (and regions within countries) offering the most cost-effective locations for exploiting the integrated market.

To some extent, the industrial hinterland of the United States and Southern Ontario in Canada may be compared with the core industrial countries in the EC, with most of Mexico and most of the rest of Canada being likened to the outer ring of European countries and regions (Spain and Portugal in Mexico's case; Denmark and parts of the United Kingdom, Germany and Italy in Canada's case). In so far as distance seems likely to be negatively correlated with the ripple effects of integration, it might be supposed that, apart from (natural-)resource-intensive FDI, the regions of Mexico and Canada furthest removed from the major markets of the NAFTA will benefit least from new MNE activity, and could indeed be net losers from integration. Furthermore, as a reduction in trade and investment barriers between two countries with very different factor endowments may lead to a substantial relocation of economic activity, the economies of the regions adjacent to the Mexican–US border are likely to incur significant adjustment costs.

However, although primarily a trading agreement, the NAFTA does embrace some of the ingredients of a customs union, and goes considerably further in its attempt to lower non-tariff barriers and harmonize trade and investment relationships than did Mark I EC integration. To this extent, the effect of the NAFTA on some sectors – including service sectors – unaffected by pre-1992 European integration may be quite pronounced, particularly in the later 1990s.

Table 6.5 summarizes some of the main responses of the intra- and extra-EC MNEs to European integration described in the previous sections, and some possible reactions of intra- and extra-NAFTA MNEs to North America's integration.

In conclusion, I have two final, and possibly controversial, thoughts. The first is that I find it difficult to perceive that the kind of economic gains enjoyed by the member states of the EC over the past thirty-five years are likely to be repeated in the NAFTA. This is because in 1957, the political, cultural and social framework of Europe was far more divisive and damaging to its economic health than the contemporary situation in Canada, Mexico and the United States. If the United States itself consisted of several countries, each with its own language, political and legal systems and cultures, then the gains of economic integration might be expected to be

Table 6.5 EC and NAFTA: a summary of the actual or likely responses of MNEs

EC	*NAFTA*
Intra-EC MNE activity	
• Prior to the mid-1980s this was limited owing largely to intra-EC non-tariff barriers and relative ease of exporting goods (but not services) within EC. There has been a substantial increase in this kind of MNE activity and EC related strategic alliances over the past 5–8 years. Predominantly, this has been of an efficiency- or strategic asset-seeking kind, except that in the less developed countries (or regions within countries of the EC), there has been some natural-resource-seeking (including low-cost labour) FDI. Such limited data as are available suggest that some of the smaller EC countries, e.g. Belgium and the Netherlands, have gained a relatively larger share of efficiency-seeking (import-substituting) FDI since 1958	• A considerable increase in all kinds of intra-North American FDI, except defensive market-seeking investment, is anticipated. However, the types of composition are likely to be country specific, and also related to the extent of non-tariff barriers that remain. The future of peripheral areas in Canada and Mexico is less secure, unless they can evolve 'clusters' of economic activity. Infrastructure and the availability of human and physical capital are likely to become more important determinants of the location of intra-North American FDI
Extra-EC MNE activity	
• **Inward** This has been largely of an import-substituting or strategic asset-acquiring kind when viewing the EC as a single market, but its location within the EC has primarily been driven by resource- or efficiency-seeking criteria. (This applies equally to *de novo* and to sequential FDI)	• **Inward** The effect on inward efficiency-seeking investment is unlikely to be as substantial as in the EC, although both Mexico and Canada are expected to attract some non-EC investment (in rather different sectors) in order to gain access to US markets. Especially in Mexico there is also likely to be an increase in market-seeking investment, including that destined for Latin American countries with whom Mexico has, or is likely to have, agreement. Strategic-acquiring FDI is unlikely to be greatly affected by the NAFTA
• **Outward** While the competitiveness of European firms has improved over the past thirty years, it is difficult to pinpoint how much of this is due to the EC initiative. One hypothesis is that prior to 1992, by its competitive enhancing effects, US FDI in the EC has helped European firms to upgrade their capability to become MNEs or increase their foreign investments. The removal of tariff barriers in post-1992 integration is likely to improve European competitiveness as a result of intra-European or Japanese FDI	• **Outward** The competitive position of the United States is likely to be only marginally affected by the NAFTA. Mexico's ability to become an outward direct investor is likely to be enhanced. The impact of the NAFTA on Canadian competitiveness will depend on its effect on Canada's high-value activities in each of the main industrial sectors

much greater – even though much of this would probably be of an intra-US nature. One suspects, then, that the effects of the NAFTA on the combined GNP of the three participating countries will be less pronounced and considerably more geographically concentrated. It may also be that FDI (and other transborder associations, e.g. strategic alliances) will play a more important role in affecting the level and distribution of intra-NAFTA value-added activity than it did – at least in the early days of European integration – within the EC.

The second thought is that, whereas regional integration in the 1960s and 1970s was best seen in the context of a politically and economically fragmented world in which cross-border corporate integration was the exception rather than the rule, the scenario in the early 1990s is totally different. We now live in a globally integrated economy and, increasingly, both corporations and governments are viewing their economic strategies towards regional integration in that light. In their reactions to the NAFTA – far more than in their response to Mark I EC (but not Mark II EC) – both sets of actors are looking at its implications for their international competitiveness. The extent to which the NAFTA leads to more Japanese FDI in Mexico or more Canadian MNE activity in the United States will then rest on the extent to which companies perceive their global goals to be better advanced by this strategy. Similarly, the US, Mexican and Canadian governments are likely to view any extension of the NAFTA in terms of how it may further affect the competitive position of their resources and firms, *vis-à-vis* those of their main trading rivals. To this extent, the objectives and evaluation of regional integration are now very different from those embraced in earlier times, and these differences are likely to become even more pronounced as we move towards the twenty-first century.

NOTES

* As this chapter is a revision of a paper first written in 1994, and prior to the formation of the European Union, the term Community is retained throughout.

1 For a review of some of the major regional integrative schemes of recent years, see Jovanovic (1992), UNCTAD (1993a) and Robson (1993).

2 This point is taken up more fully by Raymond Vernon (1994). In particular, one might conceive of two kinds of intraregional economic relationships emerging from integration. One is best described as a 'hub and spoke' relationship in which a core country dominates economic activity in the region, but there is another relationship as well – an asymmetric relationship between it and the other nations. The other is a 'spider's web' relationship in which there is no dominant member state, but rather an intricate interpenetration of resource flows and markets by firms of the participating nations.

3 This point and others related to the effects of regional integration on the location of economic activity are taken up in more detail in Eaton *et al.* (1994).

4 Thus, *ceteris paribus*, the greater the cross-border marketing costs (which reflect psychic or economic distance), the lower the proportional effect of any tariff reduction.

5 See Table 2.1 of USITC (1993).

6 The NAFTA agreement is unclear as to the extent to which non-tariff barriers between the participating countries will be removed. Some government-induced barriers, for example restrictive procurement policies, are mentioned in the

treaty, but others, for example with respect to fiscal harmonization, are not. (See Table 6.2.)

7 For an analysis of the differences between structurally distorting and endemic market failure, see Chapter 4 of Dunning (1993a).

8 For an examination of the patterns of FDI in these countries and how these are related to the revealed comparative advantages of natural resources and created assets, see Chapters by Juhl, Dunning and Simoes in Dunning (1985).

9 The role of government in affecting the location of FDI in a global economy is discussed in Dunning (1993b).

10 Indeed, the primary rationale behind EC 92 was to provide a more favourable economic environment for European firms in their bid to sustain their global market positions *vis-à-vis* their US and Japanese competitors.

11 Some details are given by Hagedoorn and Schakenraad (1990).

12 Formerly the UNCTC.

13 At the same time, through subcontracting and other networking arrangements, they may stimulate the output of smaller non-MNEs in Mexico, Canada and the United States.

14 Especially those to do with cross-border culturally related transaction costs.

15 As detailed at length in Cecchini *et al.* (1988).

16 For further details, see the volume edited by Mason and Encarnation (1994).

17 This was in spite of the dramatic recovery of the German economy in the 1960s and 1970s. For further details of the shares of European exports accounted for by the affiliates of US MNEs and other (mainly European) companies in the EC, see Dunning (1988b: Chapter 5).

18 Of course, not all of the recent growth of intra-European M&As is attributable to European integration. Among other reasons noted by Walter (1992) for the M&A boom in Europe are: (i) an overdue need for industrial restructuring in Europe, (ii) the availability of financial resources, (iii) the transfer to Europe of much of the M&A know-how that accumulated in the United States during the 1980s, and (iv) the increasing liberalization of capital markets in Europe (itself being part and parcel of European integration).

19 For further details, see Encarnation (1994).

20 See also Westney (1994).

21 For example, the cost of intra-American border controls is less than their pre-1992 intra-EC equivalents, while US and Canadian technical standards are broadly comparable.

22 For non-EC investors, several EC countries still limit or regulate the conditions of entry into the finance, insurance, telecommunications, publishing, airlines, maritime transport, nuclear power and armament sectors. For further details see OECD (1991).

23 For example, hardly any mention is made of the likely impact of EC 92 on foreign investment into or out of the Community by the Cecchini report.

24 See especially UNCTAD (1993a) and Dunning (1992, 1993a). In particular, it is possible that countries like the United Kingdom, Germany and Italy would have adopted less liberal policies towards inward investment in the absence of the EC. This is simply because MNEs would have had less opportunity to engage in efficiency-seeking investment. In other words, their affiliates would most likely have been more responsive.

25 For further details and an analysis of these issues, see Graham and Warner (1994).

26 Noticeably, FDI has grown fastest in those sectors in which intra-European and intrafirm trade has expanded the most, for example electronics, pharmaceuticals, office machinery, transport equipment, etc.

27 A result broadly confirmed in a longitudinal multi-regressional study by Clegg (1995) of US FDI in the EC between 1970 and 1988. When Clegg added a dummy variable to proxy the internal market, he found this made only insignificant difference to the explanatory power of his equation.

28 For example, Italian housewives traditionally prefer top-loading machines while German and UK housewives prefer front-loading machines.

29 For a recent analysis of European integration and FDI in developing countries see Agarwal, Hiemenz and Nunnenkamp (1995).

REFERENCES

Agarwal, J.P., Hiemenz, U. and Nunnenkamp, P. (1995) *European Integration: A Threat of Foreign Investment in Developing Countries?*, Kiel: Institut für Weltwirtschaft an der Universitat Kiel, Discussion Paper No.46, March.

Baden-Fuller, C. W. F. and Stopford, J. M. (1991) 'Globalization frustrated: the case of white goods,' *Strategic Management Journal* 12: 493–507.

Buiges, P., Ilzkovitz, F. and Lebrun, J. (1990) 'The impact of the internal market by industrial sector; the challenge of member states', *European Economy* Special Edition: 1–114.

Buiges, P. and Jacquemin, A. (1994) 'Foreign investment and exports to the European Community', in M. Mason and D. Encarnation (eds) *Does Ownership Matter?*, Oxford: Clarendon Press.

Cantwell, J. A. (1992) 'The effects of integration on the structure of multinational corporation activity in the EC', in M. W. Klein and P. J. Welfens (eds) *Multinationals in the New Europe and Global Trade*, pp. 193–236, Berlin and New York: Springer- Verlag.

Cecchini, P., Catinat, M. and Jacquemin, A. (1988) *The European Challenge 1992. The Benefits of a Single Market*, Aldershot: Wildwood House.

Chakravarthy, B. S. and Perlmutter, H. V. (1985) 'Strategic planning for a global business', *Columbia Journal of World Business* 20: 3–10.

Clegg, J. (1995) 'The determinants of United States foreign direct investment in the European Community: a critical appraisal', University of Bath (mimeo).

De Long, G., Smith, R. C. and Walker, I. (1996) *Global Merger and Acquisition Tables, 1995*, New York: New York University (mimeo).

Doz, Y. (1986) *Strategic Management in Multinational Companies*, Oxford: Pergamon.

Doz, Y. and Prahalad, C. K. (1987) 'A process model of strategic redirection in large complex firms: the case of multinational corporations', in A. Pettigrew (ed.) *The Management of Strategic Change*, pp. 63–83. Oxford: Basil Blackwell.

Dunning, J. H. (1985) 'The United Kingdom', in J. H. Dunning (ed.) *Multinational Enterprises, Economic Structure and International Competitiveness*, pp. 13–56, Chichester and New York: John Wiley.

——(1986) *Japanese Participation in British Industry*, London: Croom Helm.

——(1988a) *Explaining International Production*, London and Boston: Unwin Hyman.

——(1988b) *Multinationals, Technology and Competitiveness*, London: Allen & Unwin.

——(1992) 'The global economy, domestic governance strategies and transnational corporations: interactions and policy implications', *Transnational Corporations* 1 (3): 7– 46.

——(1993a) *Multinational Enterprises and the Global Economy*, Wokingham, England, and Reading, MA: Addison Wesley.

——(1993b) *The Globalization of Business: The Challenge of the 1990s*, London and New York: Routledge.

Economists Advisory Group (1996) *Foreign Direct Investment Flows and the Completion of the Internal Market*, report prepared for the European Commission, London (mimeo).

Eaton, B. C., Lipsey, R. G. and Safarian, A.E. (1994) 'The theory of multinational plant behaviour: agglomerations and disagglomerations', in L. Eden (ed.) *Multinationals in North America*, pp. 79–102 Alberta, Canada: University of Calgary Press.

Encarnation, D. J. (1994) 'Intra-firm trade in North America and the European Community', in L. Eden (ed.), *Multinationals in North America*, pp. 309–34, Alberta, Canada: University of Calgary Press.

Goldberg, M. A. (1972) 'The determinants of US direct investment in the EEC: a comment', *American Economic Review* 62, September: 692–9.

Graham, E. M. and Warner, M. A. A. (1994) 'Multinationals and competition policy in North America', in L. Eden (ed.) *Multinationals in North America*, pp. 463–508, Alberta, Canada: University of Calgary Press.

Hagedoorn, J. and Schakenraad, J. (1990) 'Strategic partnering and technological cooperation', in B. Dankbaar, J. Groenewegen and H. Schenk (eds) *Perspectives in Industrial Economics*, Dordrecht: Kluwer.

Jovanovic, M. N. (1992) *International Economic Integration*, London and New York: Routledge.

Mason, M. and Encarnation, D. J. (eds) (1994) *Does Ownership Matter? Japanese Multinationals in Europe*, Oxford: Clarendon Press.

Mytelka, L. K. and Delapierre, M. (1987) 'The alliance strategies of European firms and the role of ESPRIT', *Journal of Common Market Studies* 26: 231–55.

OECD (1991) *Measures Affecting Direct Investment in OECD Countries*, Paris: OECD.

Ozawa, T. (1991) 'Japanese multinationals and 1992', in B. Burgenmeier and J. L. Mucchielli (eds) *Multinationals and Europe 1992*, pp. 135–54, London and New York: Routledge.

Pain, N. and Lansburg, M. (1996) 'The impact of the internal market on the evolution of European direct investment', London: NIESR (mimeo).

Panic, M. (1992) 'The impact of multinationals on national economic policies', in B. Burgenmeier and J. L. Mucchielli (eds) *Multinationals and Europe 1992*, pp. 204–222, London and New York: Routledge.

——(1995) 'International economic integration and the changing role of national governments', in H.-J. Chang and R. Rowthorn (eds) *The Role of the State in Economic Change*, Oxford: Clarendon Press.

Porter, M. E. (1990) *The Competitive Advantage of Nations*, New York: The Free Press.

Robinson, J. (1983) *Multinationals and Political Control*, Aldershot: Gower.

Robson, P. (ed.) (1993) *Transnational Corporations and Economic Integration. United Nations Library on Transnational Corporations*, London: Routledge.

Shelburne, R. C. (1991) *The North American Free Trade Agreement: Comparisons with and Lessons from Southern EC Enlargement*, Washington, DC: US Department of Labor Economic Discussion Paper No. 39.

Sweeney, R. J. (1993) 'The competition for foreign direct investment', in L. Oxelheim (ed.) *The Global Race for Foreign Direct Investment in the 1990s*, pp. 71–106, New York: Springer-Verlag.

UNCTAD (1993a) *From the Common Market to EC 1992*, New York: UN.

——(1993b) *Explaining and Forecasting Regional Flows of Foreign Direct Investment*, New York: UN.

US Department of Commerce (1995) *US Direct Investments Abroad, Provisional Results, 1993*, Washington, D.C.: US Government Printing office.
Vernon, R. (1994) 'Multinationals and governments: key actors in the NAFTA', in L. Eden (ed.) *Multinationals in North America*, pp. 25–52, Alberta, Canada: University of Calgary Press.
Walter, I. (1993) 'Patterns of mergers and acquisitions, 1985–90', in L. Oxelheim (ed.) *The Global Race for Foreign Direct Investment in the 1990s*, pp. 151–76, Berlin and New York: Springer-Verlag.
Westney, D. E. (1994) 'Japanese multinationals in North America', in L. Eden (ed.) *Multinationals in North America*, pp. 253–70, Alberta, Canada: University of Calgary Press.

7

GLOBALIZATION, TECHNOLOGICAL CHANGE AND THE SPATIAL ORGANIZATION OF ECONOMIC ACTIVITY

INTRODUCTION

One of the most distinctive features of the globalizing economy of the early 1990s is the extent to which the cross-border movement of created assets is internalized either within multinational hierarchies or between two or more separately owned, but interrelated, firms[1] located in different countries. It is the contention of this chapter that the resulting international division of labour, and the nature of the competitive advantages of both firms and countries, is fundamentally different from that determined by the disposition of locationally immobile assets and the transactions between independent buyers and sellers.

For much of the past century, most of the explanations for the international specialization of value-added activity have been based upon the uneven spatial distribution of natural resources. But, today, the competitive and comparative advantages of countries are increasingly determined by the ability of governments and firms to create and organize the deployment of created assets, and from the trade in foreign direct investment (FDI) arising from these assets. At the same time, the significance of intrafirm and interfirm alliance trade is also increasing.

The metamorphosis in the organization of natural and created assets, and of international transactions, is having critical implications for both the ownership and location of economic activity. This is most conspicuously shown by the increasing role of multinational enterprises (MNEs) in global production and trade (UNCTAD 1995). It is true that new organizational systems are favouring the participation of small firms, but there are strong suggestions that those involved in the most dynamic sectors of the international economy are most likely to be part of a business district or cross-border network of activities, in which the pivotal role is played by large multi-activity and multi-locational corporations (Harrison 1994).

EXPLAINING CHANGES IN THE SPATIAL ALLOCATION OF ECONOMIC ACTIVITY

Under classical and neo-classical theories of trade, the international division of labour was determined entirely by the geographical disposition of natural resources and the stock of capital. Changes in economic activity were presumed only to occur as a result of the increase or depletion of such resources. Trade in capital and intermediate products, like that of finished goods and services was assumed to be arm's length; otherwise assets were perceived to be completely location bound. There was no reason for FDI to exist, as there were no incentives for firms to internalize cross-border markets. Neither was there any necessity for firms to engage in cross-border alliances or networks.[2]

The treatment of technology in neo-classical theory was ambiguous. Either it was ignored altogether or it was assumed to be freely available to all firms, and instantaneously transferable across national boundaries. The transborder locational consequences of technological change were rarely considered in the literature, although, in part, this deficiency was partly remedied by the neo-technology theories of trade of the 1950s.[3]

A central feature of received trade theory was the complete disregard of the firm, or interfirm alliances, as institutional entities and of the costs of organizing economic activity. The competitiveness of a country was judged by the ability of its economic system to allocate resources in a way which maximized their comparative advantage. It is, perhaps, worth emphasizing that *international economics* – as a distinctive discipline – originated because of the presumed differences in the determinants and outcomes of the allocation of resources *within* a nation as compared with those *between* nations. In turn, these were postulated to arise because, beyond the jurisdictional boundaries of nations, all resources were perceived to be completely immobile. It was also assumed that each country processed a distinctive pattern of resource endowments.

In the neo-classical tradition, trade economists gave little attention to the distribution of international economic activity *within* countries. This lacuna was taken up by locational economists. However, their focus of interest was rather different. Rather than asking the question 'What determines the optimum mix of activities for a subnational location?', they asked the question 'What determines the optimum location for a particular mix of activities?' Partly, this lack of concern with issues central to international economics is reflected in the fact that resources were assumed to be fully mobile within countries. Consequently, the dominant paradigm of locational economics became the principle of *absolute* competitive advantage, rather than that of *comparative* competitive advantage.

In contrast to trade theory, the unit of analysis in locational economics was the firm, and most of the neo-classical models constructed, for example by Von Thunen (1876), Weber (1929), Hotelling (1929), Losch (1940) and Hoover (1948), were extensions of the profit-maximizing theory of the firm. Given a particular market, the optimum location was that which minimized production plus transport costs. In imperfect markets, firms had to balance the spatial implications for maximizing revenue with those of minimizing costs. No such spatial choice was allowed firms between a domestic and foreign location.

For the most part, the dichotomy between intra- and intercountry spatial economics remains. One notable exception is the work of Bertil Ohlin, who, perhaps, more than any other economist, tried to bridge the gap[4] between the two intellectual strands. In 1976, he organized a symposium in Stockholm to which he invited some leading economists, geographers and regional scientists to share their thoughts on the determinants of the international allocation of economic activity. However, for the most part, the papers presented, and the ensuing discussion (later published in book form by Ohlin *et al.* 1977), proceeded on parallel lines with few interdisciplinary bridges being built. Trade economists stuck to their last and apart from our own contribution, which gave birth to the eclectic paradigm of international production, there was no attempt to take on board either organizational issues or the implications of the growing mobility of intangible assets.[5]

Over the past two decades, there has been a gradual shift of emphasis away from *country*- to *firm*-specific considerations in exploring the territorial spread of business activity. Indeed, with a few notable exceptions, which are detailed elsewhere in this chapter, the main advances in our understanding of this phenomenon have come not from scholars versed in extant international economics, but from those working on the boundaries of that subject of institutional and technological economics, organizational theory and business strategy.

At the same time, most of the mainstream thinking scholars from these disciplines have not embraced an international dimension and, as a result, our understanding of the way resources are organized and distributed across national boundaries has been constricted.[6] But, the globalization of economic activity is likely to force scholars, working both in traditional trade and locational economics and those in a variety of business-oriented disciplines, to search for a more common paradigmatic approach.

What then might be the intellectual components of any future explanation of the spatial organization of economic activity? In this chapter, we propose to examine a number of features of the globalizing economy and how they are affecting the extant paradigms and theories of a variety of disciplines – and also to speculate a little on the future direction of both uni- and interdisciplinary research in the later 1990s.

THE ROLE OF CREATED ASSETS IN TRADITIONAL THINKING

As countries move along their development paths, the role of *created*, relative to *natural*, assets as the main generators of future income increases. As their name implies, created assets embrace all forms of wealth produced from natural resources. More particularly, they include accumulated knowledge, skills, learning and experience, and organizational competence, which are embodied in human beings, proprietary rights, institutions and physical capacity. Some scholars may add to these other 'softer' assets, such as an entrepreneurial spirit, an ability to benefit from co-operative alliances and networking, and a mentality which favours wealth creation, and a continual upgrading in quality and efficiency of existing assets. Unlike natural resources – notably land, power sources and climate – many, but not all, created assets are transportable over space, although the precise way in which they are packaged may not be.[7] Unlike natural assets too, most created assets are likely to be the privileged possession of particular private or public institutions. These two characteristics of created assets – namely, their mobility and their ownership specificity – cut right across the assumptions of neo-classical international economics[8] and are forcing scholars to reappraise their explanations of spatial activity.

For the most part, *organizational scholars* have paid only limited attention to the underlying characteristics of created assets. Two notable exceptions are Alfred Chandler and David Teece, who, in their various writings,[9] have distinguished between the competitive advantages of firms arising from their possession of a core asset, for example a patent, brand name or the exclusive access to a market, and those which arise from the efficient co-ordination of these assets with complementary assets owned by other firms. In Chandler's view, it is the access to and efficient deployment of the latter kind of competence, which has been one of the key components of corporate success over the past century, and, by inference, that of nations as well. However, while examining some of the country-specific features which might lead to the creation of co-ordinating assets, neither Chandler nor Teece has given much attention to the spatial implications of the governance of interrelated assets; except, perhaps, to suggest that these might aid, rather than inhibit, industrial clustering and the concentration of economic activity.[10]

In contrast to organizational scholars, *scholars in the Schumpterian tradition* have placed rather more emphasis on the possession and accumulation of technological assets as a firm-specific advantage, and of the role of innovatory systems as a country-specific advantage. More recently, as attention has become focused on the learning experiences, technological trajectories and innovatory strategies of firms, the interests of the neo-Schumpterians, such as Antonelli, Chesnais, Dosi, Freeman and Pavitt, and those of the organizational and business strategists, such as Teece, Hedlund, Bartlett and Ghoshal, have begun to converge. Both approaches have paid some attention to the spatial implications of technological innovation. In particular, building on the work of Ray Vernon (1970) and Gary Hufbauer (1965, 1970), Dosi *et al.* (1990) have incorporated this variable, at a *country* level, into extant trade theory. Several Italian scholars, notably Cainarca *et al.* (1988), Antonelli (1991) and Archibugi and Pianta (1993), have examined the international and intraregional diffusion of technological activity, while Bartlett and Ghoshal (1989) have argued that MNEs which successfully co-ordinated and integrated their technological strategies are those most likely to record the most creditable performances as international direct investors.

For their part, until recently, *international economists* have tended to treat created assets as a country-, rather than a firm-, specific competitive advantage. Using such indices as R&D expenditure as a proxy for created assets, and patents or technology-intensive products as the output of such assets, they have sought to incorporate this variable into H–O- type models – and undertake some evaluation of its importance.[11] In his explanation of Japanese direct investment abroad, Kojima (1978, 1990) argued that *countries* which had a comparative advantage in the *creation* of technological assets, but not in their *use*, should export technology as an intermediate product, and import those products which required other created, or natural, assets in which they were comparatively disadvantaged. Only in his more recent writings (e.g. Kojima 1992) has Kojima considered the mode by which technology is exported as a factor influencing the spatial distribution of economic activity.[12]

Until the 1970s, relatively little attention was given to the competitive advantages of firms by *micro-economists*. In the heritage of Edward Chamberlin (1933), Joan Robinson (1933) and Joe Bain (1956), any advantage one firm was supposed to have over another was presumed to reflect the form and degree of its monopoly power. Only in the last twenty years or so has the emphasis on firm-specific advantages switched to the firm's ability to create to acquire assets which yield competitive enhancing results. The work of Michael Porter (1980, 1985), following in the tradition of industrial economics, and that of Barney (1986), Dierickx and Cool (1989) and Rumelt (1984), which has helped refocus attention on the resource-based theory of the firm (Penrose 1959), are examples of two schools of thought which specifically address the question of why some firms are more successful at creating and sustaining core competencies than others.

To what extent is it possible – or indeed desirable – to integrate these various approaches? Our own preference is first to accept that, at any given moment of time, each firm possesses a unique portfolio of accumulated assets – including those which may be located outside its national boundaries – and that the way these assets are organized is determined by the trajectory chosen by the management of the firm to advance its time-related objectives and its position on that path. These assets we term ownership-specific (O) for, in the last resort, it is ownership which determines the jurisdictional boundaries of a firm. In turn, however, the fecundity of assets may be influenced by the extent and type of activity in which a firm engages, the region or country in which it operates and the characteristics of the firm, other than its ownership.

We have suggested in Chapter 5 that in its explanation of the international allocation of economic activity, neo-classical trade theory treats firms as 'black boxes', and only immobile country-specific assets are taken to determine the trading patterns of nations. Both the asset portfolios and the products supplied by competing firms are assumed to be homogeneous, and all firms are presumed to engage in only a single activity, and to be price takers. Even the concept of dynamic comparative advantage pays little attention to the growth of the firm. However, in practice, we know that the propensity of firms, within a particular sector and of a particular nationality, to engage in intra- and international activity varies a great deal, and this is because of their distinctive asset portfolios and/or the way in which they organize and manage such assets.

Now, if it were possible to identify a 'best practice' asset structure and a 'best practice' usage of a dynamic firm, normalizing for such variables as its nationality, size and product range, one could presumably incorporate these ownership-specific characteristics into any macro-model of spatial activity. The problem is to define what *is* the 'best practice' firm, when each firm is moving along a different trajectory of innovatory activity, product specialization or spatial diversification.[13] In an uncertain world, only with hindsight can the optimum behaviour of a firm be identified and, most certainly, yesterday's 'best practice' firm is not necessarily a guide to tomorrow's 'best practice' firm. This makes the incorporation of firm-specific behaviour into any *normative* theory of the spatial allocation of economic activity a very difficult thing to do.[14] Indeed, it may be questionable how productive such an effort might be!

Yet, in explaining the spatial activity of resources, as it *is*, as opposed to how it *ought* to be, it is surely incumbent on scholars at least to identify – if not to evaluate – the way in which the O-specific asset portfolios of firms affect both their ability to compete in spatial markets and their preference for siting their value-added activities in different locations. But, for the most part, this has not been done. For example, while it is generally acknowledged that patent protection may confer an O advantage on the patenting firm, without a knowledge of the asset portfolios, production functions, interfirm relationships and strategies of that firm and those of its competitors, it is impossible to gauge the consequences of that patent protection for either the industry of that firm or the country in which it is domiciled. Thus, for example, the impact of patent protection on the competitiveness of an auto firm engaging in scale production may be very different from that on one pursuing a more flexible manufacturing strategy. On the other hand, it may be reasonable to hypothesize that, in the absence of patent protection, there would be less incentive to engage in research and development in the first place, and, if and when countries differ in their national innovatory systems, this could have considerable spatial consequences.

It is possible to analyse the spatial consequences of other O-specific advantages in a similar way. However, it may be conceptually useful to distinguish between those advantages which arise from the privileged access to specific assets and those which stem from the way in which such assets, and those which are more generally available, are organized. We shall consider the spatial implications of these latter assets in our next section.

We would, however, make one further point about firm-specific assets. Much of received spatial economics rests on the assumptions that the sole objective of firms is to maximize profits and that there is minimal market failure. In practice, neither assumption is legitimate. However, where competitive pressures exist, then, as the theory suggests, firms are forced to look more closely at ways and means of lowering production costs and/or increasing revenues, and of organizing their assets in a way which minimizes transaction costs. A similar argument applies to reaping economies of scale. To overcome the costs of market failure, it may be inevitable that some concentration of competitive advantages among firms arises. So long as the privileged firms are not protected, that is, markets are contestable, this may be an optimum solution as the most analogous to the perfect market model which is assumed by received theory.

So far in our analysis of the spatial implications of firm-specific advantages, we have been concerned with those which, independently, arise directly from a firm's *own* asset portfolio and management. But, sometimes, these advantages may, themselves, be influenced by its participation in interfirm networks and its locational choices. The gains to be derived from the geographical concentration, agglomeration or clustering of related activities have been well acknowledged by industrial and locational economists, at least since the time of Alfred Marshall.[15] By contrast, until recently they had been largely ignored by trade economists, mainly, we suspect, because of the latter's narrow interpretation of the boundaries of a firm and their reluctance to embrace endemic market failure (in this case arising from externalities) into their models or theories.

However, over the last decade, a systemic approach to the dynamics of the firm, and its interaction with related firms located in close proximity to each other, has gained increasing attention by scholars from economics, organization theory, business strategy, geography and sociology.[16] Owing to the increased ease with which products, assets and people can move across national boundaries, the traditional paradigms of the micro-organization of business activity, and their spatial implications, are becoming increasingly inappropriate. In particular, as flexible and network-related production systems tend to place Fordist-type hierarchies as the dominant systems of value-added activity, the concept of 'neo-Marshallian' subnational spatial areas, for example the business or industrial district as a critical unit of economic organization, is gaining ground. We have already alluded to the main feature of the globalizing economy as the replacement of an 'arm's length' international division of labour by one largely characterized by trading and production relationships between related parties.[17] It is also evident that this leads both to some clustering of value-added activities by foreign direct investors in particular countries – very much on the lines earlier observed by Knickerbocker (1973)[18] – and to an increasing spatial concentration of such activities – and particularly innovatory activities – between countries.

The renaissance of the Marshallian agglomerative economies has been acknowledged by several scholars, including Michael Porter (1990) and Paul Krugman (1991), both of whom assign it considerable importance in affecting the competitive advantages both of the participating firms and of the regions and countries of which they are a part. The point at issue here is the extent to which firms with O-specific assets, and particularly those which advance global competitiveness, need to be in close proximity to other firms supplying complementary assets in order to minimize their transaction and co-ordination costs.

It is not difficult to find historical or contemporary examples of the way in which agglomerative economies have added to the O advantages of the participating firms; and also to the competitiveness of the regions and countries. Among the best known are the square mile (= City) of London and Silicon Valley in California, the Geneva watch and the Solingen cutlery industries.[19] However, there are strong suggestions that, in spite of (or perhaps it is because of) advances in transportation and communication technologies, the value of agglomerative economies is increasing.[20] This is especially so in the more dynamic and service-intensive industrial sectors, in which there is usually an above-average representation of smaller and entrepreneurial firms, which are likely to gain particular benefit from networking with other firms, and the near presence of diverse, yet complementary, assets.[21] It also reflects the increasing need of firms producing or using complementary assets at the top end of the value chain to keep in close touch with each other,[22] and is encouraged by various facets of innovatory-led production, including the desire of firms to keep inventories to the minimum. One of the fastest growing sectors of economic activity is that of industrial and science parks. Here, too, there is a good deal of intraindustry FDI in research and development activity, as the major MNEs seek to acquire, as well as to exploit, already existing knowledge.[23]

It is difficult, if not impossible, to define an optimum space of a regional cluster, as this will critically depend on the composition of the activities making up the cluster. But, one noticeable result of European integration is the realignment of the geography of agglomeration, which, *inter alia*, is leading to the emergence of new cross-border networks. Examples include those parts of the Low Countries and Germany adjacent to the Ruhr Valley, and along the borders of Northern Italy and France. It is most conspicuous in sectors no longer encumbered by non-tariff barriers; in those which gain most benefit from labour pooling and the common availability of specialized inputs and services; in those which comprise activities which are technologically or organizationally synergistic to each other; and in those which are faced with relatively insignificant transport and communications costs.

Trade liberalization has also affected the location of economic activity in other regions of the world. In his study of the Mexican economy, for example, Hanson (1994) found that the introduction of more market-oriented policies of the Mexican government has led to a relocation of the geographical clustering of manufacturing activity from Mexico City to the US border region. Trade liberalization has also tended to compress regional wage differentials.

THE GROWING SIGNIFICANCE OF THE CO-ORDINATING AND TRANSACTION FUNCTIONS OF FIRMS

We have already observed that neo-classical economists regarded the firm solely as a production unit, and markets to be the optimal modality for the exchange of inputs and outputs relevant to that production. Prior to Knight (1921), Schumpeter (1947) and Penrose (1959), the co-ordinating role of the entrepreneur was given little attention, except that it was generally accepted by micro-economists that, in conditions of perfect competition, the eventual limit to the size of firms was the rising costs of co-ordination.

Yet, as several scholars from a wide range of disciplines have demonstrated, the relative significance of the transaction and co-ordinating costs (cf. e.g. production costs) of economic activity tends to increase with economic development.[24] This is essentially because, as the division of labour becomes more specialized, the likelihood of learning constraints, information asymmetries and opportunism between independent transacting parties increases. Where it is perceived that these costs are higher than those of internal, or quasi-internal,[25] organizational mechanisms, then individual hierarchies, or groups of related firms, will replace the market as an organizational mode. Hence, the growth of multi-activity firms and networks is directly correlated with the growth of market-related transaction and co-ordination costs, and also with advances in organizational and communications technology.

The geographical specialization of economic activities across space is likely to lead to additional transport and co-ordinating costs, both of the market and of firms. Sometimes – as in the case of some service-intensive activities, for example R&D and merchant banking, where face-to-face contact between producers and users is imperative – such costs are infinite. Initially, economists measured distance costs entirely by the direct costs of traversing space. But again, owing to technological advances and a more complex division of labour, these costs, relative to market-related transaction and co-ordinating costs, have fallen. Increasingly, the locational preferences of firms are being set by their ability to organize spatially dispersed or spatially concentrated activities.

Although *international economists* have largely ignored them, *international business* (IB) scholars have long recognized that the distinction between cross-border and domestic value-added activities lies in the presence of transnational market failures. These include not only the most obvious co-ordinating costs and learning and information constraints firms have to incur when they commence production in a less familiar, and perhaps riskier, economic and political environment, but also those to do with establishing and fostering relationships between individuals and institutions in countries with different historical and institutional backgrounds, legal systems, lifestyles, political and religious ideologies and business customs.

Historically, cultural distance[26] has been one of the key variables determining the geographical pattern of economic activity, notably between metropolitan countries and their colonies, and between countries with comparable legal systems and commercial practices. Almost certainly, the globalizing economy is eroding some types of cultural distance and causing a realignment of spatial preferences among firms. On the other hand, where, to acquire the intermediate products or complementary assets necessary to protect or advance their own competitive advantages, firms perceive a need to be part of a subnational network, this could add to their spatial specific co-ordination and transaction costs. Whether the resulting spatial realignment is predominantly centripetal or centrifugal will obviously reflect a balance between the production, transaction and co-ordinating costs of clustering particular kinds of economic activities, and those of decentralizing such activities.

While scholars have long since recognized that the gains to be derived from agglomerative economies are activity specific, rather less attention has been paid to the role of subnational or country-specific variables in determining such clusters. To some extent, Michael Porter (1990) rectifies this deficiency, and correctly points to the growing importance of subnational clusters as a variable influencing the competitiveness of firms and countries. Building on Porter's analysis, we would like to suggest that the capability of countries to develop and sustain efficient clusters rests, first, on the macro-economic and organizational policies of governments; second, on the innovating and marketing strategies of the participating firms; third, on the willingness and ability of those firms to capture the benefits and minimize the costs of clustering; and fourth, on the availability and quality of complementary assets – notably R&D, transport and communication infrastructure and a flexible labour market. Such a capability may well become one of the most important location-bound and country-specific characteristics determining the competitive advantages of particular activities and the composition of a country's economic activities in the emerging age of alliance capitalism.[27]

To what extent, then, have scholars embraced the spatial consequences of the inability of arm's length markets to maximize the net benefits of the co-ordinating and transaction functions of a market economy? As far as much of extant *international trade* theory is concerned, the answer is very little,[28] although there have been some brave attempts to integrate theories of trade and international production.[29] As for *international direct investment* theory, the record is much better. Indeed, perhaps the critical contribution of international business scholars over the past two decades has been to develop a firm-level theory of international direct investment, by explaining the situations in which firms will internalize cross-border intermediate product markets – the so-called internalization (I) paradigm[30] – and also why firms should opt to undertake the value-added activities arising from such internalization from one location rather than another.

At the same time, IB scholars have paid much less attention to the ways in which the intracountry allocation of economic activity might affect the competitive advantages of firms or nations; or indeed to the significance of agglomerative economies in explaining the intracountry distribution of FDI.[31] This deficiency is in the process of being partially corrected by economic geographers,[32] and by economists interested in the spatial distribution of technological innovation.[33] We say 'partially' for although this group of scholars has sought to identify the reasons why particular activities tend to agglomerate together, there has been little rigorous evaluation either of the origins or the significance of systemic market failure leading to the clusters, or to how these failures may differ between industrial sectors.[34] And, although *organizational scholars* have considerably advanced our knowledge about the nature and determinants of networks or related activities,[35] and of the management of innovatory systems,[36] they, too, have been slow to embrace the spatial dimension in their models.

Business analysts, notably Chandler (1977, 1990) and Porter (1990), have, in general, confined their attention to examining the attributes of industrial clusters of activities within a country, although, in his work, Porter has made some attempt to relate the location-bound characteristics of countries to the kind of subnational clusters they generate. Porter, however, does not draw much on the market failure paradigm for his explanation of why a group of firms with synergistic O assets may wish to be clustered in one region or country rather than another; nor how this clustering may vary, according to country-specific characteristics, and to the asset management strategy of the participating firms.

What, then, can one glean from these rather diffuse disciplinary perspectives? To what extent is it possible to evaluate the role of organizational structures as they affect the competitiveness of firms and countries and the location of economic activity? We would suggest a three-pronged approach. The first, drawing mainly on organizational theory and industrial economics, is to identify which kinds of co-ordination and transaction costs are most likely to be space related, and how far these costs are likely to vary between different types of activities and/or countries. The second, which combines the work of scholars on the dynamics of the firm, technological accumulation and business strategy, is to look more closely at the determinants of the asset portfolios of firms, and the strategic management of these portfolios, so as to identify the critical firm-specific characteristics influencing the location of activity.

The third prong is to relate the findings of the first two prongs to the received theories of trade and location, and to see whether country-and firm-specific co-ordinating and transaction costs can be incorporated into these theories. This, like the inclusion of created assets – and particularly firm-specific mobile assets – into existing explanations of the spatial allocation of resources is a tall order!

THE ROLE OF GOVERNMENTS IN AFFECTING THE SPATIAL ORGANIZATION OF ACTIVITY

We now consider the consequences of globalization for the actions of national and subnational governments,[37] and of supranational institutions and regimes, in so far as they affect the locational choices of the dynamic firm – or groups of firms. Again, historically, *international economics* – and neo-classical economics in particular – has ignored the macro-organizational (as opposed to the macro-economic)[38] role of government. This is mainly because in a Pareto-optimal world, markets are assumed not to fail, and only where structural distortions occur is any government intervention considered necessary.[39]

More recently, this analytical lacuna has, at least partly, been overcome by the work of two groups of scholars. The first – typified by the writings of Paul Krugman (1986, 1994) – has injected new life into international trade theory by extending the tools of industrial economics to explain how strategic trade policy by governments might affect the location of economic activity. The second is the ongoing research of a group of mainly US scholars, notably Ray Vernon, Fred Bergsten, Gary Hufbauer and Monty Graham, on the changing interface between trade, FDI and global business activity, and its implications for a whole range of domestic economic and other issues. Nevertheless, neither group of scholars has given much attention to the ways in which governments might interact with firms and markets to lessen or circumvent the endemic failure of different organizational forms of economic activity, and how these, in turn, might affect the international and intranational disposition of national and created assets.

Turning to *locational economics* and *geography* – including that part of it concerned with the extranational activities of firms – we see a much greater willingness of scholars to tackle head-on the role of government-related variables, notably fiscal penalties and incentives. Indeed, in recent work on the determinants of the locational preferences of MNEs,[40] the role of host governments, and particularly their ability to affect the co-ordinating and transaction costs[41] of economic activity, has been shown to be a critical one. Much of this latter research has been undertaken by *economic geographers*, *regional scientists*, *urban economists* and *international business specialists*, but it is, perhaps, the international marketing scholars[42] who have gone furthest in their attempts to embrace psychic distance (which includes non-economic spatial market failures, many of which are government influenced) into their thinking. Economists interested in the interaction between MNE activity and the pattern and path of technological accumulation are increasingly acknowledging the decisive role of national innovatory systems as a competitive enhancing instrument of governments (Chesnais 1993, Nelson 1993).

By contrast, *organization theory* has generally neglected government-related and other exogenous variables in its examination of the decision-making practices of firms. The same charge may also be levelled at much of the strategic management literature,[43] notwithstanding a copious volume of research which has sought to analyse the way in which business strategy may be affected by a firm's external environment. Since, in the past, both organization and management theory has been geared towards explaining the internal functioning of firms operating largely within their national boundaries, this neglect is, perhaps, understandable. But in today's globalizing economy, where governments exercise so much influence on the extent and pattern of cross-border market failure,[44] this neglect – even at the most micro level of analysis – is quite unacceptable.

It is difficult to conclude from the above paragraphs that the role of government as an organizer and co-ordinator of economic activity has, in the past, been given the attention it deserves.[45] There are signs that this is changing and this, we believe, is primarily due to the effect the globalizing economy is having on the costs and benefits of alternative organizational modes – and particularly on the role of governments as facilitators of efficient markets.

The concept of government as a superintendent of the organization of economic activity, and the instruments which government may use to facilitate an efficient market system, are now being much more closely examined by *political scientists*, *economists*, *organizational scholars* and *business strategists* alike.[46] This, as we have already said, is because the kind of co-ordination and transaction costs most influenced by the actions of governments are exercising a more important part in the locational decision process of firms and networks than once they did. This, in turn, reflects the convergence of many kinds of production costs across national boundaries – particularly among advanced industrialized countries – and the increasing role of created assets in the production process.

The macro-organizational actions of government – and elsewhere (Dunning 1994b) we have explored the situations in which government action to reduce market failure is likely to be the most cost effective[47] – are clearly likely to be discriminatory in their impact, both between firms and types of economic activity. Of the former, those most likely to be affected are those whose competitiveness rests on continuous product innovation and improvement; new ventures, especially in relatively high-risk sectors; those whose assets are most spatially mobile; and those most dependent on the kind of complementary assets, which are critically influenced by government actions. Viewed from a functional or strategic perspective, the influence of government is most likely to affect the decisions of firms about expenditure on R&D and training, the extent of vertical integration or horizontal diversification and the locational configuration of high-value-added activities.

The subject matter of this chapter embraces several of these areas and the ways in which they interact with each other. To tackle these effectively, government action must be more explicitly considered as a critical explanatory variable, and much more rigorous work needs to be done on the consequences of collective and specific macro-organizational strategies on the ownership, organization and competitiveness of firms, and on the location of different types of economic activity.

CONCLUDING REMARKS

The key message of this chapter is that globalization – and more particularly the forces driving it and its consequences – is affecting the costs and benefits of the four main modalities of organizing economic activity in capitalist economies, namely markets, hierarchies, interfirm alliances and governments. It further argues that, while in the past these modalities have largely been viewed as alternatives to each other, the growing economic interdependence of domestic and cross-border activities and the increasing significance of co-operative ventures, both between firms and between firms and governments, are requiring scholars to search for a more macro-systemic approach to the organization of resources and capabilities in which markets, hierarchies, networks and governments each have complementary roles to play.

Such a macro-systemic approach is especially relevant when considering the interaction between the dynamic firm and its external environment, and especially between the former and firms supplying goods and services, the price and quality of which influences its own competitiveness. The chapter has further suggested that the introduction of flexible production systems and alliance capitalism is causing firms to reorganize their asset portfolios, *inter alia*, by externalizing some of their internal markets, but, at the same time, reinternalizing them among a network of related firms. Finally, we have argued that both the intra- and international locations of economic activity are being increasingly guided by the desire of firms to reduce the costs of market failure and/or to capture the synergies offered by business districts and other spatially related networks of firms, and by the actions of governments designed to promote the competitiveness of their location-bound assets and that of their own MNEs.

None of the traditional disciplines analysing the behaviour of firms has yet fully embraced the features and consequences of globalization in their paradigms and theories. In particular, the significance of firm-specific competencies and management strategies, not to mention the growing cross-border mobility of assets, has still not engaged the attention of mainstream economists. On the other hand, the need for a more systemic approach in addressing issues relating to the growth of firms and groups of firms, the role of governments and the organization and management of a complex bundle of assets, is forcing a reassessment of our ideas about the very nature of economic activity, and the relationships between the major institutional entities.

While it seems probable that, barring catastrophes, the forces currently driving globalization will continue in the foreseeable future, it is less certain how these will affect the organization of created assets between and within firms, the dynamics of technological accumulation and the location of economic activity. As far as the leading global players are concerned, there are suggestions of a flattening of organizational structures and a divestment of activities which do not directly enhance their core competences. At the same time, firms are becoming increasingly aware of the need to balance the advantages of a centralized control of financial assets, R&D and of markets, with those of the decentralization of entrepreneurial initiative and managerial competence, and the need to adapt asset usage to local needs and customs.

While lean and flexible organizational structures are likely to follow – and sometimes lead – the techno-economic system of flexible production and the socio-institutional system of alliance capitalism, and some of the advantages of hierarchical capitalism may disappear, it is probably premature to predict that today's successful large corporations will become tomorrow's dinosaurs. At the same time, as well as studying the production and co-ordinating functions of individual firms, economists should give more attention to the concept of a systemic group or network of firms as a unit of analysis,[48] and of the positioning of individual firms in that grouping or network. It is, indeed, quite possible that some of the economies of scope and co-ordination enjoyed by independent firms will be transferred to the 'flagship' or lead firms in a network, while, concurrently, some of the erstwhile functions of large firms will be contracted out to medium and small-sized firms in the network.

The impact of future technological and organizational advances on the location of economic activity is also unclear. While there is some indication that the leading MNEs are decentralizing some of their production and innovatory activities, this is largely taking place in the same countries or regions from which other MNEs, namely Japan, the United States and the EC, are decentralizing their activities. Moreover, as we have seen, despite advances in telematics, the need for close, if not face-to-face, contact between the managers, administrators, scientists and technologists of inter-related firms – particularly at the top end of the value-added chain and between the factory and the research laboratory – is encouraging centripetal tendencies. Across countries and regions, too, there are suggestions that the principle of comparative advantage may be applied to explaining different clusters or networks of activities;[49] the willingness and ability of firms to embrace alliance capitalism, and the macro-organizational policies of national and regional governments come into play.

There are also suggestions that the forces affecting the geography of innovatory activities are also encouraging similar networks or firms producing at different stages of the same value-added chain. There is nothing particularly new in this phenomenon. What, perhaps, is new is the extent to which the composition and character of such clusters has been affected by inward and outward direct investment. Indeed, one especially interesting feature of networks in the auto and electronics sectors, as for example fashioned by Japanese MNE activity in the EC and the United States, is the extent to which horizontal cross-border linkages have been formed between particular component manufacturers in the host countries and their opposite numbers in Japan.

What of the role of the developing economies in the emerging global economy? This could easily be a subject for a separate volume, although we have touched upon some of the relevant issues in Chapter 1 and will do so again in Chapter 9. But, just as the presence of created complementary assets – and particularly in those which are government induced – and a market-facilitating environment are becoming increasingly important determinants of both domestic and inbound investment in developed countries, so these location-bound characteristics are also the prerequisites for the upgrading of economic activity in most developing countries – especially in those which compete with each other. But, as Porter (1990) and others have shown, because of the limited size of their domestic markets, it is much more difficult for the poorer nations to create the educational and infrastructure needed to participate in global trade and investment. While the examples of Singapore and Hong Kong are salutary, it is difficult to perceive how the smaller developing nations, especially in sub-Saharan Africa and Latin America, can expect to experience the benefits of their counterparts in Europe, either by forging networks with foreign firms or by participating in regional integration schemes.

In conclusion, and returning to the main theme of this volume, there are several indications that alliance capitalism is requiring a reappraisal of the appropriate or optimum spatial unit of organizational governance, and that the economic transformation now being fashioned by globalization is likely to upgrade the role of subnational units of governance, and downgrade that of national governments.

Certainly, scholars from a variety of disciplines are beginning to explore or re-explore issues such as regional business cultures, regional institutional building, the learning or intelligent region, regional competitiveness, regional industrial policy, and interregional policy co-ordination (Storper and Scott 1995, Florida 1995). Increasingly, regions are being perceived as ministates.[50] Indeed, Kenichi Ohmae (1993, 1995) has gone as far as to suggest that (what he calls) region states may supplant nation states as the core unit of spatial governance. To quote directly,

> The nation state has become an unnatural, even dysfunctional unit for organizing human activity and managing economic endeavor in a borderless world. It represents no genuine, shared community of economic interests; it defines no meaningful flows of economic activity. . . . On the global economic map the lines that now matter are those defining what may be called 'region states.' . . . Region states are natural economic zones. They may or may not fall within the geographic limits of a particular nation – whether they do is an accident of history. Sometimes these distinct economic units are formed by parts of states. . . . At other times they may be formed by economic patterns that overlap existing national boundaries. . . . In today's borderless world, these are natural economic zones and what matters is that each possesses, in one or another combination, the key ingredients for successful participation in the global economy.
>
> (Ohmae 1993: 78–9)

Whether Ohmae's vision is realized remains to be seen. What is, however, already occurring is a realignment of the geography both of the activities of individual and networks of business units and of the jurisdiction of governments. Apropos the former, Amin and Thrift (1994: 13) refer to centres of geographical agglomeration as becoming 'centres of representation, interaction and innovation within global production filiers'. This, they argue, is leading to a spatial reconfiguration of territorial embeddedness based upon the ability of regions to exploit their location-specific advantages. Certainly the idea that geography is dead, as avowed by some scholars (e.g. O'Brien 1992), with respect to the operation of global financial markets, is more than counter-balanced by the emergence of new localized industrial clusters bound together by the need to minimize distant-sensitive transaction costs, such as those associated with irregular idiocyncratic, uncertain and time-dependent transactions (Storper and Scott 1995).

Yet the appropriate form of spatial networking remains a matter of debate among scholars. Ann Markusen (1994), for example, has distinguished between four ways of organizing regional business activity, each of which is likely to make a different contribution to the prosperity of the 'sticky' places[51] of which they are a part.[52] These are (i) the *flexible specialization* rubric, as exampled by the Italian textile industry in Prato, Northern Italy, and the watch industry of Switzerland; (ii), the *hub and spoke* industrial districts where the pattern of economic activity is centred on a number of 'flagship' corporations or strategic centres, for example, Toyota City in Japan and the Seattle industrial district (Gray *et al.* 1996); (iii) the *satellite industrial platform*, which is mainly made up of the affiliates of extra regional firms, such as in export-processing zones in developing countries; and (iv) the *non-market centred district* where the local economy revolves around either a group of top-ranking educational institutions or a number of major government-owned administrative or research installations, as along Route 128 in the United States and the M4 corridor in the United Kingdom.

Apropos the latter, scholarly opinions vary from those of political scientists who predict an increasing 'squeezing' or 'hollowing out' of national governments as both subnational and supranational administrative structures become more important to those that believe that, however much their functions may be reconstructed, national governments will continue to be the dominant fashioners and monitors of economic systems.[53]

NOTES

1 Interrelated in the sense that the participating firms incur certain costs and enjoy certain benefits which are internal to the relationship, for example a strategic alliance or network, but external to their own activities.
2 Although the presence of intranational networks has long been acknowledged, for example by Alfred Marshall (1919).
3 For a review of these and other trade theories of the time, see Hufbauer (1970) and Stern (1975).

4 See especially his classic volume on interregional and international trade (Ohlin 1933).

5 Although, in his paper, Hla Myint (1977) did discuss the role of institutional factors in economic development.

6 There are, of course, notable exceptions, including the work of James Markusen, Bruce Kogut, David Teece, Gunner Hedlund, Yves Doz, Sumantra Ghoshal and Christopher Bartlett.

7 One example of a package of assets which is not transportable is the macro-organizational strategies of domestic governments.

8 Although not necessarily of the predictions of international economics. See Dunning (1994a).

9 See, for example, Chandler (1962, 1977, 1990) and Teece (1986, 1992a).

10 Teece, however, has written on the implications of cross-border transfer of technology to the competitive advantages of the transferring firms (Teece 1977).

11 See, for example, Vernon (1966), Keesing (1966) and Gruber *et al.* (1970).

12 See also the next section of this chapter.

13 The problem is composed when the unit of analysis is extended to an alliance or network of firms.

14 There are other areas of imperfect competition and the appropriate behaviour of strategic oligopolists which cloud the issue even further!

15 See especially Marshall (1919).

16 See, for example, Piore and Sabel (1984), Best (1990), Casson (1991), Gerlach (1992), Patel and Pavitt (1992), Cantwell (1992), Archibugi and Pianta (1993), Harrison *et al.* (1993), Enright (1944), Harrison (1994), Scott (1994), and various contributions to an edited volume by Grabher (1993).

17 The relationship might be by non-equity ownership, or by some form of co-operative agreement.

18 More recent examples include the 'follow my leader' behaviour by Japanese consumer electronics and auto MNEs into the United States and Europe.

19 Other examples are given by Enright (1994).

20 Venables (1994) has demonstrated that the forces of agglomeration in vertically linked industries are likely to be most pronounced at intermediate levels of transport costs. He suggests that beyond a certain point, lower transport costs will cause industries to operate in multiple locations, which will lead to a spatial convergence, rather than a concentration, of economic activity.

21 In a study on employment growth of industrial sectors in major US cities and countries, Henderson (1994) found that employment gains from dynamic externalities were most marked in cities and counties which offered the most diversified range of complementary assets to their core activities.

22 The kind of face-to-face contact which has always characterized transactions in the City of London (which, in its square mile, probably comprises the most intimate network of firms in the world) seems now to be increasingly valued by firms in the dynamic manufacturing sectors, and particularly those whose technologies and organizational competencies are complementary to each other. In a recent paper, dealing with intra-US geographical clustering and using employment data for three two-digit industrial sectors and four US cities, Hagen and Hammond (1994) found that asset sharing produces significant localization economies, while the economies of labour pooling tend to be most significant in rapidly growing labour markets.

23 Archibugi and Michie (1993) refer to technological acquirers as 'polyp' firms which 'acquire from each country its excellence in research rather than to decentralize their brains'.

24 Notably, Emile Durkheim (1964) from sociology, Douglass North (1990) from economic history, Alfred Chandler (1990) from business strategy, Oliver Williamson (1975, 1990) from organizational theory and Ronald Coase (1937, 1960), Edith Penrose (1959) and Kenneth Arrow (1969, 1974) from economics. An interesting collection of cross-disciplinary essays on the nature of the firm is contained in Gustafsson and Williamson (1990) and Williamson and Winter (1991).

25 Quasi-internal embraces relationships between related parties other than those arising from the ownership of one party by the other. These include non-equity co-operative agreements and networks.

26 The concept of business-related cultural distance is broadly similar to that of psychic differences between countries.

27 See also Chapters 1 and 2 of this volume.

28 This is not to say trade economists, notably Paul Krugman, have not concerned themselves with market imperfections and the strategic behaviour of firms; but to the best of our knowledge, they have not embraced transaction and co-ordination costs in their analyses.

29 Notably by Ethier (1986), Horstman and Markusen (1987) and Gray (1992).

30 See especially the various writings of Peter Buckley and Mark Casson, of Alan Rugman and of Jean Francois Hennart, as set out in Dunning (1993).

31 There are some exceptions, noticeably Teece (1992b) in his study of FDI in California, and Wilkins (1979) in a study of FDI in Florida.

32 See, for example, the various contributions of Allen Scott, that of Malecki (1985), Thwaites and Oakey (1985), Hall *et al.* (1987), Howells (1990) and Feldman (1993). See also several of the contributions to Krugman and Venables (1994) and especially those of Audretsch and Feldman, Hagen and Hammond, Henderson, and Venables.

33 See especially references set out in footnote 16 and in OECD (1992) and Kenney and Florida (1994). In their contribution to the Krugman and Venables volume, David Audretsch and Maryann Feldman (1994) found that the propensity of innovatory activity to cluster spatially was greater in industries in which the creation of knowledge spillovers is important, and in which university researchers provide important inputs for such knowledge.

34 The concept of hierarchical failure is rarely discussed in the literature. Yet, it seems to us that the existence of networks rests on the failure of both markets and industrial hierarchies to generate the relational or agglomerative economies which networks provide. The more significant these benefits are to protecting or advancing the core competencies of firms, and the greater the costs of engaging in vertical or horizontal integration, the more networks and/or bilateral alliances are likely to replace or supplement hierarchies and markets as an organizational form.

35 See especially the work of the Uppsala scholars (e.g. Johanson and Mattson 1987).

36 See, for example, Bartlett and Ghoshal (1990).

37 We are using action of governments as a proxy for all actions affecting the allocations which are not taken by the constituents of a market system.

38 The macro-economic role is concerned with the level or economic activity, unemployment, prices, exchange rates; the macro-organizational (sometimes called micro-economic) role is concerned with the allocation of economic activity via industrial, trade, innovation, education, transport, fiscal, environment, etc., policies, and the response of such activity to changes in demand and supply conditions. For a contemporary examination of the macro-organizational role of

government see Dunning (1992, 1994b), Stopford (1994) and Stopford and Strange (1991).

39 In other words, governments act to correct market imperfections rather than to prevent market imperfections.

40 As, for example, described in Dunning (1993) and Loree and Guisinger (1995).

41 Or what we have elsewhere described as the 'hassle' costs of doing business (Dunning 1992).

42 See, for example, Johanson and Vahlne (1977, 1990), Nordström (1991), Reid (1984), Welch and Luostarinen (1988) and Vahlne and Nordström (1992).

43 Although, in some thinking (e.g. Teece 1986), more stress is being given to the ways in which governments may affect the provision of complementary assets necessary to the efficient exploitation of the O advantages of firms. A recent paper by Kobrin (1993) also tackles the interface between networks and government behaviour.

44 Illustrations include the strategic trade policies of individual governments; the formation of regional economic blocs; and the role of GATT in setting the rules of the game for international commerce.

45 This may seem a strange statement, as governments have always acted as regulatory agencies, as well as initiating and monitoring the economic system, which is responsible for the allocation of scarce resources. But, rarely have governments attempted to optimally coordinate the alternative modes of organization of economic activity. Perhaps this is an impossible dream!

46 See, for example, Krueger (1990), Stopford and Strange (1991), Audretsch (1989), McKenzie and Lee (1991), Wolf (1988) and Osborne and Gaebler (1992).

47 The costs of government intervention have been extensively discussed in the literature; see especially Wolf (1988), Audretsch (1989) and Krueger (1990). For a more in-depth analysis of the comparative advantage of governments as organizing mechanisms (cf. unaided markets and hierarchies) see Wade (1988), World Bank (1993) and Hämäläinen (1994).

48 Of course, there have been various attempts by economists in the past to classify firms into groups, and for various reasons. Yet such terms as 'industry', 'strategic groups' and 'clusters' do not encompass the idea that firms become part of a larger entity in order to capture the external economies which are internal to the entity, and that they perceive this as a preferable way to advance their competitiveness than by engaging in vertical or horizontal integration. Marshall's concept of 'agglomerative economies' and the Japanese *keiretsu* system of relational enterprises come closest to what we have in mind.

49 To this extent, we do not agree with Porter (1990) that his analysis negates the validity of the concept of comparative advantage; but rather that it suggests that the components and determinants of that advantage have changed.

50 A good example is Richard Florida's analysis of the refashioning of the dominant micro-production system from mass production to knowledge production based (Florida 1995).

51 So called because particular spatial units have flourished despite the increasing mobility of firm-specific assets. Such mobility, however, needs to be set against the rising need of firms to use a group of complementary but regional-specific immobile assets. This makes for spatial embeddedness or stickiness.

52 For an alternative classification of relational structures, see Storper and Harrison (1991) and Miles and Snow (1992).

53 For a discussion of these views, see various chapters – and particularly the one by John Stopford in Dunning (1996).

REFERENCES

Amin, A and Thrift, N. (eds) (1994) *Globalization, Institutions and Regional Development in Europe*, Oxford: Oxford University Press.

Antonelli, C. (1991) *The Diffusion of Advanced Telecommunications in Developing Countries*, Paris: OECD Development Centre.

Archibugi, D. and Michie, J. (1993) *The Globalization of Technology: Myths and Realities*, Cambridge: Judge Institute of Management Studies, 1992–3, No. 18, May.

Archibugi, D. and Pianta, M. (1993) 'Patterns of technological specialization and growth of innovatory activities in advanced countries', in K. Hughes (ed.) *European Competitiveness*, Cambridge: Cambridge University Press.

Arrow, K. J. (1969) *The Organization of Economic Activity: Issues Pertinent to the Choice of Market versus Non-market Allocation*. Testimony presented to the Joint Economic Committee, 31st Congress, 1st Session, 'The analysis and evolution of public expenditures: the PPB system', Washington: US Government Printing Office.

——(1974) *The Limits of Organization*, New York: W. W. Norton.

Audretsch, D. B. (1989) *The State and the Market*, New York and London: Harvester Wheatsheaf.

Audretsch, D. B. and Feldman, M. P. (1994) 'External economies and spatial clustering', in P. Krugman and A. Venables (eds) *The Location of Economic Activity: New Theories and Evidence*, London: Centre of Economic Policy Research (CPER).

Bain, J. (1956) *Barriers to Competition*, Cambridge, MA: Harvard University Press.

Barney, J. B. (1986) 'Strategic factor markets: expectations, luck and business strategy', *Management Science* 32: 1232–41.

Bartlett, C. G. and Ghoshal, S. (1989) *Managing Across Borders: The Transnational Solution*, pp. 215–255, Boston: Harvard Business School Press.

——(1990) 'Managing innovation in the transnational corporation', in C. A. Bartlett, Y. Doz and G. Hedlund (eds) *Managing the Global Firm*, London and New York: Routledge.

Best, M. (1990) *The New Competition: Institutions of Restructuring*, Cambridge, MA: Harvard University Press.

Cainarca, G. C., Colombo, M. G. and Mariotti, S. (1988) *Cooperative Agreements in the Information and Communication Industrial System*, Milan: Politecnico de Milano.

Cantwell, J. A. (1992) 'The internationalization of technological activity and its implications for competitiveness', in O. Granstrand, L. Hakanson and S. Sjölander (eds) *Technology, Management and International Business: Internationalization of R&D and Technology*, pp. 75–96, Chichester: John Wiley.

Casson, M. (1991) 'Internalization theory and beyond', in P. J. Buckley (ed.) *Recent Research on the Multinational Enterprise*, pp. 4–27, Cheltenham: Edward Elgar.

Chamberlin, E. (1933) *The Theory of Monopolistic Competition*, Cambridge, MA: MIT Press.

Chandler, A. D. Jr (1962) *Strategy and Structure: The History of American Industrial Enterprise*, Cambridge, MA: MIT Press.

——(1977) *The Invisible Hand: The Managerial Revolution in American Business*, Cambridge, MA: Harvard University Press.

——(1990) *Scale and Scope: The Dynamics of Industrial Capitalism*, Cambridge, MA: Harvard University Press.

Chesnais, F. (1993) *National Systems of Innovation, Foreign Direct Investment and the Operations of Multinational Enterprises* (mimeo).
Coase, R. H. (1937) 'The nature of the firm', *Economica* (New Series) 4, November: 386–405.
——(1960) 'The problem of social cost', *Journal of Law and Economics* 3: 1–10.
Dierickx, I. and Cool, K. (1989) 'Assets, stock accumulation and sustainability of competitive advantage', *Management Science* 35: 1504–11.
Dosi, G., Pavitt, K. and Soete, L. (1990) *Technical Change and International Trade*, New York: Harvester Wheatsheaf.
Dunning, J. H. (1992) 'The global economy, domestic governance, strategies and transnational corporations; interactions and policy recommendations', *Transnational Corporations* 1: 7– 45, December.
——(1993) *Multinational Enterprises and the Global Economy*, Wokingham: Addison Wesley.
——(1994a) 'What's wrong – and right – with trade theory?', *International Trade Journal* IX(2): 153–202.
——(1994b) *Globalization: The Challenge for National Economic Regimes*, Dublin: The Economic and Social Research Council.
——(1997) *Governments, Globalization and International Business*, Oxford: Oxford University Press.
Durkheim, E. (1964) *The Division of Labor in Society*, New York: The Free Press (originally published in German in 1893).
Enright, M. J. (1994) *Regional Clusters and Firm Strategy*, Paper presented to Prince Bertil Symposium on *The Dynamic Firm, The Role of Regions, Technology, Strategy and Organization*, Stockholm, June.
Ethier, W. J. (1986) 'The multinational firm', *Quarterly Journal of Economics* 101: 806–33.
Feldman, M. P. (1993) 'An examination of the geography of innovation', *Industrial and Corporate Change* 2: 451–70.
Florida, R. (1995) 'Towards the learning region,' *Futures* 27(5): 527–36.
Gerlach, M. L. (1992) *Alliance Capitalism: The Social Organization of Japanese Business*, Oxford: Oxford University Press.
Grabher, G. (ed.) (1993) *The Embedded Firm*, London and New York: Routledge.
Gray, H. P. (1992) 'The interface between the theories of trade and production', in P. J. Buckley and M. Casson (ed.) *Multinational Enterprises in the World Economy*, pp. 41–53, Brookfield, VT and Aldershot, Edward Elgar.
Gray, M., Golob, E. and Markusen, A. (1996) 'Big firms, long arms, wide shoulders. The "hub and spoke" industrial district of the Seattle region', *Regional Studies*, forthcoming.
Gruber, W., Mehta, D. and Vernon, R. (1967) 'The R&D factor in international trade and international investment of United States industries', in R. Vernon (ed.) *The Technology Factor in International Trade*, New York: Columbia University Press.
Gustafsson, B. and Williamson, O. E. (1990) *The Firm as a Nexus of Treaties*, London and Newbury Park, CA: Sage.
Hagen, Jürgen von and Hammond, G. (1994) 'An empirical test of the Marshall/Krugman hypothesis', in P. Krugman and A. Venables (eds) *The Location of Economic Activity: New Theories and Evidence*, London: Centre of Economic Policy Research (CPER).
Hall, B., Breheny, M., McQuaid, R. and Hart, D. (1987) *Western Sunrise*, Hemel Hemspread: Allen & Unwin.
Hämäläinen, T. (1994) *The Evolving Role of Government in Economic Organization*, Newark, NJ: Rutgers University (mimeo).

Hanson, G. H. (1994) 'Increasing returns and regional structure of wages', in P. Krugman and A. Venables (eds) *The Location of Economic Activity: New Theories and Evidence*, London: Centre of Economic Policy Research (CPER).
Harrison, B. (1994) *Lean and Mean: The Changing Landscape of Corporate Power in the Age of Flexibility*, New York: Basic Books.
Harrison, B., Kelley, M. and Appold, S. J. (1993) *Spatially Distributed and Proximate Interorganizational Networks, Agglomeration and Technological Performance in US Manufacturing*, Pittsburgh: Heinz School of Public Policy and Management Congress, Mellon University Working Paper 93–120.
Henderson, V. (1994) 'Externalities and industrial development', in P. Krugman and A. Venables (eds) *The Location of Economic Activity: New Theories and Evidence*, London: Centre of Economic Policy Research (CPER).
Hoover, E. M. (1948) *The Location of Economic Activity*, New York: McGraw-Hill.
Horstman, I. and Markusen, J. R. (1987) 'Strategic investments and the development of multinationals', *International Economic Review* 28: 109–21.
Hotelling, H. (1929) 'Stability in competition', *Economic Journal* 29: 41–57.
Howells, J. (1990) 'The location and organization of research and development: new horizons', *Research Policy* 19: 133–46.
Hufbauer, G. (1965) *Synthetic Materials and International Trade*, pp. 145–232, London: Duckworth.
——(1970) 'The impact of national characteristics and technology on the commodity composition of trade in manufactured goods', in R. Vernon (ed.) *The Technology Factor in International Trade*, New York: Columbia University Press.
Johanson, J. and Mattson, L. G. (1987) 'Internationalization in industrial systems: a network approach', in N. Hood and J. E. Vahlne (eds) *Strategies in Global Competition*, Chichester and New York: John Wiley.
Johanson, J. and Vahlne, J. E. (1977) 'The internationalization process of the firm: a model for knowledge development and increasing market commitments', *Journal of International Business Studies* 8: 23–32.
——(1990) 'Management of foreign market entry', *Scandinavian International Business Review* 1(3): 9–27.
Keesing, D. B. (1966) 'Labor skills and comparative advantage', *American Economic Review* Papers and Proceedings 1965 Annual Meeting.
Kenney, M. and Florida, R. (1994) 'The organization and geography of Japanese R&D: results from a survey of Japanese electronics and biotechnology firms', *Research Policy* 23: 305–23.
Knickerbocker, F. T. (1973) *Oligopolistic Reaction and the Multinational Enterprise*, Cambridge, MA: Harvard University Press.
Knight, F. (1921) *Risk, Uncertainty and Profit*, Chicago: University of Chicago Press.
Kobrin, S. J. (1993) *Beyond Geography: Inter-Firm Networks and the Structural Integration of the Global Economy*, Philadelphia: William H. Wurston Center for International Management Studies, The Wharton School Working Paper 93–10.
Kojima, K. (1978) *Direct Foreign Investment: A Japanese Model of Multinational Business Operations*, London: Croom Helm.
——(1990) *Japanese Direct Investment Abroad, Tokyo: International Christian University, Social Science Research Institute, Monograph series 1.*
——(1992) 'Internalization vs international business approach to foreign direct investment', *Hitosubashi Journal of Economics* 23: 630–40.
Krueger, A. (1990) 'Economists' changing perception of government', *Weltwirtschaftliches Archiv* 126(3): 417–31.

Krugman, P. (ed.) (1986) *Strategic Trade Policy and the New International Economics*, Cambridge, MA: MIT Press.

——(1991) *Geography and Trade*, Cambridge, MA: MIT Press.

——(1994) 'Competitiveness: a dangerous obsession', *Foreign Affairs* 73(2), March/April: 28–44.

Krugman, P. and Venables, A. (eds) (1994) *The Location of Economic Activity: New Theories and Evidence*, London: Centre of Economic Policy Research (CPER).

Loree, D. W. and Guisinger, S. E. (1995) 'Policy and non-policy determinants of US equity foreign direct investment,' *Journal of International Business Studies* 26(2): 281–300.

Losch, A. (1940) *Die Raumliche Ordnung der Wirtchaft*, trans. *The Economics of Location*, New Haven, CT: Yale University Press, 1954.

Malecki, E. J. (1985) 'Industrial location and corporate organization in high technology industries', *Economic Geography* 61(4): 345–69.

Markusen, A. R. (1994) *Sticky in Slippery Places Space: The Political Economy of Post-War Fast-Growth Regions*, New Brunswick, NJ PRIE Working Paper No. 79.

Marshall, A. (1919) *Industry and Trade*, London: Macmillan.

McKenzie, R. B. and Lee, D. R. (1991) *Quicksilver Capital*, New York: The Free Press.

Miles, R. E. and Snow, C. C. (1992) 'Causes of failure in network organization', *California Management Review* 34: 53–72.

Myint, H. (1977) 'The place of institutional change in international trade theory in the setting of the underdeveloped economies', in B. Ohlin, P. O. Hesselborn and P. M. Wijkman (eds) *The International Allocation of Economic Activity*, pp. 367–86, London: Macmillan.

Nelson, R. R. (ed.) (1993) *National Innovation Systems*, New York and Oxford: Oxford University Press.

Nordström, R. (1991) *The Internationalization Process of the Firm: Search for New Patterns and Explanations*, Stockholm: Stockholm School of Business, IIB, Dissertation.

North, D. (1990) *Institutions, International Change and Economic Performance*, Cambridge: Cambridge University Press.

O'Brien, R. (1992) *Global Financial Integration: The End of Geography*, London: Pinter.

OECD (1992) *Technology and the Economy*, Paris: OECD.

Ohlin, B. (1933) *Inter-regional and International Trade*, Cambridge, MA: Harvard University Press (Revised Edition 1967).

Ohlin, B., Hesselborn, P. O. and Wijkman, P. M. (eds) (1977) *The International Allocation of Economic Activity*, London: Macmillan.

Ohmae, K. (1993) 'The rise of the region state', *Foreign Affairs* 72(2): 78–87.

——(1995) *The End of the Nation State: The Rise of Regional Economies*, London: Harper Collins.

Osborne, D. and Gaebler, T. (1992) *Reinventing Government*, Reading, MA: Addison Wesley.

Patel, P. and Pavitt, K. (1992) 'The innovatory performance of the world's largest firms: some new evidence', *Economic Innovation and New Technology* 2: 91–102.

Penrose, E. (1959) *The Theory of the Growth of the Firm*, Oxford, Basil Blackwell.

Piore, M. and Sabel, C. (1984) *The Second Industrial Divide: Possibilities for Prosperity*, New York: Basic Books.

Porter, M. (1980) *Competitive Behavior*, New York: The Free Press.

——(1985) *Competitive Advantage*, New York: The Free Press.

——(1990) *The Competitive Advantage of Nations*, New York: The Free Press.
Reid, S. D. (1984) 'Market expansion and firm internationalization', in E. Kaynak (ed.), *International Marketing Management*, pp. 197–206, New York: Praeger.
Robinson, J. (1933) *The Economics of Imperfect Competition*, London: Macmillan.
Rumelt, R. P. (1984) 'Towards a strategic theory of the firm', in R. B. Lamb (ed.) *Competitive Strategic Management*, Englewood Cliffs, pp. 556–70, NJ: Prentice Hall.
Schumpeter, J. A. (1947) *Capitalism, Socialism and Democracy*, New York: Harper & Row.
Scott, A. J. (1994) 'The geographic foundations of industrial performance', Paper presented to the Prince Bertil Symposium on *The Dynamic Firm, the Role of Regions, Technology Strategy and Organization*, Stockholm, June.
Stern, R. M. (1975) 'Testing trade theories', in P. B. Kenen (ed.) *International Trade and Finance*, Cambridge: Cambridge University Press.
Stopford, J. (1994) 'The growing interdependence between transnational corporations and governments', *Transnational Corporations* 3(1): 53–76.
Stopford, J. and Strange, S. (1991) *Rival States, Rival Firms: Competition for World Market Shares*, Cambridge: Cambridge University Press.
Storper, M. and Harrison, B. (1991) 'Flexibility, hierarchy and regional development: the changing structure of industrial production systems and their forms of governance in the 1990s', *Researcher Policy* 20: 207–422.
Storper, M. and Scott, A. J. (1995) 'The wealth of regions', *Futures* 27(5): 505–26.
Teece, D. J. (1977) *The Multinational Corporation and the Resource Cost of International Technology Transfer*, Cambridge, MA: Ballinger.
——(1986) *Profiting from Technological Innovation Research Policy* 15(6): 286–305.
——(1992a) 'Competition, cooperation and innovation', *Journal of Economic Behavior and Organization* 18: 1–25.
——(1992b) 'Foreign investment and technological development in Silicon Valley', *California Management Review* Winter: 88–106.
Thwaites, A. T. and Oakey, R. P. (eds) (1985) *The Regional Economic Impact of Technological Change*, New York: St Martins Press.
UNCTAD (1995) *World Investment Report 1995, Transnational Corporations and Competitiveness*, New York and Geneva: UN.
Vahlne, J. E. and Nordström, K. A. (1992) *Is the Globe Shrinking? Psychic Distance and the Establishment of Swedish Sales Subsidiaries During the Last 100 Years*, Stockholm (mimeo).
Venables, A. (1994) 'Equilibrium locations of vertically linked industries', in P. Krugman and A. Venables (eds) *The Location of Economic Activity: New Theories and Evidence*, London: Centre of Economic Policy Research (CPER).
Vernon, R. (1966) 'International investment and international trade in the product cycle', *Quarterly Journal of Economics* 80: 190–207.
——(ed.) (1970) *The Technology Factor in International Trade*, New York: Columbia University Press.
Von Thunen, J. H. (1876) 'Der Isolierte Stoat', English trans. in P. Hall (ed) *Von Tulden's Isolated State*, Oxford: Oxford University Press.
Wade, R. (1988) 'The role of government in overcoming market failure in Taiwan, Republic of Korea and Japan', in H. Hughes (ed.) *Achieving Industrialization in East Asia*, Cambridge: Cambridge University Press.
Weber, A. (1929) *Über den Standort der Industrien*, trans. *The Theory of Location of Industries*, Chicago: University of Chicago Press.
Welch, L. S. and Luostarinen, R. (1988) 'Internationalization: evolution of a concept', *Journal of General Management* 14(2), Winter: 34–55.

Wilkins, M. (1979) *Foreign Enterprise in Florida*, Gainesville: University of Florida Press.

Williamson, O. E. (1975) *Markets and Hierarchies, Analysis and Antitrust Implications*, New York: The Free Press.

——(1990) *Organization Theory*, New York: The Free Press.

Williamson, O. E. and Winter, S. G. (eds) (1991) *The Nature of the Firm*, Oxford: Oxford University Press.

Wolf, C. (1988) *Markets or Governments*, Cambridge, MA: MIT Press.

World Bank (1993) *The East Asian Miracle*, Oxford: Oxford University Press.

Part III

FDI, INDUSTRIAL RESTRUCTURING AND COMPETITIVENESS

8

RE-EVALUATING THE BENEFITS OF FOREIGN DIRECT INVESTMENT

INTRODUCTION

Thirty-eight years ago, the first comprehensive analysis on the consequences of inbound foreign direct investment (FDI) for a host country was published (Dunning 1958). The subject of study was the UK; since that date, similar investigations have been undertaken – with varying degrees of sophistication – for almost every country in the world.[1] Hundreds of books, theses and government reports, and thousands of papers in academic and professional journals have been written on the topic,[2] and scarcely a day goes by without some newspaper or magazine article lauding or denigrating the globalization of business activity.

Why, then, do we need to revisit the subject? Hasn't everything worth while already been said or written about the role of MNEs in economic development? Well, quite apart from its spectacular growth over the past decade,[3] we would offer two sets of reasons for the current resurgence of interest. Each reflects the changes in attitudes towards the costs and benefits of FDI which have occurred over the past twenty years: the first is by *countries* and the second by *firms* – and particularly by MNEs.[4]

THE CHANGING ATTITUDES OF COUNTRIES

In the mid-1990s, most governments are acclaiming FDI as 'good news', after a period of being highly critical – if not downright hostile – to it in the 1970s and early 1980s. There are a number of possible explanations for this change of heart. Some of these are set out in Exhibit 8.1. The first is the renewed faith of most countries in the workings of the market economy, as demonstrated, for example, by the wholesale privatization of state-owned assets, and the deregulation and liberalization of markets over the last 8–10 years. While these events are being most vividly played out in Central and Eastern Europe and in China, the need to remove structural market distortions has also been acknowledged in many other parts of the world – notably in the European Community, India, Mexico and Vietnam.

The second explanation is the increasing globalization of economic activity and the integration of international production and cross-border markets by MNEs (UNCTAD 1993). The third reason is that the key ingredients of contemporary economic growth of created assets, such as technology, intellectual capital, learning experience and organizational competence, are not only becoming more mobile across national boundaries, but becoming increasingly housed in MNE systems.[5]

Exhibit 8.1 The changing world of Foreign Direct Investment

(a) *From a country's perspective*

- Renaissance of the market system.
- Globalization of economic activity.
- Enhanced mobility of wealth-creating assets.
- Increasing number of countries approaching 'take-off' stage in development.
- Convergence of economic structures among advanced countries, and some industrializing countries.
- Changing criteria by which governments evaluate FDI.
- Better appreciation by governments of the costs and benefits of FDI.

(b) *From a firm's perspective*

- Increasing need to exploit global markets (e.g. to cover escalating R&D costs).
- Competitive pressures to procure inputs (raw materials, components, etc.) from cheapest possible source.
- Regional integration has prompted more efficiency-seeking investment.
- Growing ease of transborder communications and reduced transport costs.
- Heightened oligopolistic competition among leading firms.
- Opening up new territorial opportunities for FDI.
- Need to 'tap into' foreign sources of technology and organizational capabilities; and to exploit economies of agglomeration.
- New incentives to conclude alliances with foreign firms.
- Changes in significance of particular locational costs and benefits.
- Need to balance better the advantages of globalization with those of localization.

The fourth reason why governments are modifying their attitudes towards FDI is that a growing number of economies – especially in East Asia – are now approaching the 'take-off' stage in their economic development, and that, as a result, the competition for the world's scarce resources of capital, technology and organizational skills is becoming increasingly intensive. The fifth is that the economic structures of the major industrialized nations are converging, one result of which is that competition between firms from these nations is becoming both more intraindustry and more pronounced.

The sixth explanation is that the criterion for judging the success of FDI by host governments has changed over the years, and changed in a way which has made for a less confrontational and a more co-operative stance between themselves and foreign investors. More particularly, the emphasis of evaluating inbound MNE activity over the past two decades has switched from the direct contribution of foreign affiliates to its wider impact on the upgrading of the competitiveness of a host country's indigenous capabilities and the promotion of its dynamic comparative advantage. And the last reason is that the learning experience of countries about what MNEs can and cannot do for host countries has enabled their governments better to understand and assess its consequences, and to take action to ensure that it more efficiently promotes their economic and social goals.

The world economy in the mid-1990s is, indeed, a very different place from that of even a decade ago, and the changes which have occurred have had implications both for the responses of individual nation states to FDI and for the very character of FDI itself.

THE CHANGING BEHAVIOUR OF FIRMS

The events just outlined have also affected the attitudes, organizational structures and behaviour of business corporations. Such enterprises, for example, have found it increasingly necessary to capture new markets to finance the escalating costs of their research and development and marketing activities, both of which are considered essential to preserve or advance their competitiveness.[6] Cross-border strategic alliances and networks have been prompted for similar reasons, and to encapsulate the time it takes to innovate and learn about new products, processes and management cultures. Firms have no less been pressured to reduce the cost and improve the quality of their raw materials and components. As a growing number of countries are building their own arsenals of skilled labour and technological capacity, foreign investors are finding it more and more desirable to diversify geographically their information-gathering and learning capabilities. Competition in internationally oriented industries has become increasingly oligopolistic, while – as is described in more detail later – the nature of the competitive advantages of firms, and the factors influencing their locational choices, are very different in the early 1990s to those only a decade or so ago.

Finally, in the more complex global environment of the 1990s, MNEs are being forced to pay more attention to achieving the optimal balance between the forces making for the global integration of their activities, and those requiring them to be more oriented to, and sensitive of, localized supply capabilities and consumer tastes and needs – what Akio Norita of Sony has referred to as 'glocalization'. For, alongside the acknowledged benefits of globalization, there is a growing awareness, particularly among the citizens of smaller countries, of the need to preserve – and indeed promote, as a comparative advantage – their distinctive cultures, institutional structures, lifestyles, working relationships and consumption preferences. MNEs ignore these country-specific differences – which many observers (e.g. Naisbitt 1994) believe will become important in the future – at their peril.[7]

At one time, firms used to engage in international transactions primarily through arm's length exporting and importing. Today, the main vehicle is FDI and co-operative alliances. Initially, these latter forms of cross-border commerce were driven by trade; today, they largely determine trade. Outside the primary sector, upwards of two-thirds of the world's exports of goods and services are accounted for by MNEs, and 30–40 per cent of these take place within these same institutions – 60–70 per cent in the case of intangible assets such as technology and organizational skills (Dunning 1993a, UNCTAD 1993, 1994).

In the 1990s, MNEs are the main producers and organizers of the knowledge-based assets now primarily responsible for advancing global economic prosperity, and they are the principal cross-border disseminators of the fruits of these assets. It is true that the ambience of innovatory activities, the availability of risk capital and the educational infrastructure are strongly influenced by the actions of governments. It is true, too, that a myriad of small firms and individual entrepreneurs are significant seed-beds of new ideas and inventions. However, increasingly, economic progress is being shaped by the way new knowledge and organizational techniques are systematized and disseminated. Sometimes, the market system is able to perform this task satisfactorily by itself, but, because many emerging innovations are both generic and multi-purpose, and have to be co-ordinated with other assets to be fully productive, firms frequently find it beneficial to supplement or supplant external markets by their own governance systems. Sometimes, too, the efficient production and use of created assets requires firms to co-operate with each other, and even to be located in close proximity to each other.[8]

To some extent, this has always been the case. One of the earliest definitions of a business enterprise was that it was a 'coordinated unit of decision taking',[9] but, today, the firm is better described as 'a coordinator of a network of interrelated value-added activities' (Dunning 1993b). At one time, the boundaries of the firm were firmly determined by its ownership. Now, as Chapter 4 has suggested, they are much fuzzier, as their sphere of influence over the way resources may be used is being extended to embrace a variety of co-operative arrangements and networking agreements.[10] The more activities a firm pursues, the greater the number of coalitions it concludes with other firms, and the more countries in which it produces, then the more its global competitiveness is likely to rest on its ability to integrate these activities systemically.

The 'systemic' view of the MNE implies very different governance structures than those implemented by traditional foreign investors. Rather than acting as an owner of a number of fairly autonomous or 'stand-alone' foreign affiliates, each of which is expected to earn the maximum economic rent on the resources invested in it, the systemic MNE aims to manage its portfolio of spatially diffused human and physical assets – including those owned by other firms over which it has some property rights – as a holistic production, sourcing, financial and marketing system. Of course, there are costs of co-ordinating intra-and interfirm cross-border activities, and these will ultimately determine the extent and diversity of a firm's territorial expansion. But recent advances in international transport and telecommunication technology have pushed out these limits. In cases where corporations have shed some of their foreign assets, this has been mainly done to reduce the scope or range, rather than the geography, of their activities.

A final feature of the FDI of the 1980s and 1990s, which accords with the systemic view of MNE activity, is that probably as much as 90 per cent of it is currently undertaken by already established MNEs; that is, it is *sequential* rather than *initial* investment. This is not to deny that new MNEs are emerging all the time – probably at the rate of 4,000 to 5,000 a year,[11] and increasingly from developing countries, notably China – but, as yet, the total foreign capital stake of these companies is thought to be quite small. Now, research has established that *sequential* FDI – which, as far as a particular country is concerned, might be a first-time investment – is likely not only to be more geared to the interests of the rest of the investing company's value activities, but to generate its own unique costs and benefits – that is, over and above those generated by an initial investment (Kogut 1983, Buckley and Casson 1985). These essentially arise from the consequences of multinationality *per se*. They embrace such gains as those arising from the diversification of exchange risk and economic uncertainty, the spreading of environmental volatility, and the opportunity to exploit better the economies of geographical scope and specialization. They also include the costs of co-ordinating the activities and markets of foreign affiliates in widely different business cultures and political regimes (Kogut and Kulatihala 1988), and those associated with the setting up and sustaining of a cross-border network of intra-and interfirm relationships.

TYPES OF FDI AND COUNTRIES

Global economic events of the last decade or so, and particularly those driven by technological advances, regional integration and the refashioning of economic systems and policies, have fundamentally altered the perception of governments of host countries about how FDI may contribute towards their economic and social goals. These same events have also caused a reappraisal of firms of *why* and *how* – and, indeed, *where* – they need to engage in international transactions. It is for these reasons that the current generation of scholars – not to mention governments and firms – continue to want to know more about the benefits (and costs!) of FDI. To what extent and in what way is the global economy causing these to change; and what may national and regional administrations do to ensure that inward MNE activity contributes the most benefits it possibly can to their economic and social needs and aspirations?[12]

With these introductory remarks in mind, let us go on to make two very simple statements, which are probably as timely today as they were twenty years ago, and which policy makers concerned with assessing the benefits of FDI would do well to bear in mind constantly. We shall then proceed to elaborate on both of these statements:

The first statement is:

> **History and geography matter. Policy makers should seek to learn from their successes and failures of the past, and from those of other countries. But, they should not be slaves to these successes and failures. In the light of the perceived contribution of FDI, they should devise and implement the macro-organizational strategies most suited to their own unique situations and needs.**

The second statement is:

> **Policy makers should be cautious about expecting easy generalizations about the consequences of FDI. Not only will its effects vary according to the kinds of FDI undertaken, but they will depend on the economic and other objectives set by governments, the economic policies pursued by them, and the alternatives to FDI open to them.**

In order to focus better the rest of this chapter, let us assume that the principal criterion by which national administrations evaluate inbound FDI in the 1990s is by *its perceived contribution to the improvement of the competitiveness of the resources and asset-creating capabilities located within their areas of jurisdiction.*[13] This, indeed, is probably the single most important medium-to long-term economic objective of governments of most nations, and particularly of those which are most dependent on foreign-owned created assets and foreign markets for their prosperity.

How, then, might competitiveness of a country be advanced? Exhibit 8.2 identifies five main ways. The first is for a country's firms to produce more efficiently whatever they are currently producing, for example by reducing organizational costs and/or raising labour or capital productivity. The second is by the innovation of new, or the continuous improvement of the quality of existing, products, production processes, and of organizational structures and procedures. The third is by the reallocation of resources and capabilities to produce goods and services which are in better accord with the country's dynamic comparative advantage. The fourth is by capturing new foreign markets – providing this is cost effective. And the fifth is by reducing the costs, or speeding up the process, of structural adjustment to changes in global demand and supply conditions.

Exhibit 8.2 The five ways for a nation to upgrade the productivity and comparative advantage of its resources and capabilities

1 **Increase efficiency of its existing asset deployment by more effective quality control procedures,** e.g. by networking with other firms; by more cost-effective sourcing; by reducing lead times; by raising labour and capital productivity.
2 **Innovate new products, processes and organizational structures,** e.g. by improving national innovatory systems; by better exploiting the economies of the spatial clustering of related activities; by ensuring risk capital is available for start-up firms.
3 **Improve the allocation of its resources and capabilities,** e.g. from less productive to more productive activities, and towards those in which perceived dynamic comparative advantage is increasing.
4 **Capture new markets,** e.g. by improving knowledge about foreign markets and about customer needs and by better marketing and distribution techniques.
5 **Reduce the costs and/or increase the speed of structural adjustment,** e.g. by encouraging flexible labour markets; by enhancing the quality of retraining programmes; by minimizing bureaucratic inefficiencies; by appropriate fiscal and other incentives for industrial restructuring; by a greater willingness to accept, and adjust to, change.

The potential contribution of inbound FDI to each of these ways or vectors of upgrading competitiveness is fairly self-evident. It may provide resources or capabilities otherwise unattainable or only attainable at a higher cost. It may steer economic activity towards the production of goods and services deemed most appropriate by domestic and international markets. It may boost R&D, and introduce new organizational techniques. It may accelerate the learning process of indigenous firms. It may stimulate the efficiency of suppliers and competitors, raise quality standards, introduce new working practices, and open up new and cheaper sources of procurement. It may provide additional markets. It may better enable a host country to tap into, or monitor, the competitive advantages of other nations. It may inject new managerial skills, profession excellence and entrepreneurial initiatives and work cultures. It may encourage the formation of cross-border co-operative alliances, technological systems and inter-firm networking. It may foster the geographical clustering of related activities that generate their own agglomerative economies. In short, it may interact with the *existing* competitive advantages of host nations and affect their *future* competitive advantages in a variety of ways.

Some of these ways are summarized in a schema set out in Figure 8.1. This figure is an adaptation and extension of Michael Porter's diamond of competitive advantage (Porter 1990).[14] It suggests that inbound FDI may affect not only the four facets of the diamond, but the actions of host governments, and the mentality of competitiveness of the constituents in the host country. This it may do, for example, by injecting more

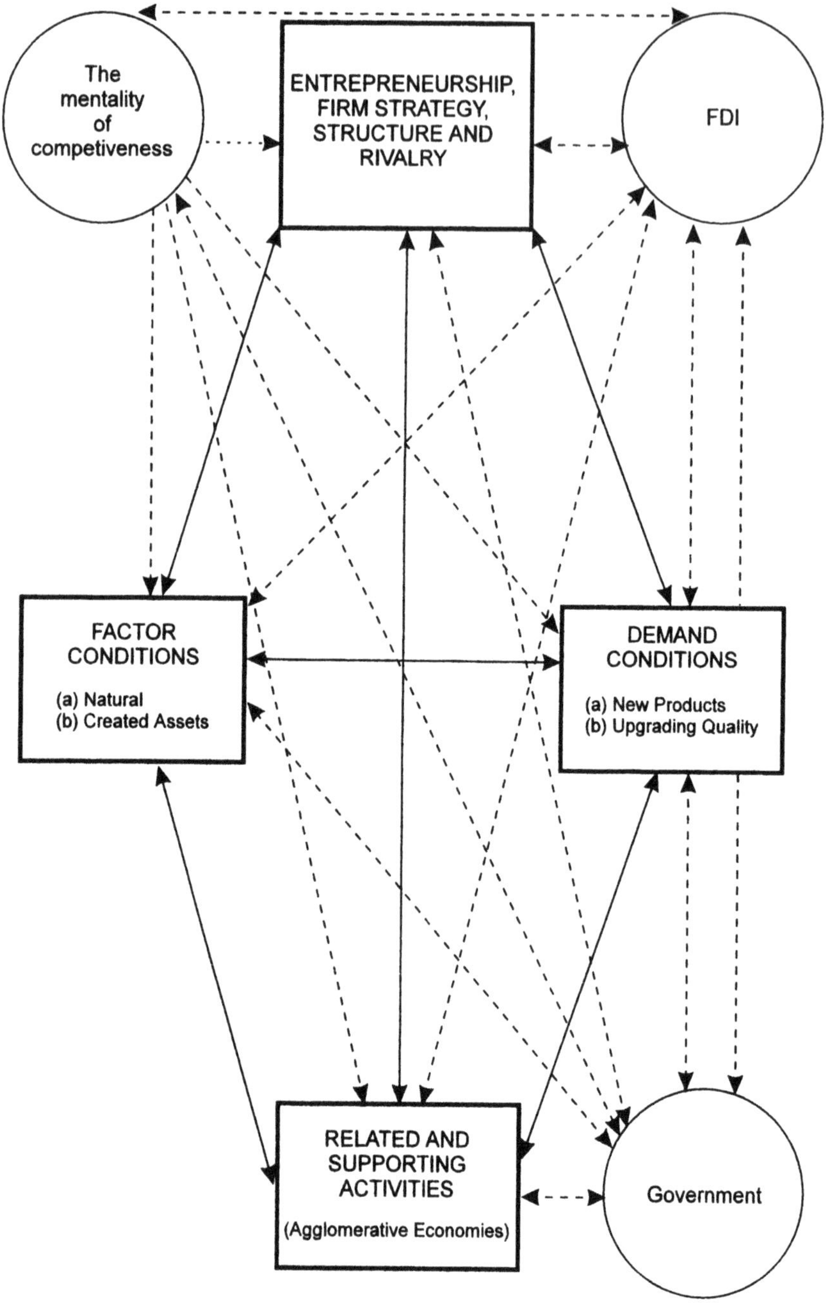

Figure 8.1 The diamond of competitive advantage
Source: Porter (1990) as modified by the author

market-oriented beliefs and practices by encouraging more harmonious labour relations, raising the quality standards expected by consumers.

It is worth noting that the significance of the individual attributes of the 'diamond' of competitive advantage may vary not only between countries, but within a particular country over time. Thus, for example, the relative importance of the production and efficient deployment of created assets, and the means by which these are transmitted over space, has increased as the world economy has become more globalized. Similarly, there are suggestions that the ways in which complementary activities are organized along the value-added chain, and the agglomerative economies to be derived from a spatial clustering of these and other related activities, are becoming more significant. By contrast, the optimum number of domestic firms competing in their home market is probably falling as the geographical focus of competition becomes more regional or global, while, with a few exceptions (e.g. oil-rich Middle Eastern states), the availability of domestic natural resources is probably a less critical competitive advantage than once it was.

We would be the first to accept that most of the competitive advantages just described are also available to domestic firms, but it is our contention that the unique attributes of FDI – and especially those which arise from the multinationality of the investing firms – offer financial, production, marketing and organizational benefits over and above those which indigenous firms may posses or can acquire.

At the same time, there are costs to a host country of inbound MNE activity. These can be divided into two groups. The first comprises various payments (e.g. profits, interest, dividends, royalties, management fees) which have to be made to attract the foreign investor or maintain the FDI. These will vary along a continuum. At one extreme, there are the payments below which a non-resident firm is unwilling to invest; and at the other, the payments above which a country is not prepared to accept the investment. The payments *actually* made will depend on the bargaining skills and negotiating power of the MNEs and of the recipient governments. These, in turn, will depend on the price which a host country would have to pay to acquire the benefits of FDI by alternative means, and the options open to the investing companies to locate their activities elsewhere. In the 1960s and 1970s, the main anxiety of host governments was that the monopoly power of foreign MNEs would enable the latter to extract unacceptably high shares of the value added by their affiliates. Today, the greater concern is that, without the inbound investment, host countries might be deprived of the advantages of being part of an integrated international production and marketing system (UNCTAD 1993).

The second type of cost associated with FDI arises whenever the behaviour of the investing firms, which is typically geared to advance their global objectives, is perceived to produce unwelcome consequences for the host country. These include the restrictions which a parent company may impose on the sourcing of raw materials and components by its affiliates, and the markets these affiliates may serve. The affiliates may also be limited in the range of products they produce, the production processes they employ, the amount and kind of research and development (R&D) they undertake, and the pattern of their networking with indigenous firms. Through transfer pricing manipulation, it is also possible that income earned in the host country might be syphoned off to the home (or some tax haven) country.

SOME DETERMINANTS OF THE BENEFITS OF FDI

What determines the net benefits of inbound FDI? What can national (and regional) governments do to ensure that such investment best contributes to the upgrading of the indigenous resources and capabilities within their jurisdiction? The short – but hardly satisfactory – answer is that it all depends on the kind of FDI, the conditions which prompted it, the existing competitive advantages of the host country, and the economic policies pursued by the host and other governments. But, fortunately, the economist can go a little further than this by identifying the situations in which a specific host country – or region within a host country[15] – is likely to gain the most from FDI, and, in suboptimal situations, what that country might do to increase this gain. In particular, we will argue that the benefits to be reaped from FDI critically depend on, first, the types and age of the investment, second, the economic characteristics of the host countries (or regions), and third, the macro-economic and organizational strategies pursued by host governments.

Types of FDI

Table 8.1 sets out the main types of FDI, the classification being based on the *raison d'être* for the investment. The first two, namely *resource-seeking* and *market-seeking* investments, represent the two main motives for an initial foreign entry by a firm – be it in the primary, secondary or tertiary sectors. The latter two embrace the two main modes of expansion by established foreign investors. These 'sequential' investments are frequently aimed at increasing the efficiency of the regional or global activities of MNEs by the integration of its assets, production and markets; these are called *efficiency-seeking* investments. However, sequential, and occasionally first-time, investments are increasingly taking the form of *strategic asset-seeking* investments, the main purpose of which is to acquire resources and capabilities which the investing firms believe will sustain or augment their core competencies in regional or global markets. These assets may range from innovatory capabilities, managerial expertise and organizational procedures, to accessing foreign distribution channels and a better appreciation of the needs of consumers in unfamiliar markets. Strategic asset-seeking

investment is frequently the most expeditious way of acquiring these kinds of competitive advantages (Wendt 1993).

Table 8.1 Four main types of foreign direct investment

1 *(Natural) Resource seeking* (a) Physical resources (b) Human resources 2 *Market seeking* (a) Domestic markets (b) Adjacent (e.g. regional) markets	Mainly motives for *initial* FDI
3 *Efficiency seeking* Rationalization of production to exploit economies of specialization and scope (a) Across value chains (i.e. product specialization) (b) Along value chains (i.e. process specialization) 4 *Strategic (created) asset seeking* To advance regional or global strategy (a) Technology (b) Organizational capabilities (c) Markets	Mainly motives for *sequential* FDI

In the 1960s and 1970s, most FDI was of the first or second types, although regional integration in Europe and Latin America was beginning to lead to some efficiency-seeking (or rationalized) FDI, particularly by large US MNEs in sectors like autos, consumer electronics and office equipment. There was also a small amount of strategic asset-seeking investment – usually by US firms which had not been among the first of their industry to invest in Europe, but, encouraged by the prospects of market growth, were seeking a speedy means of catching up with their rivals.

In the 1980s and early 1990s, FDI has been increasingly of the third and fourth type. Exceptions include first-time investments by MNEs from developing countries and a new generation of small and medium-sized MNEs from the First World. But, upwards of 75 per cent of all intra-Triad MNE activity since the mid-1980s has been by established European or US MNEs, and by Japanese companies, that, from the start of their internationalizing programmes, have sought to co-ordinate the deployment of their domestic and foreign assets. These firms have viewed each of their foreign affiliates, and frequently their associated suppliers and industrial customers, not as self-contained entities, but as part of a regional or global network of activities.

While FDI in developing countries – which in the period 1988–93 accounted for about one-third (UNCTAD 1994) of all new FDI (UNCTAD 1995) – remains primarily of a market- or resource-seeking kind, this, too, is changing. Increasingly, the liberalization of markets and regional integration in Asia and Latin America is enabling foreign MNEs to view their production and sourcing strategies from a regional, rather than a national, perspective. The subregion comprising the eastern coastline of China, Hong Kong, Taiwan and Indo-China is a case in point. More and more, too, many developing countries are being drawn into the hinterland of the globalizing firms from First World countries, as, in their bid to remain competitive, these firms are continually seeking new markets and cheaper, better-quality and more stable sources of supply.

However, unlike the 1960s and 1970s, most investments now taking place in developing countries by First World MNEs are not autonomous investments. Rather, they are part of an integrated network of activities (UNCTAD 1993). This means that the decisions of an MNE of *what to* produce in a particular country, *where to* source its inputs from and *who to* sell its output to, are based not only on the locational attractions of that country, *vis-à-vis* other countries, but on what is perceived to advance best the global interests of the corporation, rather than the interests of one of its foreign affiliates, or group of affiliates. *Inter alia*, and we shall return to this point later, this requires governments of host countries, in the formation and implementation of their domestic macro-economic strategies – and especially those which affect the decisions of foreign direct investors – to be cognizant of the strategies of governments of other countries whose firms are competing for the same resources and markets.

In Table 8.2, we identify some of the attributes of each type of inbound direct investment which are most likely to enhance the competitive advantages of recipient countries. In practice, the precise contribution of each type of investment will be both activity and firm specific. It is also likely to vary according to age of the investment – generally speaking, the local value added of a foreign affiliate is positively correlated with its age – and, perhaps most important of all, it will depend on the organizational strategies and economic policies adopted by the host government. We shall examine some of these strategies and policies later in this chapter, but, in compiling Table 8.2, we have assumed that they are broadly consistent with the dictates of the international market-place, and that they are primarily directed towards enhancing the dynamic competitive and comparative advantages of the resources and capabilities within their jurisdiction.

The conclusions of the tables, which summarize the research findings of scholars,[16] and the experience of national authorities, are self-evident. Each type of FDI has its own particular contribution to make to the five ways of upgrading competitiveness, identified in Exhibit 8.2 and the four facets of Porter's diamond illustrated in Figure 8.1. For example, by the resources and capabilities they transfer, and their transactions with domestic firms, both market- and resource-seeking FDI have the potential to raise the productivity of indigenous resources and capabilities, improve quality standards and stimulate economic growth. In the right circumstances, effi-

Table 8.2 Some likely contributions of different kinds of FDI to the upgrading of competitiveness of host countries

1 Natural resource seeking	(a) Provides complementary assets (technology, management and organizational competence)
	(b) Provides access to foreign markets
	(c) May or may not lead to local 'spin-off' effects on industrial customers, e.g. secondary processing activities
	(d) Raises standards of product quality
	(e) May or may not foster clusters of resource-based related activities
2 Market seeking	(a) As 1(a) above
	(b) Fosters backward supply linkages and clusters of specialized labour markets and agglomerative economies
	(c) As 1(d) and also raises domestic consumers' expectations of indigenous competitors
	(d) Stimulates local entrepreneurship and domestic rivalry
3 Efficiency seeking	(a) Improves international division of labour and cross-border networking; entices comparative advantage of host country
	(b) Provides access to foreign markets and/or sources of supply
	(c) As 2(b) above
	(d) As 1(d) and 2(e) above
	(e) Aids structural adjustment
4 Strategic asset seeking	(a) Provides new finance capital and complementary assets
	(b) As 1(b) above
	(c) As 2(d) above
	(d) As 3(a) above

ciency-seeking FDI can assist the host country to restructure its economic activities more in line with their dynamic comparative advantage; it can reduce the costs of structural adjustment; and it can foster more demanding purchasing standards both by industrial and personal consumers. Strategic asset-seeking investment may help integrate the competitive advantages of the acquired firm with those of the acquiring firm, and make for additional rivalry between domestic firms. However, this type of FDI, unlike the other three, may be undertaken with the specific purpose of transferring the assets acquired from the host to the home country, and this may work to the disadvantage of the competitiveness of the former country.[17]

The contribution of each type of MNE activity will also vary according to the part, or parts, of the value chain in which it is undertaken. In turn, investment in each part may be differently motivated. For example, some kinds of foreign-owned research and development (R&D) activities are truncated replicas of those of the parent companies; some are akin to efficiency-seeking foreign production; and some are designed to gain an insight into the innovatory advantages of the host country, and, where permitted, to participate in foreign research consortia.[18] This latter motive explains the presence of foreign MNEs in regional clusters of R&D activities in the United States, the EC and Japan. However, in general, inbound investment, providing it helps advance the dynamic comparative advantage of the host country, is likely to have its most beneficial effects where it is directed to those stages of the value chain where the potential for upgrading productivity is the greatest.

Spatial and country influences

What, then, are the important factors determining the location of MNE activity in the 1990s? How do they differ from those of twenty years ago? What determines the kind of competitive advantages offered by countries seeking to attract FDI? What should be the attitude and policies of national governments or regional authorities towards FDI in the light of globalization? And, how do these attitudes and policies differ from those displayed in the 1960s and 1970s?

In answer to the first question, Exhibit 8.3 sets out some generic spatial characteristics which scholarly research has shown to most affect the geography of MNE activity. These characteristics – each of which embraces a number of more specific cost- or revenue-determining variables – will impact differently on each of the kinds of FDI just described.[19] They are also likely to vary according to the industry[20] of, and the asset portfolios and stratègies pursued by, the investing firms.[21] And, their significance as inbound FDI determinants will also depend on the attributes of particular host countries, such as their size, stage of economic development, industrial structure, degree of economic interdependence with the rest of the world, and the physical and psychic distance from the main investing countries.

Most of these spatial characteristics and the industry-, firm- and the country-specific contextual variables which influence them are well known both to scholars and to business enterprises alike. Yet, in the past, the expectations of governments – and particularly governments of low-income countries – have been shattered because they have not sufficiently taken into account the uniqueness of their own resources and organizational capabilities. The benefits of inward FDI for Nigeria or Taiwan are unlikely to be the same as those for India; those now experienced by Chile and Vietnam are quite different from what they were ten to fifteen years ago; those currently gained in Malaysia and Botswana from efficiency-seeking FDI are scarcely comparable with each other; while those which result from market- and resource-seeking FDI are likely to be highly dependent on the

Exhibit 8.3 Some country-specific attributes affecting FDI by firms

1 THOSE WHICH CHIEFLY IMPACT ON DIRECT PRODUCTION COSTS AND BENEFITS

- Spatial distribution of natural resources, created assets and markets.
- Input prices, quality and productivity (e.g. labour, energy, materials, components, semi-finished goods).
- Investment incentives and disincentives (including performance requirements etc.).
- Comparative economies of centralization versus decentralization of different segments of value chain, (e.g. R & D, production and marketing).

2 THOSE WHICH CHIEFLY IMPACT ON TRANSACTION AND CO-ORDINATING COSTS AND BENEFITS

- Cross-border transport and communication costs.
- Artificial barriers (e.g. import controls) to trade in goods and services.
- Societal and infrastructural provisions (commercial, legal, educational, transport and communication).
- Differences in cross-country political ideologies, language, culture, business, customs and the ethos of competitiveness.
- Economic system and policies of host governments. The organizational and institutional framework for resource allocation.
- The opportunities to exploit the agglomerative economies of industrial districts.

Source: Adapted from Table 4.1 in Dunning (1993a)

development and macro-organizational policies of host governments, relative to those implemented by other governments competing for the same FDI.

With respect to the second question, the significance of the spatially related variables set out in Exhibit 8.3 has changed considerably over the last two decades. As their share of total production costs has declined, the drawing power of natural resources and unskilled labour has declined while that of created assets and the opportunities of networking with local firms has risen.[22] As the unique competitive advantages of MNEs have become both more mobile and systemic, so such firms have increasingly chosen to locate their value-added activities in countries which can offer the most cost-effective complementary assets, and the quality of infrastructural support which an integrated international production or marketing strategy requires. In this connection, intending investors usually place their need for state-of-the-art facilities for the cross-border transmission of information, technology and finance at the top of their locational priorities. An effective and trustworthy legal framework – particularly in its ability to enforce property rights and resolve contractual disputes – comes a close second. At higher levels of economic development, the quality of a country's educational and technological infrastructure becomes more critical.

More generally, as the organizational and transaction costs of economic activity have become relatively more important – and there is some evidence (Stiglitz 1989, Wallis and North 1986) that these are also positively related to the complexity of a nation's industrial structure – countries which can offer a business environment that is conducive to minimizing these costs are, *ceteris paribus*, likely to gain an increasing share of inbound investment. In the early 1990s, two surveys were conducted – one on the determinants of Japanese direct investment in UK manufacturing and the other on the location of international offices (Dunning 1991). In both surveys, variables related to transaction and co-ordinating costs, for example those to do with interpersonal relations, information asymmetries, language and culture, searching for and dealing with subcontractors, learning about the quality of communications and adapting to local business practices and customer needs, and bureaucratic controls were ranked considerably higher as investment determinants than were traditional variables related to production costs.[23]

Host government policies

The literature on FDI is replete with examples on the ways in which the actions of national governments might influence – for good or bad – the location and structure of MNE activities. In this chapter, we shall focus only on the main changes in host government organizational strategies, over the past two decades, which have most affected the level and distribution of FDI.

Foremost among these changes has been a softening in the attitudes of governments towards FDI. This has resulted in a widespread liberalization of policies which previously constrained FDI. These are described in UNCTAD (1995).[24] In addition, as we have already mentioned, the criterion by which most countries evaluate inbound MNE activity has shifted from its direct contribution to local value added to its longer-term consequences for the competitiveness of indigenous resources and capabilities. This reassessment has occurred at a time when governments – both of developed and developing countries – have been rethinking their own economic functions in the light of political changes and the globalization of the world economy. The most obvious manifestation of this rethinking has been a widespread deregulation and liberalization of markets and the privatization of many state-owned sectors, and the removal, or reduction of, a wide range of government-imposed market imperfections, for example subsidies, tariff and non-tariff barriers, price controls and all manner of rules and regulations.

However, the fact that governments have lessened their direct intervention in markets does not mean that they have abdicated – or indeed should abdicate – their responsibility as *catalysts* and *steerers* and monitors of wealth-creating activities, or as *facilitators* of the private enterprise system. Indeed, as firm-specific assets become more internationally mobile, while others increasingly take on the form of public goods,[25] the role of government as a co-ordinator of markets and hierarchies is becoming a more, rather than a less, critical one. Moreover, because of the demands of modern technology and competitive pressures, the organization of economic activity has become more pluralistic. This places additional responsibilities on governments to ensure the synergistic benefits from alliance or co-operative capitalism are fully exploited.

To a large extent, this reconstructed role of governments – be they subnational, national or supranational – reflects the changes now taking place in the relative efficiency of the different modes of organizing economic activity. The market – as a systemic organizational entity – has been reinstated and upgraded, except in the case of public goods and strategically sensitive products. The current philosophy is that decisions on what is to be produced in a particular country, and how it is produced, are best left to the collective will of thousands of firms and hundreds of thousands, or millions, of consumers. At the same time, this philosophy also presumes that, underpinning and sustaining the market as a resource allocative mechanism, is the visible hand of government. For without the complementary assets of an efficient and up-to-date legal, financial and commercial infrastructure, an educated labour force, an adequate transportation and telecommunications network, a strong anti-monopoly policy, a sound macro-economic policy, and a wealth-creating culture, the market cannot do the job expected of it. We believe that besides its various social and strategic responsibilities, it is the government's task to cultivate and support – though not necessarily undertake – all of these market-enabling activities.

Possibly, what we have so far written is not contentious. Indeed, the policy implications may seem all too familiar. However, the real challenge facing governments is how best to implement these policies. The particular point we wish to emphasize is that the globalizing economy of the 1990s is forcing national governments – be they large or small – developed or developing – to re-examine their domestic economic strategies, in the light of the fact that they are increasingly competing for competitive enhancing assets which are much more footloose than they used to be.[26] Macro-organizational policies which, at one time, only affected the domestic allocation and use of resources, are now as likely to affect trade, FDI and cross-border alliances as much as any tariff, exchange rate change or interest rate hike. If nothing else, the world economy of the 1990s is obliging governments to realign their domestic economic strategies more closely to the needs of the international market-place.

It is our strong contention that governments which are successful in reducing – or helping hierarchies to reduce – the transaction and co-ordinating costs of economic activity, and which best enable their firms to surmount the obstacles to structural change, are, *ceteris paribus*, likely to be the most successful, not only in attracting the right kind of FDI, but to do so at the least real costs. It is surely no accident that the countries which have recorded the most impressive economic performances over the last two decades are also those which have (i) designed and implemented a macro-organizational strategy consistent with upgrading the competitiveness and the dynamic comparative advantage of their location-bound resources, and (ii) ensured that the kind of inward FDI, which best advanced these objectives,[27] was attracted to their midst.

One final difference between the domestic economic policies now being required of governments in a world of increasingly mobile firm-specific assets,[28] and those practised in the 1960s and 1970s, is that, except for cultural or strategic reasons, there is little case for discriminatory action by governments, either in favour of, or against, inbound MNE activity. Though not always admitted, and except for particular types of incentives and performance requirements, most governments have downgraded the significance of FDI policies *per se*. Instead, they are preferring to re-examine the appropriateness of their general macro-economic and macro-organizational strategies *in the light of the globalization of the economic activity and the growing mobility of the critical wealth-creating assets, and on the understanding that FDI and FDI-related trade are the chief modalities by which countries are linked together.* It is, then, the interaction between these policies and the strategies pursued by MNEs that will determine the extent to which inbound FDI is able to upgrade a particular country's competitive advantage.

CONCLUSIONS; AND SOME CAVEATS

This chapter has sought to identify the main contributions which inbound FDI can make to the competitiveness of host countries, and the conditions which must prevail if that contribution is to be optimized. It has also reviewed the changes which have taken place over the past twenty years, in both the determinants affecting MNE activity and the attitudes of governments towards it.

Among the most important of these changes has been the emergence of the global economy, and the deeper structural integration of the world's markets and production systems. This new international division of labour, an integral part of which is the growing mobility of intrafirm intermediate products between countries, is demanding a reappraisal of the economic philosophies and policies of national governments. In particular, the widening locational options of MNEs and the convergence of the industrial structures and trade patterns of advanced countries are forcing national administrations to pay more attention to ensuring that the quality of their location-bound resources and capabilities do not fall behind those of their competitors.

In pursuance of these goals, governments have other critical roles to play, including the elimination of structural and institutional impediments to efficient resource usage; the active promotion of market-facilitating measures; and the encouragement of an ethos of competitiveness among their constitutents. It is the administrations which have gone the furthest in implementing these changes which have been the most successful, not only in attracting inbound FDI, but – much more important – in using it in a way which best advances its national interests in a globalizing economy.

However, we feel it is necessary to conclude this chapter by offering a couple of caveats to what has been written. The first caveat takes us back to some of the possible costs of FDI as a competitive enhancing vehicle. There is a saying, much beloved by Western economists, that there is no such thing as a free lunch. That means all good things have to be paid for; there is a price. This is certainly true of FDI; the only question is whether the price attached to it is a fair and reasonable one. One difficulty faced by many governments in formulating and implementing policies which affect the costs and benefits of inbound FDI is that they either do not have the knowledge, or are uncertain, about what these costs and benefits actually are. This is partly because most decisions, the outcome of which affects the behaviour of foreign-owned affiliates, are taken by their parent companies on the basis of information and expectations known only to them. This is not to say that these globally oriented decisions necessarily work against the interests of host countries, but it does make life more difficult for a government seeking to optimize the level and pattern of inward FDI and its effects on domestic competitiveness.

We might summarize the main points made in this chapter by reference to Exhibit 8.4, which sets out the main costs and benefits of FDI as have been experienced by host countries over the past two decades or more. The balance between the costs and benefits of each kind of contribution will vary according to the types of investment identified in Exhibit 8.1, to a variety of *firm*- and *industry*-specific features, some of which we have identified in this chapter, and to the age and nationality of the FDI. It will also depend on the characteristics of host countries – and especially, as we have seen, the policies of host governments. Some of these latter characteristics are set out in the third column of the exhibit.

A second caveat we wish to make relates to the nature of a country's competitiveness. As we will show in Chapter 10, the term competitiveness is a relative concept and it is used by analysts to compare the economic performance between firms, industries or countries, or that of the same firm, industry or country over time. However, whether a country whose firms are uncompetitive in the production of a particular range of goods or services should encourage inbound FDI to upgrade that competitiveness is a debatable point. Very rarely – if ever – can one country expect to be competitive in the production of all goods and services. Obvious examples

Exhibit 8.4 Some possible contributions of inbound FDI: the upgrading of the competitive advantages of host countries

Positive	*Negative*	*Host country characteristics which favour positive effects*
1 By providing additional resources and capabilities, i.e. capital, technology management skills, access to markets.	May provide too few, or the wrong kind of, resources and assets. Can cut off foreign markets, cf. those serviced by domestic firms. Can fail to adjust to localized capabilities and needs.	Availability of local resources and capabilities at low real cost, particularly those complementary to those provided by foreign firms. Minimal structural distortions or institutional impediments to upgrading of indigenous assets. Development strategies which help promote dynamic comparative advantage.
2 By injecting new entrepreneurship, management styles, work cultures and more dynamic competitive practices.	An inability of foreign entrepreneurship, management styles and working practices to accommodate to, or where appropriate change, local business cultures. The introduction of foreign industrial relations procedures may lead to industrial unrest. By the pursuance of anti-competitive practices, it may lead to an unacceptable degree of market concentration.	The policies pursued by host governments to promote local entrepreneurship and a keen and customer-driven work ethic; the character and efficiency of capital markets; the effectiveness of appropriate market-facilitating policies. Larger countries may find it easier to introduce some of these conditions than smaller countries.
3 By a more efficient resource allocation, competitive stimulus and spill-over effects on suppliers and/or customers, it can help upgrade domestic resources and capabilities, and the productivity of indigenous firms; it can also foster clusters of related activities to the benefit of the participating firms.	Can limit the upgrading of indigenous resources and capabilities by restricting local production to low-value activities, and importing the major proportion of higher-value intermediate products. It may also reduce the opportunities for domestic agglomerative economies by confining its linkages to foreign suppliers and industrial customers.	The form and efficiency of macro-organizational policies and administrative regimes. In particular, the benefits likely to be derived from FDI rest on host governments providing an adequate legal, commercial and assigning priority to policies which help upgrade human and technological capabilities, and encouraging regional clusters of related activities, e.g. science and industrial parks.

Exhibit 8.4 (cont)

Positive	*Negative*	*Host country characteristics which favour positive effects*
4 By adding to the host nation's gross domestic product (GDP), via 1–3 above, and by providing additional tax revenue for government.	By restricting the growth of GDP via 1–3 above, and by transfer pricing (TP) other devices to lower taxes paid by host governments.	See 1–3 above, and by suitable policies by the tax authorities of host governments to minimize TP abuse. Countries which have most to offer MNEs are likely to be more successful in implementing these policies.
5 By improving the balance of payments (b of p), through import substitution, export generating or FDI efficiency-seeking investment.	By worsening the b of p, through limiting exports and promoting imports and outcompeting indigenous firms which export more and import less.	Need to take a long view of importing and exporting behaviour of foreign affiliates. The key issue is not the b of p *per se*, but the contribution of FDI to economic efficiency, growth and stability. However, countries with a chronic b of p deficit may find it difficult to completely liberalize their b of p policies.
6 By better linking the host economy with the global market-place, and helping to advance economic growth by fostering a more efficient international division of labor (d of l).	By promoting a d of l based on what the investing firm perceives to be in its global interests, which may be inconsistent with dynamic comparative advantage, as perceived by host country.	As 3 above – and in particular the extent to which host country governments can pursue policies which encourage investing firms to upgrade their value-adding activities, and invest in activities which enhance the dynamic comparative advantage of indigenous resources. The gains from 6 are particularly important for smaller countries.
7 By more directly exposing the host economy to the political and economic systems of other countries; the values and demand structures of foreign households; to the attitudes to work practices, incentives and industrial relations and foreign workers; and to the many different customs and behavioural norms of foreign societies.	By causing political, social and cultural unrest or divisiveness; by the introduction of unacceptable values (e.g. respect to advertising, business customs, labour practices and environmental standards); and by the direct interference of foreign companies in the political regime or electoral process of the host country.	Extent to which society is strong and stable enough to adjust smoothly to technological and political change. Also, the strength and quality of government-determined regulations and norms; the nature of the host country's goals and its perceived trade-off between (e.g.) economic growth, political sovereignty and cultural autonomy. The difficulties in optimizing the benefits of the openness induced by FDI are likely to be greatest in countries which are most culturally distinct from their trading or investing partners.

include growing bananas in Iceland and producing sophisticated electronic equipment in Chad. One of the tasks of the international market-place – backed by the appropriate government policies – is to allocate resources and capabilities such that each country engages in the kind of economic activities to which it is *comparatively* best suited. FDI can play a useful – and sometimes a decisive – part in this process. What, however, it should not be used for is to 'prop up' activities which can never be internationally competitive. Resources must be directed to where they can be most productively used. After all, one of the functions of trade is to allow a country to import products which it is relatively unsuited to produce for itself and pay for these with products which other countries are relatively unsuited to produce. The success or otherwise of FDI in upgrading the *competitive* advantage of a country's resources and its *comparative* advantage in the international market-place should also be judged by this criterion.

NOTES

1 Of the more substantive studies, we might mention those for Canada (Safarian, 1966), Australia (Brash 1966), Norway (Stonehill, 1965), New Zealand (Deane 1970), the Netherlands (Stubenitsky 1970), Kenya (Langdon 1981), Singapore (Mirza, 1986), the United States (Graham and Krugman, 1989), India (Kumar 1990), Mexico (Peres-Nuñez, 1990) and Central and Eastern Europe (Artisien *et al.* 1993).

2 In 1991, the Center on Transnational Corporations (as it was then called) identified over 3,000 books, reports and articles published between 1988 and 1990 alone (UNCTC 1991).

3 As documented, for example, in various editions of *World Investment Report* and in Chapter 2 of this volume.

4 Some of these changes in attitudes and values are reflected in the publications of the UN Center on Transnational Corporations (now the Transnational Corporations and Management Division of UNCTAD in Geneva), since its inception in 1974. In particular, the initial focus on the actions of MNEs, which might constrain the sovereignty of national governments, has gradually been replaced by an examination of the ways in which host governments and foreign direct investors can work together to promote sustainable economic development and the competitiveness of domestic resources and capabilities. The contemporary mood which stresses the complementarity between governments, firms and markets is also echoed in several of the reports of the World Bank (see especially World Bank 1991, 1993).

5 The expression 'MNE systems' is used deliberately, because although there is a good deal of evidence that uninational – and particularly small to medium-size uninational – firms continue to play an important role in the generation of created assets, sooner or later these firms are forced into a network of complementary activities in which the larger MNEs act as the lead or flagship firms. This idea is further explored in Van Tulder and Junne (1988), Gugler and Dunning (1993), D'Cruz and Rugman (1993) and Harrison (1994).

6 This is especially so in the case of dynamic industries where product life cycles are shortening and the urgency to innovate new products and introduce more cost-effective production techniques is particularly intense.

7 For some illustrations of the failures of MNEs to acknowledge the significance of intercountry cultural differences, and for some ways in which MNEs may, themselves, build upon these differences to their advantage, see an excellent book by the ex-chairman of Smith Kline Beecham (Wendt 1993).

8 The gains of spatial agglomeration or clustering of related industries are one of the four critical variables influencing the competitiveness of firms and countries, as identified by Michael Porter (1990).

9 This definition was popularized in the 1930s, when the nature of the firm as an organizational unit was hotly debated among British economists.

10 These include strategic alliances and long-term contractual relations with suppliers. The widening scope of firms to control at least partially the use of resources and capabilities of other firms in which they have no ownership, and vice versa, is encouraging scholars to return to the idea of *groups* of related firms as a critical unit of micro-economic analysis.

11 Estimates of the universe of MNEs, and their affiliates, are constantly being revised upwards. The latest estimates by UNCTAD are that, in the early 1990s, there were at least 39,000 MNEs and 250,000 foreign affiliates (UNCTAD 1995).

12 While this chapter concentrates on the relations to inbound direct investment, an increasing number of governments are also reassessing the benefits of outbound direct investment. Indeed, as we have frequently stressed, the globalizing economy is forcing governments to take a more integrated view of outward and inward MNE activity, in exactly the way they do of international trade.

13 As, for example, usually measured by gross national product (GNP) per head or rate of increase in GNP.

14 For further details, see Dunning (1992). In our diagram, we have replaced Porter's 'chance' variable by a 'mentality of competitiveness' variable, as we believe this to be a more critically important country-specific factor, which not only is exogenous to each of the four attributes of the diamond, but is closely linked to the government and FDI variables.

15 Much of what is written in this chapter applies equally to the regional dimension of economic activity as to the national dimension. See Chapter 7 of this volume.

16 For a summary of these, see Dunning, (1993a). For a more recent empirical investigation into the impact of FDI on the manufacturing productivity of fifteen advanced industrial nations, see OECD (1994). This study showed that foreign-owned firms in these countries were typically more efficient than domestic firms in both absolute levels and in rates of productivity growth. The study also revealed that in ten out of the fifteen countries studied, foreign affiliates created new employment more rapidly than did their domestically owned counterparts.

17 But not necessarily, as much would depend on how the owners of the acquired firm spend the proceeds of the transaction, and how the location-bound resources released by the acquired firm are subsequently deployed.

18 For a recent examination of the structure of FDI in US R&D facilities, see Dunning and Narula (1995).

19 Thus, for example, artificial barriers to trade might encourage defensive market-seeking FDI, but deter efficiency-seeking FDI. Both resource- and efficiency-seeking investors are less interested in the size and character of the local market, which is the main concern of market-seeking investors. Investment incentives and disincentives have been found to be most significant in influencing efficiency-seeking FDI, while sequential investors are less likely to be concerned about cross-country ideological, language and cultural differences than first-time market-seeking investors. Strategic asset-seeking investors are unlikely to be

influenced by input prices or cross-border consumer transport costs to the same extent as are efficiency-seeking investors, while the opportunity to exploit scale economies is likely to be positively correlated with efficiency-seeking FDI, and negatively correlated with market-seeking FDI.

20 According, for example, to differences in input requirements, costs of transporting intermediate and final products, the extent to which products need to be adapted to local customer requirements, the advantages offered by networking with local firms, the behaviour of competitors, and the need to be sensitive to government mandates and policies.

21 Asset portfolios are the accumulated tangible and intangible assets which a firm owns, or to which it has privileged access. It is these portfolios, and the firm's strategic response to them, which will determine the kind and range of products it produces, the extent to which it is vertically integrated, the number and character of its associations with other firms, and the geographical distribution of its activities. In turn, the strategy of a firm will be affected by its age, size, organizational competences and long-term objectives.

22 Exceptions include some resource-seeking and manufacturing assembling investments in the poorer developing countries.

23 See especially Dunning (1991, 1992, 1993b, 1994).

24 Especially interesting are the policies now being introduced by the Indian government, although, of the larger developing economies, India still remains reluctant to embrace fully the FDI strategies of her eastern neighbours.

25 Examples include many capital- and knowledge-intensive products and those which, in their exchange, yield external costs and benefits, that is to non-market participants.

26 The idea of 'competing' governments has a very respectable intellectual heritage. It has, so far, been used by public choice economists to explain how individuals by 'voting with their feet' can act as a constraint to governments in the tax policies, and in the services they offer their tax payers. See, for example, Brennan and Buchanan (1985). But, the idea could be easily extended to explain how a whole range of actions by governments which affect the profitability of firms may also influence their locational preferences.

27 There are examples of countries which have attracted FDI, but have not grown, and vice versa. But, sensible macro-economic and macro-organizational policies have led to FDI being attracted to most competitive sections of the economy or those which are potentially the most competitive.

28 The fact that many firm-specific assets are increasingly mobile does not deny the fact that other vital created assets to economic prosperity are becoming less mobile, for example an efficient domestic and cross-border telecommunications infrastructure.

REFERENCES

Artisien, P. M., Rojec, M. and Svetlicic, M. (eds) (1993) *Foreign Investment in Central and Eastern Europe*, New York: St Martins Press.

Brash, D. T. (1966) *American Investment in Australian Industry*, Canberra: Australian University Press.

Brennan, G. and Buchanan, J. M. (1985) *The Power to Tax*, Cambridge: Cambridge University Press.

Buckley, P. J. and Casson, M. C. (1985) *The Economic Theory of the Multinational Enterprise*, London: Macmillan.

D'Cruz, J. R. and Rugman, A. M. (1993) 'Business networks, telecommunications and international competitiveness', *Development and International Cooperation* IX, December: 223–61.

Deane, R. S. (1970) *Foreign Investment in New Zealand Manufacturing*, Wellington: Sweet & Maxwell.

Dunning, J. H. (1958) *American Investment in British Manufacturing Industry*, London: George Allen & Unwin, reprinted by Arno Press, New York.

——(1991) 'Governments, economic organization and international competitiveness', in L. G. Mattson and B. Stymne (eds) *Corporate and Industry Strategies for Europe*, pp. 41–74, Rotterdam: Elsevier Science,

——(1992) 'The competitive advantage of nations and MNE activities', *Transnational Corporations*, February 1: 135–68,

——(1993a) *Multinational Enterprises and the Global Economy*, Wokingham, England, and Reading, MA: Addison Wesley.

——(1993b) *The Globalization of Business*, London and New York: Routledge.

——(1994) *Globalization: The Challenge for National Economic Regimes* (The Geary Lecture for 1993), Dublin: Economic and Social Council.

Dunning, J. H. and Narula, R. (1995) 'The r&d activities of foreign firms in the US', *International Studies of Management and Organization* 25: 39–74.

Gerlach, M. (1992) *Alliance Capitalism*, Oxford and New York: Oxford University Press.

Graham, E. M. and Krugman, P. R. (1991) *Foreign Direct Investment in the United States*, 2nd Edition, Washington, Institute for International Economics.

Gugler, P. and Dunning, J. H. (1993) 'Technology based cross-border alliances', in R. Culpan (ed.) *Multinational Strategic Alliances*, pp. 123–65, Binghamton, NY: International Business Press.

Harrison, B. (1994) *Lean and Mean: The Changing Landscape of Power in the Age of Flexibility*, New York: Basic Books.

Kogut, B. (1983) 'Foreign direct investment as a sequential process', in C. P. Kindleberger and D. Audretsch (eds) *The Multinational Corporation in the 1980s*, Cambridge, MA: MIT Press.

Kogut, B. and Kulatihala, N. (1988) *Multinational Flexibility and the Theory of Foreign Direct Investment*, Philadelphia: Reginald H. Jones Center for Management Policy, University of Pennsylvania (mimeo).

Kumar, N. (1990) *Multinational Enterprises in India*, London: Routledge.

Langdon, S. W. (1981) *Multinational Corporations in the Political Economy of Kenya*, London: Macmillan.

Mirza, H. (1986) *Multinationals and the Growth of the Singapore Economy*, New York: St Martins Press.

Naisbitt, J. (1994) *Global Paradox*, New York: William Morrow.

OECD (1994) *The Performance of Foreign Affiliates in the OECD Countries*, Paris: OECD.

Peres-Nuñez, N. (1990) *Foreign Direct Investments and International Development in Mexico*, Paris: OECD Development Centre.

Porter, M. E. (1990) *The Competitive Advantage of Nations*, New York: The Free Press.

Safarian, A. E. (1966) *Foreign Ownership of Canadian Industry*, Toronto: University of Toronto Press.

Stiglitz, J. (1989) *The Economic Role of the State*, Oxford: Basil Blackwell.

Stonehill, A. (1965) *Foreign Ownership in Norwegian Enterprises*, Oslo: Central Bureau of Statistics.

Stubenitsky, F. (1970) *American Direct Investment in Netherlands Industry*, Rotterdam: Rotterdam University Press.

UNCTAD (1993) *World Investment Report 1993, Transnational Corporations and Integrated International Production*, New York and Geneva: UN.

——*World Investment Report 1994, Transnational Corporations, Employment and the Workplace*, New York and Geneva: UN.

——*World Investment Report 1995, Transnational Corporations and Competitiveness*, New York and Geneva: UN.

UNCTC (1991) *Transnational Corporations: A Select Bibliography*, New York: UN.

Van Tulder, R. and Junne, G. (1988) *European Multinationals in Core Technologies*, Chichester: John Wiley/IRM.

Wallis, J. J. and North, D. C. (1986) 'Measuring the transaction sector in the American economy 1870–1970', in S. L. Engerman and R. E. Gallman (eds) *Long Term Factors in American Economic Growth*, pp. 95–164, Chicago: University of Chicago Press.

Wendt, H. (1993) *Global Embrace*, New York: Harper Business.

World Bank (1992) *World Development Report*, Oxford and New York: Oxford University Press.

——(1993) *The East Asian Miracle*, Oxford and New York: Oxford University Press.

9

THE INVESTMENT DEVELOPMENT PATH REVISITED

INTRODUCTION

This chapter considers the interaction between inward and outward direct investment, the role of governments, and the upgrading and restructuring of the indigenous assets of countries, from a dynamic or developmental perspective. It particularly examines the impact of some changes now occurring in the global economy on the nature and course of economic development and restructuring, and on the role which both governments and MNEs can play in influencing that development and restructuring.

SOME THEORETICAL ISSUES

The nature of the investment development path

The notion that the outward and inward direct investment position of a country is systematically related to its economic development, relative to the rest of the world, was first put forward by the present writer in 1979, at a conference on 'Multinational Enterprises from Developing Countries' which took place at the East West Center at Honolulu.[1]

Since then the concept of the investment development path (IDP)[2] has been revised and extended in several papers and books (Dunning 1981, 1986, 1988a, 1993, Narula 1993, 1996, Dunning and Narula 1994). The following paragraphs summarize the state of thinking on the nature and characteristics of the IDP.

The IDP suggests that countries tend to go through five main stages of development and that these stages can be usefully classified according to the propensity of those countries to be outward and/or inward direct investors. In turn, this propensity will rest on the extent and pattern of the competitive or ownership-specific (O) advantages of the indigenous firms of the countries concerned, relative to those of firms of other countries; the competitiveness of the location-bound resources and capabilities of that country, relative to those of other countries (the L-specific advantages of

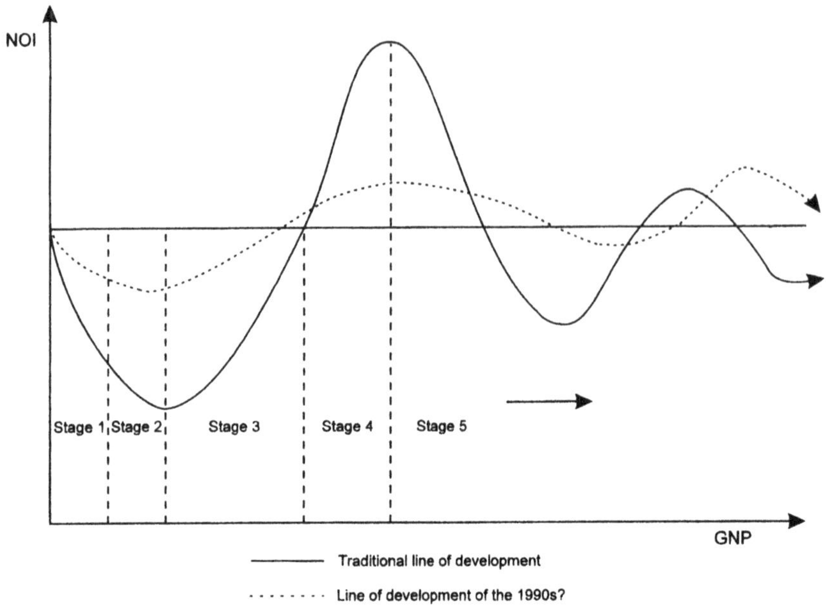

Figure 9.1 The pattern of the investment development path
Note: Not drawn to scale – for illustrative purposes only

that country); and the extent to which indigenous and foreign firms choose to utilize their O-specific advantages jointly with the location-bound endowments of home or foreign countries through internalizing the cross-border market for these advantages,[3] rather than by some other organizational route (i.e. their perceived I advantages).

A diagrammatic representation of the IDP, which relates the net outward investment (NOI) position of countries (i.e. the gross outward direct investment stock less the gross inward direct investment stock) – as a continuous line – is presented in Figure 9.1. We shall briefly summarize the main features of these stages, but pay particular attention to Stage 5, which we did not consider in our earlier writings.

Stage 1

During the first stage of the IDP path, the L-specific advantages of a country are presumed to be insufficient to attract inward direct investment, with the exception of those arising from its possession of *natural* assets. Its deficiency in location-bound *created* assets[4] may reflect limited domestic markets – demand levels are minimal because of the low per capita income – inappropriate economic systems or government policies; inadequate infrastructure such as transportation and communication facilities; and, perhaps most important of all, a poorly educated, trained or motivated labour force. At this stage of the IDP, there is likely to be very little outward direct investment. *Ceteris paribus*, foreign firms will prefer to export to and import from this market, or conclude co-operative non-equity arrangements with indigenous firms. This is because the O-specific advantages of domestic firms are few and far between, as there is little or no indigenous technology accumulation and hence few created assets. Those that exist will be in labour-intensive manufacturing and the primary product sector (such as mining and agriculture), and may be government influenced through infant industry protection such as import controls.

Government intervention during Stage 1 will normally take two forms. First it may be the main means of providing basic infrastructure, and the upgrading of human capital via education and training. Governments will attempt to reduce some of the endemic market failure holding back development. Second, they engage in a variety of economic and social policies, which, for good or bad, will affect the structure of markets. Import protection, domestic content policies and export subsidies are examples of such intervention at this stage of development. At this stage, however, there is likely to be only limited government involvement in the upgrading of the country's created assets, for example innovatory capacity.

Stage 2

In Stage 2, inward direct investment starts to rise, while outward investment remains low or negligible. Domestic markets may have grown either in size or in purchasing power, making some local production by foreign firms a viable proposition. Initially this is likely to take the form of import-substituting manufacturing investment – based upon their possession of intangible assets, for example technology, trademarks, managerial skills, etc. Frequently such inbound FDI is stimulated by host governments imposing tariff and non-tariff barriers. In the case of export-oriented industries (at this stage of development, such inward direct investment will still largely be in natural resource intensive sectors with some forward vertical integration into labour-intensive low technology and light manufactures) the extent to which the host country is able to offer the necessary infrastructure (transportation, communications facilities and supplies of skilled and unskilled labour) will be a decisive factor. In short, a country must possess some desirable L characteristics to attract inward direct investment, although the extent to which these can be effectively exploited will depend on that country's development strategy and the extent to which it prefers to develop the technological capabilities of its domestic firms.

The O advantages of domestic firms will have increased from the previous stage, wherever national government policies have generated a virtuous circle of created asset accumulation. These O advantages will exist owing to the development of support industries clustered around primary industries, and production will move towards semi-skilled and moderately knowledge-intensive consumer goods. Outward direct investment emerges at this stage. This may be either of a market-seeking or trade-related type in adjacent territories, or of a strategic asset-seeking type in developed countries. The former will be characteristically undertaken in countries that are either further back in their IDP than the home country, or, when the acquisition of created assets is the prime motive, these are likely to be directed towards countries further along the path.

The extent to which outward direct investment is undertaken will be influenced by the home country government-induced 'push' factors such as subsidies for exports, and technology development or acquisition (which influence the I advantages of domestic firms), as well as the changing (non-government-induced) L advantages such as relative production costs. However, the rate of outward direct investment growth is likely to be insufficient to offset the rising rate of growth of inward direct investment. As a consequence, during the second stage of development, countries will increase their net inward investment (i.e. their NOI position will worsen), although towards the latter part of the second stage, the growth rates of outward direct investment and inward direct investment will begin to converge.

Stage 3

Countries in Stage 3 are marked by a gradual decrease in the rate of growth of inward direct investment, and an increase in the rate of growth of outward direct investment that results in increasing NOI. The technological capabilities of the country are increasingly geared towards the production of standardized goods. With rising incomes, consumers begin to demand higher-quality goods, fuelled in part by the growing competitiveness among the supplying firms. The comparative advantage of labour-intensive activities will deteriorate, domestic wages will rise, and outward direct investment will be directed more to countries at lower stages in their IDP. The original O advantages of foreign firms also begin to be eroded, as domestic firms acquire their own competitive advantages and compete with them in the same sectors.

The initial O advantages of foreign firms will also begin to change, as the domestic firms compete directly with them in these sectors. This is supported by the growing stock of created assets of the host country due to increased expenditure on education, vocational training and innovatory activities. These will be replaced by new technological, managerial or marketing innovations in order to compete with domestic firms. These O advantages are likely to be based on the possession of intangible knowledge, and the public good nature of such assets will mean that foreign firms will increasingly prefer to exploit them through cross-border hierarchies. Growing L advantages such as an enlarged market and improved domestic innovatory capacity will make for economies of scale, and, with rising wage costs, will encourage more technology-intensive manufacturing as well as higher value added locally. The motives of inward direct investment will shift towards efficiency-seeking production and away from import-substituting production. In industries where domestic firms have a competitive advantage, there may be some inward direct investment directed towards strategic asset-acquiring activities.

Domestic firms' O advantages will have changed too, and will be based less on government-induced action. Partly owing to the increase in their multinationality, the character of the O advantages of foreign firms will increasingly reflect their ability to manage and co-ordinate geographically dispersed assets. At this stage of development, their O advantages based on possession of proprietary assets will be similar to those of firms from developed countries in all except the most technology-intensive sectors. There will be increased outward direct investment directed to Stage 1 and 2 countries, both as market-seeking investment and as export platforms, as prior domestic L advantages in resource-intensive production are eroded. Outward direct investment will also occur in Stage 3 and 4 countries, partly as a market-seeking strategy, but also to acquire strategic assets to protect or upgrade the O advantages of the investing firms (Dunning, van Hoesel and Narula 1996).

The role of government-induced O advantages is likely to be less significant in Stage 3, as those of FDI-induced O advantages take on more importance. Although the significance of location-bound created assets will rise relative to those of natural assets, government policies will continue to be directed to reducing structural market imperfections in resource-intensive industries. Thus governments may attempt to attract inward direct investment in those sectors in which the comparative O advantages of enterprises are the weakest, but the comparative advantages of location-bound assets are the strongest. At the same time, they might seek to encourage their country's own enterprises to invest abroad in those sectors in which the O advantages are the strongest, and the comparative L advantages are the weakest. Structural adjustment will be required if the country is to move to the next stage of development, with declining industries (such as labour-intensive ones) undertaking direct investment abroad.

Stage 4

Stage 4 is reached when a country's outward direct investment stock exceeds or equals the inward investment stock from foreign-owned firms, and the rate of growth of outward FDI is still rising faster than that of inward FDI. At this stage, domestic firms not only can now effectively compete with foreign-owned firms in domestic sectors in which the home country has developed a competitive advantage, but they are able to penetrate foreign markets as well. Production processes and products will be state of the art, using capital-intensive production techniques as the cost of capital will be lower than that of labour. In other words, the L advantages will be based almost completely on created assets. Inward direct investment into Stage 4 countries is increasingly sequential and directed towards rationalized and asset-seeking investment by firms from other Stage 4 countries. The O-specific advantages of these firms tend to be more 'transaction' than 'asset' related, and to be derived from their multinationality *per se*. Some inward direct investment will originate from countries at lower stages of development, and is likely to be of a market-seeking, trade-related and asset-seeking nature.

Outward direct investment will continue to grow, as firms seek to maintain their competitive advantage by moving operations which are losing their competitiveness to offshore locations (in countries at lower stages), as well as responding to trade barriers installed by both countries at Stage 4, as well as countries at lower stages. Firms will have an increasing propensity to internalize the market for their O advantages by engaging in FDI rather than exports. Since the O advantages of countries at this stage are broadly similar, intraindustry production will become relatively more important, and generally follows prior growth in intraindustry trade. However, both intraindustry trade and production will tend to be increasingly conducted *within* multinational enterprises (MNEs).

The role of government is also likely to change in Stage 4. While continuing its supervisory and regulatory function, to reduce market imperfections and maintain competition, it will give more attention to the structural adjustment of its location-bound assets and technological capabilities, for example by fostering asset upgrading in infant industries (i.e. promoting a virtuous circle) and phasing out declining industries (i.e. promoting a vicious circle). Put another way, the role of government is now moving towards reducing transaction costs of economic activity and facilitating markets to operate efficiently. At this stage too, because of the increasing competition between countries with similar structures of resources and capabilities, governments begin taking a more strategic posture in their policy formation. Direct intervention is likely to be replaced by measures designed to aid the upgrading of domestic resources and capabilities, and to curb the market-distorting behaviour of private economic agents.

Stage 5

As illustrated in Figure 9.1, in Stage 5, the NOI position of a country first falls and later fluctuates around the zero level. At the same time, both inward and outward FDI are likely to continue to increase. This is the scenario which advanced industrial nations are now approaching as the century draws to a close, and it possesses two key features. First, there is an increasing propensity for cross-border transactions to be conducted not through the market but internalized by and within MNEs. Second, as countries converge in the structure of their location-bound assets, their international direct investment positions are likely to become more evenly balanced. It has been suggested in chapter 5 and elsewhere (Dunning 1993) that these phenomena represent a natural and predictable progress of the internationalization of firms and economies. Thus the nature and scope of activity gradually shifts from arm's length trade between nations producing very different goods and services (Hecksher–Ohlin trade) to trade within hierarchies (or co-operative ventures) between countries producing very similar products.

Unlike previous stages, Stage 5 of the IDP represents a situation in which no single country has an absolute hegemony of created assets. Moreover, the O advantages of MNEs will be less dependent on their country's natural resources but more on their ability to acquire assets and on the ability of firms to organize their advantages efficiently and to exploit the gains of cross-border common governance. Another feature of Stage 5 is that as firms become globalized their nationalities become blurred. As MNEs bridge geographical and political divides and practise a policy of transnational integration, they no longer operate principally with the interests of their home nation in mind, as they trade, source and manufacture in various locations, exploiting created and natural assets wherever it is in their best interests to do so. Increasingly, MNEs, through their arbitraging functions, come to behave like mini-markets. However, the ownership and territorial boundaries of firms become obscured[5] as they engage in an increasingly complex web of transborder co-operative agreements.[6]

The tendency for income levels to converge among the Triad countries has been noted, among others, by Abramovitz (1986), Baumol (1986), Dowrick and Gemmell (1991) and Alam (1992). Indeed, during the 1970s and 1980s, Japan, the EC and EFTA countries have experienced a 'catching up' in their productivity and growth relative to the United States (the 'lead' country), while a range of the newly industrializing countries began to move from Stage 2 to Stage 3 in their IDP.

As a result of these developments, the economic structures of many industrial economies have become increasingly similar. Countries which were once the lead countries in Stage 4 now find themselves joined by others. This tends to reduce their NOI position and pushes them into Stage 5 of the IDP. At the same time, there has also been a 'catching-up' effect among MNEs since the 1970s. Firms that have had relatively low levels of international operations have been internationalizing at faster rates than their more geographically diversified counterparts. These two effects are not unrelated; firms have had to compensate for slowing economic growth in their home country by seeking new markets overseas. Given the similarity in income levels, the factors of production are broadly similar, and, as Cantwell and Randaccio (1990) have shown, firms that are trying to catch up seek to imitate competitors and develop similar O advantages as their competitors in the same industry, *but not necessarily in the same country.*

To take this argument a step further, as income levels, economic structures and patterns of international production among the Triad countries converge, the relative attractions of a particular location will depend less on the availability, quality and price of their natural assets and more on those of their created assets. It has been noted elsewhere that the prosperity of modern industrial economies is increasingly dependent on their capacity to upgrade continually, or make better use of their technological capacity and human resources (Cantwell and Dunning 1991). Since many of these advantages are transferable across national boundaries, it may be predicted that, in the long run, this should lead to a more balanced international investment position, and to an increasing convergence of created asset L advantages.

However, the ability of a country to upgrade its technological and human capabilities is a function of its own location-bound endowments and, in particular, of its natural assets, the characteristics of its markets and the macro-organizational strategies of its government. We believe the role of government in affecting dynamic economic restructuring cannot be overstated. In a myriad of ways, governments can promote new trajectories of economic growth which some countries are better able to cope with than others. This has been amply illustrated by the evolution of Japan's economy compared with that of the United States, especially in the 1980s.

In terms of their gross inward and outward direct investment positions, Stage 5 countries, after an initial burst of new inward direct investment (e.g. as occurred in the United States in the 1980s), may be expected to settle down to a fluctuating equilibrium around a roughly equal amount of inward and outward investment. Inward investment will be of two kinds. The first will come from countries at lower stages of the IDP and will be essentially of the market-seeking and knowledge-seeking type. The second will be from Stage 4 (or Stage 5) countries whose firms will continue to indulge in rationalized investment among themselves, as well as making outward direct investments in less developed countries, especially in the natural-resource-intensive sectors. In other words, truly rationalized or efficiency-seeking MNE activity will occur as plant and product specialization is encouraged in sectors where economies of scale and scope are important.

As the world economy begins to resemble a global village, strategic asset-seeking investments may also be expected to rise, and this, too, will lead to increasing convergence among countries as firms seek to improve their O advantages by cross-border mergers and acquisitions (M&As) or strategic alliances. Therefore, in the shorter time frame, inward and outward investment will fluctuate depending on relative innovatory and organizational strength of the participating countries. However as Cantwell has noted,

> The sectoral pattern of innovative activity gradually changes as new industries develop and new technical linkages are forged between sectors. Yet this is a slow process which in general only slightly disturbed the pattern of technological advantages held by firms of the major industrialized countries in the 20 years between the early 1960s and the early 1980s.
>
> (Cantwell 1989: 45)

Thus, *pro tem*, at least, it is possible for one country to be a net outward investor compared with another. But over time, according to the extent and speed at which created assets are transferable, the investment gap will again close, leading to a fluctuating investment position around an equilibrium level. It is within this context that the fifth stage will exist.

In other words, an equilibrium of sorts will be perpetuated, but it will not be a stable equilibrium as the relative comparative and competitive advantages of countries and firms are likely to be continually shifting. Hence, along with these fluctuations in relative comparative advantages, when combined with external and internal changes in the domestic economy, gradually the number of countries at Stage 5 will fluctuate.

The acquisition, diffusion and transfer of O advantages will be influenced by the cumulative causation in trade, production and technology, and whether the industry or sector in each of the countries at Stage 5 experiences a 'vicious' or a 'virtuous' circle (Dunning 1988b, Cantwell 1989). In the former case, it may serve to increase technological divergences between countries; in the latter, it may strengthen the technological linkages between them.

In summary, Stage 5 is marked by a gradual convergence of industrial structures among countries and a change in the character of international transactions. MNE activity, in particular, will be directed to efficiency-seeking investment with greater emphasis on cross-border alliances, mergers and acquisitions, and the governance and equity position of MNEs will become increasingly pluralistic. The success of countries in accumulating technology, as well as inducing continued economic growth, will depend increasingly on the ability of their firms to co-ordinate their resources and capabilities at a regional and global level. The economic convergence of industrialized countries on one hand, and high rate of intra-Triad FDI growth on the other, may be expected to foster regional and/or global integration as well as lessening the role of natural assets as a country-specific determinant of FDI. In Stage 5, governments will increasingly assume the role of strategic oligopolists, taking into account the behaviour of other governments in the formation and execution of their own macro-organizational strategies. In this stage too, governments are likely to play a more pro-active role in the fostering of efficient markets, and co-operating with business enterprises to reduce structural adjustment and other transaction costs.

We conclude. Beyond a certain point in the IDP, the absolute size of GNP is no longer a reliable guide of a country's competitiveness; neither, indeed, is its NOI position. This is for two reasons. First the competitiveness of a country is better measured by the rate and character of growth of GNP *vis-à-vis* that of its major competitors. Second, as the motivation of FDI has evolved away from being primarily geared to the exploitation of existing O advantages to the acquisition of new O advantages, countries which offer the appropriate location-bound resources for the creation of such advantages may increase their attractiveness to inbound FDI. Investments made to acquire or exploit indigenous competitive advantage, far from representing a weakness of the recipient country, could represent a strength. Certainly, recent evidence seems to suggest that in the Triad at least, inbound and outbound FDI are increasingly complementary to each other, especially at a sectoral level (UNCTAD 1993).

Most of the empirical testing of the basic proposition of the IDP, namely that there is a systematic relationship between a country's inward and outward investment and its GNP per capita, has used cross-sectional data, and is generally supportive of the proposition.[7] However, new cross-sectional and time series data – some of which are set out in Dunning and Narula (1996) – seem to be pointing to two things. The first is that the shape and position of the IDP probably varies much more between individual countries than it was originally thought. In particular, the economic structure of countries, and the development strategies and macro-organizational policies of governments, appear to be critical in influencing both the role of MNEs in a country's economy at a given moment of time, and how inward and outward direct investment may help fashion the growth and structure of the economy over time (Dunning 1993). The second is that the underlying nature of the IDP for all countries appears to be undergoing some change, owing to a series of events in the global economy, which leads us to revise some of our hypotheses about its trajectory. This issue is taken up in greater detail later in this chapter.

Country-specific factors and the IDP

As in previous contributions (e.g. Dunning 1986, 1993) we have written extensively about the interaction between inbound and outbound FDI and the level, composition and growth of the GNP of countries, we will need to add comparatively little at this point about country-specific factors. It may, however, be appropriate to remind ourselves that the IDP was first put forward to illustrate the relevance of the eclectic paradigm of international production in explaining the NOI position of countries. It follows, then, that any predictions about the IDP must rest on the contents of the paradigm itself.

Now, as stated earlier, the paradigm avers that a country will attract inbound FDI when (i) foreign firms possess certain O-specific advantages over and above those of indigenous firms; (ii) its L-bound resources and capabilities favour the deployment of these competitive advantages, relative to those offered by other countries; and (iii) foreign firms perceive that it is to their benefit to internalize the intermediate product markets for these advantages, rather than selling them via the external market, or by a co-operative arrangement, to domestic firms in the host country. Similarly the paradigm hypothesizes that the propensity of a country to be an outward direct investor will rest on the strength and character of the O advantages of its indigenous firms, and the extent to which these might best be exploited by adding value to them in a foreign location, and organized through an MNE hierarchy rather than through a non-equity relationship with a foreign firm.

The eclectic paradigm further suggests some of the ways in which, over time, inbound and outbound investment may affect the trajectory of a country's development path. This it might do by its impact both on the composition and productivity of domestic economic activity, and the ease or difficulty with which a country is able to restructure its resources and capabilities to meet the needs of endogenous and exogenous change. The critical role played by inbound FDI in the upgrading of Singaporean indigenous endowments, and that of outbound FDI in the dynamic restructuring of Japan's post-war development, are two cases in point, although other examples show that FDI does not always have such salutary affects on economic welfare.[8]

Over the past thirty years, there have been a large number of studies on the impact of both outbound and inbound MNE activity on the development and economic restructuring of the countries in which they operate. The overwhelming consensus of these studies is that, for good or bad, this is critically dependent on three main variables, namely (i) the type of FDI undertaken, (ii) the structure of the indigenous resources and capabilities of the countries concerned, and (iii) the macro-economic and organizational policies pursued by governments.[9] We would then expect the shape and position of the IDP of countries – which traces the interaction between inbound and outbound FDI and advances in the prosperity of those countries – to be determined by the same variables.

We have suggested that one of the characteristics of economic development identified by several writers (e.g. Porter 1990, Ozawa 1992, Narula 1996, Dunning and Narula 1994) is that, as development proceeds, the significance of indigenous assets relative to *natural* assets as a locational attraction to inbound FDI increases. Ozawa (1992), in describing the post-war development of Japan, identifies four distinct stages, namely those of labour-intensive manufacturing, scale-economies-based production of heavy and chemical industries, assembly-based mass production of consumer durables, and mechatronics-based flexible manufacturing. For his part, Porter (1990) writes about the nature of competitive advantages of a country according to whether they are factor driven, investment driven, innovation driven or wealth driven. While the prosperity of most poor countries is largely resource driven, that of the richest is largely innovation or wealth driven. Naturally, the precise balance of a country's natural and created assets will vary depending on the extent to which it is endowed with the former (cf. Canada with Japan, and Kuwait with Singapore) but as Ohmae (1987) has powerfully shown, even the value of natural resources such as minerals and agricultural products can be dramatically increased by secondary processing and astute marketing, both of which require the input of created assets.

In view of the fact that an increasing number of countries are now at the innovation stage of their IDP – indeed, as we shall suggest later, innovation-led production is changing the trajectory of global economic development – it is not surprising that both outward and inward FDI are being increasingly evaluated by national governments in terms of their perceived contribution to technological capacity and human resource development (Dunning 1994). Governments, too, are becoming aware that, if their FDI is properly to achieve their objectives, they need to provide the location-bound resources and capabilities essential for the efficient creation and deployment of the O-specific advantages of both foreign investors and their own MNEs. An appropriate combination of the competitive advantages of firms and countries is likely to make for a *virtuous* cycle of upgrading economic development, with each advantage fostering the other. An inappropriate combination of such advantages – or the lack of one or both – is likely to lead to a vicious cycle to the detriment of economic development.

Structural changes and the IDP

Let us now turn to the main focus of the first part of this chapter, which is to consider the ways in which recent technological and organizational changes, as they have impinged upon the governance of both firms and national economies, have affected our thinking about the shape and character of the IDP.

Some shifts in the rationale for FDI

Most of the received literature on MNE-related activity tends to assume that firms engage in FDI in order to exploit best, or organize more efficiently, their existing competitive advantages. Sometimes, these resources and capabilities are combined with foreign location-bound assets to supply domestic or adjacent markets, and sometimes to service more distant markets. In some instances, too, inbound FDI may be used to restructure the existing portfolio of foreign value-added activities by MNEs. Such sequential investment is best thought of as efficiency-seeking transborder activity, as contrasted with market- or resource-seeking transborder activity.

In the last decade or more, however, MNE activity has been increasingly motivated by the desire to acquire new competitive advantages, or protect existing advantages. Such strategic asset-acquiring FDI has been particularly pronounced within the Triad of advanced industrial countries, and is most dramatically shown by the spate of cross-border mergers and acquisitions (M&As) which have occurred since the mid- and late 1980s.[10] Essentially, such M&As have been (and still are) undertaken by firms for five main reasons: (i) the rising costs of innovation and of entry into unfamiliar markets, (ii) competitive pressures for firms to be more cost effective, (iii) the growing need to tap into complementary technologies and to capture the economies of scale and scope expected from the merger or acquisition, (iv) a desire to protect or advance their global markets, *vis-à-vis* oligopolistic competitors, and (v) the need to encapsulate the time of the innovating or market entry process.

Such strategic asset-acquiring FDI implies that firms may engage in outward FDI from a position of weakness, and that countries may attract inbound FDI because their resources and capabilities offer competitive advantages to foreign MNEs. Thus, part of the contemporary outbound MNE activity directed to the United States is designed to gain access to the technological capabilities of US firms, and their privileged access to US or adjacent (e.g. NAFTA) markets. Such FDI is likely to be determined by a different configuration of O and L advantages than those facing traditional market or resource-seeking MNEs.

The effect of strategic asset-seeking investment on the IDP is that it is likely to increase the level of outward investment of all countries, but particularly that from medium-income and fast-growing industrializing nations, as they seek to establish a speedy presence in the most innovatory and dynamic markets of the world. Frequently, firms from developing countries do not have the full range of resources and capabilities to promote a fully blown 'stand-alone' competitive strategy, and certainly not one which would help them penetrate unfamiliar global markets. Depending on their particular strengths and weaknesses, their liquidity position and the type of assets to which they need access, the mode of foreign involvement by firms is likely to vary between an FDI, a minority joint venture and some form of co-operative alliance. However, *ceteris paribus*, the first of these routes is most likely to be preferred whenever the assets sought are perceived to be critical to protect or advance the core competencies of the investing firms.

As yet, there has been little systematic research into the significance of strategic asset-acquiring FDI, relative to that of other kinds. But, taking inbound FDI in the United States as an example, it is generally agreed by scholars that, although the resurgence of activity by European firms in the 1970s and much of the greenfield investment by Japanese firms in the 1980s reflected the growing O advantages of these firms, relative to those of US firms, many of the transatlantic European M&As in the late 1980s and early 1990s have been geared towards strengthening the O advantages of the investing firms (or diminishing those of their competitors) by buying into US resources and capabilities, and/or markets. One suspects that had it been feasible, there would also have been a substantial amount of M&A activity by US and European firms in Japan during this period.

The presence of strategic asset-acquiring FDI is then tending to raise the level of inward investment of industrialized countries – and particularly those which are the leading repositories of advanced created assets. It is also tending to increase the outward investment of these countries – but not to the same extent as inward investment – while raising the outbound FDI by industrializing developing countries, as they seek to aid and accelerate the entry of their firms into global markets. In short, the presence and growth of asset-acquiring MNE activity is leading to a flattening out of the NOI position of countries, as compared with that suggested by the traditional version of IDP; namely, at lower levels of GNP the net *inward* investment position will be less, and at high levels of income the NOI position will be lower, than in the absence of such investment.[11] The suggested reshaping of the IDP is portrayed by the dotted line in Figure 9.1.

The emergence of alliance capitalism

Another feature of the last decade has been the growth in non-equity collaborative arrangements of one kind or another. Sometimes, these are being pursued as alternatives to FDI, but, for the most part, they are complementary to it. Increasingly, cross-border *intra*firm FDI and *inter*firm co-operative schemes are being perceived as part of a holistic and multi-modal strategy of the leading global players.

It is possible to identify many different kinds of collaborative schemes, but the vast majority fall into two categories. The first take the form of strategic alliances which are specifically intended to gain access (or preclude a competitor from gaining access) to foreign assets or markets. The second embrace a galaxy of international subcontracting relationships, in which interfirm co-operation goes beyond the production of materials, parts and components, to the design and development of new materials, parts and components. In each case, too, it would seem that the terms of any collaboration are contained less in a formal contract and more by a sense of agreed mission and mutual commitment.

It is the latter characteristic of interfirm relationships which has led to the coining of the term 'alliance' capitalism.[12] As we have seen, alliance capitalism differs from hierarchical capitalism in that, whereas in the case of the former, the co-ordination of economic activity is determined primarily by arm's length markets and interfirm co-operation, in the latter it is decided primarily by arm's length markets and hierarchical *intra*firm fiat.[13]

While alliance capitalism has long since been a prominent feature of many East Asian economies – most noticeably Japan and South Korea – in the mid-1990s it is spreading – albeit in a modified form – to other parts of the world. This is for three main reasons. The first reflects the lack of experience of hierarchical capitalism by the transition economies of Central and Eastern Europe and China. As these countries struggle to embrace the discipline of free markets, they are finding that the speediest and most effective way to upgrade their natural and created assets is for their newly privatized firms to form co-operative alliances with other domestic, or foreign, firms, rather than to pursue the route of internal economic growth. Second, it reflects the increasing inability of firms to pursue 'stand-alone' strategies in situations in which their core competencies need to be efficiently combined with those of other firms if they – the former – are to be fully effective.

Third, one of the features of the emerging techno-economic paradigm of micro-economic activity, namely flexible and innovation-led production, is that it requires a symbiotic and continuing relationship between the various participants in the production process, and that this is likely to be most effective if it is based on mutually agreed upon goals and on active and purposeful co-operation, rather than on administrative fiat. Thus, although many firms are currently downsizing the range of their activities in order to concentrate on those central to their core competencies, that is becoming *less* hierarchical, they are also concluding new strategic alliances with their critical suppliers and industrial customers along the value chain, and with their competitors across value chains. This they are doing both to leverage more effectively their own special capabilities and to ensure, by appropriate control procedures, that the goods and services they transact with other firms, and which critically affect these capabilities, are provided at the highest quality and/or the lowest cost.[14]

What are the implications of the advent of alliance capitalism on the international direct investment position of countries and their IDP? Perhaps the main implication is that such non-equity forms of cross-border production are becoming too important to be ignored in discussing the export and import of resources and capabilities, and the way in which their use is influenced either by hierarchical or by co-operative arrangements involving foreign firms. Here what scant evidence we have[15] suggests that, apart from situations in which inbound and/or outbound FDI is disallowed or regulated by governments, cross-border alliance formation to gain access to new technologies and markets, or to exploit the economies of scale and synergy, tends to involve a two-way exchange of resources and capabilities between firms from advanced industrial countries. By contrast, other kinds of alliances, and especially those which involve firms from both developed and developing countries, are primarily concluded in order to facilitate a transfer of resources and capabilities from the former to the latter countries.[16]

Incorporating such alliances into the IDP would then suggest that inbound transfer MNE activity[17] of the poor or middle-income countries would increase, but in the case of the richer countries, one might predict an increase of both inbound and outbound resource transfer. Unfortunately, apart from some data on cross-border interfirm royalties and fees, it is extremely difficult to quantify either the extent to which alliances *do* transfer resources and capabilities, or the consequence of such transfers on the welfare of the exporting and importing countries. As a subject for further research, the relationships between alliance formation, economic structure and development surely demand some degree of priority.

The role of non-market country-specific differences in explaining the IDP

In our earlier testing of the hypothesis that a country's outward and inward FDI is systematically related to its stage of development (Dunning 1981, 1986, 1988a), we identified a number of contextual variables which could explain why the shape and position of the IDP differs between countries. *Inter alia*, our research showed that industrial or industrializing countries were likely to generate more outward direct investment at any given level of GNP per head than the natural-resource-based economies.[18] At the same time, we made the general assumption that countries – or, more specifically, the governments of countries – pursued market-friendly economic strategies, and intervened as little as possible in the organization and allocation of resources within their jurisdiction.

In retrospect, it is clear that, throughout the last three decades, by a bevy of macro-economic and organizational policies, national governments have considerably affected the structure of the IDP of their countries. This they have done both by specific actions to influence the level and composition of inbound and outbound FDI, and by their general economic and social policies, which impact the attractiveness of their location-bound resources and markets to foreign investors. Moreover, notwithstanding the liberalization and deregulation of many markets over the past decade, national governments continue to exercise a powerful influence on a country's international investment position and the profile of its IDP.

Several country case studies contained in Dunning and Narula (1996) confirm this proposition. It is most obviously seen in the case of centrally planned and East Asian economies. But, as revealed by some quite dramatic shifts in the outward and inward FDI position of particular countries – which have often occurred as a direct result of a reorientation in government economic policy – it is no less evident in economies such as the United Kingdom, France, Sweden, Greece and Portugal in Europe; Chile, Columbia, Argentina, Jamaica, Mexico and Venezuela in Latin America; China, India, the Philippines, Vietnam and South Korea in Asia; Canada in North America; Morocco, Egypt, Nigeria and South Africa in Africa; and in Iran in the Middle East.

There is already a good deal of evidence that the liberalization and privatization of markets, and the attempts by many governments to increase inbound investment, have led to an increased flow and restructuring of inward investment into many countries, and, *pari passu*, an increased flow of outward investment from other countries.[19] It is also apparent that the role of national governments in affecting the price and quality of location-bound resources within their jurisdictions, and the motivation and capabilities of their own firms to be outward investors, is becoming increasingly significant – and especially in so far as inter-Triad strategic asset- and efficiency-seeking investment is concerned. Thus, for example, government policies which aim to upgrade the quality of indigenous resources and capabilities to meet the demands of the international market-place are likely to engage in more cross-border transactions (e.g. FDI, trade and co-operative alliances) than those which are designed to promote economic self-reliance.[20]

It follows from the above paragraphs that the relationship between FDI and income levels using cross-sectional country data may well be expected to vary at different points of time because of changes in the role of governments in affecting inward and outward investment. It is also likely to fluctuate according to the direction and character of technological advances and the country from which they originate. Such advances, by their impact on the competitive advantages of firms of a particular nationality, on the cost-effectiveness of the location-bound resources and capabilities of countries, and on the way in which economic activity is organized, are likely to lead to a repositioning of the IDPs of countries. At the same time, longitudinal data show that variations in the trajectory of a country's IDP may occur because of changes in the actions of national governments. In short, then, although we have some ideas about the interaction of the behaviour of governments and inward and outward investment, we need to explore this in a more systematic and rigorous way.

The theory: some concluding remarks

In this chapter, we have suggested that some of the propositions initially put forward to relate the inward and outward direct investment position of countries to their stages of development need reconsideration. Partly, we have argued that this is because the *raison d'être* and character of FDI has undergone some important changes. Partly it is because other forms of cross-border involvement – and notably co-operative arrangements – by MNEs need to be incorporated in the analysis; and that the interaction between these other forms and the stages of development may well be different from those of FDI. And partly we have suggested this is because differences in national government policies need to be more explicitly identified as an explanatory variable of the international direct investment of countries, before any satisfactory relationship beween outbound and inward investment and economic development can be established.

Lastly, we believe that further attention needs to be given to the form and characteristics of the fifth stage of the IDP, namely that in which the outward and inward investment positions – like those of exports and imports – fluctuate around the same level. Here the hypothesis is that the structures of the most advanced industrial economies are both similar and inextricably linked with each other. Although, for a period of time, one nation, through a series of path-breaking technological or organizational advances and/or superior macro-economic or macro-organizational policies, might gain a major competitive advantage over other nations, any marked increase in outbound direct investment may well be tempered by a corresponding rise in inbound strategic asset-seeking investment and alliance formation. Moreover, owing to the increasing ease at which knowledge, information and even organizational techniques can move across national boundaries, any lead by one country is likely to be quite quickly eroded by its competitors, and sometimes the catching-up process, itself, may be aided and abetted by inbound and outbound FDI and alliance formation.

However, little is known about the mechanism by which this is achieved. Some hints about the dynamic interplay between the O-specific advantages of firms and the L-specific advantages of countries have been given by Tolentino (1993), Dunning (1993) and Narula (1996), while Ozawa (1992) has explored some of the ways in which inbound and outbound Japanese FDI has affected the structure of Japanese economic development. The conditions under which inward and outward FDI[21] can promote the upgrading of a country's resources and capabilities and advantageously restructure its resource allocation have also been explored by several writers,[22] including Cantwell (1989) and Cantwell and Dunning (1991), who used the concepts of virtuous and vicious cycles to explore the interplay between inward FDI and the competitiveness of a particular industrial sector.

While some of the contributions in the Dunning and Narula (1996) volume take this discussion a little further, much remains to be done. Why, indeed, has inbound FDI promoted advantageous structural economic development in some countries (e.g. Singapore and Thailand) but not in others (e.g. Chile and Nigeria)? What determines whether outward direct investment helps a country to upgrade the quality of its indigenous assets, and to promote its dynamic competitive advantage, or, instead, to erode its technological strengths and human resource development? What is the impact of alliance capitalism on both the optimal mode of resource transfer and usage, and on the ways in which these may affect the structure and pace of economic development? It is questions such as these which need the attention of scholars in the years to come.

A STATISTICAL EVALUATION

Structural changes and the IDP

At the outset it is important to point out that any statistical evaluation of the IDP must necessarily be a tentative one. Any attempt to conduct a thorough empirical analysis of a complex and changing relationship has severe limitations. Given this fact, it is not our intention to develop a rigorous statistical specification and test of the IDP. In fact, our aim is almost exactly the opposite as we wish to demonstrate that a statistical evaluation of the relationship between FDI and economic development cannot be conducted on an aggregate basis across countries, as the IDP represents a paradigm which is idiosyncratic and country specific, and therefore best analysed on a country-by-country basis. We intend merely to argue that the basic relationships postulated by the IDP are still applicable, and how the lacunae regarding the extent and evolution of natural and created assets as well as the changes in the world economy affect the relationships suggested by the IDP.

Structural changes in the world economy

There have been two major developments in the world economy which have impacted the character of the IDP. The first is the introduction of Stage 5, which reflects the catching-up and convergence process of the industrialized economies. As we have discussed in the first part of this chapter and elsewhere (Narula 1993, 1996, Dunning and Narula 1994), as countries reach Stage 4 and begin to enter Stage 5, the activities and growth of their MNEs are no longer a function of just the economic conditions of their home country, but the various host countries in which they have subsidiaries. The more globalized the operations of a firm, the greater the extent to which its O advantages are likely to be firm specific, rather than determined by the economic, political and cultural conditions of its home country. Moreover, the O advantages of firms will increasingly be dependent on their ability to acquire and develop *created* assets and their ability to organize these assets efficiently in order to exploit the advantages due to common governance, making the MNE less dependent on its home country's natural resources. As such, O advantages become increasingly firm specific as MNEs become more internationalized. The consequence of this is that the outward direct investment position of a country's firms at this stage is no longer entirely dependent on the economic status and competitiveness of their home country, and increasingly affected by the conditions in the various other countries in which they operate. Therefore, after reaching a certain NOI position, a country's investment position will *not* necessarily be proportional to *its income level or relative stage of development*. To put it another way, we hypothesize that, *ceteris paribus*, a Stage 5 country will continue to experience change in its FDI position regardless of whether its relative stage of development or income levels change. This is readily apparent when examining the NOI position and GDPs of countries like the United States and the United Kingdom which have either remained at the same relative stage of development or fallen, but continue to experience high growth in both their inward and outward position. Indeed, not only has the share of total world-wide inward investment to industrialized countries increased, but a greater extent of outward investment from these countries is being directed towards other industrialized countries. (The current exception is the surge of FDI into China.)

Furthermore, the use of GDP as a proxy for development does not take into account the profound changes in the economic structure of the industrialized countries, which have shown a clear trend towards tertiary (i.e. service) sectors. In other words, while their overall economic growth has slowed over the past two decades, there has been considerable structural adjustment between sectors. This has also had an effect on the composition of their inbound and outbound FDI and, because of this, its geographical composition. Since 1980, for example, much of the growth in inward and outward FDI has been directed to the tertiary sector, and has been between industrialized countries (Narula 1996). These changes make a statistical evaluation of the relationship between NOI and GDP of Stage 4 and 5 countries an increasingly difficult exercise through an aggregate, cross-sectional test.

The growth of alternative forms of overseas value-added activity such as strategic alliances needs also to be taken into account, especially in high-technology sectors. As suggested in the first part of this chapter, strategic alliances have become an important means by which MNEs from industrialized countries have begun to engage in cross-border activities since the 1980s. The evidence suggests that there is an increasing preference for Triad-based MNEs to utilize non-equity-based co-operative agreements in preference to equity-based agreements (such as joint ventures) in their intra-Triad partnering activities in these sectors[23] (Hagedoorn and Narula

1994). Such agreements are naturally not reflected in the FDI data, and since well over 95 per cent of all strategic alliances[24] are intra-Triad in scope (Freeman and Hagedoorn 1994) the use of FDI data for industrialized countries without allowing for the growth of strategic alliances may make the results questionable.

The second consequence of changes in the world economy has been the growing divergence of at least some of the developing economies away from the industrialized economies. The catching-up process described earlier has not occurred among the poorer countries, who have diverged as a group from the wealthier countries and are not exhibiting a tendency to converge in relation to the world leaders (Dowrick and Gemmel 1991, Dowrick 1992, Verspagen 1993), and are in fact 'falling behind'. The effect on the FDI activities of developing countries is that less inward direct investment is from industrialized countries, and those developing countries that are outward investors prefer to invest in the industrialized countries, wherever possible, to acquire created assets. However, the 'falling-behind' effect is associated primarily with Stage 1 and 2 countries, while a handful of developing countries that are regarded as newly industrializing economies (Stage 3) have been shown to be 'catching up' with the industrialized economies. Indeed, data on FDI flows indicate that the four Asian NICs account for 57.6 per cent of total outward flows from non-oil-exporting developing countries between 1980 and 1990, and 83 per cent over 1988–90.

The idiosyncratic nature of countries

Most previous tests of the validity of the IDP have used a cross-sectional study across countries as a surrogate for longitudinal analysis. As various country studies in Dunning and Narula (1996) show, the exact circumstance of each country is unique, and while there are some general similarities between groups of countries, the explanatory power of the 'ideal' IDP based on cross-sectional analysis of a large group of countries is severely limited. This aggregation of countries for a given time period assumes that countries follow a broadly similar IDP, whereas, in fact, each country follows its own particular path which is determined by three main variables: (i) the extent and nature of its created and natural assets, (ii) its strategy of economic development, and (iii) the role of government. These factors essentially determine the nature and extent of the firm-specific assets of both foreign MNEs and domestic firms operating within its borders.

The character of a country's resource endowments

The extent and nature of a country's natural and created assets are determined by two main issues: (i) its resource structure and (ii) its size.

Resource structure

A country may possess a significant comparative advantage, or an absolute advantage, in primary commodities. Such a country is likely to spawn domestic firms that possess O advantages in the exploitation of such assets. However, especially if such an advantage is a near absolute one, it is likely to be the recipient of considerable inward investment from MNEs that wish to internalize the supply of primary products to their upstream activities located in other countries, and the extent of this inward investment will almost continue to rise as the other L advantages associated with the host country develop. These L advantages include the availability of skilled labour and other infrastructural facilities, and may lead to sequential vertical investment in upstream activities by both domestic firms and MNEs. As a result, a comparative advantage in a natural-resource-based industry may be sustained even when the income levels rise to developed country standards. Such a scenario would result in an NOI position that continues to be negative even when its economy is developed, as for example in Australia. Any outward investment would also tend to be in industries that are either in or related to the primary sector, but would be dwarfed by the increasing extent of inward investment. Such countries would tend to have a much lower (i.e. negative) level of NOI at considerably advanced stages of development.

The *lack* of a natural resource base (i.e. a comparative disadvantage in primary commodities) would, *ceteris paribus*, result in the opposite effect. Inward investment at earlier stages would be muted, and outward investment might begin at an earlier stage to secure the availability of necessary natural resources. Such a country is also more likely to begin strategic asset-seeking investment at an earlier stage (e.g. Japan). Overall, these countries would become net outward investors at a considerably earlier stage of development than well endowed with natural resources.

Market size

Countries that possess small domestic market size, such as Hong Kong, Singapore and Switzerland, are likely to have not just limited natural resources such as primary commodities, but limited attraction in terms of market size. Thus the lack of economies of scale will inhibit inward foreign investment in earlier stages. As their human capital and infrastructure improves, some inward investment may occur for export processing purposes. The small populations may mean not just small aggregate consumption, but that domestic firms would need to seek overseas markets in order to achieve economies of scale. This not only would result in outward direct investment at earlier stages of development, but also suggests that as income levels rise, domestic investors that were involved in export-oriented production will seek overseas locations to compensate for the shortage of low-wage human capital for labour-intensive production. Such countries will reach (and remain at) a positive NOI position at a considerably earlier stage of their development. The opposite scenario would apply for large countries, which would attract larger amounts of inward investment due to the attractions of their large markets, and domestic firms may not have as much incentive to seek overseas markets since economies of scale can be achieved at home.

The dynamics of the natural/created asset evolution are primarily determined by those associated with the economic, social and political environment issues that are generally a direct result of the actions of governments. A statistical analysis of the IDP cannot, given the static nature of a cross-sectional test, capture the dynamic development of created assets. The role of government is even more idiosyncratic and peculiar to each country, and it is exceedingly difficult to translate this into a general variable, or to group countries into distinct groups according to the role of governments in influencing the created/natural asset balance. However, since these issues are dealt with in considerable detail in the country studies in Dunning and Narula (1996), we will briefly discuss the two main issues that primarily influence the dynamics of created asset development.

Economic system

The economic orientation of a country may be outward looking, export oriented (OL–EO) or inward looking, import substituting (IL–IS) (Ozawa 1992). Depending on the orientation of an economy, the use of either (or a hybrid of the two) will substantially affect both economic development and the extent and pattern of FDI, and hence the nature of the path taken by a particular country. An OL–EO regime is likely to achieve faster growth and structural upgrading. Ozawa (1992) argues that an OL–EO regime is a necessary condition for FDI-facilitated development. We suggest here that although it is not a necessary condition for growth in the first two stages, the greater the extent of OL–EO policy orientation, the faster the process of structural adjustment and economic growth and the quicker a country's progress through the stages of the IDP. Our earlier discussion of the various stages assumes an OL–EO type of policy regime beyond the second stage, but not for the first two. IL–IS countries would tend to have relatively little inward and outward FDI activity.

The failure of countries to proceed beyond the second stage is associated with the vicious cycle of poverty (VCP). This, when applied in the traditional sense, is explained as follows: low income levels in less developed countries are associated with low savings rates which, in turn, result in low capital investment, thereby keeping income levels low. In the parlance of the eclectic paradigm there is a lack of ownership advantages of domestic firms and location advantages of the country, as well as an inability to develop or acquire these. The O advantages referred to here include financial assets as well as the Oa and Ot types of advantages, whereas the L advantages are those of infrastructure. This cycle can be broken, *inter alia*, through the infusion of capital through FDI, which allows for technological spillovers and financial capital.

Governments and organizations of economic activity

Although the kind of economic system associated with a country broadly determines the path taken by a country, the nature of government policy associated with a particular system can vary between countries with the same economic system and at the same stage of development. There are two main areas of government strategy which directly impinge on the nature of the IDP of a country: macro-economic strategy and macro-organizational strategy (Dunning 1992). The role of governments in determining macro-economic policy is relatively well defined, and is often associated with the economic system. On the other hand, there is considerable variance among countries in the role of governments in determining macro-organizational strategy. Macro-organizational strategy primarily influences the structure and organization of economic activity, and the nature of the policies most appropriate at a particular stage should, in an 'ideal' situation, change as the economy evolves, reflecting the nature of market imperfections that the policy is designed to circumvent (Hämäläinen 1993). Essentially, in such a best-world scenario, government plays a market-facilitating role in its macro-organizational policy dynamically evolves over time. Increasing economic specialisation associated with economic development leads to a growth in market failures and increases the potential benefits of government macro-organizational policy (Durkheim 1964). However, as Hämäläinen (1993) points out, governments may also fail, and society is often faced with a choice between imperfect markets and imperfect governments. Given that macro-organizational policy embraces a wide variety of issues,[25] and the fact that there is little agreement on what the optimal involvement of government should be, the macro-organizational policy stance varies widely among countries. The differences between the macro-organizational strategy of countries at the same stage of development influence both the structure of markets and the extent to which economic activity is efficiently conducted, thereby affecting the specialization and economic structure of the country, as well as the extent of FDI activity associated with it.

Evaluating the IDP

As we have earlier indicated, it is not our intention to develop a rigorous specification of the IDP, but merely to examine whether a causal relationship exists between FDI and economic development for 1992, and to illustrate the deviation from the 'ideal' path due to the extent of natural and created assets, as well as those due to structural changes in the world economy. We shall utilize data on FDI stocks published in UNCTAD (1994). GDP and population data are derived from World Bank (1994). All data are in nominal US dollars. All FDI and GDP figures are normalized by population. Inward FDI per capita is denoted as IWK, outward FDI as OWK, NOI per capita as NOIK, and GDP per capita is denoted as GDPK. In conducting the analysis, we shall also attempt to illustrate that the nature of the relationship varies with the extent of natural and created assets associated with a country.

The extent of natural/created assets is based on a twofold criterion to allow for differences due to resources intensity as well as differences in country size. High natural asset countries are defined as those countries whose primary exports as a percentage of total exports (PRX) are greater than or equal to 50 per cent or whose area is greater than 1.9 million km^2.[26] Since most developing countries tend to have a comparative advantage in primary commodities, the sample tends to consist largely of this group of countries. Although it would be more appropriate to include only those countries which have an absolute advantage in natural resources, rather than those with a comparative advantage, it is exceedingly difficult to find such measure. Low natural asset countries are assumed to represent countries with a high created asset base, or have a potential to become economies with a created asset base. This group is defined as countries for which PRX $\leqslant$ 20 per cent or area is less than 5,000 km^2.

Net outward investment

We examine the relationship between NOI and GDP utilizing a quadratic specification. This allows for the fact that the dependent variable changes over time and stages, but it also assumes that the rate of change is more or less constant. Apart from running regressions for the entire sample (ALL) we also do so for a smaller subsample that excludes the most industrialized countries. This has two purposes. First, since we have not developed a specification for the fifth stage of the IDP, by excluding the countries that are most likely to be in Stage 5, we are able to test whether in fact the J-curve initially proposed by Dunning (1981) is still valid for the pre-Stage 5 countries. Second, by excluding the Stage 5 countries we are able to avoid 'stretching' of the IDP due to the cluster of a large number of developing countries at the origin and the spread of the industrialized countries around the *X*-axis, due to the process of convergence and divergence. This would make the second NOI = 0 point be further to the right than might actually be the case. The cut-off point for this sample is taken to be the first industrialized country with an NOI > 0. Figure 9.2 shows the plot of NOI per capita against GDP per capita for 1992. We also run regressions

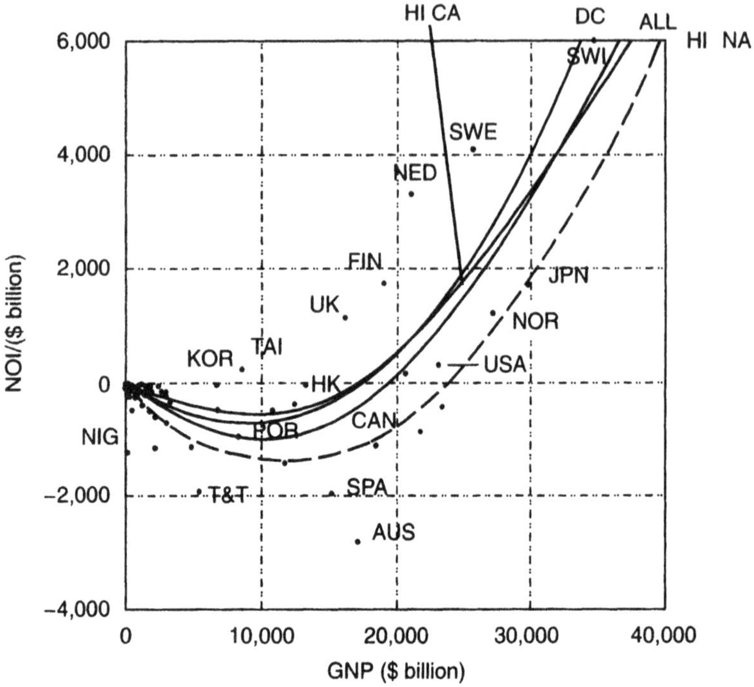

Figure 9.2 Net outward investment and GDP of selected countries, 1992
Source: as for Table 9.2

for two other subsamples, the created asset countries (HI CA) and the natural asset countries (HI NA). These four curves have been superimposed on Figure 9.2 while the results of these regressions are given in Table 9.1. We have not included the results for 1980 here since these are broadly similar to those for 1992. None the less, there are broad differences in the distribution of the observations for the developing countries and the industrialized countries that are due to the catching-up and falling-behind scenarios due to convergence and divergence which have been evaluated using some simple measures in Table 9.2. In the case of the industrialized countries, which dominate much of the graph, there has been an increasing trend towards a wider distribution along the *Y*-axis since 1980. The mean NOI has become more positive, increasing by a factor of 10.2, while the mean GDP has increased by a factor of just 2.1. Furthermore, the ratio of the standard deviation to the mean of NOI has fallen from 9.2 in 1980 to 2.4 in 1992 for industrialized countries, while this ratio for GDP have remained constant at 0.2. This suggests that convergence phenomena regarding GDP have halted, while the NOI positions of these countries have become increasing similar.

The high growth rate of NOI relative to GDP for the industrialized countries can be contrasted with that of the non- industrial countries (Table

Table 9.1 Linear regression equations for NOI with GDP based on a quadratic statistical relationship

Sample	*GDPK*	*GDPK²*	*ADJ.R²*	*F-value*	*N*
ALL	−0.1872***	0.957×10^{-5}***	0.542	51.69	88
DC	−0.1767***	0.102×10^{-4}***	0.418	26.35	73
NA	−0.2292***	0.962×10^{-5}***	0.582	36.64	53
CA	−0.1329**	0.789×10^{-5}***	0.579	16.33	24

*** Significant at the 1% level
** Significant at the 2.5% level

Table 9.2 International direct investment and GDP for selected countries, 1980 and 1992

	1980			*1992*				
	Mean ($ billion)	*Standard deviation*	*Ratio*	*Mean ($ billion)*	*Standard deviation*	*Ratio*	*Ratio of means*	*Ratio of standard deviations*
	(i)	(ii)	(i)/(ii)	(iii)	(iv)	(iii)/(iv)	(i)/(iii)	(ii)/(iv)
All countries								
Inward FDI	246	386	1.6	783	1,263	1.6	3.2	3.3
Outward FDI	164	533	3.2	721	1,783	2.5	4.4	3.3
NOI	−84	402	−4.8	−62	1,076	−17.4	0.7	2.7
GDP	3,453	4,200	1.2	6,231	8,717	1.4	1.8	2.1
Industrialized countries								
Inward FDI	749	525	0.7	2,671	1,746	0.7	3.6	3.3
Outward FDI	837	985	1.2	3,562	2,717	0.8	4.3	2.8
NOI	87	804	9.2	890	2,157	2.4	10.2	2.7
GDP	10,919	2,167	0.2	22,816	4,804	0.2	2.1	2.2
Non-industrialized countries								
Inward FDI	128	223	1.7	363	574	1.6	2.8	2.6
Outward FDI	6	26	4.2	90	338	3.8	14.8	13.2
NOI	−124	217	−1.7	−273	429	−1.6	2.2	2.0
GDP	1,696	2,088	1.2	2,545	3,533	1.4	1.5	1.7
Stage 3 countries								
Inward FDI	556	789	1.4	2,694	4,414	1.6	4.8	5.6
Outward FDI	40	84	2.1	727	954	1.3	18.2	11.4
NOI	−515	711	−1.4	−1,966	3,815	−1.9	3.8	5.4
GDP	5,402	2,975	0.6	11,118	3,671	0.3	2.1	1.2
Stage 1 and 2 countries								
Inward FDI	97	183	1.9	221	347	1.6	2.3	1.9
Outward FDI 5	5	26	5.5	12	35	2.8	2.6	1.4
NOI	−94	177	-1.9	−208	335	−1.6	2.2	1.9
GDP	1,110	1,095	1.0	1,285	1,182	0.9	1.2	1.1

Note: All values are normalized by population

9.2). The mean NOI levels for the non-industrial countries have become more negative but only by a factor of 2.2, whereas their mean GDP levels have increased by a factor of 1.5. The ratio of the standard deviation to the mean of NOI has decreased only slightly, while that of GDP has increased from 1.2 to 1.4 between 1980 and 1992. This suggests there is an increasing variation in the income levels of these countries as a whole, while their NOI positions have remained at the same level of dispersion.

However, as Figure 9.2 illustrates, there seem to be two groups of pre-Stage 4 countries. The majority of developing countries seem to be clustered at the origin, while just a handful of countries are more widely distributed, and roughly correspond to the newly industrializing countries (NICs). If we extract this group, we are able to distinguish between the Stage 1 and 2 countries, and the Stage 3 countries, identified separately in Table 9.2. It is readily apparent that much of the growth associated with the entire sample of non-industrialized countries was primarily associated with the NICs. The mean level of GDP for Stage 1 and 2 countries between 1980 and 1992 has shown only a marginal increase even in nominal terms by a factor of just 1.2, implying that there may even have been a decline in real terms. As for the Stage 3 countries, their GDP growth rate was equivalent to that of the industrial countries. The mean NOI level for Stage 1 and 2 countries doubled over the same period, becoming more negative, while NOI for Stage 3 became more positive, growing by a factor of 3.8.

The change in distribution over time lends support to our earlier comments regarding the changes in the world economy. None the less, there are only minor differences in the regressions between 1980 and 1992, and therefore we shall only present those for the most recent period.

The results of the regressions, set out in Table 9.1 and plotted on Figure 9.2, confirm our hypotheses. By excluding the industrialized countries from our analysis, the results of the regressions seem to be weaker. The curve (labelled as 'DC') provides a better estimation of the true relationship between NOI and GDP for non-industrialized countries.

As Figure 9.2 shows, the results of our regressions also confirm our hypotheses regarding the differences in the 'idealized' IDP due to the differences in the extent of natural and created assets. Countries with above-average natural assets tend to demonstrate a lower level of NOI for any given value of GDP relative to the average expected path. Countries with above-average created assets, on the other hand, demonstrate a much higher value of NOI relative to the average expected path, and to the natural-asset-type countries. It is interesting to note, however, that although there are differences in NOI for any given level of GDP between the two groups, the difference narrows considerably at higher levels of GDP.

Inward and outward FDI

The effects noted above regarding changes to the extent of NOI are more apparent when examining the two components of NOI separately. As Table

9.2 shows, the mean outward FDI for the industrialized countries increased by a factor of 4.3 between 1980 and 1992 – twice that of the growth of GDP. The ratio of the standard deviation to the mean has also fallen, implying that the level of outward FDI has tended to converge among this group of countries. The mean inward FDI has also increased by a factor of 3.6, but the level of disparity has remained constant.

For pre-Stage 4 countries, outward FDI grew faster than inward FDI between 1980 and 1992, but even in 1992 the extent of outward investment remained at very low levels. It is interesting to note that the ratio of the standard deviation to the mean for outward FDI for developing countries has fallen from 5.5 to 2.8, implying that a larger number of developing countries have begun to engage in outward FDI since 1980. The Stage 3 countries, on the other hand, have shown an eighteen-fold increase in their outward investment levels, and a fall in the ratio of the standard deviation to the mean from 2.1 to 1.3. Inward investment into the NICs also grew twice as rapidly as that into other developing countries. Thus, as expected, the Stage 3 countries have demonstrated growth of both inward and outward FDI at a much higher pace than both the developing countries and the industrialized ones. Their GDP has grown at the same rate as that of the industrialized countries, and twice as fast as the developing countries. The ratio of the standard deviation to the mean of GDP for the NICs is almost the same as that for the industrialized countries, implying that, as a group, their levels of GDP have converged.

Table 9.3 Log–linear regression equations for inward and outward FDI against GDP

Independent variable	*Sample*	*Constant*	*LOGGDPK*	*ADJ.R^2*	*F-value*	*N*
LOGOWK	ALL	−11.866***	1.9487***	0.866	342.58	54
LOGOWK	NA	−10.812***	1.8199***	0.809	115.63	28
LOGOWK	CA	−14.572***	2.2457***	0.768	57.35	18
LOGIWK	ALL	−3.7024***	1.1626***	0.746	256.85	88
LOGIWK	NA	−4.2996***	1.2751***	0.705	127.39	54
LOGIWK	CA	−4.166***	1.176***	0.755	68.87	23

*** Significant at the 1% level
** Significant at the 2.5% level

In running regressions for gross inward and outward direct investment, we have utilized a log–linear specification as originally suggested by Dunning (1981). We have done so for three samples – all countries (ALL), the natural asset countries (NA) and the created asset countries (CA) and the results are set out in Table 9.3 and graphed against the data in log form on Figures 9.3 and 9.4. Since a large number of developing countries have no outward investment, there is a considerable loss of sample size when outward direct investment per capita (OWK) is logged. As a result of this, the estimated value of the intercept is inaccurate. In the case of inward direct investment per capita (IWK), although theoretically a constant term is not required, since there is no country for which GDP = 0, it is necessary to include one. It is therefore not meaningful to reconvert the data back into linear form. None the less, it is significant to note that the intercept terms for IWK equations are considerably lower than for OWK, which confirms that in fact inward FDI tends to precede outward FDI.

As Table 9.3 shows, the results are highly significant for all six regressions at the 1 per cent level, with values greater than 0.7 in all cases. In the case of inward FDI, as hypothesized, created asset countries demonstrate a lower rate of growth of inward FDI than do natural asset countries, while created asset countries have a higher slope for outward FDI than do natural asset countries.

CONCLUSIONS

The current version of the IDP, in introducing dynamic aspects to its framework, represents a paradigm that encapsulates complex phenomena

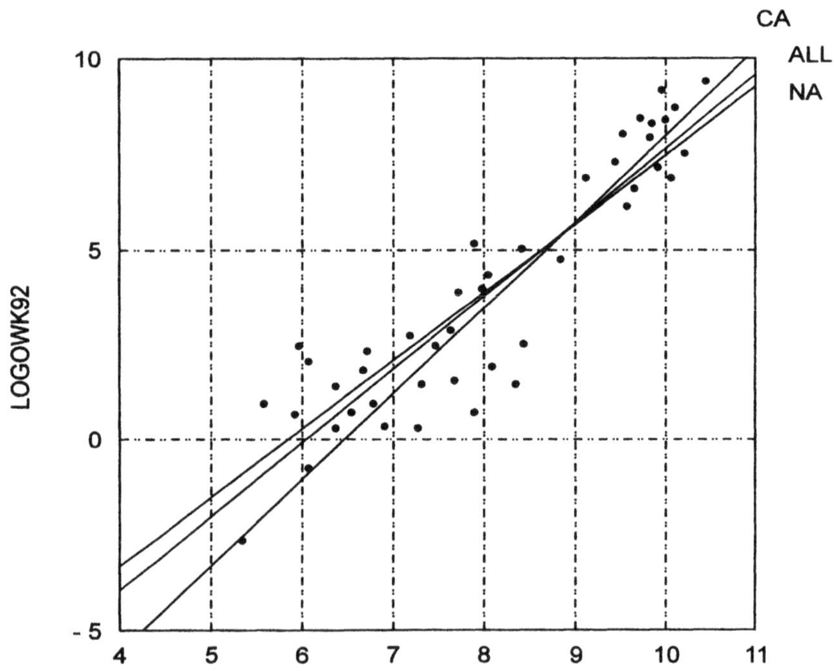

Figure 9.3 Outward Foreign Direct Investment and GDP, 1992 (log–linear)

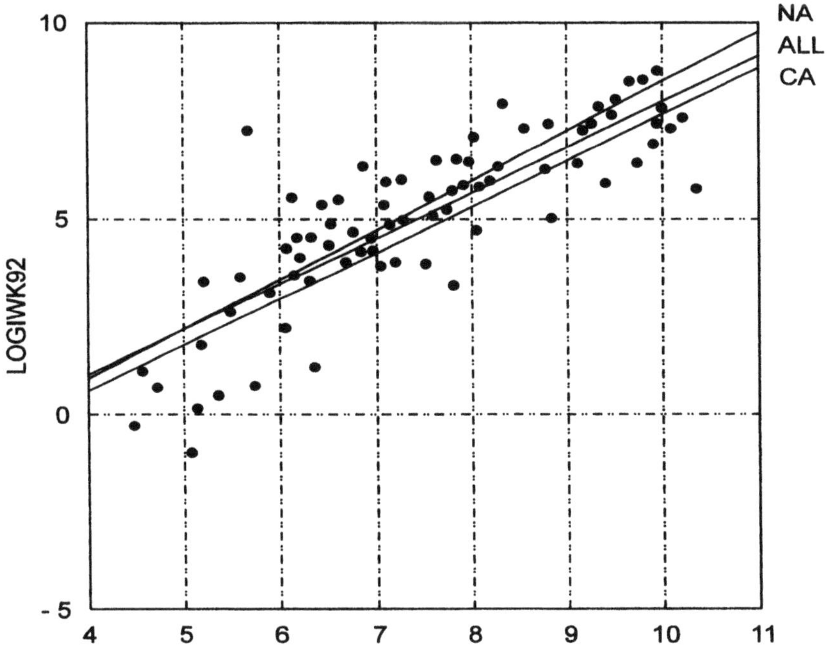

Figure 9.4 Inward Foreign Direct Investment and GDP, 1992 (log–linear)

which are exceedingly averse to aggregation. The relationship between FDI and economic development requires the comparison of two phenomena at different levels of economic analysis. While FDI is primarily a micro-economic or firm-specific activity, economic development is a macro-economic or country-specific phenomenon (Gray 1982). The examination of FDI as a country-specific variable requires the assumption that the activities of domestic and foreign MNEs can be aggregated in terms of their motivation, both within industrial sectors and across industrial sectors. Such aggregation can only be justified in countries where the nature, mode and motivation of MNE activity are relatively homogeneous, and the extent of their value-adding activities remains at relatively low levels, such as in the lesser developed countries. However, as MNEs become more globalized and engage in more complex investment activity the importance of firm-specific factors in determining the FDI profile of a country becomes increasingly significant. This increasing complexity, together with the differences in measuring FDI between countries, makes any such analysis a hazardous one.

In addition, some of the data reviewed confirm that there have been profound changes in the world economy as a whole, as well as among particular groups of countries and within these countries. The process of catching up and falling behind has resulted in a polarization of countries into three distinct groups. The first group consists of the industrialized countries, which have been shown to have a convergence within the group of income levels, but considerable growth in income levels in the past fifteen years. On average, their NOI positions have become increasingly positive, while their levels of gross inward and outward FDI are tending to converge. The second group consists of a handful of economies that can be regarded as being in Stage 3, which are exhibiting high growth in income levels and have become larger net outward investors since the 1980s. Their income levels also show signs of converging as a group, as well as with the industrialized countries. More significantly from our point of view, however, is the fact that their inward and outward FDI has been growing at a rate that outstrips even that of the industrialized countries. The third group consists of the Stage 1 and 2 countries which have experienced a divergence of income levels away from those of the industrialized countries as well as from the Stage 3 countries. Income levels have grown only marginally even in nominal terms, although the extent of FDI activity associated with these countries continues to grow faster than their domestic economies. None the less, their NOI position has become increasingly negative, and both their inward and outward FDI positions have grown at a slower pace than that of either of the other two groups.

Despite the limitations associated with a static analysis of a dynamic phenomenon, changes in the world economy as well as the large differences between countries, the data reviewed in this chapter indicate that there continues to be a relatively strong causal relationship between FDI activity and economic development. Furthermore, we have also been able to examine, albeit simplistically, the hypotheses regarding how the extent of natural/created assets determines the shape of the IDP. Countries that are relatively well endowed in natural assets have a higher growth rate of inward FDI, but a much lower growth rate of outward FDI, than countries that do not have a strong natural asset position as well as those countries with a strong created asset position. In terms of the traditional J-relationship between NOI and development, the J-curve continues to be valid for pre-Stage 5 countries. Natural-asset-type countries tend to have a considerably higher NOI position relative to the created asset countries at any given income level.

Both parts of this chapter have sought to show that cross-sectional analysis is not an appropriate tool to capture the dynamic character of the IDP. This requires an oversimplification of complex economic activity into a few general and aggregated variables, an exercise which cannot be undertaken without great caution. For instance, if we restrict ourselves to using GDP as a single indicator of development, the process of economic restructuring as well as the growth of the technological competitiveness of countries are not taken into account. Likewise, the growth of strategic alliances as an alternative mode of international value-added activity and the growth of the activities of governments in the organization of economic activity cannot be usefully included in an aggregate analysis across countries.

NOTES

1 See Kumar and McLeod (1981).
2 Earlier called 'cycle'.
3 Or the right to their use.
4 *Natural assets* consists of the 'fruits of the earth' and the stock of unskilled labour. *Created assets* are those derived from the upgrading of natural assets. For further details, see earlier chapters of this volume and Narula (1996).
5 See the article by Reich (1990) for a succinct discussion on this issue.
6 See Gugler (1991).
7 For a review of the various empirical studies, see Narula (1993).
8 Cited, for example, in Dunning (1993): Chapters 11–19.
9 As reviewed, for example, in Dunning (1993).
10 Acquisitions accounted for 83.2 per cent of the outlays by foreign direct investors in the United States between 1986 and 1992 (Fahim-Nader and Bargas 1993).
11 Put another way, in their search for created assets and markets which they perceive necessary to advance their objectives, both firms and countries are acquiring these resources and capabilities by buying out (or investing in) foreign firms, in addition to being bought out (or invested in) by foreign firms. The extent to which these routes are complements to, or substitutes for, each other has not been explored in the literature.
12 Also called 'collective' capitalism (Lazonick 1992) and the 'new' capitalism (Best 1990).
13 What one writer (Maister 1993) has referred to as a 'farmer' rather than a 'hunter' organizational management style.
14 Other motives for strategic outsourcing include the need to capture the specialized professional capabilities of suppliers, to shorten cycle times, and to respond better to customers. Examples of firms engaging in 'close' control procurement strategies include Marks and Spencer, Nike and Honda (Quinn and Hilmer 1994).
15 Notably from the work of John Hagedoorn and his colleagues at MERIT. For recent contributions see Hagedoorn and Schakenraad (1991, 1992, 1994) and Hagedoorn (1992, 1993).
16 For example, host governments may compel foreign firms to conclude co-operative arrangements with indigenous firms if they wish to produce within their boundaries, and/or force domestic firms to conclude such arrangements with foreign firms if they wish to transfer their O advantages abroad.
17 It is also worth recalling that the greater part of non-equity technology and organizational transference between countries is undertaken by MNEs.
18 Primarily because the *created* to *natural* asset ratio of the former countries was higher.
19 See especially Contractor (1990).
20 This proposition is explored in more detail in Dunning (1992, 1994).
21 Thus to quite a large extent the US net inward investment position in the 1960s has been eroded by the catching up of many European countries, while the seemingly invincible economic prowess of Japan in several sectors is now being challenged by the United States and Europe.

22 For a review of these, see Dunning (1993), especially the writers mentioned in Chapter 10. See also Dunning (1994).
23 Freeman and Hagedoorn (1994) suggest that between 1980 and 1989, almost 70 per cent of strategic technology partnering agreements between Triad firms and developing country firms were equity based, while for intra-Triad agreements, it was less than 50 per cent.
24 These data only cover strategic technology partnering for the period 1980–9.
25 See Dunning (1992, 1993).
26 These data are both derived from the World Bank (1994).

REFERENCES

Abramovitz, M. (1986) 'Catching up, forging ahead, and falling behind', *Journal of Economic History* XLVI: 385–406.
Alam, M. S. (1992) 'Convergence in developed countries: an empirical investigation', *Weltwirtshaftliches Arachiv* 128: 189–200.
Baumol, W. (1986) 'Productivity growth, convergence, and welfare: what the long-run data show', *American Economic Review* 76: 1072–85.
Best, M. (1990) *The New Competition: Institutions of Restructuring*, Cambridge, MA: Harvard University Press.
Cantwell, J. (1989) *Technological Innovation and Multinational Corporations*, Oxford: Basil Blackwell.
Cantwell, J. A. and Dunning, J. H. (1991) 'Multinationals, technology and the competitiveness of European industries', *Aussenwirtschaft* 46(1): 45–65.
Cantwell, J. and Randaccio, F. (1990) 'The growth of multinationals and the catching up effect', *Economic Notes* 19: 1–23.
Contractor, F. (1990) 'Ownership patterns of US joint ventures abroad and the liberalization of foreign government regulation in the 1980s: evidence from the benchmark surveys', *Journal of International Business Studies* 21: 55–73.
Dowrick, S. (1992) 'Technological catch up and diverging incomes: patterns of economic growth 1960–88', *The Economic Journal* 102: 600–10.
Dowrick, S. and Gemmell, N. (1991) 'Industrialization, catching up and economic growth: a comparative study across the world's capitalist economies', *Economic Journal* 101: 263–75.
Dunning, J. H. (1981) 'Explaining the international direct investment position of countries: towards a dynamic or developmental approach', *Weltwirtschaftliches Archiv* 119: 30–64.
——(1986) 'The investment development cycle revisited', *Weltwirtshaftliches Archiv* 122: 667–77.
——(1988a) *Explaining International Production*, London: Unwin Hyman.
——(1988b) *Multinationals, Technology and Competitiveness*, London: Unwin Hyman.
——(1992) 'The global economy, domestic governance, strategies and transnational corporations: interactions and policy recommendations', *Transnational Corporations* 1, December: 7–45.
——(1993) *Multinational Enterprises and the Global Economy*, Wokingham, England, and Reading, MA: Addison Wesley.
——(1994) 'Reevaluating the benefits of foreign direct investment', *Transnational Corporations* 3 February : 23–52.
Dunning, J. H. and Narula, R. (1994) 'Transpacific FDI and the investment development path: the record assessed', *University of South Carolina Essays in International Business* May No. 10: 69.

——(eds) (1996) *Foreign Direct Investment and Governments*, London and New York: Routledge.

Durkheim, E. (1964) *The Division of Labour in Society*, New York: The Free Press.

Fahim-Nader, M. and Bargas, S. E. (1993) 'US business enterprises acquired or established by foreign direct investors in 1992', *Survey of Current Business* May: 113–23.

Freeman, C. and Hagedoorn, J. (1994) 'Catching up or falling behind: patterns in international interfirm technology partnering', *World Development* 22: 771–80.

Gray, H. P. (1982) 'Macroeconomic theories of foreign direct investment: an assessment,' in A. Rugman (ed.) *New Theories of the Multinational Enterprise*, London: Croom Helm.

Gugler, P. (1991) *Les Alliances Strategiques Transnationales*, Fribourg: Editions Universitaires.

Hagedoorn, J. (1992) 'Organizational modes of inter-firm cooperation and technology transfer', *Technovation* 10: 17– 30.

——(1993) 'Understanding the rationale of strategic technology partnering: interorganizational modes of cooperation and sectoral differences', *Strategic Management Journal* 14: 371–85.

Hagedoorn, J. and Narula, R. (1994) *Choosing Modes of Governance for Strategic Technology Partnering: International and Sectoral Differences*, MERIT Working Paper Series No. 94-025.

Hagedoorn, J. and Schakenraad, J. (1991) 'The internationalization of the economy, global strategies and strategic technology alliances', *Nouvelles de la Science et des Technologies* 9: 29–41.

——(1992) 'Leading companies in networks of strategic alliances in information technologies', *Research Policy* 21: 163–90.

——(1994) 'The effects of strategic technology alliances on company performance', *Strategic Management Journal* 15: 291–309.

Hämäläinen, T. (1993) *The Evolving Role of Government in Economic Organization*, Newark, NJ: Rutgers University (mimeo).

Kumar, K. and McLeod, M. (eds) (1981) *Multinationals from Developing Countries*, Lexington, MA: D. C. Heath.

Lazonick, W. (1992) 'Business organization and competitive advantage: capitalist transformation in the twentieth century', in G. Dosi, R. Giannetti and P. A. Toninelli (eds) *Technology and Enterprise in a Historical Perspective*, pp. 119–63, Oxford: Clarendon Press.

Maister, D. H. (1993) *Managing the Professional Service Firm*, New York: The Free Press/Macmillan.

Narula, R. (1993) 'An Examination of the Evolution and Interdependence of Foreign Direct Investment and Economic Structure: The Case of Industrialized Countries', PhD Thesis, Newark, NJ: Rutgers University.

——(1996) *Multinational Investment and Economic Structure*, London: Routledge.

Ohmae, K. (1987) *The Borderless World*, New York: The Free Press.

Ozawa, T. (1992) 'FDI and economic development', *Transnational Corporations* 1: 27–54.

Porter, M. E. (1990) *The Competitive Advantage of Nations*, New York: The Free Press.

Quinn, J. B. and Hilmer, F. G. (1994) 'Strategic outsourcing', *Sloan Management Review* 35, Summer: 43–55.

Reich, R. (1990) 'Who is us?', *Harvard Business Review* January–February: 53–64.

Tolentino, P. (1993) *Technological Innovation and Third World Multinationals*, London: Routledge.

UNCTAD (1993) *World Investment Report 1993, Transnational Corporations and Integrated International Production*, New York and Geneva: UN.
——(1994) *World Investment Report 1994, Transnational Corporations Employment and the Workplace*, New York and Geneva: UN.
Verspagen, B. (1993) *Uneven Growth Between Interdependent Economies*, Avebury: Aldershot.
World Bank (1994) *World Development Report 1994*, Oxford: Oxford University Press.

10

THE CONCEPT OF COUNTRY COMPETITIVENESS

INTRODUCTION

Competitiveness is about benchmarking economic performance. Performance may be variously defined, as indeed may be the benchmark, for comparison. From the perspective of the business enterprise, performance is usually taken to mean its productivity, profitability, market share or rate of growth of sales, while its benchmark for comparison is the performance of its major competitors – and, more particularly, those perceived to utilize 'best practice' techniques and strategies. From the perspective of a government of a country, the most widely accepted measure of national performance is gross national product (GNP) per head of population, or the change in GNP per head over time, while national competitiveness is usually assessed by comparing the performance of one country with that of the countries serving similar world markets – although the countries benchmarked may vary according to the industrial sectors and markets being considered.[1]

We believe that benchmarking the performance of both firms and countries is a worthwhile exercise *wherever it is expected that the knowledge so gained may help improve that performance*. Competitiveness should not be regarded as an end in itself. It is quite possible for a country's citizens to be relatively better off than those of another country, yet, in terms of GNP per head, to be worse off. By the same token, its citizens may be absolutely better off in these latter terms, but, relative to those of another country, they may have a lower standard of living. Similarly, at a sectoral level, an increase in competitiveness will only raise economic welfare if the resources used to achieve this goal could not have been better deployed in other directions.

It must also be acknowledged that the goals and the territorial boundaries of firms and countries are not the same. The main interest of the former is to identify how well they are performing – independently of the location of their productive facilities – relative to their competitors, and to establish ways and means of improving that performance; governments, on the other hand, are chiefly concerned with increasing the welfare of the citizens who live *within the boundaries of their jurisdiction* – however, they may use inward and outward direct investment or cross-border strategic alliances to foster this goal.[2]

In a number of recent writings, Professor Paul Krugman (1994a, b, c) has questioned the usefulness of benchmarking the competitiveness of countries – specifically at a sectoral level. He believes that the fact that the productivity of (say) the pharmaceutical or airline industry in country A is lower or higher than the same industry in country B offers us no guidance as to whether more resources ought to be allocated to country A's industry. We agree; but, we suggest, this is not because the benchmarking of productivity is a meaningless exercise, but because, without a proper understanding of the reasons why the productivity of the industries in the two countries is different, no prognosis on what (if anything) should be done about these differences can be made.

But, it would appear that Professor Krugman wishes to go further, as he castigates those scholars who assert that such comparisons *may* be useful. In doing so, he seems to be making the implicit assumption that each and every firm in each and every country is already producing at its best practice level, that is at maximum efficiency. In this event, the only way in which the competitiveness of a country can be raised is by a better allocation of resources – that is, one which is more in accord with the comparative advantage of the country's resources. Krugman also makes no explicit distinction between the appropriateness of evaluating *static* and *dynamic* competitiveness of countries.[3] Finally, by ignoring (implicitly, at least) the role of non-tradable goods in affecting the economic welfare of a country, he also seems to be caught up in the strait-jacket of the neoclassical trade economics.

WHEN IS THE CONCEPT OF COUNTRY COMPETITIVENESS IRRELEVANT?

It is perhaps worth rehearsing the assumptions underlying the contention that comparisons between the economic performance of countries serve no useful purpose. Six of these are:

1 **All domestic resources and capabilities[4] are being efficiently deployed in their present use.** This means that whatever they are producing, all firms are operating on their optimum production functions and at the frontier of these functions, and that, given the state of technology and knowledge, such firms could not improve their performance – either in the short or long run.
2 **Any intercountry differences in the performance of firms or industrial sectors are unavoidable.** This means that all intercountry productivity differences – whether of tradable or non-tradable products – reflect

differences in the availability or quality in the location-bound resources and capabilities and/or markets between countries.

3 **(Following from 2.) All resources and capabilities are immobile between countries.**

4 **The extent to which a country creates new resources and capabilities or upgrades its existing resources and capabilities (e.g. by innovation, education and training) is minimal and/or such assets are instantaneously and costlessly available to all firms.**

5 **There is little or no structural or endemic market failure, and all firms compete under conditions of perfect competition.** *Interalia*, this situation allows no latitude for firm-specific proprietary advantages or strategies.

6 **There is no unemployment or unused capacity of resources.** Although traditional neo-classical economics does not spell out this condition, most of its exponents implicitly assume that, as long as countries allocate resources under conditions of perfect competition, either there will be no unemployment or unemployment will be lower than it otherwise might be.

It will be readily recognized that these six assumptions are also those used by neo-classical trade economists in their assertion that, if global economic welfare is to be maximized, each country should produce those goods and services which require the input of those (immobile) resources and capabilities in which it has a comparative advantage and, in exchange for exporting these goods and services, import those which require resources and capabilities in which it has a comparative disadvantage. In this model, the *only* question of interest to scholars is the appropriate allocation of resources between the production of different tradable goods, that is *allocative* or *sectoral* productivity. Implicitly, at least, the model assumes that market forces compel firms to produce the relevant goods and services in the most efficient way – there is no *technical* or X inefficiency.

At the same time, neo-classical economists take no account of *other* kinds of productivity, notably those arising from *scale* economies, which can only be achieved in imperfect markets. Neither are they interested in identifying or explaining the optimum path of increasing productivity through innovation. And finally, they completely ignore the transition and co-ordination costs associated with the adjustment of markets to changes in supply or demand conditions.

ALLOWING FOR MARKET FAILURE AND THE MOBILITY OF ASSETS

Once one allows for firm-specific differences in efficiency, the mobility of assets across national boundaries, and the introduction of innovation into the picture, the benchmarking of productivity (i.e. evaluating competitiveness) *may* become a legitimate exercise in learning. And, while we would be first to accept that the differences in the competitiveness of countries are *not* always avoidable, we believe that efforts designed to determine why, and in which direction, productivity may vary between firms, industries and countries – engaged in similar activities – are entirely worth while. We would further contend that, in the globalizing economy of the 1990s – when the productivity of a country, or of a particular industry in a country, rests on the ability of its firms and government to upgrade its existing assets (e.g. human capital) and to create new ones (e.g. information and technology) and where such assets are mobile across national boundaries – an analysis of the performance of the firms or governments (acting on behalf of their constituents) of different countries may provide a helpful basis for guiding actions and policies which determine the *future* productivity of a country's resources and capabilities. To this extent then, competitiveness *does* matter.

Let us further argue our case by considering two possible scenarios. The first is the traditional neo-classical two-commodity scenario. Both commodities are assumed to be tradable. Country A is particularly good at producing wool and country B is particularly good at producing wine. Producers in both countries are operating on their optimum production functions, and producing and selling their products in perfect market conditions. Resources are immobile between country A and country B, and there is no government intervention in either country which may affect the exchange of goods and services as determined by the market. In such a scenario, making comparisons between the performance of country A's and country B's firms, or between the GNPs of country A and country B, is a totally unhelpful exercise. Any increase in the prosperity of firms and countries is entirely dependent on their ability as domestic producers to upgrade the productivity of their resources. In such a scenario, we completely endorse Krugman's views on the competitiveness of countries, and of industries of countries.

The second scenario is where countries A and B both produce very similar goods, some of which are not tradable. Trade, itself, is mainly of an intraindustry character. At least some resources and capabilities are mobile between the two countries, largely, let us assume, as a result of the activities of their multinational enterprises (MNEs) and/or of cross-border and strategic alliances. The competitive advantages of country A's and country B's firms are based on their abilities to upgrade their core competencies of (say) technological and organizational capabilities, and part of this rests on the successful innovating activities of their foreign subsidiaries. Endemic market failure exists within and between both economies. There are considerable market externalities, and neither country A's nor country B's firms can achieve their full economies of scale and scope without some degree of market imperfection. Many goods produced involve high fixed costs and are of a public goods character. The leading firms in both economies are producing in oligopolistic markets, and their long-term prosperity rests as much on their abilities to innovate new products successfully as it does on their abilities to maximize their static efficiencies. By utilizing a range of macro-organizational policy tools, for example with respect to education and training, innovation, competition, taxation, trade and the environment, governments may affect the competitiveness of their own firms both at home and abroad. Governments can also influence the extent to which foreign-owned firms, as well as domestic firms, prefer to locate their 'footloose' activities within their national boundaries. Finally, the future prosperity of both country A and country B is assumed to be dependent on successful firm-specific innovatory and management strategies, deployed in imperfect and uncertain global market conditions. Also, especially in dynamic sectors, firms rarely attain an equilibrium situation, if for no other reason than that asset upgrading – including learning and experience – is a continuous process. For these reasons, an optimum production or pricing strategy may be difficult to identify.

In this second scenario – which is one which seems more appropriate than the first to describe the kind of competitive environment currently existing between the major industrial powers – the relevance of competitiveness or absolute competitive advantage is very real indeed. Of course, to compare the competitiveness of countries, one also has to examine the performance of firms. But, the goals and territorial jurisdiction of firms and countries are not the same. Moreover, to imply from this that governments have no interest in these performances, and that governments cannot (or indeed should not) influence them, is as misleading as the supposition that, by itself, benchmarking or sectoral competitiveness necessarily provides guidance to governments on how best to raise the productivity of the resources within their jurisdiction.

A comparison between both the overall and sectoral productivity of countries is, then, relevant in so far as it is a first step in helping us to identify whether or not a country's firms are as efficient as they might be – or if indigenous resources and capabilities are being optimally allocated. Now, while some commentators may argue that this is a matter for the firms themselves, there can surely be no denying that this same efficiency is at least partly dependent on exogenous factors, and especially on the role of governments as overseers of the economic environment within their jurisdiction. Moreover, it is worth observing that this role is not neutral in its sectoral effects. Innovatory and educational policies tend to affect the efficiency of high-skill and technology-intensive sectors and firms, relatively more than they do the efficiency of low-skill and less technology-intensive sectors. Thus, the competitiveness with which location-bound assets are created is relevant to our understanding of why firms from different countries may have varying levels of efficiency.

The presumption that extramarket factors are playing an increasingly important role in affecting the competitiveness of firms, and that the associated effects are not evenly spread, rests on the proposition that, in modern economies, there is a good deal of endemic market failure, and this failure may impede the competitiveness of countries. *Ceteris paribus*, the more dynamic an economy is, the more likely markets are to fail, and the more likely it is that countries can learn from the experiences and mistakes of other countries. Most economists accept that firms do this all the time. But, is it no less the case that national governments, on behalf of the constituents they represent, also have the right – indeed, the duty – to do so?

MOBILITY OF ASSETS AND COMPETITIVE ADVANTAGE

There is another reason why making a comparative analysis of the productivity of a nation's location-bound resources matters. Namely, there is a growing significance of mobile assets in the production process. In neoclassical trade theory, firms are assumed to be completely constrained in their locational choice, as all assets used in the production process are country specific. No MNEs exist, for, no enterprise of one nationality is presumed to possess any competitive advantage over the firms in the country in which it might be contemplating a foreign direct investment. It follows from this analysis that GNP is equal to GDP, and that the competitive advantages (see footnote 1) of national firms are internalized by the residents of the countries in which they produce.

The possibility of asset mobility, however, means that the competitive advantages of firms may be used outside their home countries. The likelihood of inward and outward direct investment affecting GNP per head suggests that countries may directly compete for such investment by the quality of the complementary or supporting resources and capabilities they offer to MNEs – and, in particular, those perceived to be necessary to exploit effectively the MNE's core assets. Frequently, these investments are discriminatory in their impact on the competitiveness of particular firms and sectors. At the same time, their creation and utilization is often decided by non-market forces, which may lead to external economies or diseconomies. Finally, although these resources are location bound, there is potentially a great deal of X inefficiency, which may mean that making comparisons between countries may lead to improvements of the productivity of domestic resources.

For national governments wishing to retain or attract the right kind of mobile income-creating assets to their territories, the need is to offer a set of complementary assets, for example telecommunications, roads, airports and other facilities, at least as good as those of their foreign competitors. Often, these assets (and their output) are non-tradable. Nevertheless, it may be useful to compare their availability and their performance with those of their competitors, and then proceed to establish how far it is desirable to upgrade the competitiveness of these assets.

EXPLAINING COUNTRY-SPECIFIC DIFFERENCES IN THE PERFORMANCE OF FIRMS

Another reason for viewing competitiveness from a country perspective is that many of the competitive advantages of firms are themselves country specific, and it is thus appropriate to consider these country-specific differences as explanatory variables. Moreover, although these variables may impact differently on different kinds of activities, they are likely to affect both the efficiency of all activities and the allocation of resources between different activities.

Once again, the assumption that it is possible to learn something from comparing particular country-specific differences in the performance of firms (i.e. that particular advantages may at least be partially transferable across countries) is critical to the analysis. Accordingly, several studies on the competitiveness of UK and German firms have pointed to the differential expenditure on training in the two economies; differences in the manufacturing systems between the Japanese and US auto industry have been used to explain the latter's superior performance; differences in level and structure of corporate taxes have been frequently hypothesized to explain differences in the rates of growth of both developed and developing countries; and the character of national innovatory systems has been shown to affect critically the amount and disposition of asset creation between countries.

These are just a few examples of the relevance of making intercountry comparisons of productivity. But, our point will have been made if we have demonstrated that the knowledge gained from comparing country-specific differences as factors influencing performance can be used to improve *technical* or *allocative* efficiency of the relatively poorer-performing countries.

THE DYNAMICS OF COMPETITIVE ADVANTAGE; THE ROLE OF NON-MARKET ACTORS

There is one other reason why evaluating the competitiveness of countries matters. This is where there is reason to suppose that any one system of national governance may learn from another on the 'best' way to help its firms improve their competitiveness. To a large extent, this comes down to the appropriate non-market and particularly government policies towards upgrading human capital and innovation, both of which are produced under conditions of market failure. However, it could easily be broadened to embrace other government-related actions in so far as they may affect the competitiveness of firms.

Many economists would appear to ignore the role of national governments in influencing the competitiveness of countries – except in so far as it is directed to reducing structural market imperfections. But, it is a fact that national governments can also affect the competitive advantages of firms located in their boundaries, by lessening endemic market failure. This they may do in a variety of ways – some of which were set out in Chapter 2 – and most noticeably by providing the infrastructure for the efficient creation of firm-specific assets and by fostering the conditions for their optimal deployment.

The other aspect of the role of governments concerns their attempts to attract footloose value-added activities into their own jurisdiction – particularly in cases where governments believe the competitive advantages of their resources require upgrading. Once again, we accept that in conditions of perfect competition and full employment this is a fruitless exercise. However, wherever market failure is present and is best countered, or compensated for, by government action, and where unemployment exists, it may be perfectly legitimate for governments to identify ways and means by which they can upgrade the quality of their indigenous resources. This can be done, in part, by drawing upon the experiences of the governments of other countries. Of course, it does not follow that these actions will always be welfare enhancing; indeed, they might generate negative externalities.[5] On the other hand, by facilitating markets and by providing complementary assets necessary to enhance the core competencies of their firms, governments may help to promote the competitiveness of their location-bound resources.

CONCLUSIONS

The measurement of the competitiveness of a country's resources and capabilities is, then, a legitimate exercise wherever there is reason to suppose that, given the external economic and other constraints within which they operate, indigenous firms are not utilizing their resources and capabilities efficiently, or are not upgrading their assets at an optimum rate. It is also relevant where a government wishes to attract or maintain mobile intangible assets to improve the productivity of its own location-bound assets, or where it wishes to discourage the hollowing out of firms who might otherwise locate their activities outside its national boundaries.

The competitiveness of a country's location-bound created assets, then, *does* matter, simply because these assets cannot be taken to be at a fixed and optimum value. This is especially the case when one considers the variables affecting dynamic competitiveness, and especially the actions of governments in affecting the value of these variables. Hence, an examination of the comparative competencies of the firms and governments of countries to generate new productive capabilities and to upgrade the quality of existing products – and an explanation of the sources of the differences in these competencies – is an entirely justifiable, and often a worthwhile, exercise.

NOTES

1 For example, the United States' main competitors in supplying high-technology products are Japan, Germany, France and the United Kingdom; in medium-technology products the newly industrializing countries of South East Asia and Mexico; and in labour-intensive products, other Latin American and Asian countries.

2 In this respect it is important to distinguish between the GNP and gross domestic product (GDP) of a country. GDP is defined as the output produced within the national boundaries of a country divided by the population of that country. GNP is the output produced by the residents of a country both inside and outside its national boundaries. GNP is equal to GDP plus income earned by a country's own residents outside its national boundaries (e.g. profits on overseas direct investment) less income accruing to foreign residents within its domestic territory (e.g profits earned by the affiliates of foreign enterprises).

3 Static competitiveness refers to the relative performance of a country at a given moment of time: dynamic competitiveness refers to the relative performance of a country over a period of time. Included in this latter measure of competitiveness is the ability of a country to restructure the allocation of resources to meet changes in global demand and supply conditions.

4 For the purpose of this chapter, we define resources as natural endowments (e.g. unskilled labour, land, etc.); tangible created assets (e.g. buildings, R&D laboratories, etc.); and capabilities as intangible *created* assets (e.g. information, labour skills and experience, technology, organizational competence, entrepreneurship, etc).

5 An example is following the 'beggar my neighbour' policies of the interwar years.

REFERENCES

Krugman, P. (1994a) 'Competitiveness: does it matter?', in P. Krugman *Peddling Prosperity: Economic Sense and Nonsense*, pp. 28–44, New York: W. W. Norton.

——(1994b) 'Competitiveness: a dangerous obsession', *Foreign Affairs* March/April.

——(1994c) *Peddling Prosperity: Economic Sense and Nonsense*, New York: W. W. Norton.

11

THE GEOGRAPHICAL SOURCES OF THE COMPETITIVENESS OF FIRMS

Some results of a new survey[1]

INTRODUCTION

This chapter presents some of the results of a new field study on the geographical sources of firm-specific competitiveness, as perceived by executives of 144 of the world's 500 largest industrial corporations.[2] Full details of the sample and the way in which the survey was organized are set out in the appendix to this chapter.

In 1993, the sample firms were responsible for two-fifths of the global sales of the largest 500 industrial corporations and nearly two-fifths of the foreign direct investment (FDI) stake in all primary and secondary economic activity. For some sectors (e.g. autos, petroleum refining, tobacco, electronics and computers) and for some countries (e.g. Japan, Sweden and the United Kingdom), our coverage is particularly good; for others, it is less so, but from the country and sector groups presented in this chapter, it is entirely acceptable.

The purpose of the field survey was to gain the opinions of senior business executives[3] about the geographical origin of the kind of firm-specific competitive advantages or core competencies[4] identified by the literature.[5] There has been much debate, in recent years, over the extent to which the competitive advantages of firms stem from the location-bound characteristics of their home countries – some of which may be internalized by the firms themselves – or whether, as FDI and strategic alliances have become increasingly directed to acquiring created assets,[6] and as firms (and, particularly, the larger and established MNEs) have been increasing their degree of multinationality,[7] competitive advantages have been increasingly sourced from outside their home countries, or in Michael Porter's terminology, 'multiple home bases'.

As the analytical basis for our study, we shall use the concept of the 'double' diamond of competitive advantage, as developed by Alan Rugman and his colleagues over the past three or four years.[8] Essentially, the Rugman approach extends the concept of Porter's 'single' diamond of competitive advantage[9] – which argues that a firm's competitive advantages are essentially a function of the domestic economic environment – whether or not the attributes of this environment are owned by the firm or available to it. Rugman and others, including the author of this chapter,[10] have argued that the deepening structural integration of the world economy and the burgeoning of alliance capitalism are widening the geographical scope for creating or acquiring competitive advantages, and that any attempt to identify the geographical sources of such advantages must embrace the diamonds of other countries, and particularly those with which the home country firms have the most dealings, by way of trade, FDI and non-equity co-operative ventures.

Our field study aims to offer some new evidence to that recorded by a number of country case studies[11] which, in the main, have confirmed the Rugman/Dunning hypothesis. The uniqueness of the present contribution lies in six directions. First, it obtains the information directly from firms themselves.[12] Second, it attempts to classify the competitive advantages identified in the literature into a number of groups, and, in doing so, uses the four components of Porter's diamond as its framework. Third, our study attempts to relate its findings to a number of critical firm-specific variables, namely size of firm, degree of multinationality, country (or region) of origin and industrial sector. Fourth, it seeks to identify which foreign countries provide the main access to non-domestic competitive advantages which complement those offered by the home country. Fifth, it ranks the significance of the three main modes of involvement of the sample firms in acquiring competitive advantages from a foreign location. And lastly, it sets out the perceptions of the sample firms about the positive or negative influences of different components of home government policy on their global competitiveness.

To contain this chapter to manageable dimensions, we shall adopt a threefold classification of industries, based upon their degree of R&D intensity in the United States. Thus, we define high-technology (HT) sectors as those which recorded an average R&D expenditure as a percentage of sales of 4 per cent or more where scientists and engineers employed in R&D were 2 per cent or more of total employment.[13] Medium-technology (MT) sectors cover those where the corresponding ratios vary between 2 and 3.9 per cent and 1 and 1.9 per cent; and low-technology (LT) sectors embrace those ratios under 2 per cent and under 1 per cent. As to home country or region of origin, we shall consider six main groups, namely large European countries,[14] smaller European countries,[15] the United States, Japan, developing countries,[16] and other countries.[17]

We shall also group our sample firms by their degrees of multinationality. This was obtained by averaging out (for each firm) the percentage of their global assets and global employment,[18] accounted for by their foreign affiliates[19] and then classifying firms into four groups, namely under 15 per cent (low), 15–29 per cent (medium–low), 30–59 per cent (medium–high) and 60 per cent and over (high).

Finally, although all of our sample firms were large companies, their global sales in 1993 varied from $0.22 billion to $138.2 billion. For the purposes of our analysis, we shall categorize our firms into four size groups, namely medium-size firms defined as those with sales of under $5 billion of scale in 1993; large firms: $5 billion to $24.9 billion of sales; very large firms: $25 billion to 49 billion of sales; and mega firms: $50 billion and over of sales.

In later research, we intend to undertake some econometric analysis on the relationship between these four contextual variables and the competitive advantages of firms as, with few exceptions, we have data for each of the 144 firms. In this chapter, we shall confine ourselves to identifying and exploring a number of possible bivariant (and occasionally trivariant) relationships between the sources of competitiveness and firms and/or country-specific characteristics, which – at the very least – may help point the way to more rigorous statistical evaluation.

THE SAMPLE FIRMS: SOME DETAILS

Tables 11.1 to 11.3 set out some details about the characteristics of the sample firms. In general, they mirror our knowledge about the industrial and geographical composition, and the size and degree of multinationality of MNEs as, for example, has been set out in various publications of the UNCTAD (DTCI) (previously UNCTC).[20] For the most part, too, the data set out in the tables are self-explanatory. We would, however, highlight just three points:

1 Although 82 per cent of the sales of our sample firms were within the HT or MT sectors, the degree of technological intensity would not appear to affect significantly the extent of their multinationality. There were, indeed, as wide differences between industries in the three broad sectors identified (compare, for example, aerospace with chemicals in Table 11.1) as between the sectors.
2 The degree to which firms undertake R&D activities in their foreign affiliates is on average about one-half that of their overall activities, although this does vary between sectors (see Table 11.1). Table 11.2, however, shows that the R&D multinationality ratio varies very considerably between countries (compare, for example, Japan and developing countries with the United Kingdom and Sweden).

Table 11.1 Industrial distribution and extent of multinationality of sample firms (1993)

Sector	*N*	*Sales ($ billion)*	*Sales (%)*	*Extent of multinationality*		
				Assets	*Employment*	*R&D*
High technology	53	892.02	35.99	38.20	39.79	22.74
of which: Aerospace	5	73.10	2.95	6.50	6.25	2.00
Chemicals and pharm.	19	215.91	8.71	51.28	54.18	26.61
Computers	9	213.90	8.63	28.87	28.67	9.60
Electronics	20	389.11	15.70	38.84	39.22	27.52
Medium technology	34	1,152.20	46.48	39.65	39.42	15.44
of which: Industrial equipment	8	73.80	2.98	28.00	39.13	12.70
Motor vehicles	12	580.00	23.40	32.20	35.47	7.50
Petroleum refining	14	498.40	20.11	49.75	42.92	24.33
Low technology	57	434.55	17.53	41.70	45.51	28.46
of which: Food, drink and tobacco	20	244.30	9.86	50.42	58.14	32.53
Paper	10	38.96	1.57	22.44	20.89	8.14
Building materials	5	16.43	0.66	49.60	46.40	39.67
Metals and metal production	14	107.30	4.33	35.01	38.00	24.65
Other	8	27.56	1.11	53.50	59.57	45.60
Total	144	2,478.77	100.00	40.01	41.80	23.34

Source: All data contained in this and subsequent tables are derived from our field survey

Table 11.2 Distribution of sample firms by region or country of origin and extent of multinationality (1993)

Region/country	*N*	*Sales ($ billion)*	*Sales (%)*	*Extent of multinationality*		
				Assets	*Employment*	*R&D*
Large European	44	922.87	37.23	49.13	49.95	32.05
of which: Germany	13	359.55	14.51	39.71	45.99	23.11
UK + UK/ Neth.	23	400.32	16.15	57.28	57.95	38.58
Other	8	163.00	6.58	28.83	32.14	27.78
Small European	21	164.46	6.63	55.24	56.81	32.72
of which: Sweden	7	31.96	1.29	70.00	70.29	53.00
Switzerland	5	68.90	2.78	58.00	61.80	33.20
Other	9	63.60	2.57	46.13	43.56	19.75
United States	31	710.20	28.65	36.12	34.48	14.67
Japan	26	606.35	24.46	19.48	28.69	5.99
Developing countries	14	42.49	1.71	27.22	25.42	15.63
Other countries	8	32.4	1.31	30.50	30.57	18.33
Total	144	2,478.77	100.00	40.01	41.80	23.34

Table 11.3 Distribution of sample firms by size and extent of multinationality (1993)

Size (sales)	*N*	*Sales ($ billion)*	*Sales (%)*	*Extent of multinationality*		
		Assets			*Employment*	*R&D*
Medium (<5 billion)	56	141.62	5.71	40.60	39.68	20.10
Large (5–24.9 billion)	58	706.20	28.49	37.30	41.12	26.55
Very large (25–49.9 billion)	16	561.55	22.65	46.09	45.00	29.00
Mega (>50 billion)	14	1069.40	43.14	42.31	49.54	12.80
Total	144	2,478.77	100.00	40.01	41.80	23.34

3 Table 11.3 shows that size of firm does not appear to be a significant influence on the degree of multinationality.[21] Somewhat surprisingly, however, the mega firms – although the most multinational in terms of their sales and assets – were the least multinational in terms of their R&D expenditures.

THE GEOGRAPHICAL SOURCES OF COMPETITIVENESS

The next set of tables (Tables 11.4–11.7) present the views of the respondents of the sample firms of the extent to which they currently derive a number of identified specific competitive advantages as a direct result of their FDIs and/or strategic alliances with foreign firms. They were asked to use a scale of 1 to 7 in their evaluations. They were informed that a rank of 1 would indicate that their competitive advantages were *entirely* derived from the resources, capabilities, markets and interfirm rivalries specific to their home countries, while a rank of 7 would indicate that such advantages were derived entirely from the location-specific attributes of foreign countries. A rank of 4 would suggest that, in the firm's opinion, the origin of the competitive advantages stemmed equally from home and foreign locations.[22]

Sector-specific differences

Table 11.4 considers four groups of competitive advantages which broadly correspond to Michael Porter's fourfold diamond of the competitive advantages of nations.[23] We have further subdivided three of these four groups into a number of more specific advantages, identified by other scholars. In this table, we have classified our firms into high-, medium- and low-technology-intensity sectors. Economic theory would suggest that firms should seek to acquire competitive assets from those locations which provide these assets at lowest cost and with the greatest security.

Essentially, the Porter hypothesis is that HT firms will create (obtain) their core assets (e.g. innovatory capacity) (Group 1 [iv]) in their home

Table 11.4 The sourcing of competitive advantages classified by technological intensity of sample firms (1993)

	All	*HT*	*MT*	*LT*
Group 1	3.54	3.46	3.48	3.65
Access to resources and assets	(1.39)	(1.20)	(1.03)	(1.71)
(i) Natural resources	4.24	3.67	4.44	4.62
	(1.70)	(1.36)	(1.67)	(1.88)
(ii) Unskilled labour	3.98	4.10	3.79	3.99
	(1.70)	(1.55)	(1.65)	(1.89)
(iii) Skilled and professional labour	2.98	2.98	2.76	3.12
	(1.27)	(1.06)	(1.17)	(1.50)
(iv) Innovatory capacity	2.88	2.75	2.71	3.11
	(1.40)	(1.16)	(1.17)	(1.70)
(v) Organizational capacity	3.12	3.21	2.88	3.18
	(1.32)	(1.13)	(1.04)	(1.61)
(vi) Managerial expertise	3.24	3.19	3.12	3.38
	(1.42)	(1.32)	(1.37)	(1.56)
(vii) Relational skills	3.75	4.00	3.41	3.71
	(1.62)	(1.64)	(1.33)	(1.73)
Group 2	3.94	4.06	3.37	4.15
Consumer demand	(1.59)	(1.36)	(1.50)	(1.81)
(i) Upgrading of product quality	3.31	3.40	2.94	3.44
	(1.37)	(1.36)	(1.14)	(1.49)
(ii) Making for more product innovation	3.44	3.40	3.06	3.71
	(1.45)	(1.26)	(1.50)	(1.55)
Group 3	4.60	4.68	4.56	4.55
Interfirm competition/rivalry	(1.67)	(1.61)	(1.65)	(1.75)
Group 4	4.10	4.19	3.68	4.29
Linkages with foriegn or domestic firms and institutions	(1.37)	(1.32)	(1.12)	(1.52)
(i) Related firms (agglomerative economies)				
(ii) Universities and other research institutions	3.29 (1.30)	3.27 (1.25)	3.21 (1.17)	3.38 (1.43)

Note: Unless otherwise indicated, in all subsequent tables the figures reported are mean responses with standard deviations in parentheses

countries, and that MT or LT firms (which, in general, are more likely to be natural resource intensive, or influenced by the characteristics of consumer demand) will tend to assign lower rankings to these and related variables. Such firms will also tend to be more internationally oriented; hence their predicted higher ranking of cross-border, *vis-à-vis* domestic, competition. The contrasting hypothesis, set out by Rugman, Dunning and other scholars researching into the behaviour of MNEs, is that, as firms become more multinational and globally integrated in their value-added activities, they are likely to derive an increasing proportion of their core assets from outside national boundaries, and, indeed, may deliberately seek out foreign assets which they perceive to be supportive of, or help augment, their own core competencies.

The data in Table 11.4 reveal a mixed picture, although, taken as a whole, they do suggest that the sample firms derive an important part of their competitive advantages – on average between 40 and 50 per cent[24] – from their presence in foreign countries, either by way of FDI or by strategic alliances. The access provided by a foreign location (cf. a domestic location) to natural resources (including unskilled labour), linkages with suppliers, industrial competitors and other foreign producers, and the benefits of larger markets and more stringent consumer demands, were all ranked particularly high (3.44 or above). By contrast, and in line with received theory and the data on innovatory activity, the sample firms perceived that their domestic operations and/or the indigenous resources and capabilities of their home countries continued to provide the main source of competitiveness – and especially so in the case of technological capacity and of skilled and professional labour.

Predictably, there were some differences in the perceptions of firms according to the technological intensity of their main activities. Most noticeably, the LT firms claimed to obtain a higher proportion of their created assets (Group 1 [iii–vii]) from foreign sources than did MT or HT firms, particularly so in the case of innovatory capacity. *Inter alia*, this finding tends to support the proposition that at least part of the competitive advantages of firms obtained from foreign sources is likely to be different from (and complementary to) those obtained from domestic sources. Nevertheless, the table strongly suggests that for each of the advantages identified, a multiple (or at least a dual) location of value-added activities was perceived to yield positive gains.[25] It thus seems reasonable to conclude that, in the opinion of the leading industrial companies, FDI and/or cross-border strategic alliances *do* provide an entry to significant competitive advantages.[26]

Country-specific differences

Table 11.5 reclassifies the data set out in Table 11.4 by the source region or country of the sample firms. The data reveal few significant differences in the perceptions among the sample firms. As might be reasonably predicted, firms from high-wage economies (e.g. the United States and smaller European countries),[27] rank the foreign sourcing of unskilled labour relatively more highly than those from low-wage and, particularly, developing countries. Likewise, and consistent with the principle of comparative advantage, is the above-average reliance of Japanese firms on foreign natural resources, and the below-average reliance of 'other' developed country firms (in our sample survey, these were all from resource-rich countries[28]) on such resources. Relative to Japanese firms, too, European and US firms appear to value the access to foreign-based created assets (e.g. organiza-

Table 11.5 The sourcing of competitive advantages classified by region or country of origin of sample firms (1993)

	All	*Large European*	*Small European*	*USA*	*Japan*	*Other developed*	*Developing*
Group 1	3.54	3.80	3.90	3.61	3.21	2.63	3.21
Access to resources and assets	(1.39)	(1.25)	(1.41)	(1.43)	(1.35)	(1.30)	(1.63)
(i) Natural resources	4.24	4.26	3.65	4.03	4.87	3.39	4.86
	(1.70)	(1.58)	(1.81)	(1.61)	(1.63)	(2.14)	(1.66)
(ii) Unskilled labour	3.98	3.81	4.10	4.37	3.75	4.00	3.92
	(1.70)	(1.63)	(1.77)	(1.50)	(1.80)	(1.91)	(2.10)
(iii) Skilled and	2.98	3.18	3.30	3.27	2.46	3.00	2.21
professional labour	(1.27)	(1.22)	(1.45)	(1.15)	(1.26)	(1.26)	(1.01)
(iv) Innovatory	2.88	2.95	3.38	2.94	2.23	3.29	2.79
capacity	(1.40)	(1.31)	(1.56)	(1.39)	(1.34)	(1.25)	(1.37)
(v) Organizational	3.12	3.30	3.43	3.35	2.85	2.43	2.43
capacity	(1.32)	(1.37)	(1.12)	(1.05)	(1.54)	(1.27)	(1.28)
(vi) Managerial	3.24	3.30	3.86	3.29	3.12	3.14	2.36
expertise	(1.42)	(1.49)	(1.39)	(1.10)	(1.70)	(0.90)	(1.22)
(vii) Relational skills	3.75	3.98	4.43	3.90	3.46	3.29	2.43
	(1.62)	(1.56)	(1.69)	(1.35)	(1.70)	(1.70)	(1.28)
Group 2	3.94	4.39	4.22	3.78	2.96	5.20	3.83
Consumer demand	(1.59)	(1.64)	(1.73)	(1.53)	(1.19)	(1.10)	(1.40)
(i) Upgrading of product quality	3.31	3.65	3.67	3.20	2.36	4.29	3.14
	(1.37)	(1.46)	(1.53)	(1.16)	(1.04)	(0.95)	(1.17)
(ii) Making for more	3.44	3.58	3.90	3.33	2.76	4.14	3.43
product innovation	(1.45)	(1.48)	(1.30)	(1.37)	(1.48)	(1.07)	(1.50)
Group 3	4.60	5.43	5.38	4.23	3.23	4.29	4.36
Interfirm competition/ rivalry	(1.67)	(1.34)	(1.72)	(1.23)	(1.45)	(0.49)	(2.17)
Group 4	4.10	4.41	4.95	3.84	3.65	3.86	3.43
Linkages with foreign or domestic firms and institutions	(1.37)	(1.39)	(1.36)	(1.07)	(1.29)	(1.46)	(1.40)
(i) Related firms (agglomerative economies)							
(ii) Universities	3.29	3.40	3.52	3.32	3.17	2.83	3.00
and other research institutions	(1.30)	(1.14)	(1.29)	(1.40)	(1.46)	(1.47)	(1.30)

tional capacity, management, expertise and relational skills) more highly, although, in general, the competitive advantages of Japanese firms were perceived to be more home specific than those of their major competitors. (This also reflects their lower degree of multinationality; see the next section.)

In respect of each of the other three components of Porter's diamond, European-owned firms appear to rely more on foreign, than on domestic, sources of competitiveness than do their US and Japanese counterparts.

This is especially seen to be so in respect of interfirm competition, and, for smaller European firms, of linkages with related firms.

Notwithstanding the below-average significance attached by the sample firms to the acquisition of, or access to, foreign created assets, the rankings – even for MNEs from countries such as Germany and the United States, which record a comparative patenting advantage in HT products (Cantwell and Hodson 1991) – suggest that large MNEs in the HT and MT sectors are increasingly seeking a technology-related presence[29] in each of the main Triad countries or regions, for example US firms in the European Community (EU) and Japan; Japanese firms in the EU and the United States; and EU firms in Japan and the United States.

Degrees of multinationality

Perhaps the most frequently cited hypothesis about the propensity of firms to derive competitive advantages from their foreign operations is that the former will be positively related to the extent and the depth of the latter, relative to that of their domestic operations. In this part of our chapter, we attempt two exercises. One is to group the data already presented according to the four bands of multinationality set out earlier. The second is to relate the extent of the two measures of multinationality earlier identified (i.e. (i) the average percentage of global assets and employment employed outside the home country and (ii) the average percentage of global R&D expenditure undertaken outside the home country) to the values placed on Porter's four facets of competitive advantages (our groups 1 to 4), in a series of bivariate relationships.

Table 11.6 shows quite clearly that a greater degree of multinationality of firms is likely to be associated with the perception that an increasing proportion of global competitive advantages is derived from foreign sources. This, of all the tables presented in this chapter, is the most striking in its findings. It would also appear that for created assets (i.e. Group 1 [iii–vii]) the biggest rise in the significance of foreign operations for global competitiveness occurs when the average degree of multinationality (of assets and employment) is 30 per cent or above. However, for innovatory capacity, it is only where the degree of multinationality exceeds 60 per cent that the (average) ranking exceeds 3.00, while, as far as the influence of consumer demand and interfirm rivalry is concerned, it exceeds 5.00. The distinction between the sources of competitive advantages perceived to be derived from FDI and cross-border strategic alliances is particularly noticeable in the case of firms with low and high degrees of multinationality.

Table 11.7 sets out some bivariate correlation coefficients between the two measures of multinationality and six indices of competitive advantage. It suggests that for the main measure of multinationality (A in Table 11.7),

Table 11.6 The sourcing of competitive advantages classified by extent of multinationality* of sample firms (1993)

	All	*Low*	*Medium–Low*	*Medium–High*	*High*
Group 1	3.54	2.33	2.83	3.76	4.50
Access to resouces and assets	(1.39)	(1.28)	(1.13)	(1.00)	(1.31)
(i) Natural resources	4.24	3.82	3.90	4.21	4.62
	(1.70)	(2.01)	(1.84)	(1.34)	(1.84)
(ii) Unskilled labour	3.98	2.26	3.57	4.38	4.52
	(1.70)	(1.58)	(1.80)	(1.44)	(1.60)
(iii) Skilled and professional	2.98	2.06	2.48	3.33	3.48
labour	(1.27)	(1.18)	(0.90)	(1.19)	(1.20)
(iv) Innovatory capacity	2.88	2.82	2.67	2.80	3.43
	(1.40)	(1.81)	(1.20)	(1.32)	(1.22)
(v) Organizational capacity	3.12	1.94	2.88	3.37	3.57
	(1.32)	(1.25)	(1.26)	(1.09)	(1.19)
(vi) Managerial expertise	3.24	2.35	2.71	3.55	3.73
	(1.42)	(1.27)	(1.30)	(1.29)	(1.28)
(vii) Relational skills	3.75	2.35	3.21	4.13	4.43
	(1.62)	(1.84)	(1.38)	(1.29)	(1.48)
Group 2	3.94	3.27	3.32	3.98	4.96
Consumer demand	(1.59)	(1.98)	(1.39)	(1.43)	(1.49)
(i) Upgrading of product	3.31	3.00	2.79	3.34	4.18
quality	(1.37)	(1.80)	(1.28)	(1.11)	(1.33)
(ii) Making for more	3.44	2.94	3.17	3.49	4.04
product innovation	(1.45)	(1.48)	(1.46)	(1.36)	(1.32)
Group 3	4.60	4.29	4.08	4.68	5.37
Interfirm competition/rivalry	(1.67)	(1.79)	(1.67)	(1.56)	(1.43)
Group 4	4.10	3.06	3.50	4.27	4.87
Linkages with foreign or domestic firms and institutions	(1.37)	(1.48)	(1.25)	(1.25)	(1.14)
(i) Related firms (agglomerative economies)					
(ii) Universities and other	3.29	2.12	2.87	3.54	3.90
research institutions	(1.30)	(0.93)	(1.55)	(1.15)	(1.11)

* For more precise definitions of extent of multinationality see the introduction

the coefficients are positive and significant at a 99 per cent level or above, and that the most likely benefits of increased multinationality are likely to arise from an access to foreign organizational capacity and managerial expertise, and the linkages forged with foreign firms.

The results for the second measure of multinationality, the foreign R&D ratio (B in Table 11.7), are virtually identical to the results obtained for the first measure. Except for the correlation with natural assets (Group 1 [i–ii]), all of the coefficients are positive and significant at the 99 per cent level or above. Not surprisingly, the two measures of multinationality are also significantly positively correlated with each other (0.69, $p < 0.0001$), confirming that they essentially measure aspects of the same phenomenon.[30]

Table 11.7 Bivariate correlation coefficients between perceived competitive advantages derived from foreign activities by extent of multinationality of sample firms (1993)

	A	*B*
(a) Natural assets (Group 1 [i–iii])	0.31982	0.18998
(b) Created assets (technological) (Group 1 [iii–v])	0.36478	0.37895
(c) Created assets (managerial) (Group 1 [vi–viii])	0.43228	0.39619
(d) Consumer demand (Group 2)	0.36339	0.35007
(e) Interfirm rivalry (Group 3)	0.27146	0.28016
(f) Linkages with related firms (Group 4 [i])	0.46452	0.39511

A: Extent of multinationality = average share of foreign employment and assets to all employment assets.
B: Extent of multinationality = average share of foreign in all R&D

Size of firm

The final contextual variable – which to some extent is correlated with the degree of multinationality[31] – is size of firm. While it is not obvious why size, itself, should be related to the geographical sourcing of competitive-enhancing assets, the literature[32] does suggest that large firms are more likely to engage in FDI than smaller firms, and that multinationality, itself, helps a corporation to maintain, or increase, its share of global markets.

At the same time, it might be hypothesized that medium-size firms are likely to be more specialized in their portfolio of global assets, and, hence, more reliant on foreign sources to enhance or complement this portfolio. However, in recent years, the evidence suggests that very large firms are just as likely to engage in merger and acquisition (M&A) activities as are their smaller competitors. Finally, it might be predicted that the portfolio of foreign competitive-enhancing assets sought by medium-size firms,[33] relative to larger firms, may have more to do with gaining access to specialized resources, capabilities and markets, and/or establishing linkages with local foreign firms, although they may be expected to engage in less competition with foreign-owned firms than their larger counterparts.

Table 11.8 presents the results of our survey. It shows that size of firm is only of marginal importance in affecting the sourcing of most categories of competitive advantage.

WHICH FOREIGN COUNTRIES PROVIDE THE MOST VALUABLE ASSETS TO UPGRADING COMPETITIVENESS?

The next part of this chapter gives some details of the foreign countries most frequently identified by the sample firms as sources of competitive-enhancing assets. Here, it is not possible to evaluate the relative importance

Table 11.8 The sourcing of competitive advantages (classified by size of sample firms 1993)

	All	*Medium*	*Large (<5–24.9 bn)*	*Very Large (25–49.9 bn)*	*Mega (> 50 bn)*
Group 1	3.54	3.58	3.53	3.57	3.43
Access to resources and assets	(1.39)	(1.54)	(1.44)	(1.09)	(0.94)
(i) Natural resources	4.24	3.96	4.41	4.20	4.69
	(1.70)	(1.79)	(1.76)	(1.61)	(1.03)
(ii) Unskilled labour	3.98	4.03	3.89	4.25	3.86
	(1.70)	(1.68)	(1.92)	(1.39)	(1.17)
(iii) Skilled and professional	2.98	2.96	3.06	2.88	2.86
labour	(1.27)	(1.28)	(1.41)	(1.12)	(0.77)
(iv) Innovatory capacity	2.88	2.71	2.98	3.25	2.71
	(1.40)	(1.41)	(1.49)	(1.13)	(1.20)
(v) Organizational capacity	3.12	3.13	3.22	3.00	2.79
	(1.32)	(1.39)	(1.39)	(1.15)	(0.89)
(vi) Managerial experties	3.24	3.45	3.09	3.19	3.14
	(1.42)	(1.56)	(1.38)	(1.42)	(0.95)
(vii) Relational skills	3.75	3.82	3.78	3.50	3.64
	(1.62)	(1.66)	(1.72)	(1.59)	(1.08)
Group 2	3.94	4.07	3.90	3.93	3.67
Consumer demand	(1.59)	(1.68)	(1.63)	(1.58)	(1.15)
(i) Upgrading of product	3.31	3.30	3.40	3.13	3.14
quality	(1.37)	(1.38)	(1.46)	(1.25)	(1.17)
(ii) Making for more product	3.44	3.57	3.33	3.53	3.29
innovation	(1.45)	(1.46)	(1.48)	(1.46)	(1.33)
Group 3	4.60	4.58	4.72	4.50	4.29
Interfirm competition/rivalry	(1.67)	(1.85)	(1.60)	(1.26)	(1.68)
Group 4	4.10	4.24	4.07	4.25	3.57
Linkages with foreign or	(1.37)	(1.36)	(1.45)	(1.29)	(1.16)
domestic firms and institutions					
(i) Related firms					
(agglomerative economies)					
(ii) Universities and other	3.29	3.28	3.30	3.20	3.43
research institutions	(1.30)	(1.29)	(1.41)	(1.08)	(1.16)

of one source country relative to another; instead, we have chosen to identify which kind of competitive advantage is likely to be most closely associated with each country.

What would the received theories of trade and investment predict in this respect? The answer is that much will depend on the type of FDI undertaken (e.g. is it market seeking, resource seeking, efficiency seeking, or strategic asset seeking?), and on the static and dynamic competitive advantages of the home and host countries. Also, like trade, FDI and alliance formation might be either inter- or intraindustry. If the former, then one might expect the countries recipient to FDI to provide assets in which the home country is deficient; if the latter, then FDI is likely to be more efficiency enhancing and strategic asset seeking, in which case the foreign country will tend to provide assets similar to those in which the investing firm (or country) has a competitive edge.

In the course of our survey, every respondent was asked to name (up to) three foreign countries which were host to their affiliates, and which they perceived had the most positive impact on their own competitiveness. Table 11.9 presents some of the results by relating each of the competitive advantages identified to the number of times a particular host country was mentioned.

The data in the table confirm most of our predictions. Thus, developing countries clearly have a competitive advantage in affording access to natural resources, while Germany and Japan provided more than the average share of technological assets, and the United States more than the average share of managerial assets and consumer demand conditions favouring competitiveness (e.g. large markets). US firms were also perceived to offer relatively more competitive stimulus than other firms, while relative to other countries, Germany, Japan and the United States were perceived as good locations for establishing linkages with other firms.

One surprise of our survey was the frequency with which developing countries were identified as providing access to created assets and to Group 3 and 4 competitive advantage. Although mostly this is the result of pooling a number of countries at different stages of development into the same group, China and Brazil were both mentioned a number of times as providing a locale for more efficient production via economies of scale.[34] As might be expected, the host countries named varied with both the industry of the investing MNEs and their home countries. Thus, for example, firms in HT sectors accounted for 45–57 per cent of all mentions in the HT countries, for example the United States, Germany, Japan and the United Kingdom. Taking European-, US- and Japanese-owned firms as a group, 25.3 per cent of the countries mentioned by the respondents were located elsewhere in the Triad. (Or, alternatively, nearly three-quarters of their advantages were derived from within the Triad.)

THE MODES OF FOREIGN ENTRY MOST LIKELY TO ADVANCE COMPETITIVE ADVANTAGES

The respondents of our sample firms was asked to rank on a scale of 1 to 7 the importance of each of three modes of acquiring and/or tapping into the resources and capabilities of foreign countries, that is foreign diamonds of competitive advantage. These modes were (a) foreign direct investment, (b) non-equity co-operative agreements (e.g. strategic alliances, management contracts, licensing and franchising agreements, etc.) and (c) arm's length transactions (in both intermediate and final goods and services).

The hypothesis here is that 'deeper' forms of cross-border structural integration, for example (a) and (b), are more likely to result in an addition of competitive advantages to the home company (and country) than 'shallower' forms of transactions, for example arm's length trade. It might also

Table 11.9 The sourcing of competitive advantages classified by region or country (number of times countries mentioned among three most important sources of advantages 1993)

	Europe				*North America*		*Japan*	*Rest of world*		*Totals*
	France	*Germany*	*UK*	*Other*	*USA*	*Canada*		*Developed*	*Developing*	
Group 1 Access to resources Natural assets	0.50	2.00	5.00	4.00	6.00	2.00	0.50	2.50	30.00	52.50
Created assets (technological)	1.33	12.33	6.67	9.00	18.00	1.33	7.33	1.67	7.67	65.33
Created assets (managerial)	1.00	4.33	6.00	3.67	10.00	2.67	3.33	1.33	6.33	38.66
Group 2 Consumer demand	0.00	4.00	4.00	0.00	8.00	0.00	0.00	0.00	3.00	19.00
Group 3 Interfirm rivalry	2.00	4.00	4.00	5.00	16.00	1.00	2.00	1.00	4.00	39.00
Group 4 Linkages with related firms	6.00	8.00	7.00	4.00	17.00	1.00	9.00	0.00	4.00	56.00
Totals	10.83	34.66	32.67	25.67	75.00	8.00	22.16	6.50	55.00	270.49
(*n*)	(139)	(131)	(125)	(116)	(113)	(138)	(118)	(142)	(130)	

(*n*) = number of firms in the sample excluding firms from the host country

be predicted that firms are more likely to wish to internalize their assets in sectors which are technology intensive, than those which are not. A related hypothesis is that non-equity co-operative ventures are likely to be ranked higher as a modality for acquiring competitive advantages by firms in low-technology-intensive sectors. Because of their needs to integrate their global operations, it might be expected that the most multinational of firms may be expected to rank FDI relatively higher than firms whose foreign operations are less significant to their overall prosperity. Finally, it might be supposed that firms from countries (e.g. the United States whose domestic institutions are organized on hierarchical lines are more likely to rank FDI as a (foreign) asset-acquiring route than their counterparts from countries (e.g. Japan) whose institutions practise a more co-operative mode of governance.

Tables 11.10 and 11.11 offer evidence to assess these hypotheses. Overall, it is clearly true that the 'deeper' forms of integration are perceived to offer the most benefits as regards the acquisition of competitive advantages abroad. In Table 11.10, the average rankings for each of the three modalities are classified according to the technological intensity of the firm. While the LT and MT firms behaved as expected, in other words FDI was perceived to offer the most advantages while arm's length transactions would offer the least, and that arm's length trade would be relatively more important to LT firms and FDI to MT firms, the HT firms actually derived more advantages from co-operative alliances than from FDI.

Also somewhat contrary to our expectations, the medium–low and medium–high multinationalization firms actually derived more advantages from all three modalities of foreign involvement than did firms in the high multinationalization group. Whether this is another manifestation of the law of diminishing returns or of the differences in the first-mover vs. late-mover experiences, remains to be seen. More in line with our expectations, the connection between internationalization and size was confirmed, as the figures in Table 11.10 would seem to indicate that the gains from FDI accrue predominantly to the largest firms, whereas the benefits from co-operative alliances or trade do not exhibit any obvious pattern.

Finally, Table 11.11 sheds some light on the advantages derived from the different modalities classified by the nationality of the firm. The results here contradict the hypothesis that firms from countries with typically hierarchical organizational structures would prefer FDI, as the Japanese firms stand out in their perception of the advantages derived not only from FDI, but from co-operative ventures and arm's length trade as well. In summary, although FDI is most likely to be the preferred route by which the domestic and foreign diamonds of competitive advantage are linked, the relative significance of this route is greatest in the case of (large) firms which are (i) medium to high technology and (ii) moderately to highly multinational.

Table 11.10 Perceptions of the importance of the mode of foreign involvement of sample firms by technological intensity, extent of multinationality and size (1993)

	(a) FDI	*(b) Non-equity*	*(c) Arm's length*
All firms	5.22 (1.63)	4.66 (1.46)	3.96 (1.45)
High technology	5.23 (1.63)	5.31 (1.08)	4.27 (1.59)
Medium technology	5.53 (1.42)	4.62 (1.41)	3.55 (1.28)
Low technology	5.02 (1.74)	4.07 (1.57)	3.92 (1.36)
Low multinationality	4.06 (2.19)	4.71 (1.69)	3.59 (1.62)
Medium–low multinationality	5.46 (1.67)	5.25 (1.07)	4.25 (1.26)
Medium–high multinationality	5.44 (1.38)	4.83 (1.28)	4.12 (1.53)
High multinationality	5.28 (1.67)	3.93 (1.65)	3.55 (1.21)
Medium size	4.83 (1.84)	4.48 (1.50)	4.00 (1.41)
Large	5.19 (1.61)	4.69 (1.31)	3.95 (1.46)
Very large	6.07 (0.80)	5.07 (1.79)	4.13 (1.46)
Mega	5.93 (0.92)	4.79 (1.58)	3.71 (1.64)

Table 11.11 Perceptions of the importance of the mode of foreign involvement of sample firms by region or country of origin (1993)

	(a) FDI	*(b) Non-equity*	*(c) Arm's length*
All firms	5.22 (1.63)	4.66 (1.46)	3.96 (1.45)
Large European	5.47 (1.42)	4.60 (1.45)	3.81 (1.24)
Small European	4.70 (1.95)	4.81 (1.63)	4.32 (1.34)
United States	4.97 (1.80)	4.58 (1.26)	3.29 (1.64)
Japan	5.96 (1.17)	5.36 (1.41)	4.88 (1.26)
Developing countries	4.79 (1.37)	4.29 (1.14)	4.21 (1.25)
Other countries	4.57 (2.15)	3.14 (1.57)	3.29 (1.38)

THE DYNAMICS OF THE GEOGRAPHICAL SOURCING OF COMPETITIVE ADVANTAGE

To what extent do firms perceive that their access to foreign diamonds of competitive advantage is becoming a more important contribution to their overall competitive advantages? It might be reasonably hypothesized that, as firms increase their degree of multinationality, they will derive increasingly more competitive advantages from their FDIs or strategic alliances. Of course, the reverse may also be the case. In the course of our survey, firms were asked to rank, on a scale of –3 to +3, whether they perceived their competitive advantages were becoming less (–) or more (+) dependent on their foreign operations.

The results presented in Table 11.12 essentially confirm the impressions already gained from Tables 11.10 and 11.11 concerning the benefits derived from internationalization. Although, overall, the firms perceived that the foreign sourcing of competitive advantages had become more important

Table 11.12 Perceptions of firms as to whether foreign sourcing of competitive advantages has become relatively more important in recent years (1993)

All	*1.50 (1.36)*
High technology	1.69 (1.35)
Medium technology	1.79 (0.95)
Low technology	1.16 (1.51)
Large European	1.64 (1.27)
Small European	1.90 (1.04)
United States	1.26 (1.53)
Japan	1.62 (1.39)
Developing	1.43 (0.85)
Other	0.38 (2.00)
Medium size	1.47 (1.32)
Large	1.31 (1.55)
Very large	1.87 (0.83)
Mega	2.00 (0.96)
Low multinationality	0.94 (1.55)
Medium–low	1.29 (1.37)
Medium–high	1.62 (1.44)
High	1.96 (0.92)

over time, MT and HT firms were clearly the most positive, as were the very large and mega firms. When classified by their region of origin, firms from small European countries were the most positive in their responses, which may reflect in part the aftermath of the wave of investment created by the perceived threat of a 'Fortress Europe' in 1992 for the countries outside of the Union. Not surprisingly, the firms that were the most multinational also saw the foreign sourcing of competitive advantages as being relatively more important.

HOME GOVERNMENTS AND COMPETITIVENESS

The role of governments in affecting the competitiveness of firms is a subject which has long been of fascination to economists and other scholars.[35] In the present context, we are interested in the perceived influences of home governments on the ability and willingness of our sample firms to be globally competitive. In our questionnaire, we identified eighteen possible ways in which governments might exert such an influence. For each of these ways, we asked the firms to assign a figure ranging from –3 to +3, according to whether, in their opinion, home governments had influenced their *global* competitiveness negatively or positively between 1988 and 1993 (0 = no influence at all). Table 11.13 presents our findings classified by the three groups of industrial sectors identified in this chapter. Table 11.14 does the same for firms classified by different nationalities and Table 11.15 for firms classified by their degree of multinationality.

Table 11.13 Perceived influence of home governments on the competitive advantages of the sample firms by technological intensity (1993)

	All	*HT*	*MT*	*LT*
1 Provision and upgrading of infrastructure	0.52 (1.00)	0.48 (1.08)	0.60 (1.00)	0.51 (0.93)
2 Social policies	–0.13 (1.44)	–0.10 (1.47)	–0.31 (1.42)	–0.05 (1.43)
3 Monetary and exchange rate policies	–0.11 (2.16)	–0.04 (1.94)	–0.73 (2.00)	0.20 (2.40)
4 Trade policies	0.35 (1.45)	0.26 (1.40)	–0.12 (1.52)	0.70 (1.39)
5 Industrial and technology policies	0.36 (2.08)	0.35 (2.11)	0.06 (2.46)	0.54 (1.80)
6 Education and training policies	0.09 (1.25)	0.15 (1.43)	0.03 (1.29)	0.07 (1.04)
7 Environmental policies	–0.06 (1.24)	–0.34 (1.22)	0.09 (1.33)	0.13 (1.16)
8 Market-facilitating policies	–0.37 (1.99)	–0.38 (2.05)	–0.55 (2.15)	–0.25 (1.85)
9 Promoting an ethos of competitiveness	0.28 (2.91)	0.53 (3.57)	0.13 (2.72)	0.13 (2.30)
10 Promoting a culture of investment and saving	0.18 (1.91)	0.51 (2.12)	–0.09 (2.07)	0.04 (1.56

Table 11.13 shows that, on average, the sample firms thought that actions by their home governments had had either a marginally beneficial effect on their global competitiveness (e.g. provision of infrastructure, trade and industrial and technology policies) or a marginally adverse effect on market-facilitating and social policies. There were few consistent differences between sectors, except that LT firms thought more favourably of most government actions (notably trade, industrial, technology, monetary and exchange rate policies) than either HT or MT firms.

More interesting differences are revealed in Table 11.14. While US and European firms perceived that their home governments pursued macroeconomic and trade policies marginally favourable to their competitiveness, Japanese firms considered these same policies of their government to work to their disadvantage. By contrast, Japanese firms believed that most macro-organizational policies of their government (e.g. environmental, industrial and technology policies), together with the promotion of a culture of investment and saving, aided their global competitiveness, while US respondents generally thought their government worked to the detriment of their competitiveness. Respondents of firms from small European and developing countries were generally more favourably disposed to the actions of their home governments than those of firms from other countries. Rather sur-

Table 11.14 Perceived influence of home governments on the competitive advantages of the sample firms by region or country of origin (1993)

	All	*Large European*	*Small European*	*USA*	*Japan*	*Other developed*	*Developing*
1 Provision and upgrading of infrastructure	0.52 (1.00)	0.68 (1.03)	0.81 (0.96)	–0.08 (0.85)	0.44 (0.96)	0.67 (0.67)	1.00 (0.99)
2 Social policies	–0.13 (1.44)	–0.45 (1.50)	0.38 (1.50)	–0.74 (1.37)	0.20 (1.00)	–0.13 (1.55)	0.92 (1.12)
3 Monetary and exchange rate policies	–0.11 (2.16)	0.21 (2.33)	0.52 (2.46)	0.29 (1.44)	–1.62 (1.77)	–0.13 (1.81)	–0.08 (2.43)
4 Trade policies	0.35 (1.45)	0.30 (1.15)	0.29 (1.95)	0.19 (1.49)	–0.19 (1.47)	1.13 (0.64)	1.54 (0.88)
5 Industrial and technology policies	0.36 (2.08)	–0.12 (1.87)	1.19 (2.40)	–0.53 (1.96)	0.72 (2.03)	0.13 (1.46)	2.08 (1.38)
6 Education and training policies	0.09 (1.25)	0.07 (1.32)	0.81 (1.47)	–0.58 (0.81)	0.12 (0.95)	0.00 (0.93)	0.62 (1.50)
7 Environmental policies	–0.06 (1.24)	–0.14 (1.32)	0.00 (1.00)	–0.55 (1.36)	0.50 (0.86)	–0.25 (1.39)	0.31 (1.18)
8 Market-facilitating policies	–0.37 (1.99)	–0.37 (2.02)	–0.14 (2.31)	–1.13 (1.87)	–0.54 (1.79)	–0.25 (1.39)	1.31 (1.38)
9 Promoting an ethos of competitiveness	0.28 (2.91)	0.21 (3.00)	0.57 (3.65)	0.10 (3.28)	0.19 (1.30)	–0.50 (2.20)	1.17 (3.41)
10 Promoting a culture of investment and saving	0.18 (1.91)	0.29 (2.00)	0.38 (1.72)	–0.77 (1.81)	0.84 (1.70)	–0.50 (1.07)	0.85 (2.19)

prisingly, while firms from all the major investing countries believed their governments did little to facilitate the efficient operation of markets, firms from developing countries were noticeably more appreciative of the role of governments.

Table 11.15 suggests that there is no consistent pattern in the reactions of firms to their own government's actions according to the degree of multinationality of the former. Thus, while the least multinational of firms regarded the impact of industrial and technology policies, and the promotion of an investment and savings culture, more favourably than did the most multinational firms, the reverse appeared to be the case for macroeconomic and social policies. Here, however, bivariant comparisons of this kind tend to break down as it so happens that Japanese firms are the least multinational, and it could be (and most likely is) that the country of the respondent firms is the more important determinant of the role of government than the degree of their multinationality. It is precisely for this and

Table 11.15 Perceived influence of home governments on the competitive advantages of the sample firms by extent of multinationality (1993)

	All	*Low*	*Medium–low*	*Medium–high*	*High*
1 Provision and upgrading of infrastructure	0.52 (1.00)	0.67 (1.12)	0.67 (0.87)	0.37 (1.03)	0.61 (0.87)
2 Social policies	–0.13 (1.44)	–0.39 (1.20)	0.10 (1.64)	–0.27 (1.39)	0.03 (1.59)
3 Monetary and exchange rate policies	–0.11 (2.16)	–0.39 (2.35)	–0.68 (1.89)	–0.03 (2.09)	0.83 (2.19)
4 Trade policies	0.35 (1.45)	0.50 (1.62)	0.32 (1.59)	0.27 (1.41)	0.60 (1.38)
5 Industrial and technology policies	0.36 (2.08)	1.33 (1.97)	0.59 (2.17)	0.17 (1.96)	–0.13 (2.13)
6 Education and training policies	0.09 (1.25)	0.28 (1.49)	–0.09 (1.06)	0.17 (1.15)	–0.10 (1.45)
7 Environmental policies	–0.06 (1.24)	–0.06 (1.43)	0.00 (0.98)	–0.08 (1.39)	–0.07 (1.08)
8 Market-facilitating policies	–0.37 (1.99)	–0.06 (1.66)	–0.41 (1.44)	–0.53 (2.18)	–0.40 (2.03)
9 Promoting an ethos of competitiveness	0.28 (2.91)	0.24 (2.25)	0.32 (2.93)	0.33 (2.79)	0.13 (3.73)
10 Promoting a culture of investment and saving	0.18 (1.91)	0.72 (1.84)	0.23 (2.43)	–0.02 (1.59)	0.03 (2.18)

related reasons why a multivariant approach is necessary to complement the descriptive interpretation of the data set out in this chapter.

SUMMARY AND CONCLUSIONS

This chapter has shown that a not insignificant part of the competitive advantages of some of the world's leading industrial corporations is derived from their foreign-based activities. It has also revealed that the extent to which a firm's competitive advantages are so derived is dependent on (i) the kind of competitive advantages and the types of FDI and/or cross-border alliances engaged in by firms, (ii) the technology intensity of the sectors in which they are engaged, (iii) the countries from which they emanate, and (iv) – and most particularly – on the degree of their multinationality.

Our data also reveal that an overwhelming majority of firms from all sectors and countries believed that the importance of the foreign sourcing of their competitive advantages had increased in recent years, and that FDI was the favoured modality (followed by that of interfirm co-operative agreements) for acquiring such advantages.

A final section of the chapter touched on the role of home governments in influencing the global competitive advantages of the sample firms. In general, this was not perceived to be of critical significance, but there were noticeable differences observed by firms of different nationalities, which, *inter alia*, reflect some very distinctive country-specific philosophies of the role of governments, hierarchies and markets between larger Western nations (particularly the United States) and Eastern nations (particularly Japan) and some smaller European nations (particularly Sweden).

APPENDIX: CHARACTERISTICS OF THE SAMPLE

The sample consists of a total of 144 responses, which come from 131 different firms. For those firms that provided multiple responses, the statistics on size and degree of multinationality, as well as industry classification, follow those of the largest corporate unit. Outside of these classification variables, all of the multiple responses received are unique, and are treated as individual responses in the analyses.

Of the 144 responses to the survey, 110 come from firms that are ranked in the *Fortune* 500 (based on 1993 sales). The remaining firms were contacted to improve the industrial and/or geographical representativeness of the data, and they are all among the largest multinationals of their respective home countries.

One firm in the sample could not be classified by industry sector, as the identity of the firm was concealed; however, values for the other classification variables were obtained.

NOTES

1 I am much indebted to Sarianna Lundan of Reading University for research assistance in the preparation of this chapter.
2 As identified by *Fortune* magazine, 25 July 1994.
3 Mainly Vice-Presidents or Directors of Foreign Operations.
4 Sometimes called ownership-specific advantages of firms.
5 For a summary of the competitive advantages identified by economists, see, for example, Dunning (1993a: Chapter 4), and for those identified by business strategists, for example, see Porter (1990) and Peteraf (1993).
6 The aim of strategic asset-acquiring FDI is to gain access to assets which protect or advance the acquiring firm's competitive advantages and/or reduce the competitive advantages of its rivals. In the language of the eclectic paradigm, firms engage in FDI not to exploit existing ownership (O) advantages, but to acquire such advantages, which, when deployed with their existing O advantages, help sustain or further their global competitive advantages.
7 As documented, for example, in the various editions of the *World Investment Reports* (UNCTAD). The most recent US data (Mataloni 1995) show that in 1993 the foreign affiliate sales of non-bank US MNEs were 45.0 per cent of their parent sales. This figure compares with a 1983 figure of 37.3 per cent.
8 See especially a special issue of *Management International Review* (No. 33, 1993) edited by Alan Rugman (Rugman *et al.* 1995).
9 First set out in Porter (1990).

10 See, for example, Dunning (1993b).
11 Including those of Australia, Canada, Denmark, Korea, Mexico and New Zealand. See Rugman (1993).
12 We fully recognize the drawbacks of such a procedure and, in particular, the inevitable subjectivity of the opinions expressed.
13 More specifically, HT sectors include aerospace, chemicals, computers, electronics and pharmaceuticals; MT sectors include industrial equipment, motor vehicles, petroleum refining, soap and cosmetics; and LT sectors include beverages, building materials, food, metal products, paper, publishing and printing, rubber and plastics, textiles and tobacco.
14 These include France, Germany, Italy, Spain, the United Kingdom and UK/Netherlands.
15 These include Belgium, Denmark, Finland, the Netherlands, Sweden and Switzerland.
16 These include Brazil, Chile, Hong Kong, South Korea and Taiwan.
17 These include Canada, Australia and New Zealand.
18 Or one of these when data on either employment or assets were given. Additionally, for some firms sales data from Worldscope/Disclosure was used.
19 As defined by the firms themselves.
20 See especially their annual *World Investment Reports* (1991–5) and the *World Investment Directory* (4 volumes, 1992–3).
21 But, again, we would remind the reader that all the firms in the sample are large, compared with the great majority of the 38,000 firms identified by UNCTAD as having foreign direct investments. See its *World Investment Report* (1995).
22 The comparison in this exercise is between advantages thought to emanate from the portfolio of assets located in the home country and that in all other countries.
23 Namely, factor conditions, demand conditions, firm strategy, structure and rivalry, and related and supporting industries (see Porter 1990).
24 Each ranking being expressed as a percentage of 7 (which would suggest that all their advantages were derived from outside their national boundaries).
25 A later paper will attempt to relate the performance of the sample firms to the sources of their competencies.
26 We accept that these data do not, in themselves, indicate whether, if the FDI had *not* taken place, or the alliances had *not* been formed, the overall competitive position of the respondent firms would have been better or worse.
27 Notably Sweden and Switzerland.
28 Namely, Canada, Australia and New Zealand.
29 By this is meant either the pursuance of R&D-related activities by the foreign subsidiaries and/or alliances with foreign firms, or the monitoring of the innovatory activities of foreign firms.
30 Since the Group 1–4 variables are not continuous, the significance levels reported here should be taken as indicators of a possible relationship (to be investigated further in a later paper) rather than any form of final analysis.
31 Although the (Pearson) correlation coefficient between size and multinationality is not significantly different from zero.
32 See, for example, Dunning (1993a: Chapter 6).
33 Remembering that all the firms in our sample are large, relative to the universe of firms, but that some are much larger than others!
34 The figures in Table 11.9 somewhat understate the importance of scale economies, as the figure for Group 2 indicates the overall importance of consumer demand conditions, and not scale economies specifically.

35 For a recent appraisal, see various contributions to an edited volume by the author to be published in 1997 (Dunning 1997).

REFERENCES

Cantwell, J. and Hodson, C. (1991) 'Global R&D and UK competitiveness', in M. Casson (ed.) *Global Research Strategy and International Competitiveness*, Oxford: Basil Blackwell pp. 133–82.

Dunning, J. H. (1993a) *Multinational Enterprises and the Global Economy*, Workingham: Addison Wesley.

——(1993b) 'Internationalizing Porter's Diamond', *Management International Review* 33, Special Issue No. 2: 7–15.

——(ed.) (1997) *Governments, Globalization and International Business*, Oxford: Oxford University Press.

Mataloni, R. (1995) 'U.S. multinational companies: operations in 1993', *Survey of Current Business* June: 31–51.

Peteraf, M. (1993) 'The cornerstones of competitive advantage: a resource based view', *Strategic Management Journal* 14: 179–91.

Porter, M. E. (1990) *The Competitive Advantage of Nations*, New York: The Free Press.

Rugman, A. M. (ed.) (1993) *Management International Review* 33, spring, No. 2 (Special Edition on Michael Porter's, 'Diamond of competitive advantage').

Rugman, A. M., Van den Broeck, J. and Verbeke, A. (eds) (1995) *Beyond the Diamond: Research in Global Management*, Vol. 5, Greenwich, CT: JAI Press.

UNCTAD (1991–5) *World Investment Reports 1991–95* (annual publication), Geneva and New York: UN.

——(1992–3) *World Investment Directory* (4 vols, 1992–3).

——(1995) *World Investment Report 1995, Transnational Corporations and Competitiveness*, Geneva and New York: UN.

Part IV

THE JAPANESE CONNECTION

12

RECENT FOREIGN DIRECT INVESTMENT IN JAPAN AND THE UNITED STATES

A comparative analysis

INTRODUCTION

Twenty years ago, the post-war hegemony of the United States as an unrivalled economic power was coming to an end as US firms gradually lost.their competitive ground to firms from Europe. By the early 1980s the competitive or ownership-specific advantages of European firms had grown sufficiently large for them to compete effectively against US producers in their home market. The subsequent wave of market- and strategic asset-seeking foreign direct investment (FDI) from Europe was joined by increasing investment from Japan in the 1980s.

As a result, the stock of total inward investment in the United States grew nearly equal to the stock of outward investment in 1989, and since then the net balance of inward and outward investment flows has hovered around zero. In terms of the investment development path (IDP), the United States had entered the fifth stage of development. Chapter 9 has shown that in the fifth stage, a nation's FDI balance is affected not only by the market- or resource-seeking investment by foreign firms, but also by the strategic acquisition of indigenous O advantages by foreign investors. In other words, if in Stages 1 and 2 of the IDP, a net inward investment balance was due to the relatively poor O advantages of indigenous firms and the locational attractiveness of natural resources for foreign investors, in the fifth stage a net inward investment balance might equally well be caused by the desire on behalf of foreign firms to assimilate some or the knowledge advantages of the indigenous firms (Dunning and Narula 1994).[1]

At the same time, Japan has followed an investment path quite unlike that of the other developed countries (or at least most Western European nations). Japan's export-led growth strategy combined with a history of limits to inward (and initially outward) investment followed by a period of aggressive outward FDI in the 1980s resulted in a starkly positive total FDI balance.

Figure 12.1(a) Net Outward Investment (NOI) stocks for US 1970–93
Source: UNCTAD (1992), US Department of Commerce (1994b)

The investment development paths of Japan and the United States are depicted in Figures 12.1(a) and 12.1(b), respectively. The figures are drawn following the original form of the IDP, which associates net outward investment position (stocks) with GDP. Since growth in GDP is not con-

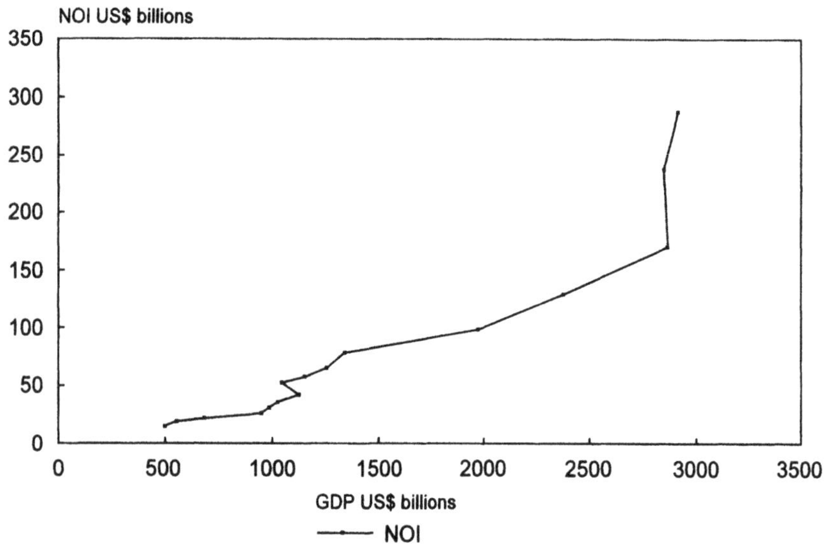

Figure 12.1(b) Net Outward Investment (NOI) stocks for Japan 1970–90
Source: UNCTAD (1992), US Department of commerce (1994b)

stant over time, and in fact can be negative as the figure for Japan illustrates, the observations in the diagram are not equidistant from one another. However, this makes little difference in the shape of the curve as virtually the same shape is observed if the net NOI position is plotted over time.

As predicted by the IDP, substantial inward investment into the United States took place in the 1980s both from Europe and a bit later from Japan, and eventually surpassed the outward flows of FDI, bringing the NOI stock position close to zero. These flows can be seen in Figures 12.2(a) and 12.2(b), which also indicate the NOI position from a flow perspective. The unstable equilibrium suggested by Dunning in Chapter 9 as characteristic of Stage 5 countries (i.e. the United States) is evident in Figure 12.2(a) which shows the alternating positive and negative balances of the inward and outward flows.[2]

The rationale for the increased inward FDI flows in Stage 5 stems from the increasing convergence of Stage 4 nations in terms of both GDP per capita and their created endowments. In fact, the basis for the dynamism of the IDP arises from this cross-border learning process which moves nations from one stage of development to another.[3] However, an increase in inward investment could have two different explanations. On one hand, an increase could be seen as evidence of the declining O advantages of US firms *vis-à-vis* their foreign counterparts. On the other hand, it could be due to the improved locational attractiveness of the United States as a production location. Or, indeed, it could be combination of both factors.

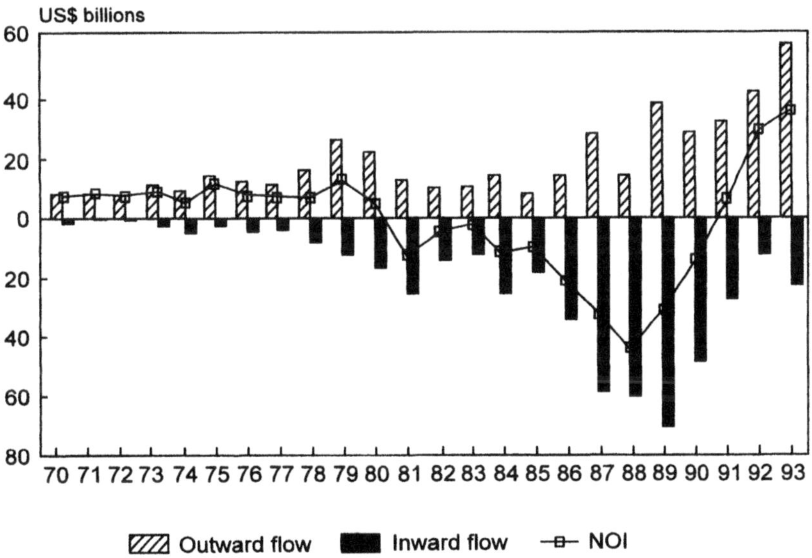

Figure 12.2(a) FDI flows to and from the US 1970–93
Source: UNCTAD (1992), US Department of Commerce (1994b)

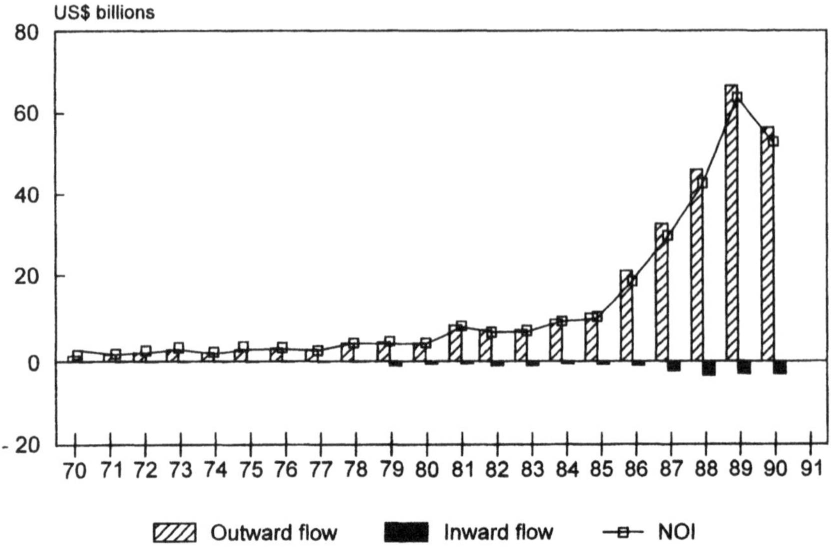

Figure 12.2(b) FDI flows to and from Japan 1970–90
Source: UNCTAD (1992)

In the case of EC investment to the United States, the European firms had indeed acquired substantial O advantages *vis-à-vis* their American counterparts by the early 1980s, and EC investment stock in the United States reached parity with US investment in the EC in 1982 (Dunning 1993). In part, this expansion was due to European firms' improved ability to seek markets outside of Europe, and in part to an increasing degree it involved sequential investment from multinationals already established in the United States.

The strategic asset-seeking investment can be hypothesized to arise from the countries of the EC catching up with the United States (and each other) in terms of GDP per capita, and their consequent move towards the fifth stage of the IDP, which is characterized by global rationalization of MNE production. The change in the motivation of FDI from market-seeking to strategic asset-seeking investment has at least two implications for the analysis.

First, it is no longer necessary for inward investment to result from weaknesses in the O advantages of indigenous firms, but rather from the advantages that arise from the incorporation of these O-specific capabilities to globally rationalized production. Second, strategic asset-seeking investment also carries implications concerning the mode of entry, which towards the end of the 1980s shifted towards mergers and acquisitions and strategic alliances.[4] An increase in sequential investment may also change the composition of the incoming investment from equity to retained earnings, and as Graham (1996) points out, these changes can be large enough to warrant inclusion in the analysis.

The initial investment from Japan, described by Gittelman and Dunning (1991) as 'defensive market-seeking investment', was fuelled by growing trade tensions, evidence of which was found in the US imposition of voluntary export restraints (VERs) on Japanese automobiles. Towards the end of the 1980s, the Japanese expansion to the US market employed what could be termed a 'late-mover' strategy, whereby Japanese firms used mergers and acquisitions to gain quicker access, in particular to enter some culturally sensitive areas, such as entertainment, in which they possessed no self-evident ownership-specific advantages (Gittelman and Dunning 1991). The Japanese also engaged in considerable real estate investment, and together these investments were indicative of a change in motivation of Japanese FDI into the United States from market-seeking to strategic asset-seeking investment.

Despite the inroads the Japanese have made into the US markets, inward investment to Japan continues to be low. To address the issue of why FDI to Japan is so low, and to what extent the experience of the United States in the 1980s can be used as a guide to try to predict the future of FDI into Japan, this chapter will first evaluate the ownership-specific advantages of foreign *vis-à-vis* Japanese firms and then evaluate the attractiveness of Japan as a location from which to exploit such advantages. Particular attention is paid to the ownership-specific advantages of US firms, and the modalities in which these advantages have been exploited in Japan, and conversely the modalities in which Japanese O advantages have been exploited in the United States.

THEORETICAL PREDICTIONS

If foreign firms possessed few O-specific advantages over Japanese firms, or if the exploitation of such advantages in Japan would be less advantageous than serving the Japanese market though exports, the dearth of FDI to Japan would follow directly from the predictions of the received theory. This section will assess the record to date and the likelihood that a lack of ownership-specific advantages exploitable in Japan can be accepted as a possible explanation for the low level of FDI to Japan.

Ownership advantages of foreign vs. Japanese firms

One possible explanation for the low FDI into Japan could be that foreign firms possess few competitive or O-specific advantages *vis-à-vis* their Japanese competitors (Dunning 1996). However, evidence of the penetration of US investment in transportation, electrical machinery, chemicals and fabricated metal products in Japan in the period 1983–90 would seem to negate this possibility.

Table 12.1(a) Sales of US foreign affiliates in Japan and US exports to Japan, 1989 (US$ billions)

Industry	*1** *Aff. sales*	*2*** *US aff. imports*	*3* *Exports to Japan*	*4**** *Exports to aff.*	*5* *Total (1-2)+(3-4)*	*6* *Sales/X (1-2)+(3-4)*
Food and kindred products	3.2	n/a	7.4	n/a	10.6	0.4
Chemical and allied products	10.5	n/a	4.7	0.5	14.7	2.5
Primary and fabricated metals	1.4	n/a	2.5	n/a	3.9	0.6
Machinery, except electrical	15.3	n/a	2.5	1.2	16.6	11.8
Electric and electronic equipment	5.7	0.2	6.6	n/a	12.1	0.8
Transportation equipment	38.9	8.2	0.9	n/a	31.6	29.8
Other manufacturing	9.2	n/a	8.7	0.6	17.3	1.1
Total manufacturing	84.3	10.3	33.3	3.1	104.2	2.5
Wholesale trade	21.8	0.8	n/a	4.7	25.7	n/a
Finance	8.2	n/a	n/a	n/a	n/a	n/a
Services	2.6	n/a	n/a	n/a	n/a	n/a
All industries	145.7	11.1	42.8	7.9	169.5	3.9

* Non-bank affiliates
** Non-bank affiliates, sales to both parents and non-affiliated firms
*** Shipped to non-bank affiliates by US parents
Sources: Dunning (1996), US Department of Commerce (1992) *US Direct Investment Abroad*, US Department of Commerce (1994a) *US Foreign Trade Highlights*

Table 12.1(a) illustrates this point by comparing the sales of US affiliates in Japan to exports to Japan. These figures should be contrasted with Table 12.1(b), which illustrates the affiliate sales of Japanese firms in the United States and Japanese exports to the United States.[5] Further indication of the existence of US O advantages is found in Tables 12.2(a) and (b), which contrast the outward investment from the United States to Europe in several industries to US direct investment in Japan. These data would suggest that at least part of the reason for the low penetration of US firms in the Japanese market is due to factors other than lack of ownership-specific advantages.

It should also be noted that some of the investment occurred in sectors with a marked Japanese competitive advantage, such as fabricated metal products and electrical machinery, indicating that the US firms were both exploiting existing advantages as well as acquiring new ones in this period (Dunning and Narula 1994).

In fact, when compared with the situation in the United States in the early 1970s, it is likely (although no data are offered here) that the number of potential entrants to the United States with a revealed comparative advantage *vis-à-vis* US firms was much less than the number of firms (from an increasingly larger pool of countries) that presently have the

Table 12.1(b) Sales of Japanese foreign affiliates in the United States and Japanese exports to the United States, 1990 (US$ billions)

Industry	*1 Aff. sales*	*2 Japan aff. imports*	*3 Exports to USA*	*4 Exports to aff.*	*5 Total (1-2)+(3-4)*	*6 Sales/X (1-2)+(3-4)*
Food and kindred products	2.5	n/a	0.3	n/a	2.8	8.3
Chemical and allied products	5.5	0.7	2.4	n/a	7.2	5.2
Primary and fabricated metal	12.3	n/a	n/a	0.8	n/a	n/a
Machinery, except electrical	12.2	1.7	70.0*	5.0	91.6	0.4
Electric and electronic equipment	5.0	0.8	n/a	1.6	n/a	n/a
Transportation equipment	11.1	n/a	n/a	4.8	n/a	n/a
Other manufacturing	10.6	1.3	n/a	1.5	n/a	n/a
Total manufacturing	59.3	5.3	89.1	14.0	129.1	0.7
Wholesale trade	219.4	33.5	n/a	73.4	n/a	n/a
Finance	12.3	n/a	n/a	n/a	n/a	n/a
Services	6.6	n/a	n/a	n/a	n/a	n/a
All industries	313.1	39.1	89.7	87.7	276.0	137.0

* Machinery and transportation equipment
Sources: US Department of Commerce (1993) *FDI in the U.S.: An Update*, US Department of Commerce (1994a) *U.S. Foreign Trade Highlights*
Note: All data are for non-bank affiliates

technical and organizational abilities that could usefully be exploited in a foreign location, Japan among those. As mentioned earlier, this is at least partly due to the fact that the increasing convergence of GDP/capita in the developed world has brought about an increasing number of multinationals in the mature stages of their internationalization process. In many cases this process leads towards globally rationalized production, creating a 'push' factor for more firms to utilize Japan as a location of production.[6]

Locational advantages in Japan

If foreign firms do possess advantages at par or beyond those possessed by the indigenous Japanese firms, are there particular aspects of the Japanese market that make it an attractive location for international production? Again, making the comparison with the United States in the early 1980s, once foreign (mainly European) firms had acquired the O-specific advantages necessary to compete in the US market, a strong 'pull' factor towards the United States was its large and affluent market. Japan has since then surpassed the United States in terms of GDP/capita, and Japanese consumers are sometimes characterized as the most demanding in the world. These factors should create a similar 'pull' factor for market-seeking FDI to Japan.

Table 12.2(a) Comparison of US FDI stocks in Europe and Japan by industry, 1993 (US$ billions)

Industry	*1* *US OFDI total*	*2* *US OFDI to Europe*	*3* *US OFDI to Japan*	*4* *3/2 per capita*	*5* *3/2 adj. for GDP*
Food and kindred products	22.6	10.0	0.8	0.2	0.1
Chemical and allied products	46.1	25.4	3.2	0.4	0.3
Primary and fabricated metals	9.9	4.9	0.3	0.2	0.1
Machinery, except electrical	29.7	17.8	3.8	0.6	0.4
Electric and electronic equipment	18.4	6.5	1.6	0.7	0.4
Transportation equipment	26.2	9.8	1.8	0.6	0.4
Other manufacturing	46.5	22.4	2.1	0.3	0.2
Total manufacturing	199.5	96.8	13.6	0.4	0.3
Wholesale trade	57.6	32.2	5.9	0.6	0.4
Finance	155.6	85.1	4.8	0.2	0.1
Services	18.1	12.2	0.7	0.2	0.1
All industries	548.6	269.2	31.4	0.4	0.3

Sources: US Department of Commerce (1994b), UNCTAD (1993) *World Investment Directory*, UNCTAD (1994) *World Investment Report*
Notes: Per capita factor is 373/123 = 3.03
GDP adjustment factor is 7,088/3,670 = 1.93

In addition to the draw of a large, affluent market, Japan in the 1990s offers another kind of 'pull' factor, namely that for inward FDI from other developed nations that seek to acquire and enhance their O-specific advantages through production in Japan. Such strategic asset-seeking FDI characterized much of Japanese FDI into the United States in the late 1980s, and it is apparent that the success of the Japanese economy (and that of some Japanese firms) has attracted a considerable degree of interest and a desire to learn from business practices in Japan.

A third attraction of the Japanese market may be hypothesized to lie in the high rates of return achieved by earlier successful entrants into the Japanese market.[7] In the 1970s and 1980s US affiliates consistently outperformed all other foreign investors' affiliates as well as the indigenous Japanese firms, which stands in rather stark contrast to the Japanese affiliates' rather dismal performance in the United States (Mason 1992, Wakasugi 1996). However, since such returns can be expected to arise to some degree from the relative closedness of the Japanese market that dodges all new potential investors, both domestic and foreign, in the event of a significant opening up of the Japanese market to inward FDI such supernormal returns would be likely to dissipate.

Table 12.2(b) US FDI Stocks in Japan and Japanese FDI Stocks in the United States by industry, 1993 (US$ billions)

Industry	*1* *US OFDI total*	*2* *US OFDI to Japan*	*3* *Japan OFDI total*	*4* *Japan OFDI to US*	*5* *4/2 per capita*	*6* *4/2 adj. for GDP*
Food and kindred products	22.6	0.8	4.1	1.0 x	2.5	2.0
Chemical and allied products	46.1	3.2	10.9	3.3	2.1	1.7
Primary and fabricated metals	9.9	0.3	10.3	1.5	10.2	8.1
Machinery, except electrical	29.7	3.8	7.9	4.8*	2.6	2.1
Electric and electronic equipment	18.4	1.6	20.4	n/a	n/a	n/a
Transportation equipment	26.2	1.8	10.9**	n/a	n/a	n/a
Other manufacturing	46.5	2.1	n/a	7.2	7.0	5.5
Total manufacturing	199.5	13.6	81.6***	17.7	2.6	2.1
Wholesale trade	57.6	5.9	34.7	33.9	11.7	9.3
Finance	155.6	4.8	111.1	11.2	4.7	3.8
Services	18.1	0.7	13.6	12.1	35.1	27.8
All industries	548.6	31.4	310.8	96.2	6.2	4.9

* Machinery
** Motor vehicles only
*** Includes petroleum and non-metallic minerals
Sources: US Department of Commerce (1994b), UNCTAD (1993) *World Investment Directory*, UNCTAD (1994) *World Investment Report*
Notes: Per capita factor is 250/123 = 2.03
GDP adjustment factor is 5,920/3,670 = 1.61
Figures for column 3 are for 1990

MITIGATING FACTORS

As hinted at in the previous section, the 'fundamentals' for a substantial increase of FDI into Japan are present. This section deals with some locational disadvantages particular to Japan which might mitigate the flow of FDI into Japan in the 1990s. These factors include the *keiretsu* structure of firms, restrictive government policies (which, however, are on the wane)

Table 12.2(c) FDI stock as percentage of GDP (US$ millions)

	Inward stock	%	Outward stock	%
USA (1993)	445,268	7.5	548,644	9.3
Japan (1990)	18,432	0.6	310,808	9.8

Sources: UNCTAD (1992) *World Investment Directory*, UNCTAD (1994) *World Investment Report*, US Department of Commerce (1994b)

and, more importantly, restrictive practices arising from the overall commercial infrastructure, and finally the effect of changes in the yen exchange rate on the cost of exports versus local production.

Although overt restrictions on foreign investment were gradually lifted in the 1980s, and the Japanese government now states that it welcomes foreign investment (Wakasugi 1996), the feeling particularly in the United States is that the markets are not open to foreigners, and that Japan's is a government for producers, not consumers, as is manifested in the prices Japanese consumers pay for many everyday items.

Since policy takes place in an institutional context, macro-economic or macro-organizational policies, which prima facie might not be seen as discriminatory, can effectively impede access to markets when combined with the unique institutional structure in Japan. Consequently, this section concentrates mostly on such intervening institutional factors. In the final analysis, the question to be addressed is whether the apparent neutrality of explicit policies should appease Japan's trading partners, or if in fact participation in an open trading system obliges Japan to renounce some of its nationhood characteristics to accommodate foreign business interests.[8]

Keiretsu structure

In the late 1970s, having evoked the super-301 provisions of US law, which branded Japan as an 'unfair' trading partner and allowed for the United States to impose disciplinary trade sanctions on Japanese products, the United States began talks under the Structural Impediments Initiative (SII). These talks grew out of a feeling in the United States that despite the gradual removal of nearly all legal impediments to trade and investment since Japan's 1964 entry into the OECD, the Japanese market still remained closed to exports and inward investment relative to other OECD countries.

Evidence (and counter-evidence) of the closedness of the Japanese market was found in the current account surplus Japan had run for a decade *vis-à-vis* the rest of the world, and of particular concern to the United States was the bilateral trade imbalance between the two nations. Among those who contended the market to be effectively closed were Lawrence (1991), who argued that the *keiretsu* structure of firms, whereby a large industrial conglomerate has several lower tiers of suppliers linked, but not owned, by the 'parent' company, restricted imports. He found evidence to demonstrate that these quasi-hierarchies (which also on occasion transferred employees from supplier firms to the 'parent' company) discriminated against outside suppliers. Kreinin (1988) offered further data regarding the propensity of foreign affiliates of Japanese MNEs to be staffed with home country executives and their marked preference for sourcing from other Japanese affiliates.

On the opposing side, Ohmae (1985) suggested that it was 'trade not access' that was imbalanced, and that the failure of Americans to penetrate the market was not so much a function of restrictive business practices in Japan than a lack of effort and understanding on the part of the Americans. Gray and Lundan (1993) argued that the tendency of the *keiretsu* to trade with its affiliates was akin to intrafirm trade, and that rather than being in evidence of a Japanese policy to overtake the United States, the high degree of intrafirm trade resulted from the extensive FDI undertaken by Japanese firms in the 1980s, and was a rational exploitation of the 'economies of close proximity', which such an arrangement afforded its members.

Opacity and 'administrative guidance'

Another factor often cited as restrictive of access to the Japanese market is the opacity of decision making at higher levels, and the 'administrative guidance' offered by government agencies. It is also claimed that the lack of transparency (and a considerable language barrier) makes it difficult for foreign firms to negotiate the red tape involved in the certification and standards-setting process required to gain access to the market. Again, such difficulties do not exclusively impede the foreign entrant, although it is accepted that foreign firms are likely to bear more of the burden (Yoshitomi 1995).

In a similar vein, a study by the United States–Japan Business Council (1993) concerning the 'opening up' of the financial services sector, and a study by Wakasugi (1996), both concluded that while many of the business practices in Japan were exclusionary, they did not (any longer) expressly discriminate against foreign investors.[9]

In his chronicle of US foreign investment in Japan, Mason (1992) illustrates in intricate detail how ingrained these exclusionary practices are in the overall commercial infrastructure. He demonstrates how US firms that through serendipity or insight gained a beach head in Japan in the immediate post-war era, such as Dow Chemical, TI and Coca-Cola, none the less took a long time to conquer the market, and how on the other hand some of the failures of American business in Japan can be attributed to a lack of sufficient effort and realization of the considerable differences in the business culture and institutional structure of the two nations.

Mergers and acquisitions

Another factor highlighted by both Mason (1992) and Wakasugi (1996) is the virtual non-existence of mergers and acquisitions in Japan. Both authors contend that mergers and acquisitions, particularly in the case of hostile takeovers, are a form of business activity fundamentally unsuited to the Japanese market. The cross-shareholding of large Japanese corporations together with their ties to financial institutions are set to provide Japanese corporations with the long-term relationships which have been credited with the success of Japanese firms by virtue of cultivating a 'vision' for the long run and for not managing the bottom line on a quarterly basis.[10] Given the apparent success of this system, it is not surprising that outside challenges to management would be frowned upon as indications of 'short-termism' and opportunistic buying and selling of firms, inherently incompatible with the established modes of business.[11]

As with many of the structural impediments in the Japanese market pointed out by a number of authors, the distaste for merger and acquisition activity seems to apply equally well to mergers between Japanese firms as it does to acquisitions by foreigners. However, to the extent that a merger or an acquisition might be the preferred mode of entry of foreign investors to markets whose psychic distance to the home market is extensive, and where relationships with suppliers and customers need to be cultivated over time, the non-existence of the merger option has increased the threshold of entry of foreign firms into Japan.

Commercial policy issues

The failure of the SII was in large part due to the fact that the structures that were found to violate American sensibilities regarding the functioning of fair and open markets were for the most part integral parts of Japanese society and for all practical purposes non-negotiable. While the SII obliged the Americans to seek improvement in US competitiveness through the reduction of the federal deficit, aggressive export promotion and workforce training, the demands placed on the Japanese included a comprehensive reform of land policies, dramatic increases in public spending and a reform of the pricing mechanism that impeded the Japanese consumer from enjoying competitively priced goods (United States–Japan Working Group 1990). All this amounted to nothing short of a wholesale restructuring of the institutions that make up the social and commercial infrastructure.[12]

The ongoing rift between the United States and Japan over the bilateral imbalance of trade, with its overtones of 'cultural imperialism' in the American insistence that the face of capitalism look the same all around the world, may also have contributed to the perceptions of American managers of the impenetrability of the Japanese market. The US government, having forsaken the use of the 'evil empire' as a relic of the cold war past, focused its rhetorical imagery on Japan Inc., intent on taking over the United States in a co-ordinated plot involving the government and the *keiretsu*.[13]

As the discussion proceeded from overt trade and investment barriers to non-tariff barriers and structural impediments, the evidence used to support the arguments shifted from actual discriminatory policies to the use of levels of market penetration as evidence of closeness. As Ostry (1992) points out, United States Inc.'s aggressive reciprocity was predisposed towards results-oriented rather than rule-oriented policy. In the present stage of the negotiations, Bhagwati (1994) argues that a reversal of roles has occurred, where the United States has begun to appreciate the gains from government–business co-operation, as seen in the agreement reached by the government for Motorola, and is insisting on quantitative targets, while Japan is singing the praises of free trade, and stands in strong opposition to any bilateral management of trade (im)balances and market shares. In some sense, the new focus of the United States on 'hard' trade issues, rather than cultural (i.e. structural) issues, is an unfortunate shift in focus, as the intractable sovereignty issues are precisely where a bargain should be struck in exchange for Japan's full participation in the world trading system.

Effect of exchange rates

The final factor affecting the attractiveness of Japan as a production location to be addressed has to do with the yen/dollar rate of exchange. Prior to the Plaza agreement in 1985, Japanese firms enjoyed the benefits of an 'undervalued' exchange rate in 1978–85 (relative to that which would exist under a balanced current account), owing to the persistent surplus on the current account. Although this imbalance is largely attributable to the differences in savings rates between the United States and Japan, Japanese firms' acquisitions of financial assets and FDI denominated in foreign currencies contributed to a virtuous cycle of competitiveness for Japanese firms by confirming the going exchange rate and consequently greatly increasing the price competitiveness of Japanese products abroad.[14]

While exchange rate fluctuations can be regarded as influencing the timing rather than the decision to engage in FDI in the first place, in periods when a currency misalignment persists for an extended period, such as the period preceding the Plaza agreement, the distinction between timing and intent becomes murky. Compared with the situation in the late 1980s and 1990s, the time before the Plaza agreement would certainly have favoured, *ceteris paribus*, the modality of direct investment over US exports to Japan. Conversely, the period following the Plaza agreement saw a flood of FDI from Japan to the United States to insulate Japanese sales from the effects of the yen appreciation. Since that time, the relative costs of Japan as a production location have increased further, prompting FDI from Japan to other NICs particularly in labour-intensive final assembly tasks, and the increasing specialization of Japanese manufacturing on high technology and high-skill component manufacture (Pollack 1994).

If such prolonged currency misalignments can in fact influence the decision to engage in FDI, the availability of this option in only one direction could be seen as discriminatory.[15] On the other hand, evidence from a survey of American managers by Kearney (1991) (reproduced in Ramstetter and James (1993)) places a relatively low value on the effect of currency fluctuations as impeding the access of US firms into Japan. In any event, the present appreciation of the yen can be expected, at least temporarily, to increase the relative importance of exports as a means for servicing the Japanese market.

ALTERNATIVES TO FDI

Before concluding the discussion on why FDI into Japan is lower than might be expected, and what if anything can be done to overcome some of the impediments to foreign firms' production in Japan, another issue regarding openness needs to be addressed. This is the question of whether openness should be evaluated solely in terms of the market penetration through FDI, or whether an overall measure of market openness should include other means of servicing a foreign market, namely joint ventures, strategic alliances, and other co-operative modalities, along with the market-based modalities of exports and technology licensing.

This idea is illustrated in Tables 12.3(a) and 12.3(b), which indicate the relative importance for US firms of the modalities of affiliate sales (FDI), exports and licensed sales in servicing the Japanese and UK markets in 1989 and 1992, respectively. While no change seems to have occurred since 1989, it is apparent that licensed sales and exports have played a much more important role in Japan than in the United Kingdom. In fact, this reliance

Table 12.3(a) Alternative modalities of servicing Japanese and UK markets by US firms, 1989

	US firms in Japan			
1989	*Affiliate sales*	*Exports*	*Licensed sales*	*Total*
All industries (US$ billions)	145.7	42.8	20.9	209.4
(Per capita) (US$)	1,183.6	347.7	169.8	1,722.2
(% of total)	69.6	20.4	10.0	100.0

	US firms in UK			
1989	*Affiliate sales*	*Exports*	*Licensed sales*	*Total*
All industries (US$ billions)	183.3	20.8	3.2	207.3
(Per capita) (US$)	3,204.5	363.6	55.9	3,994.7
(% of total)	88.4	10.0	1.5	100.0

Sources: Dunning (1996), US Department of Commerce (1992) *U.S. Direct Investment Abroad*.
Notes: Affiliate sales represent sales of US non-bank affiliates in the two countries
Exports represent all exports to the two countries by all US firms
Licensed sales represent royalties and fees paid by unaffiliated Japanese or UK firms to US firms multiplied by 20 (it being assumed that royalties and fees were calculated as 5% of gross sales)

Table 12.3(b) Alternative modalities of servicing Japanese and UK markets by US firms, 1992

	US firms in Japan			
1992	*Affiliate sales*	*Exports*	*Licensed sales*	*Total*
All industries (US$ billions)	161.7	47.8	29.3	238.8
(Per capita) (US$)	1,309.3	387.0	237.2	1,933.5
(% of total)	67.7	20.0	12.3	100.0

	US firms in UK			
1992	*Affiliate sales*	*Exports*	*Licensed sales*	*Total*
All industries (US$ billions)	212.5	22.8	4.5	239.8
(Per capita) (US$)	3,702.1	397.2	78.4	4,177.7
(% of total)	88.6	9.5	1.9	100.0

Sources: Dunning (1996), US Department of Commerce (1994b)
Notes: Affiliate sales represent sales of US non-bank affiliates in the two countries
Exports represent all exports to the two countries by all US firms.
Licensed sales represent royalties and fees paid by unaffiliated Japanese or UK firms to US firms multiplied by 20 (it being assumed that royalties and fees were calculated as 5% of gross sales)

on licensed technology prompted Ozawa (1996) to relabel the cross-border learning curve (IDP) of Japan as a 'technology development path' (TDP). In the opposite direction, Tables 12.4(a) and 12.4(b) reveal the higher reliance of Japanese affiliates in the United States on affiliate sales, and even more strikingly, the near absence of licensing as a modality.

Licensing

While the licensing of technology may be a viable way to derive a return from the sale of technology that is not feasibly exploited in a foreign location by the firm itself, in many cases, particularly in the case of most services and in the establishment of marketing and distribution outlets, licensing is clearly not a substitute for FDI. In cases where licensing does

Table 12.4(a) Alternative modalities of servicing the US market by Japanese firms, 1989

	Japanese firms in the USA			
1989	*Affiliate sales*	*Exports*	*Licensed sales*	*Total*
All industries (US$ billions)	271.5	97.1	2.6	371.2
(Per capita) (US$)	1,086.0	388.4	10.4	1,466.8
(% of total)	73.1	26.2	0.7	100.0

Table 12.4(b) Alternative modalities of servicing the US market by Japanese firms, 1992

	Japanese firms in the USA			
1992	*Affiliate sales*	*Exports*	*Licensed sales*	*Total*
All industries (US$ billions)	334.8	97.4	3.3	435.4
(Per capita) (US$)	1,339.2	389.6	13.2	1,742.0
(% of total)	76.9	22.4	0.7	100.0

Sources: Dunning and Narula (1994), US Department of Commerce (1993) *FDI in the U.S.: An Update*, US Department of Commerce (1994b)
Notes: Affiliate sales represent sales of US non-bank affiliates in the two countries
Exports represent all exports to the two countries by all US firms
Licensed sales represent royalties and fees paid by unaffiliated Japanese or UK firms to US firms multiplied by 20 (it being assumed that royalties and fees were calculated as 5% of gross sales)

take place, as it did to a significant extent from US to Japanese firms in the 1970s and early 1980s, it is not unforeseen that the licensee in fact outgrows its bounds and becomes a formidable competitor to the original licensor. In fact, quite a bit of disenchantment has been expressed by some US firms, who early on licensed their technology to the Japanese only to witness the remarkable success derived from the use of the licensed technology combined with Japanese management practices accruing to the licensees. Tables 12.5(a) and 12.5(b) illustrate the disparity in the use of licensing by US and Japanese firms, as well as the stronger tendency of Japanese licensing sales to go to affiliated parties in intrafirm transactions.

It is not possible to know *ex post* whether, in the case that this technology had entered the Japanese market via FDI rather than licensing, the learning and upgrading of management practices would not have occurred in the interaction of the foreign investors and indigenous firms over time. Clearly, however, in the case of FDI, the firm originating the technology has a further chance of co-evolution along with its competitors in the foreign market, whereas in a pure market exchange, no such potential remains for the licensor.

This is not to say that long-term relationships and trust do not play a role in licensing. As demonstrated by Contractor and Sagafi-Nejad (1981), this

Table 12.5(a) Royalties and licence fees received from affiliated firms in Japan by US firms (US$ millions)

	Receipts from Japan			
	Affiliated 1	*Unaffiliated 2*	*Total 1+2*	*Ratio aff./unaff. (1/2)*
1983	387	500	887	0.77
1987	1,080	723	1,803	1.49
1990	1,653	1,205	2,858	1.37
1993	2,392	1,648	4,040	1.45

Table 12.5(b) Royalties and licence fees paid to affiliated firms in Japan by US firms (US$ millions)

	Payments to Japan			
	Affiliated 3	*Unaffiliated 4*	*Total 3+4*	*Ratio aff./unaff. (3/4)*
1983	−154	38	−116	NC
1987	185	88	273	2.10
1990	349	184	533	1.90
1993	721	205	926	3.52

NC = Not calculable
Sources: Dunning and Narula (1994), US Department of Commerce (1994b)
Note: Royalties and fees given are net. Negative numbers indicate that receipts of royalties and fees by affiliates of Japanese firms from their parents exceeded payments to Japanese parents that year.

is indeed often the case, and such arrangements can substitute for the FDI option in terms of the mutual gains derived from this relationship. However, for many types of proprietary technology, its transferability is significantly compromised outside of the firm, and in the event of a transfer, the firm has to guard itself against appropriability challenges, as described by Teece (1987).

Joint ventures and strategic alliances

The remaining option for firms for which licensing of technology is unfeasible owing to the type of technology involved, is to enter into a joint venture or a non-equity alliance with a foreign firm. From the perspective of US investment into Japan, joint ventures with Japanese firms allowed for access to the market and local knowledge while providing some of the dynamic benefits of long-term association in terms of organizational learning, and in a market where mergers and acquisitions were discouraged, probably acted as the closest available substitute.

Although no direct evidence of the number of mergers and acquisitions in Japan and the United States is available here, Table 12.6(a) gives an indication of the propensity of Japanese affiliates of US firms to be wholly owned (48 per cent), or even majority owned (61 per cent). This stands in clear contrast to US affiliates in the United Kingdom as well as the average of all US affiliates world-wide. The low proportion of total ownership in Japan is also reflected in Table 12.6(b), where the gross product of US majority-owned foreign affiliates is compared internationally.[16]

Despite the problems of lack of trust and unclear responsibilities that sometimes plague joint ventures (which to some extent are solved by a singular management in the case of an acquisition), successful joint ventures could also circumvent the 'clashes of culture' sometimes experienced in

Table 12.6(a) US parents' ownership of non-bank foreign affiliates, 1992

	Number of affiliates				*Percentage of all affiliates that are:*	
	Total	*Majority owned*		*Minority owned*	*Majority owned*	*Wholly owned*
		Total	*Of which: Wholly owned*			
All countries	18,225	16,081	14,423	2,144	88	79
UK	2,150	2,025	1,906	125	94	89
Japan	828	507	397	321	61	48

Source: US Department of Commerce (1994b)

Table 12.6(b) Gross product of US non-bank majority-owned foreign affiliates as percentage of GDP, 1991

Ireland	13.5
Canada	9.2
Singapore	8.3
UK	6.8
Netherlands	4.6
Indonesia	3.1
Germany	3.1
Mexico	2.7
Italy	1.8
Sweden	1.2
Japan	0.5
India	0.1

Source: US Department of Commerce (1994b)

hostile takeovers and in that sense be preferable, particularly in nations with considerable psychic distance between the parties.

Strategic co-operative alliances are the newest form of market access to multinationals, and while it is too early to judge what the ultimate benefits of such relationships are, a few factors can be highlighted. In some sense, these relationships are akin to the co-operation achieved under a joint venture without the establishment of separate legal entity and the exercise of control via shareholding. Alliances (although requiring human resources and managerial attention) are a cost-effective and quick means to gain access to resources or markets. Their motivation can be aggressive or defensive, and they may be used as a means of pooling resources and sharing risk in R&D projects. However, unlike in the case of a takeover, access can typically only be gained to a piece of another firm's resources in the hopes that complementarities between the various pieces acquired by the firm ultimately result in something adding value.

As the number of alliances grows, it is likely that some form of diminishing returns will set in. Although a 'follow my leader' strategy is not always observed in the case of FDI, the relatively low start-up cost of alliances may precipitate a situation in which firms enter into alliances merely for the sake of eliminating uncertainty or prompted by a fear of being left out. In such a case it is unclear what, if any, tangible benefits arise from a myriad of such relationships.

It would stand to reason that the same factors that generally make for effective joint ventures, namely clearly delineated responsibilities and division of gains, as well as the existence of identifiable (complementary) competencies, would predicate a successful alliance as well. To the extent that the decision to engage in joint ventures or alliances in lieu of FDI is made by default, that is since the FDI option is not available, it is likely that such complementarity of interests will not always be present, and that effective access to the market is consequently impeded.

SUMMARY AND CONCLUSIONS

This chapter has suggested that many of the factors that attracted European and Japanese FDI into the United States in the 1970s and 1980s are present today in Japan. It has argued that foreign firms possess the kinds of ownership-specific abilities that could be gainfully exploited abroad, and that their exploitation in Japan could be profitable for a number of firms owing to the locational attractions of Japan. However, despite the 'push' of the improved competitiveness of US and European firms, as well the increasing importance of strategic asset-seeking investment, and the 'pull' of the skilled workforce and the affluent Japanese market, there are mitigating factors particular to Japan that will in all likelihood constrain the expected flow of FDI.

Foremost among these factors are institutional impediments, such as the *keiretsu* structure of firms and the non-existence of mergers and acquisitions as a mode of entry, which in many cases effectively impede the possibilities of foreign MNEs to enter the market via foreign investment. The legitimacy of such impediments is the subject of an ongoing debate between Japan and the United States, and it is suggested that whether discriminatory or not, some of the exclusionary practices in Japan should continue to be the focus of the negotiations in exchange for the continued participation of Japan in an open trading regime.

The question of market openness is finally readdressed from a wider perspective by bringing into the discussion other modalities of servicing a foreign market. It is suggested that while in terms of licensing and equity and non-equity co-operative alliances Japan isn't nearly as closed as the

FDI figures alone would suggest, it is also probable that, at least for some firms, these modalities have been entered into as a second-best solution in the absence of the FDI option, and that in such cases the institutional features of the market constitute an impediment for the establishment of foreign MNEs in Japan.

Three scenarios are offered as the likely future of FDI in Japan:

1 FDI into Japan will significantly increase akin to the experience of the United States in the 1980s, involving both market-seeking and increasingly strategic asset-seeking investment.
2 FDI will increase moderately, but no surge will take place.
3 Japan will retain its very low levels of FDI in contrast to most other developed nations.

While it seems somewhat unlikely that the first scenario will be fully realized, an outcome somewhere between 1 and 2 seems plausible. To the extent that the merger option remains largely unavailable, some of the strategic asset-seeking investment may be negatively affected.

NOTES

1 See also various contributions to Dunning and Narula (1996).
2 As pointed out by Graham (1996), contrary to earlier analyses, it seems that Stage 5 of the IDP is not necessarily characterized by an equilibrium stock value of zero, but rather by zero net flows.
3 The term 'cross-border learning curve' to describe the IDP is offered by Ozawa (1996).
4 See Walter (1992) for data on the growth of transatlantic mergers and acquisitions in the 1980s.
5 Note that affiliate sales are for all affiliates. The high affiliate sales in transportation equipment are almost completely from minority-owned affiliates.
6 Naturally the push for firms towards globally rationalized production does not just push them towards Japan, but to the extent that inward FDI to Japan has been constrained, the extant distribution does not reflect all of the preferences of location that might otherwise have ensued.
7 These entrants were and are mostly of American origin, as FDI from the United States accounted for a half of all inward FDI to Japan in 1989 (from MITI (1990), reported in Dunning and Narula (1994)).
8 See Gray and Lundan (1994) on Japanese nationhood issues.
9 At least when it is assumed that all investors face some level of adjustment costs when operating in a foreign market.
10 Close ties between firms and banks are naturally not limited to Japan. The success of German firms has been attributed to their close ties to the banks in addition to the apprenticeship system and university–industry ties (Zysman 1983). Large corporations were also linked to financial institutions in Finland throughout the post-war period, although the crisis of the Scandinavian banking system had loosened these ties somewhat.
11 However, as mentioned earlier, this has not stopped Japanese firms from acquiring firms overseas.

12 The use here of the term institutions is analogous to its use by North (1991).
13 Japan Inc. has re-emerged in two recent books, *Japan: Who governs? The rise of the developmental state* by Johnson (1995) and *Blindside: Why Japan is still on track to overtake the U.S. by the year 2000* by Fingleton (1995).
14 For a further elaboration on this virtuous cycle, see Gray and Lundan (1993).
15 It is not clear what the precise meaning of the term currency fluctuations is in terms of the elapsed time. It is argued here that if the duration of a fluctuation is extended several years, it is possible that some capital investment decisions may be affected.
16 There are two factors resulting in the very low gross product in Japan. First are the historical restrictions limiting inward FDI overall, and second is the historical preference in Japan for minority-owned affiliates.

REFERENCES

Bhagwati, Jagdish (1994) 'The U.S.–Japan rift: Samurais no more', *Foreign Affairs* 73(3): 7–12.

Contractor, Farok J. and Tagi Sagafi-Nejad (1981) 'International technology transfer: major issues and policy responses', *Journal of International Business Studies* Fall: 113–35.

Dunning, John H. (1993) *The Globalization of Business: The Challenge of the 1990s*, London: Routledge.

——(1996) 'Explaining foreign direct investment in Japan: some theoretical insights', in M. Yoshitomi and E. M. Graham (eds) *Foreign Direct Investment in Japan*, pp. 8–63, London: Edward Elgar.

Dunning, John H. and Narula, Rajneesh (1994) 'Transpacific foreign direct investment and the investment development path: the record assessed', *Essays in International Business* No. 10: 69, South Carolina, University of South Carolina.

——(1996) *Foreign Direct Investment and Governments*, London and New York: Routledge.

Fingleton, Eamonn (1995) *Blindside: Why Japan is still on track to overtake the U.S. by the year 2000*, Boston, MA: Houghton Mifflin.

Gittleman, M. and Dunning, J. H. (1991) 'Japanese multinationals in Europe and the United States: some comparisons and contrasts', in Michael W. Klein and Paul J. Welfens (eds) *Multinational Enterprises in the New Europe and Global Trade*, pp. 237–64 New York: Springer-Verlag.

Graham, Edward M. (1996) 'The United States: some musings on its international investment development path', in John H. Dunning and Rajneesh Narula (eds) *Foreign Direct Investment and Governments*, London and New York: Routledge.

Gray, H. Peter and Lundan, Sarianna (1993) 'Japanese multinationals and the stability of the GATT system', *The International Trade Journal* 7(6): 635–53.

——(1994) 'Nationhood, the GATT ideal and a workable international trading system', *Banca Nazionale del Lavoro Quarterly Review* 188, March: 99–114.

Johnson, Chalmers (1995) *Japan: Who Governs? The rise of the development state*, New York: W. W. Norton.

Kreinin, M. (1988) 'How closed is the Japanese economy? Additional evidence', *The World Economy* 11, December: 529–42.

Lawrence, R. Z. (1991) 'Efficient or exclusionist? The import behavior of Japanese corporate groups', *Brookings Papers on Economic Activity* 1: 311–30.

Mason, Mark (1992) *American Multinationals and Japan: The Political Economy of Japanese Capital Controls, 1899–1980*, Cambridge, MA: Harvard University Press.

North, Douglass C. (1991) 'Institutions', *Journal of Economic Perspectives* 5, Winter: 97–112.

Ohmae, K. (1985) *Triad Power*, New York: The Free Press.

Ostry, Sylvia (1992) 'The domestic domain: the new international policy arena', *Transnational Corporations* 1, February: 7–26.

Ozawa, Terutomo (1996) 'Japan: the macro-IDP, meso-IDPs, and the technology development path (TDP)', in John H. Dunning and Rajneesh Narula (eds) *Foreign Direct Investment and Governments*, pp. 142–73, London and New York: Routledge.

Pollack, Andrew (1994) 'Stunning changes in Japan's economy', *The New York Times*, 23 October: Section 3:1.

Ramstetter, E.D. and James, W. E. (1993) 'Japan–U.S. economic relations and economic policy: the uncomfortable reality', *Transnational Corporations* 2, December: 65–96.

Teece, D. J. (ed.) (1987) *The Competitive Challenge: Strategies for Industrial Innovation and Renewal*, Cambridge, MA: Ballinger.

UNCTAD (1992) *World Investment Directory, Vol. III: Developed Countries*, New York: UN.

——(1994) *World Investment Report: Transnational Corporations, Employment and the Workplace*, Geneva and New York: UN.

US Department of Commerce (1992) U.S. Direct Investment Abroad, Washington DC.: US Government printing office.

——(1993) FDI in the U.S.: An Update Washington DC.: US Government printing office.

——(1994a) *U.S. Foreign Trade Highlights*Washington DC.: US Government printing office.

——(1994b) *Survey of Current Business*, February, June, July, August and September.

United States–Japan Business Council (in co-operation with the US Chamber of Commerce in Japan and the Financial Services Group of the Coalition of Service Industries) (1993) *Japan's Financial Services Market: The Case for Expanded Access*, Washington, DC.

United States–Japan Working Group on the Structural Impediments Initiative (1990) *Joint Report*, Washington, DC.

Wakasugi, Ryuhei (1996) 'Why foreign firm's entry has been low in Japan: an empirical examination', in M. Yoshitomi and Edward M. Graham (eds) *Foreign Direct Investment in Japan*, London: Edward Elgar.

Walter, Ingo (1993) 'Patterns of mergers and acquisitions 1985–90', in L. Oxelheim (ed.) *The Global Race for Foreign Direct Investment in the 1990s*, pp. 151–76, Berlin and New York: Springer-Verlag.

Yoshitomi, Masaru (1995) 'Behind the low level of foreign investment in Japan', *KKC Forum: Views on International Economic Issues* 5, January: 1–4.

Zysman, John (1983) *Governments, Markets, and Growth*, Ithaca, NY: Cornell University Press.

13

THE STRATEGY OF JAPANESE AND US MANUFACTURING INVESTORS IN EUROPE*

INTRODUCTION

This chapter first examines the current patterns of Japanese-and US-owned economic activity in West European manufacturing industry. It goes on to suggest some hypotheses for the similarities and differences in these patterns, within the framework of one of the most generally accepted paradigms and some of the best-known theories of foreign direct investment (FDI) and the activities of multinational enterprises (MNEs). It then offers some exploratory evidence on the significance of the variables identified in the earlier sections. The chapter concludes by considering whether or not the distinctive structure of Japanese MNE activity in Europe is likely to continue in the later 1990s.

SOME STATISTICAL DATA

We draw upon two sets of data. The first, set out in Table 13.1, compares and contrasts the industrial distribution of the stock of US and Japanese direct investment in European manufacturing industry at the end of 1991 (in the case of US investment) and 31 March 1992 (in the case of Japanese investment). The data reveal that while both Japanese and US investment in the European manufacturing sector is largely directed to high-value-added fabricating and processing industries, producing Schumpeterian-type goods (Hirsch and Meshulach 1992), Japanese investment is relatively more concentrated in the electrical and electronic equipment and auto industries. The final column of Table 13.1 calculates a Japanese concentration coefficient (JCC), which is obtained by dividing the share of the total Japanese capital stake accounted for by a particular sector by the corresponding US share.

Overall, the direct investment stake in European manufacturing industry of Japanese MNEs was about one-fifth of that of their American counterparts at the beginning of the 1990s. However, for all sectors, the value of the

Table 13.1 Japanese and US direct investment in Europe, by industry, early 1990s

	Japan (Mar. 1992)[a]		*USA (Dec. 1991)*		*JCC*
	$m	%	*$m*	%	
1 *Manufacturing industries*					
Processing industries					
Food products	573	3.8	9,437	10.6	0.36
Chemicals and allied products	1,640	10.9	19,262	21.6	0.50
Metals	693	4.5	4,131	4.6	0.98
Textiles and clothing	1,022	6.7	1,042[b]	1.2	5.58
Wood-related products	94	0.6	313[b]	0.4	1.50
Fabricating industries					
Electrical and electronic equipment	4,823	31.7	6,013	6.7	4.73
Non-electrical machinery	2,362	15.5	19,105	21.4	0.72
Transportation	2,618	17.2	9,870	11.1	1.55
Other products	1,406	9.2	19,917	22.4	0.41
Total manufacturing	15,230	100.0	89,090	100.0	1.00
2 *Other industries*					
Services					
Wholesale trade and commerce[c]	8,329	15.6	24,875	18.6	0.84
Banking, finance, insurance and real estate	35,415	66.3	74,370	55.7	1.19
Other services	5,583	10.5	6,159	4.6	2.28
Other industry[d]	4,079	7.6	28,060	21.1	0.36
Total other industries	53,406	100.0	133,464	100.0	1.00
Total all industry	68,636	100.0	224,554	100.0	1.00

JCC = Japanese Concentration Coefficient ratio (% of Japanese investment in a particular sector divided by % of US investment in a particular sector)
[a] Represents cumulative FDI, April 1951 to March 1992
[b] Estimated on basis of stock of US direct investment set out in US Department of Commerce (1993).
[c] Note that these investments may include investments in marketing and distribution by manufacturing companies
[d] Including that not classified
Sources: Japan: Ministry of Finance (based on investments approved by the Ministry); USA: US Department of Commerce (1993)

Japanese stake in March 1992 was $68.0 billion, some 25.4 per cent of the US stake of $224.6 billion in December 1991. This relatively higher Japanese participation reflects the fact that the Japanese stake in European service industries was $49.3 billion,[1] 46.8 per cent of the US stake of $105.4 billion. In finance, insurance and property alone, the Japanese investment was $35.4 billion, 47.6 per cent of the US investment of $74.4 billion, whereas in wholesale trade, the percentage of Japanese to US capital stock was nearly twice that in manufacturing industry, namely 33.5 per cent compared to 17.1 per cent.

More detailed data are available on the employment of Japanese manufacturing affiliates in 1990 and US manufacturing affiliates in 1989. Some of these are reproduced in Table 13.2. They broadly corroborate the data in Table 13.1, but suggest that within sectors, there may be quite significant differences in the JCC ratio. Other data (JETRO 1991) also reveal that in the general machinery sector and instruments sector, it was especially high in office and photographic equipment, while in the electrical and electronic sector, it was more marked in the production of consumer goods (notably colour TV sets, video recorders, microwave ovens) than in the production of electronic components.

Table 13.2 Employment distribution of Japanese and US affiliates in European manufacturing

	Japan 1990		*US 1989*		*J/US*
		%	*000s*	%	*REA*
Processing industries					
1 Food and kindred products	453	0.50	119.7	7.95	0.06
2 Pharmaceuticals	1,823	2.01	79.5	5.28	0.38
3 Other chemical products[a]	4,800	5.29	177.7	11.81	0.45
4 Iron and steel[b]	450[c]	0.49	36.5	2.43	0.20
5 Textiles and clothing	493	0.54	30.6	2.03	0.27
6 Wood-related products	14	0.02	6.9	0.46	0.04
7 Rubber products	18,778	20.72	40.8	2.71	7.65
8 Non-ferrous materials[d]	4,010[c]	4.42	72.5	4.82	0.92
Fabricating industries					
9 General machinery	8,384	9.25	158.5	10.53	0.88
10 Electronic and electronic equipment[e]	22,981	25.36	268.6	17.85	1.42
11 Transport equipment	21,061	23.24	309.1	20.54	1.13
12 Instruments	3,905	4.31	107.2	7.12	0.61
13 Other industries	3,459	3.82	97.5	6.48	0.59
All industries	90,611	100.00	1505.1	100.00	1.00

J/US REA = Japanese/US Revealed Employment Advantage. (For definition, see text)
a Includes plastics
b Includes metal products
c MITI figures adjusted based on data from Yamawaki (1991)
d Includes glass, stone and ceramics
e Includes computers, office machinery and computers
Sources: MITI (1991), US Department of Commerce (1991), Yamawaki (1991)

The final column of Table 13.2 makes use of what we shall call the Japanese/US revealed employment advantage ratio (Japanese/US REA). This ratio is obtained by dividing the share of the total employment of US manufacturing subsidiaries accounted for by a particular sector by the share of the Japanese subsidiaries in that sector.[2] For the remainder of this chapter, Japanese/US REA is the variable which – in the absence of more detailed data on capital stock or sales – we shall take as our own proxy for the relative significance of Japanese (cf. US) direct participation in European manufacturing industry.[3]

EXPLAINING THE DIFFERENT STRUCTURE OF JAPANESE MNE ACTIVITY IN EUROPEAN MANUFACTURING INDUSTRY

Some Alternative Theories

It is, perhaps, worth recalling that, in the early 1970s, when the first wave of Japanese manufacturing investment in Europe occurred, US foreign subsidiaries were already contributing between 12 and 15 per cent of the manufacturing output of the major European industrial powers. This investment had been initiated as market-seeking investment, and was primarily prompted by the world-wide shortage of US dollars. Later, as a result of the removal of the tariff barriers between member countries of a newly formed European Economic Community (EC), the European production by US MNEs was restructured to exploit better the economies of scope and large-scale production (Cantwell 1992), and by 1977, not only were US affiliates in the EC exporting 39 per cent of their output to countries other than the United States (and mainly to elsewhere in the EC), but 59 per cent of these exports were to sister affiliates (US Department of Commerce 1981).

From the start, however, Japanese investment in the EC has been aimed at exploiting the European market as a whole. Like its US counterpart, it was (and is) essentially market seeking, and like the US MNEs in the 1950s, Japanese MNEs have been persuaded to invest in Europe earlier than they might have done by the inability of European consumers to purchase freely the imports they wanted.[4] Partly because of the moves towards regional integration, and partly because of their need to 'catch up' in the globalization process, Japanese firms have pursued a rationalized and asset-acquiring European investment strategy from the start. Especially in sectors in which there is (or was) surplus capacity, Japanese firms have entered the European market by acquiring existing producers, rather than setting up new greenfield ventures. The rubber tyre sector is a particularly good example of a sector which is strongly globalized in its orientation. Yet to serve the foreign transplants of their own motor vehicle firms, and indeed other auto producers, more efficiently, Japanese firms have chosen to acquire established – and for the most part ailing – European or US MNEs.[5]

In recent years, attempts by economists to explain the foreign activities of MNEs have mainly fallen into two groups. The first are those which seek to offer generic paradigms, within which it is possible to accommodate a variety of specific, and operationally testable, theories of FDI and the internationalization of production. The internalization and eclectic paradigms fall into this category. The second are those which identify and seek to assess the significance of a number of operationally testable variables in explaining particular kinds of aspects of MNE activity.

Our basic assertion is that the phenomenon of Japanese direct investment in Europe requires only minor modification to the existing paradigms of international production, but that the specific variables which economists have used to explain much of US direct investment in Europe in the 1960s and 1970s are not those which best explain much of current Japanese MNE activity in that area.

While we shall primarily use the framework of the eclectic paradigm of international production to support our argument, it may be helpful very briefly to review the applicability of some of the theories earlier put forward to explain outbound US FDI to our present discussion.

The product cycle thesis

In many ways, Raymond Vernon's original product cycle theory (1966) is a better explanation for much of recent Japanese investment in Europe than it is for explaining the contemporary activities of US MNEs. Goods requiring resources and capabilities in which Japan had (or managed to create for itself) a comparative advantage were first exported by Japan to countries with similar income levels and tastes, for example, much of Western Europe (Ozawa 1992). Then when, because of improved market prospects, it became more profitable to produce these goods (or part of their value added) in Europe, or barriers were placed on Japanese exports, Japanese firms set up (or acquired) production facilities in Europe. Between 1975 and 1990, for example, the ratio of cars exported from Japan to Europe to those produced by Japanese companies in Europe fell from near infinity to 6.0, and of CTV sets from 8.0 to 0.8.

The major differences between the thrust of US firms into Europe in the 1960s and that of their Japanese counterparts in the 1980s is that first, unlike their predecessors, Japanese MNEs have treated Europe as a single market and, in that light, have pursued a regionally integrated product and locational strategy; and second (as will be discussed later), the form and interaction between the competitive or ownership-specific advantages of Japanese (cf. US) firms and the competitive or location-specific advantages of Japan (cf. the United States) have led to a different industrial structure of such investment.

The 'follow my leader' thesis

Working on data on the internationalization of US-based MNEs, Knickerbocker (1973) concluded that the timing of the entry of US firms into foreign markets was bunched. He asserted that this reflected the oligopolistic behaviour of such firms. This hypothesis is, again, broadly upheld by

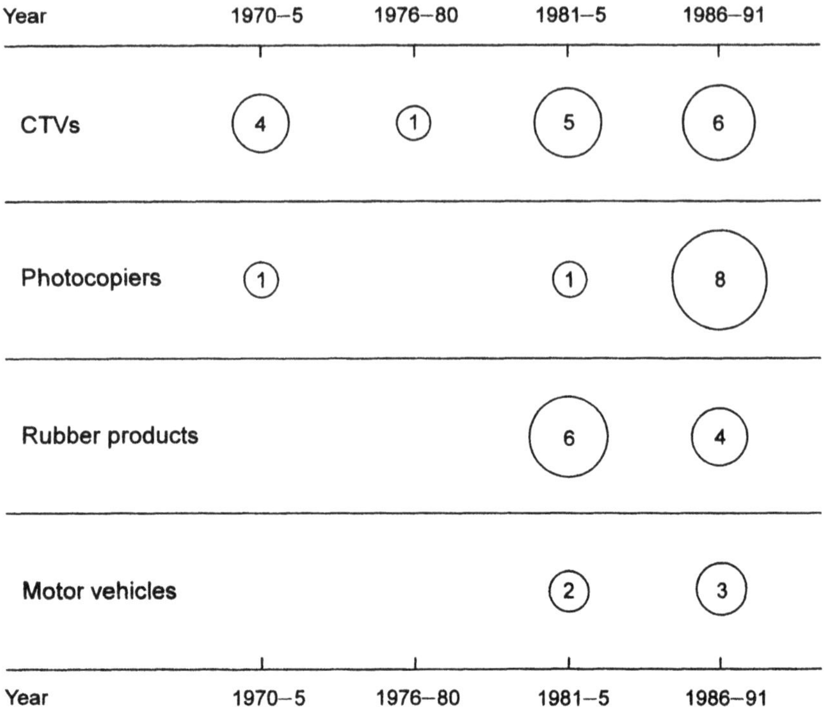

Figure 13.1 Clustering of Japanese subsidiaries in Europe 1970–91
Note: Figures in circle represent number of firms established in 5-year period

the data on the entry of Japanese foreign investors into Europe. Figure 13.1 illustrates the kind of bunching revealed by Japanese MNEs entering into the consumer electronics industry in the 1970s and the motor vehicle, rubber tyre and photocopying industries in the 1980s.[6] Again, however, it is worth noting that while Knickerbocker considered individual countries in Europe as separate (and largely independent) locations, in the case of Japanese investors, it is more appropriate to consider them as regions of an integrated Europe.

The risk-diversification thesis

The idea that the location of the foreign value-added activity of a company is a function of its propensity to diversify country-specific risk was first analysed by Rugman (1979) based upon some earlier work by Grubel (1968). We believe this has only limited explanatory relevance as far as the current wave of Japanese investment in Europe is concerned, chiefly because such investment is generally not competitive with that which might have been directed to other countries, and, apart from exchange rate fluctuations (now greatly modified by the alignment of the currencies of the EC countries), the risk premium of investing in Europe is little different from investing in Japan or the United States.

However, as in the case of US investors in the 1960s, Japanese MNEs are becoming increasingly sensitive about the distribution of their value-added activities within Europe. Partly, this is for political reasons (e.g. to pacify the French and Italians over the concentration of Japanese auto investment in the UK, and the accusation of exporting Japanese cars to France and Italy through a UK gateway!) and partly to ensure a reasonably balanced portfolio of key European currencies.

The intangible assets thesis

The idea that firms will invest abroad in those sectors in which, relative to their foreign competitors, they enjoy a favoured competitive position, is associated with the work of many scholars, including that of Hymer (1960, 1968), Caves (1971, 1974), Owen (1982), Lall (1980) and Lall and Siddarthan (1982). One of the key components of this thesis is that, in order to produce in particular countries, foreign firms need to possess a set of intangible assets (referred to by Hymer as monopolistic advantages) which are sufficient to outweigh the specific costs which they have to incur in undertaking the investment. Almost certainly, these entry costs – and especially language problems and the unfamiliarity with political, economic and legal institutions, business customs, organizational structures, supplying facilities, industrial relations and government regulations – have been (and are) higher for Japanese than for US firms; and to some extent at least, these differences explain the greater preference of the former, relative to the latter, to supply the European markets via exports.[7]

However, as has been shown elsewhere (United Nations 1992), the nature of these intangible assets is likely to be both industry and country specific; hence those which might satisfactorily explain the industry structure of US direct investment in Europe may not be appropriate to explaining Japanese investment in Europe. Moreover, as Kogut (1983) has demonstrated, the kind of advantages which lead firms initially to forage abroad may be quite different from those likely to determine the sequential growth of such investments. In particular, the literature has distinguished between the ownership-specific advantages which stem from possession of specific assets (e.g. a particular technology or type of product market), and those which arise from the cross-border governance of a collection of assets. We shall consider this distinction in more detail in a later section of this chapter.

The Kojima hypothesis

In several contributions, both Dunning (1958, 1981) and Kojima (1978, 1990) have argued that FDI should follow the principle of comparative advantage, and that firms should only engage in foreign value-added activities which require an input of natural resources or created capabilities in which the host country is comparatively well endowed relative to the home country. In the past, Kojima has consistently alleged that the geographical distribution of Japanese MNE activity more nearly meets his criteria than that of US MNE activity. However, to explain the rapid growth of Japanese FDI in Europe, and its industrial distribution, Kojima would either have to abandon his earlier assertion that Japanese investment is more trade oriented than its US counterpart, or to accept that there are other kinds of efficiency-enhancing FDI (particularly of an intraindustry variety), or to acknowledge that the kind of market imperfections (e.g. tariff barriers) imposed on US exports, or oligopolistic tactics deployed by US MNEs, are now being imposed on Japanese exports or being practised by Japanese firms. Whatever the explanation, Kojima's thesis, as initially stated, is not very helpful in explaining much of the growth of Japanese MNE activity in European manufacturing industry, and particularly that which has occurred as a result of mergers and acquisitions (M&As) in recent years.

General Paradigms

Turning to the two general economic explanations of international production, we shall concentrate on the eclectic paradigm, as it also embraces the essential features of the internalization paradigm.[8] Essentially, the paradigm avers that the propensity of firms to engage in FDI will depend on the interaction between their unique competitive and/or monopolistic (or ownership-specific (O)) advantages and the locational (L) attractions of alternative sites for the creation or use of those advantages;[9] and also on the extent to which firms find it in their interests to govern internally (I) these resources and capabilities in preference to other organizational routes, for example, the external market or co-operative arrangements.

The paradigm further suggests that the exact configuration of the OLI advantages facing firms and their strategic response to it will depend on (i) the countries of origin of the investing companies and the countries in which they are making the investment; (ii) the characteristics of the value activities financed by the FDI (usually considered as industry-specific characteristics); and (iii) the economic and behavioural attributes of the investing firms themselves – that is, characteristics *apart* from their nationality of ownership, or degree of multinationality.

For example, since the competitive advantages of enterprises are, to some extent at least, likely to reflect the location-bound characteristics of their home countries, it may be reasonable to hypothesize that the O advantages which are most pertinent to explaining US MNE activity in Europe will be different from those explaining Japanese direct investment in that region.

Similarly, the variables likely to influence the L advantages facing US firms in supplying the European market, from a US relative to a European production facility, may not be the same as those facing Japanese MNEs, while the kinds of market failure most relevant to explaining why US firms may choose to engage in FDI in Europe, rather than conclude co-operative, but non-equity, agreements with European firms, may be different from those which Japanese firms consider most appropriate in their organizational strategies.

The task of the economist seeking to explain differences in the level and composition of Japanese and US investment in Europe by use of the eclectic paradigm is twofold. First, it is to identify and evaluate which of the many possible OLI variables[10] is, or are, more likely to influence the two kinds of investment and why. Second, it is to establish how far and why such variables, and/or their values, may be different between value-added activities (in this case, industrial sectors). In pursuing both these tasks, it may be necessary for the analyst to draw upon some of the more specific theories outlined above and/or others put forward by business strategists, plus marketing and organizational scholars. Indeed, as we have repeatedly emphasized the eclectic paradigm should not be considered as a competing theory to these explanations, but rather as an integrating framework both analysing them and evaluating their validity.

To the extent that patterns of trade differ between countries, and reflect the structure of the resources and capabilities of the trading nations, it is hardly surprising that patterns of outward or inward direct investment – which are, to some extent, based on the same specific endowments – are also country specific. Raymond Vernon was one of the first economists to make use of both the neo-classical and neo-technology theories of trade to explain the characteristics of US FDI (Vernon 1966, 1970), and his seminal contributions have been followed by others which assert that the competitive advantages possessed by firms at time *t* strongly reflect the immobile resources and capabilities of the countries from which they emanate in time *t*-1. More recently, Michael Porter (1990) has offered a conceptual framework for identifying the determinants of the competitive advantages of nations, while many of the attempts to explain the economic renaissance of Japan have sought to pinpoint the unique (i.e. Japanese-specific) factors influencing the productivity and behaviour of Japanese firms.

THE OWNERSHIP ADVANTAGES OF JAPANESE AND US FIRMS IN EUROPE

Asset-Specific Advantages

Casual empiricism takes us some way in pinpointing the symptoms of Japanese economic success. Ask any European consumer why he or she buys a motor vehicle made by a Japanese firm rather than one made by a European or American firm, and the answer usually comes down to a combination of quality, price, reliability, and the technical and other attributes of the vehicle. It is now widely acknowledged that in the 1960s and 1970s, the only way the Japanese auto producers could effectively compete with the established Western car producers was either to produce a similar car at a lower price and higher quality, or to produce a car (in size, technical quality and complementary features such as cruise control, electric windows, etc.) which the existing producers were not supplying, and which consumers were signalling they wanted to buy (see e.g. Abegglen and Stalk 1985). Had the European- and US-owned car firms been producing at optimal (or X) efficiency, the entry of Japanese producers into their territories would have been much more difficult. As it is, over the last two decades, the Japanese have continuously upgraded their competitive advantages, and are now in the vanguard of product and process innovation.

It is possible to identify specific intangible assets which firms of different nationalities may possess at the same or different time periods, the origin of which, at least, partly reflects the location-bound resources of the countries which give rise to them.[11] We say partly, because some of the O advantages evolved by Japanese firms reflect those of a newcomer entering an industry in which there existed some kind of static or dynamic inefficiency – including a failure of existing producers to identify existing or future consumer needs.

The example of the auto industry can be replicated in other sectors. The point is that whereas in the 1950s and 1960s, the O-specific advantages of US firms were primarily based on their ability to innovate new products and production processes, devise more appropriate organizational structures and professionalize structures, their marketing and budgetary control techniques, the O advantages of Japanese firms in the 1970s and 1980s essentially comprised their capability to co-ordinate and manage the resources and capabilities within their jurisdiction – including those acquired from Western nations – so as to minimize their X production and transaction costs.[12]

However, these symptoms of success themselves need explaining. They also beg many questions. Why is the Japanese economic prowess limited to particular kinds of activities? And why these particular activities? Exactly how have the Japanese been able to make such inroads into markets traditionally served by North American or European producers?

Governance-Specific Advantages

To answer these questions we need to turn to a second kind of O-specific advantage which firms may possess. This may best be described as the ability systemically to organize resources and capabilities under their governance. We have described these as transaction-cost-minimizing or common governance ownership advantage (Ot).[13] Here the essential proposition is that the country of origin of an MNE is relevant in explaining the modalities of which it organizes its value-added activities, and that different modalities are more suited for some kinds of production than others. It is also likely that the *L*-specific endowments of a home country will influence an MNE's response to different types of market failure.

The questions which now arise are threefold. First, what are the particular attributes of Japanese, compared with US, firms in their governance of both internal and external transactions? Second, how do they impact on their response to different kinds of market failure? Third, given the answer to these questions, to what extent are these attributes specific to particular kinds of transactions or industrial sectors?

In answer to the first question, scholars are generally agreed that the governance of Japanese, relative to US, MNEs tends to be best marked by the ability efficiently to generate and sustain a consensus among the stakeholders involved in the production of goods and services to provide these goods and services at highest possible quality at the lowest possible cost. Put another way, their form of governance seems to be especially successful in managing idiosyncratic human-intensive transnational relations, whether they be organized within or between hierarchies. By contrast, casual inspection of the organizational structures of US MNEs suggests they have a comparative advantage in the administration of formalized, but more technical and standardized, transactional relations.

Second, it is possible to classify different kinds of market failure according to the extent to which they can be best organized through tacit or informal systems of human co-operation or by formal hierarchical control and/or interfirm contractual relationships. Some suggestions are put forward in Table 13.3. In this table, we have attempted to rank some of the reasons why firms may wish directly to control transnational relationships (whether via the hierarchical or a non-equity mode), by our perception of importance of the human intensity content relative to the technical intensity content of these relationships. For example, transactions which involve substantial search and negotiating costs, which have a high opportunistic element attached to them, which require the fullest co-operation of workers to ensure that rigorous quality control procedures are maintained, and the success of which is strongly dependent on supplier reliability and the readiness of sales agents to behave in a way which advances the interests of their principals, are among those classified as (relatively) human intensive. On the other hand, the ability of firms to engage in price discrimination, to capture the economies of interdependent activities, to compensate for the absence of futures markets, to control suppliers or market outlets, and to reduce the risks of exchange fluctuations, are all transaction-related activities which depend more on the technical characteristics of the firm and/or on the business acumen of its managers.

Third, the presence of at least some of these market failures is likely to vary between industrial sectors. Table 13.3 sets out our estimate on a scale of 1 to 3 of the relevance of different kinds of market failure to particular sectors. As the table reveals, human-related market failure is relatively most pronounced in the fabricating sectors, while technical market failure, though no less significant in these sectors, tends to be more significant than human-related market failure in the processing sectors.

Most of the literature on market failure tends to take as given the transaction costs of using external markets, and considers the conditions under which firms can lower these costs by internalizing these markets.[14] But there are other alternatives open to firms. Moreover, the extent and pattern of the failure of a particular market or the market system *in toto* may vary over time. One option to administered hierarchies – often neglected by economists – is for a firm to try to improve the efficiency of external markets by tilting the terms of exchange and conditions of demand and/or supply in their favour. For example, it might be possible for an MNE to improve the quality of a product supplied by its subcontractor or the reliability with which it is supplied by providing advice to its suppliers as to how best to remedy these deficiencies. Also, by a restructuring of incentives, a sales agent may be persuaded to work more in his or her principal's interests than the agent is currently doing. Alternatively, firms may reduce the organizational costs of markets by engaging in co-operative ventures which are 'in between' arm's length transactions and internal hierarchies.

The response of MNEs to both domestic and cross-border market failure is likely to be country, industry and firm specific. For example, the Japanese auto industry in Japan is considerably less vertically integrated than its US counterpart in the United States. There are various reasons for this, but, most surely, one of the most important is that the relationships which Japanese auto assemblers have forged with their suppliers have helped lower the (interfirm) transaction costs of using intermediate product markets (Okada 1991). In other words, by helping to reduce market failure, the Japanese auto assemblers have had less incentive to internalize such markets. Second, the suitability of using a particular organizational route may vary according to the character of the products being supplied

In our analysis of O-specific factors influencing the Japanese/US REA ratio, we shall assume that the costs and benefits of common governance economies will depend on the kind and complexity of transactions – and especially the human intensity content of them – and also the number of particular kinds of benefits.

Let us sum up this part of the chapter. The competitive or O advantages of MNEs fall into two groups. First, the possession of specific income-

Table 13.3 Estimated significance of various kinds of market failure in making for internal governance, classified by industry

	Processing sectors								Fabricating sectors			
	1	*2*	*3*	*4*	*5*	*6*	*7*	*8*	*9*	*10*	*11*	*12*
1 *Relatively human intensive*												
Search and negotiating costs	2	2	1	1	2	2	1	2	3	3	3	3
Quality control (of labour-intensive production)	2	2	2	1	3	2	2	1	3	3	3	3
Supplier reliability	2	3	1	2	2	2	1	1	3	3	3	3
Agent reliability	1	3	1	1	2	1	1	1	2	3	3	3
Opportunism in labour market etc.	1	1	1	2	2	2	1	2	3	3	3	3
2 *Relatively technical intensive*												
Protection of property rights	2	3	3	2	1	1	2	1	3	3	2	3
Protection of trademarks	3	3	2	1	2	1	3	3	1	2	2	2
Economies of scale or scope	3	2	2	2	1	2	2	3	3	3	3	1
Diversification of risks	2	3	3	2	1	1	2	1	2	2	2	2
Economics of joint supply	2	2	2	2	2	2	1	2	3	2	1	2
Arbitraging of markets	2	2	2	1	1	1	2	1	2	2	2	1
Price discrimination	3	3	2	1	2	1	2	2	2	2	2	2
Quality control (of machine-intensive production)	3	3	3	2	2	2	3	3	2	2	2	2

Key to sectors

1 Food and kindred products
2 Pharmaceuticals
3 Other chemicals
4 Iron and steel
5 Textiles and clothing
6 Wood-related products
7 Rubber products
8 Non-metallic materials
9 General machinery
10 Computers, electrical equipment and goods
11 Transport equipment and parts
12 Photographic and precision instruments

Note: The higher the figures in the table, the more important the reasons for internal governance are perceived to be.

generating assets; and second, the way in which a firm governs the organization of these assets, in response to its perceived costs and benefits of alternative modes. It is our contention that both kinds of O advantages are partly country specific, and reflect the structure of the location-based resources and capabilities of the countries of origin of MNEs, as well as those of countries in which their subsidiaries operate.[15]

In this section, we have suggested that there are reasons to suppose that differences in Japanese and US country-specific characteristics (e.g. as identified by Porter (1990)[16]) not only cause Japanese and US firms to possess (or seek to acquire) different kinds of O advantages, but that these, in turn, will affect their relative abilities to supply particular kinds of products. Thus for these reasons alone, we would expect the revealed employment advantage of Japanese and US manufacturing affiliates in Europe to be different.

More specifically, and set out as two hypotheses (H_1, H_2), we are suggesting that:

H_1 The more Japanese firms, relative to US firms, possess (or utilize efficiently) specific asset advantages, the higher the Japanese/US employment ratio in Europe is likely to be.

H_2 The greater the common governance advantages of Japanese relative to US firms, the higher the Japanese/US employment ratio in Europe is likely to be.

We are also hypothesizing that both of these advantages are also likely to be of varying importance between industrial sectors.

THE COMPARATIVE LOCATIONAL ADVANTAGES OF EUROPE AS A PRODUCTION BASE TO JAPANESE AND US FIRMS

It is one thing to identify the country-specific, competitive, or O advantages of Japanese and US firms, but quite another to conclude that the FDI structures of the two groups of firms should necessarily be different. For, given the same O advantages, it may be profitable for Japanese firms to create or utilize these advantages from a home location rather than a European location, while US firms may find it profitable to create or utilize their O advantages from a European, rather than a home, location. The Japanese/US REA ratio could, then, reflect the different locational perceptions and preferences of the two groups of firms.

The literature is replete with explanations of the variables influencing the location of the activities by MNEs (UNCTC 1992). Some are likely to be product or host country specific rather than home country (or home to host country) specific. Examples include products which need to be adapted to the needs of foreign purchasers, and non-discriminatory taxes, incentives and import controls imposed by host country governments. But others which reflect differences in the resource capabilities and endowments of the home and host countries, physical or psychic distances between these countries, and discriminatory import and investment policies of a host government towards a particular foreign country or its firms, will affect the way in which a particular market is served, and hence the revealed employment ratio of foreign subsidiaries.

Table 13.4 identifies some of these variables and estimates their likely significance as factors influencing the locational determinants by Japanese and US MNEs selling to European markets. The impact of these variables is also most likely to be activity and sector specific, and some estimates – on a scale of 1 to 3[17] – of which sectors are likely to be affected by any particular factor are also given in the table.

Our reading of the literature on the motives for Japanese and US direct investment in European industry (e.g. JETRO 1991) suggests that, besides the real exchange rate, there are four locational variables, the value of which, or the response to which, is likely to be very different between the two home countries:

1 *Productivity in the home country.* Here the hypothesis (L_1) is that the higher the productivity in Japan relative to that in the United States, the less the Japanese/US employment ratio in Europe is likely to be. (This hypothesis would be nullified if it could be shown that the differences in productivity were not country but firm specific, and that they are transferable across national borders.) For reasons set out earlier these differences are also likely to be partly industry specific. While, ideally, one would like to include all factors of production in the productivity measure, in practice, one has to make do with a labour productivity measure (see the next section).
2 *Distance costs.* These are determined by the physical and psychic distance between the exporting and importing countries and the nature of the product being supplied. Casual observation would suggest that both kinds of distance costs are likely to be greater between Japan and Europe than the United States and Europe.[18] Clearly, too, these distance costs are likely to vary between products according to such variables as weight, bulkiness, fragility or perishability of the products being transported. The hypothesis (L_2) here is that the greater the transport costs per unit of product produced the greater the Japanese/US employment ratio in Europe is likely to be, because Japanese firms would have a relatively greater incentive to supply the European market for a European location.
3 *Tariff and non-tariff barriers.* Most government-imposed barriers to imports from Japan and the United States do not discriminate by country of origin, but some do; over the past decade, most discriminatory measures have arisen as a result either of the perceived dumping by Japanese producers of such products as cameras and photocopiers, or of the

Table 13.4 Likely variables to affect the location of MNE activity, by industry

	Processing sectors								Fabricating sectors			
	1	*2*	*3*	*4*	*5*	*6*	*7*	*8*	*9*	*10*	*11*	*12*
1 *Tending to favour a home location*												
Low transport costs of finished products	1	3	2	1	3	2	2	3	2	2	1	2
Substantial plant economies of scale	2	3	3	3	2	1	1	3	3	3	3	3
Low real input prices in home (cf. host) country	1	2	1	1	2	1	1	1	1	1	1	1
Large physical or cultural distance between home and host countries	2	1	1	1	3	2	1	1	1	1	1	1
Relatively high intrafirm communication costs	2	3	3	3	2	1	2	2	2	2	2	1
High risk/commitment ratio costs of investing in a foreign location												
Near location of important inputs	3	1	1	1	1	1	1	1	2	2	2	3
2 *Tending to favour a foreign (European) location*												
Need to adapt products to local consumer needs	3	2	1	1	3	2	1	1	1	2	2	1
High transport costs of finished products	2	1	2	3	1	2	2	3	2	1	2	1
High production costs of home (cf. host) country	3	1	2	1	1	1	1	1	2	2	2	1
Tariff or non-tariff barriers	1	2	1	3	2	1	1	1	2	3	3	1
Relatively low intrafirm communication costs	1	2	2	1	2	2	1	2	3	3	2	2
Investment incentives	1	2	2	1	3	2	2	1	2	3	2	2
Good local infrastructure and/or supplier networks	2	2	2	1	1	1	2	1	2	1	3	2
Near location of important inputs	2	1	2	3	2	3	2	2	2	2	2	2

Key to sectors

1 Food and kindred products
2 Pharmaceuticals
3 Other chemicals
4 Iron and steel
5 Textiles and clothing
6 Wood-related products
7 Rubber products
8 Non-metallic materials
9 General machinery
10 Computers, electrical equipment and goods
11 Transport equipment and parts
12 Photographic and precision instruments

Note: The higher the figures in the table, the more important the reasons influencing location are perceived to be

unacceptable (speed of the) penetration of European markets by Japanese exporters of such products as autos, CTV sets, VTRs, etc. Our hypothesis (L_3) here is that the greater the discriminatory import measures against Japanese firms in any one sector, the higher the Japanese/US employment ratio in Europe is likely to be.

4 *Revealed comparative exporting advantage (RCA)*. Finally, we consider a measure which encompasses revealed comparative advantage (RCA) in exports. This represents the extent to which exports from Japan to Europe, relative to exports from the United States in particular sectors, are shown (on the basis of past data) to be higher or lower than the exports of all products from Japan to Europe, relative to exports from the United States. Here there are two conflicting hypotheses. The first (L_{4a}) is that Japanese or US exports to Europe and the European production of their subsidiaries are substitutes for each other, and that the RCA of Japanese exports is likely to be negatively correlated with the Japanese/US REA ratio in Europe (i.e. the L advantage favours the home country). The other hypothesis (L_{4b}) is that exports and foreign production are alternative indices of the competitive advantage of the exporting and investing country, and that a high RCA of Japanese exports in Europe is likely to be positively correlated with a high Japanese/US REA ratio (i.e. the L advantage favours the host country).

DO JAPANESE MNES INTERNALIZE INTERMEDIATE PRODUCT MARKETS BETWEEN JAPAN AND EUROPE MORE THAN THEIR US COUNTERPARTS?

Ethier (1986) has referred to the internalization variable as being the 'Caesar' in the OLI triumvirate explaining MNE activity. In the current exercise, it plays a less significant role. Partly this is because we have subsumed the relative ability of US and Japanese hierarchies to govern the resources and capabilities within their jurisdiction under the second group of O-specific advantages. Partly it is because there are few reasons to suppose that the transactional costs[19] of engaging in transatlantic or trans-Asian arm's length transactions should be substantially different. Exceptions might include the costs of upgrading the quality of local inputs to a differential level of quality expected by Japanese (cf. US) firms, and the identification and nurturing of appropriate distribution channels and after-sales servicing facilities.

One area in which the opportunity and incentive (as opposed to the ability) of firms to internalize cross-border markets is likely to vary according to the nationality of the investing firm relates to the extent to which it is possible for it to exploit economies of scale or scope. Clearly this opportunity is related to the size and geographical distribution of MNEs in different parts of Europe. Since US direct investment in Europe is so much larger and geographically more dispersed than its Japanese counterpart, it is reasonable to assume that the opportunities for it to exploit the benefits of process and product specialization are that much greater. The literature, for example, strongly suggests that, irrespective of their nationalities, MNEs which pursue regional or globally integrated strategies tend to internalize their cross-border markets more than those which supply products wholly for domestic markets (Doz 1986, Cantwell 1992).

One index that might be used to demonstrate the validity or otherwise of this proposition is the proportion of intrafirm European trade by Japanese (cf. US) firms in Europe. Unfortunately we only have data for the latter. Since we know, however, that the volume of intra-European exports by Japanese firms is small and that most of them are intrafirm, we may reasonably hypothesize that the Japanese/US employment ratio in Europe is likely to be positively related to the ratio between intra-European exports of Japanese subsidiaries and the intrafirm, intra-European exports of US subsidiaries.[20]

One other measure of the relative propensity of Japanese and US firms to internalize their trans-Asian and transatlantic intermediate markets relates to their respective opportunities to forge vertical or horizontal networks in Europe. This networking propensity is extremely difficult to measure, but one such index could be the extent to which a particular industrial sector is dominated by firms belonging to the six leading *keiretsu*. Because some estimates are available, we have chosen to take as our independent variable the proportion of the output of a sector supplied by the six leading *keiretsu* (Gerlach 1992). The hypothesis here (I_2) is that the higher the networking of Japanese firms (in Japan) the greater the Japanese/US employment ratio – it being somewhat heroically assumed that the benefits of networking in Japan can be transferred to a European location.

SOME EXPLORATORY TESTING

Since Japanese direct investment in Europe is still a very recent phenomenon and many of the data we need to test the kind of hypotheses set out earlier in this chapter are not disaggregated in sufficient industrial detail, we have had to abandon the kind of econometric exercise we had originally hoped to conduct. In later years, as the volume of Japanese investment increases, and its pattern becomes more geographically and industrially diversified, it may be possible to undertake some pooled cross-sectional regression or logit analysis using data from the individual European countries. We experimented with such an exercise in the course of our research but, with the exception of a significant relationship between the Japanese/US employment ratio and the revealed comparative exporting advantage (L_4), it produced completely inconclusive results.

Instead, in Tables 13.5 and 13.6, we have set some data about the values of the independent variable and the seven independent variables identified earlier in this chapter. In most cases, we have presented the actual values of the various data and then ranked these by sector. In two cases, we have compiled an estimated ranking from a composite of proxy variables.

While we would be the first to admit that this procedure leaves much to be desired, we none the less believe that the data set out in Tables 13.5 and 13.6 do tell an interesting and, for the most part, consistent story. First, it is possible to identify a number of unique characteristics associated with Japanese (cf. US) direct investment in Europe. Most certainly, some of these characteristics reflect the much more recent entry of Japanese MNEs into Europe, their relative lack of knowledge and experience of European markets, their smaller size, and their limited industrial and geographical diversification. But others, at least in the 1980s, reflect the different configuration of OLI variables facing Japanese (cf. US) firms, which specifically reflect the unique features of their respective home economies – and which, in turn, lead to distinctive production, marketing and organizational strategies on the part of Japanese MNEs.

The data in Tables 13.5 and 13.6 confirm that the industrial structures of Japanese and US manufacturing affiliates in Europe are generally positively correlated with their respective revealed patenting and common governance advantages. The main exception is the relatively large investment by Japanese firms in the rubber industry, which mainly reflects the strategic purchases by Sumitomo and Bridgestone of the Dunlop and Firestone rubber tyre plants in Europe.[21] More particularly, the value of the independent variable is highest in those sectors in which the human intensity market-related transaction costs are also higher.

The L-specific variables identified yield mixed results. The tables show that the Japanese/US employment ratio in electrical and transport equipment is positively related to the non-tariff barriers exerted on these products by European governments, while, excepting iron and steel products, there is some suggestion that Japanese and US exports are complementary with, rather than substitutable for, FDI. On the other hand, there seems to be little systematic relationship between the composition of Japanese and US MNE activities and that of domestic labour productivity or of the estimated transportation costs. Of the two proxies for internalization advantages, only the second – membership of one of the leading *keiretsu* – seems to be positively and closely ranked with the dependent variable.

It is also clear from Tables 13.5 and 13.6 that the factors influencing the Japanese/US employment ratio differ between sectors. For example, partly reflecting the distinctiveness of Japanese tastes and partly the comparatively low propensity of the Japanese to engage in foreign patenting, there is little Japanese FDI in the European food and beverage sector. This could change in the 1990s if and when the population of East Asians in Europe increases.

Table 13.5 A list of variables explaining Japanese/US employment ratios, by industry

	J/US (employment ratio)	H_1	H_2	L_1	L_2	L_3[b]	L_4	I_1	I_2
Processing industries									
Food and kindred products	0.06	0.64	7	0.61	16.6	10.26	0.03	1.30	n/a
Pharmaceuticals	0.38	0.89	12	1.11	(0.7		(0.16		46.3
Other chemicals	0.45	0.88	8	1.15	38.0)	1.52	0.36)	0.58	63.5
Iron and steel[b]	0.20	0.67	5	1.43	21.7	9.74	1.04	1.22	79.0
Textiles and clothing	0.27	0.52	6	0.85	35.7	7.26	0.79	0.24	40.3
Wood-related products	0.04	n/a	11	0.92	n/a	0.00	0.03	0.00	35.6
Rubber	7.65	1.08	9	0.90	39.4	0.52	2.49	n/a	59.9
Non-ferrous materials[b]	0.92	1.10	10	1.02	42.6	0.38	0.37	1.06	82.5
Fabricating industries									
General machinery	0.88	0.69	3	1.00	10.1	1.60	0.57	2.10	77.1
Electrical equipment[a]	1.42	1.53	2	0.87	17.1	1.72[b]	1.40	1.13	70.8
Transport equipment	1.13	1.46	1	0.93	4.3	3.15[b]	1.26	1.25	87.1
Instruments	0.59	1.57	4	0.63	5.0	n/a	0.85	0.14	30.8

H_1 = Ratio of revealed technological advantage of Japan and United States in overall innovation 1978–86 (Cantwell and Hodson 1991: table 5.10)
H_2 = Author's estimate based on an estimate of average number of transactions involved in production of goods
L_1 = Ratio of labour productivity (value added divided by average employment) in Japan and United States (1986) (United Nations 1990)
L_2 = Estimated value of transportation costs per unit value in each industry based on average value of Japanese and US exports to Germany (1989) (defined as CIF value minus FOB value) (OECD 1990)
L_3[b] = Average estimated *ad valorem* equivalents of non-tariff barriers in European countries (%) (Saxonhouse and Stern 1989: table 9.4)
L_4 = Ratio between the revealed comparative advantage of Japan and US exports (1989) (United Nations *Commodity Trade Statistics*, 1990)
I_1 = Estimate of ratios between Japanese and US intrafirm, intra-European exports to total exports (1979) (US Department of Commerce 1991, MITI 1991)
I_2 = Percentage of sales of Japanese firms accounted for by *keiretsu* (Dodwell Marketing Consultants 1986, Gerlach 1992)
[a] Includes computers and office machinery
[b] The percentage *ad valorem* in those industries does not reflect the actions of individual EC countries in restricting imports of Japanese goods

Table 13.6 The ranking of variables explaining Japanese/US employment ratios, by industry

	J/US *(employment ratio)*	H_1	H_2	L_1	L_2	L_3[b]	L_4	I_1	I_2
Processing industries									
Food and kindred products	11	10	7	12	7	3	11	2	n/a
Pharmaceuticals	8	6	12	3	11	7	10	7	8
Other chemicals	7	7	8	2	3	7	9	7	6
Iron and steel[b]	10	9	5	1	5	4	4	4	3
Textiles and clothing	9	11	6	10	4	5	6	9	9
Wood-related products	12	n/a	11	7	n/a	11	11	11	10
Rubber	1	5	10	8	2	9	1	n/a	7
Non-ferrous materials	4	4	9	4	1	10	8	6	2
Average ranking	7.8	7.4	8.5	5.9	4.7	7	7.5	6.6	6.4
Fabricating industries									
General machinery	5	8	3	5	8	6	7	1	4
Electrical equipment[a]	2	2	2	9	6	1[b]	2	5	5
Transport equipment	3	3	1	6	10	1[b]	3	3	1
Instruments	6	1	4	11	9	n/a	5	10	11
Average ranking	4.0	3.5	2.5	7.8	8.3	2.7	4.3	4.8	5.2
Rank coefficient of correlation (with J/US Emp.)	n/a	+0.737	+0.350	–0.014	+0.164	+0.137	+0.739	+0.305	+0.409

[a] Includes computers and office machinery
[b] The percentage *ad valorem* in those industries does not reflect the actions of individual EC countries in restricting imports of Japanese goods

By contrast, with the exception of transportation costs, the ranking of each of the explanatory variables for transport equipment and electronic products is either very or quite closely ranked with the Japanese/US employment ratio.

The case of rubber products is an interesting one. The Japanese do not appear to have strong O-specific advantages in this sector. Yet it is one which is dominated by large MNEs which, in the past, have tended to follow auto companies abroad. However, because of surplus capacity in rubber tyres and the relative unimportance of human-intensive transaction costs in their production, Japanese firms have preferred to invest in Europe (and the United States) by way of acquisition rather than greenfield investment. Hence their comparatively large volume of FDI and employment in this sector.

Despite relatively high transport costs and non-tariff barriers, there is little Japanese investment in the European iron and steel industry. This is a sector in which the Japanese firms enjoy relatively few O-specific advantages, *vis-à-vis* their US counterparts, but which, nevertheless, records higher labour productivity ratios in Japan. The relatively high Japanese/US employment ratio in non-ferrous materials is entirely due to a single, large Japanese FDI in a Belgian glass manufacturing company.

While Japanese firms record the highest revealed patenting advantage in instruments (including photographic equipment), their domestic productivity in this sector is the lowest. Transportation costs are relatively insignificant, as is the incentive to internalize cross-border markets. The relationships for general machinery and textiles and clothing also yield ambiguous results, although, in both cases, the mean ranking of the explanatory variables is broadly consistent with that of the Japanese/US employment ratio.

SOME UNRESOLVED ISSUES

There remain several interesting issues which only future events will resolve. We might identify just four of them; others may arise in the course of discussion. The first question concerns the extent to which the country-specific O advantages of Japanese firms are transferable to a European location. To what extent will the Japanese MNEs lose some of their competitive advantages as they are forced to engage in more international production? We are getting some hints from the experience of Japanese affiliates in both the United States and Europe that many of them are, but it is early days yet. Most Japanese affiliates are still producing at the lower value-added part of their value chain and have yet to be fully integrated into the local economies of which they are a part.

Second, to what extent are the kind of O advantages, which are the basis of Japanese direct investment in Europe, capable of being copied by their foreign competitors (and especially US and European MNEs)? Again, we have strong suggestions that in some industries – especially the colour TV and photographic equipment sector – they have been, or are being so copied. There is, for example, much less difference in the quality and reliability of the current generation of colour TVs and cameras now being marketed by firms of different nationalities than there was a decade or so ago.

Third, can one predict the kind of assets or forms of governance likely to determine the success of MNEs in the future? And even if one could – as some business scholars, such as Bartlett and Ghoshal (1989) and Doz and Prahalad (1987), have attempted – can one foretell which country-specific characteristics are most likely to give rise to these advantages? In other words, is the present structure of Japanese investment in Europe a reflection of the past competitive advantages of Japan, which might be quite different from those which are likely to be the critical determinants of future outbound activity by Japanese MNEs?

Fourth, unlike its US counterpart, much of Japanese investment in Europe is initial rather than sequential, and the literature (e.g. Kogut 1983) suggests that as firms increase their degrees of multinationality, the structure of their OLI configuration changes; in its turn, such change may affect particular sectors differently. For this reason, too, one might expect some realignment of the structure and significance of US and Japanese investment in Europe.

Much, of course, will depend on the form and pattern of growth of Japanese participation in Europe. Will growth occur along the value chain (e.g. via a deepening in the quality of such investment) or by product diversification? To what extent is Japanese investment, relative to US investment, likely to be directed to acquiring new competitive advantages (most noticeably through the joint venture and M&A route) rather than exploiting existing competitive advantages?

It would be a bold person who feels comfortable in predicting the comparative *OLI* configuration facing Japanese and US firms over the next decade. While the competitiveness convergence paradigm has much appeal, the idea of vicious and virtuous asset-generating circles (Cantwell 1989) suggests there could be considerable periods in which particular countries or firms can sustain, or even advance, their competitive positions. Certainly, the more one discerns about the commitment of the Japanese to the upgrading of human and physical capital, and their continued efforts to promote governance systems which are geared to advancing national and international competitiveness, the more one is led to infer that not only will the share of Japanese, relative to US, direct investment in European industry continue to increase, but, in those sectors which are most regionalized or globalized in their orientation, the share is likely to increase the fastest. Of course, macro-economic and other factors may completely negate this inference, but only time will tell whether this will or will not occur.

NOTES

* I am most grateful for the research assistance given by Rajeesh Narula in the preparation of this chapter, and also for the comments by Dennis Encarnation on an earlier draft.

1 The Japanese figure includes a small amount of agricultural and mining activities.

2 Namely, $E_{Ji}/E_{USi} - E_{Jt}/E_{USt}$ where i = a particular industrial sector and t = all manufacturing sectors.

3 There is an implicit assumption in this procedure that sectoral capital/labour ratios for Japanese affiliates are broadly similar to those of their US affiliates. I am grateful to Dennis Encarnation for pointing this out to me.

4 Except that in the 1980s, tariff barriers, import quotas and voluntary export restrictions limited Japanese exports to Europe in the way the high value and absolute US shortage of US dollars limited the import.

5 Examples include Bridgestone's acquisition of Firestone (US) and Sumitomo's acquisition of Dunlop (UK). Whether they be US or European companies, however, the acquired tyre makers had (and have) substantial European investments.

6 Other examples are given by Micossi and Viesti (1991). Outside manufacturing industry, there are examples of Japanese firms pursuing 'follow my leader' strategies in retail and wholesale banking.

7 In 1990, while 80 per cent of manufactured products supplied by US firms and bought by European consumers were made in Europe by US manufacturing subsidiaries, the equivalent percentage for Japanese firms was 20 per cent. These percentages have been calculated from various trade and production data published by the Department of Commerce, MITI and the Japanese Ministry of Finance.

8 For a discussion of the distinction between the two paradigms see Dunning (1991).

9 In a sense all advantages of firms are monopolistic, but it is useful to distinguish between those designed to exploit or extend a monopolistic position, and those (e.g. of a Schumpterian kind) which are designed to improve the static or dynamic efficiency of resource allocation.

10 See Chapter 2 of this volume.

11 Tying O-specific advantages to a particular country becomes difficult as a firm becomes multinational, and especially as it undertakes high-value activities outside its home country. But as far as Japanese MNEs are concerned, the great majority of innovatory activity (which results in the upgrading of the specific O assets of firms) is still undertaken in Japan.

12 The comparative competitive advantages of the Japanese and US economies is further explored in Chapter 2.

13 Distinguishing them from O advantages based upon the possession or more efficient use of a specific asset, namely Oa.

14 For a recent analysis of the costs and benefits of organizing transactions subject to different kinds of market failure see Kojima (1992).

15 This chapter does not consider this second influence on the O-specific advantage of firms.

16 In his 'diamond of competitive advantages' Porter distinguishes between four attributes: factor endowments, interfirm rivalry, presence of related and supporting industries, and quality of consumer demand. Each of these, in turn, may be affected by government and by chance. In our review of Porter's work (Dunning 1992) we added another exogenous variable, namely international business activity. It is not difficult to trace how each of these advantages may lead to

Japanese and US firms developing a different structure of Oa and Ot advantages, which, in turn, will result in a different pattern of Japanese- and US-owned domestic and foreign activity.

17 In ascending order of significance as a locational variable.

18 The sea distance from Tokyo to Southampton is approximately 15,000 miles and from New York approximately 3,000 miles.

19 As opposed to the way in which Japanese or US firms might affect these costs by endogenizing them.

20 For example, from surveys conducted by JETRO of manufacturing subsidiaries in Europe.

21 Such investment would be regarded as auto-supporting investment. The Japanese preferred the M&A route to the greenfield route of entry because of surplus capacity in the European auto industry.

REFERENCES

Abegglen, J. and Stalk, G. (1985) *Kaisha: The Japanese Corporation*, New York: Basic Books.

Bartlett, C. and Ghoshal, S. (1989) *Managing Across Borders: The Transnational Solution* Boston: Harvard Business School Press.

Cantwell, J. (1989) *Technological Innovation and the Multinational Corporation*, Oxford: Basil Blackwell.

——(1992) 'The effects of integration on the structure of multinational corporation activity in the EC', in M. Klein and P. Welfens (eds) *Multinationals in the New Europe and Global Trade*, pp. 193–236, Berlin and New York: Springer-Verlag.

Cantwell, J. and Hodson, C. (1991) 'Global R&D and UK competitiveness', in M. Casson (ed.) *Global Research Strategy and International Competitiveness*, pp. 133–82 Oxford: Basil Blackwell.

Caves, R. (1971) 'International corporations: the industrial corporations of foreign investment', *Economica* 38: 1–27.

——(1974) 'Causes of direct investment: foreign firms shares in Canadian and UK manufacturing industries', *Review of Economics and Statistics* 56: 279–93.

Dodwell Marketing Consultants (1986) *Industrial Groupings in Japan*, 7th Edition, Tokyo: Dodwell Marketing Consultants.

Doz, Y. (1986) *Strategic Management in Multinational Companies*, Oxford: Pergamon.

Doz, Y. and Prahalad, C. (1987) *The Multinational Mission*, New York: The Free Press.

Dunning, J. (1958) *American Investment in British Manufacturing Industry*, London: Allen & Unwin.

——(1981) *International Production and the Multinational Enterprise*, London: Allen & Unwin.

——(1991) 'The eclectic paradigm of international production: a personal note', in C. Pitelis and R. Sugden (eds) *The Nature of the Transnational Firm*, pp. 177–135, London and Boston: Routledge.

——(1992) 'The competitive advantages of nations and TNC activities: a review article', *Transnational Corporations* 1(1): 135–6.

Ethier, W. (1986) 'The multinational firm', *Quarterly Journal of Economics* 101: 805–33.

Gerlach, M. (1992) *The Keiretsu: A Primer*, New York: Japan Society.

Grubel, H. (1968) 'International diversified portfolios: welfare gains and capital flows', *American Economic Review* 58: 1299–314.

Hirsch, S. and Meshulach, A. (1992) 'Towards a unified theory of internationalization', Tel Aviv and Hebrew Universities (mimeo).
Hymer, S. (1960) 'The international operation of national firms: a study of direct investment', *PhD Dissertation*, MIT (published by MIT Press, 1976).
——(1968) 'La grande firme multinationale', *Revue économique* 19: 943–73.
JETRO (1990) *Sixth Survey of Japanese Manufacturing Investment in Europe*, Tokyo: Japanese External Trade Organization, International Economic and Trade Information Center.
——(1991) *Seventh Survey of European Operations of Japanese Companies in the Manufacturing Sector*, Tokyo: Japanese External Trade Organization, International Economic and Trade Information Center, March.
Knickerbocker, F. (1973) *Oligopolistic Reaction of Multinational Enterprise*, Boston: Harvard University Press.
Kogut, B. (1983) 'Foreign direct investment as a sequential process', in C. Kindleberger and D. Andretsch (eds) *Multinational Corporations in the 1980s*, 38–56 Cambridge, MA: MIT Press.
Kojima, K. (1978) *Direct Foreign Investment: A Japanese Model of Multinational Business*, London: Croom Helm.
——(1990) *Japanese Investment Abroad*, Tokyo: International Christian University, Social Science Research Institute, Monograph Series, 1.
——(1992) 'Internalization vs cooperation of MNC's business', *Hitutsubashi Journal of Economics* 33/1(June): 1–17.
Lall, S. (1980) 'Monopolistic advantages and foreign investments by US manufacturing industry', *Oxford Economic Papers* 32: 102–22.
Lall, S. and Siddarthan, N. (1982) 'The monopolistic advantages of multinationals: lessons from foreign investment in the US', *Economic Journal* 92: 668–83.
Micossi, S., and Viesti, G. (1991) 'Japanese investment in manufacturing in Europe', in L. A. Winters and A. Venables (eds) *European Integration, Trade and Industry*, pp. 200–33, Cambridge: Cambridge University Press.
Ministry of Finance (v.d.) *Japanese Direct Investment Abroad*, Tokyo.
MITI (1991) *Dai Yon Kai Kaigai Jigyo Katsudo Kihon Chosa Kaigai Toshi Tokei Soran*, Tokyo: MITI, International Policy Department, September.
OECD (1990) *Foreign Trade by Commodities, Series C*, Paris: Department of Economics and Statistics, OECD.
Okada, Y. (1991) 'Cooperative sectoral governance strategies of Japanese automobile multinationals in Asian countries', International University of Japan (mimeo).
Owen, R. (1982) 'Inter-industry determinants of foreign direct investments: a Canadian perspective', in A. Rugman (ed.) *New Theories of the Multinational Enterprise*, London: Croom Helm.
Ozawa, T. (1992) 'Cross-investments between Japan and the EC: income similarity, product variation and economies of scope', in J. Cantwell (ed.) *Multinational Investment in Modern Europe: Strategic Interaction in the Integrated Community*, pp. 13–45, Cheltenham: Edward Elgar.
Porter, M. (1990) *The Competitive Advantage of Nations*, New York: The Free Press.
Rugman, A. M. (1979) *International Diversification and the Multinational Enterprise*, Lexington, KY: Lexington Books.
Saxonhouse, G. and Stern, R. (1989) 'An analytical survey of formal and informal barriers to international trade and investment in the United States, Canada and Japan', in R. Stern (ed.) *Trade and Investment Relations among the United States, Canada and Japan*, pp. 293–364, Chicago: University of Chicago Press.
United Nations (n.d.) *Commodity Trade Statistics*, New York: UN.

——(1990) *Industrial Statistics Yearbook, 1988*, New York: UN.
UNCTC (1992) *The Determinants of Foreign Direct Investment: A Survey of the Evidence*, New York, UN Centre on Transnational Corporations.
US Department of Commerce (1981) *US Direct Investment Abroad, 1977*, Washington, DC: US Government Printing Office.
——(1990) 'US direct investment abroad: detail for position and balance of payments flows', *Survey of Current Business* August: 56–89.
——(1991) 'Provisional results of survey on US direct investment abroad, 1989', Washington, DC: US Government Printing Office.
—— (1993) 'US direct investment abroad: detail for historical cost position and balance of payments flows, 1992', *Survey of Current Business*, July: 88–124.
Vernon, R. (1966) 'International investment and international trade in the product cycle', *Quarterly Journal of Economics* 80: 190–207.
——(ed.) (1970) *The Technology Factor in International Trade*, New York: Columbia University Press.
Yamawaki, H. (1991) 'Location decisions of Japanese multinational firms in European manufacturing industries', in K. Hughes (ed.) *European Competitiveness*, Cambridge: Cambridge University Press.

Part V

THE AGE OF PARADOXES

14

SOME PARADOXES OF THE EMERGING GLOBAL ECONOMY

The multinational solution[1]

INTRODUCTION

In approaching the end of the twentieth century, one cannot but be struck by both the similarities and differences of circumstances to those faced by our forefathers a hundred years ago. Then, as now, was an era of dramatic and widespread technological change.[2] Then, as now, a new generation of telecommunication advances was shrinking the boundaries of economic activity. Then, as now, the organizational structures of firms and the socio-institutional framework of countries were in a state of flux. Then, as now, the cartography of political space was being reconfigured. Then, as now, the jurisdiction of national governments was being questioned, and the locus and composition of civic responsibilities were being redefined. Then, as now, new relationships and alliances were being forged between, and within, private and public institutions, and among different ethnic, religious and social groups.

But, to a more discerning observer, the differences between the two ages are more marked than the similarities. Key among these is that, while the events of the late nineteenth century were taking place *within* a well-established and widely accepted social and political order, those now occurring seem to be challenging long-cherished ideologies and values – and, in some cases, the very institutional fabric of society. At the same time, contemporary events are moulding a very unpredictable future – both for individuals and for institutions – and, more often than not, they are as divisive as they are unifying in their consequences. Our contemporary world is in a state of transition and turmoil. Some may view this as a form of creative destruction – of ideas, of technologies, of institutions and of cultures. Others fear that it is the beginning of an era of social and political unrest, the like of which we have not seen for many generations. The order of hierarchical capitalism which, as a wealth-creating system, has served much of the world so well over the past century, is being increasingly questioned, but no one is quite sure what is going to replace it – or indeed what should replace it.

Part of our increasing sense of bewilderment and insecurity, I suggest, arises because many of the events now occurring are paradoxical, if not antithetical, in both their characteristics and implications. Indeed, we may well be moving out of Eric Hobsbawn's 'Age of Extremes'[3] into an 'Age of Paradoxes'. Nowhere is this more clearly seen than in the globalization of economic activity. Few can surely deny that alongside an impressive array of opportunities and benefits offered by deep cross-border economic integration, it is demanding enormous and often painful adjustments, not only of corporations and governments, but of the working lives, leisure pursuits and mind sets of ordinary men and women. One political scientist, in a book published last year, with the intriguing title *Jihad vs McWorld*,[4] writes about our planet simultaneously 'falling apart and coming together', and starkly contrasts the economic and technological forces which are integrating nations into one 'gigantic and homogeneous theme park', and the frightening, but no less widespread, movement towards inter- and intrastate fragmentation along ethnic, tribal and religious lines.

In this concluding chapter, I shall consider just four paradoxes[5] or contradictions of the emerging global economy – or what the Chinese might prefer to call the 'yin' and 'yang' of globalization. I believe that the ways in which these paradoxes are approached and reconciled – if, indeed, they are reconciled – will determine the shape of our planet's political and economic future, and the social well-being of each and every one of us. I shall also suggest that hints of how the paradoxes may be managed by the international community are already contained in the strategies and actions of (successful) multinational enterprises (MNEs), just as, a century ago, the emergence of large national enterprises helped point the way to the macro-economic management of (the then emerging) hierarchical capitalism.

CO-OPERATION AND COMPETITION: THE PARADOX OF RELATIONSHIPS

At the end of the last century, the main form of interface between firms was competition. Most transactions between buyers and sellers were at spot or arm's length prices, and adversarial in nature. Apart from the conclusion of mergers, combines and other business agreements to restrict competition, rival firms perceived little need to co-operate with each other. In most advanced industrial nations, free enterprise was perceived 'to rule OK', and where markets failed, either firms or non-market entities intervened by internalizing these markets – namely, by an 'exit', rather than a 'voice', response. To the 'yin' of competition there was no counter-balancing 'yang' of co-operation.

By contrast, yet at the same time, the behaviour of national governments was predicated on the assumption that international commerce was beneficial because it enabled each country to produce goods and services which were *complementary* to each other's needs. This, after all, is what the principle of comparative advantage is all about. True, some interventionist actions – particularly by governments of later industrializing nations – were being practised,[6] but the dictum 'Firms compete but countries co-operate – and both obey the dictates of the market' was widely upheld. This was the deeply implanted order of things, which the events of the second industrial revolution of the late nineteenth century did little to disturb.

As we approach the new millennium, interfirm and internation state relationships are taking on more complex, pluralistic and contradictory forms. The last decade, in particular, has witnessed a spectacular increase in collaborative agreements between firms, both to penetrate new markets and to share the costs and speed up the process of innovation. Paradoxically, at a time of increased competition between firms in the factor and final goods markets, there has been a shedding of non-core activities by firms along and between value chains, and a replacement of them by a range of closely monitored interfirm alliances and networking arrangements. This movement has also led to another paradox – namely, the renaissance of small to medium-size firms – at a time when giant MNEs continue to engage in international mergers and acquisitions (M&As), and dominate the markets for technology-intensive and branded goods and services.

The reasons for the emerging 'yin' and 'yang' of the organization of economic activity are many, but most reduce to the rapidly rising overhead costs of production – at a time when manufacturing methods are becoming more flexible – an accelerating rate of technological obsolescence, a closer interdependence between many cutting-edge technologies, and the growing integration of different stages of the value-added chain (especially between R&D and the manufacturing departments of firms). Such events, together with the growing ease with which firms can co-operate with each other, have encouraged them to specialize in activities based on their core competencies, while, at the same time, to forge new and continuing alliances with firms now supplying inputs into these activities.

National governments, too, are finding that globalization is leading to new, and incongruous, cross-border relationships. Increasingly, in a world in which trade and FDI are within rather than between industrial sectors, unemployment is unacceptably high, human resource development is at a premium, and firm-specific assets are easily transferable across national borders. Governments are increasingly and openly competing with each other for similar resources, as well as seeking to advance their own particular social agendas. As the economic structure of countries tends to converge, so institutional and organizational factors are becoming more important location-specific endowments. Foremost among these are the actions of governments, which I will consider in more detail a little later. For the moment, I would simply note that, in contrast to the late nineteenth century scenario, where the policies of national governments were either independent of, or tended to complement, each other, those of today are a mixture of the 'yin' of competition and the 'yang' of co-operation.

Even the most cursory review of the now-emerging relationships between firms and governments suggests that, far from being antithetical, co-operation and competition each have a unique and mutually reinforcing role to play in a dynamic market economy. In and of themselves, each is a neutral concept; however, each may be deployed in a market-distorting or a market-facilitating way. There is an unacceptable face of co-operation and an unacceptable face of competition. One of the challenges of the globalizing economy is to manage and resolve the apparent contradictory nature of these two organizational forms. Clearly, the decision of *when*, *with whom* and *how* to co-operate, and *when*, *with whom* and *how* to compete, is partly determined by firm-, industry- and country-specific characteristics. Because of this, it is difficult to lay down any universal guidelines. But, in the last two decades or so, Western firms and nations have learnt a great deal about the 'yin' and 'yang' of commercial relationships and institutional arrangements practised in East Asia. The knowledge so gained is now being assiduously adapted to Western norms and needs – so much so that the expression 'alliance' capitalism is now being used to describe a new trajectory of market-based socio-economic systems. A feature of this trajectory is that it is reconstituting the concepts of competition and co-operation, from being exclusive alternatives, to being mutually reinforcing organizational forms.

In seeking to manage or resolve the paradox of relationships, I would like to suggest that nation states have much to learn from MNEs. Such corporations – at least the successful ones – are 'masters of the paradox'. They are well experienced both at translating the horns of dilemma of economic change into virtuous circles of growth and profitability, and of using competition and co-operation and strategies to obtain their long-term objectives (Baden-Fuller and Stopford 1992). While, in the last resort, most MNEs are subject to the discipline of the global market-place, an increasing number are forming alliances with other firms to innovate new products or seek out new markets. The key to achieving the right balance between competition – a 'go it alone strategy' – and co-operation – a 'do it together strategy' – seems to rest on the perception of managers about the nature and strength of their distinctive or core competitive advantages, relative to those of their competitors, and that of the other (i.e. complementary) assets which need to be combined with these critical capabilities if they are to exploit them effectively.[7] Research suggests that firms are most likely to co-operate with each other to reduce their resource commitments in acquiring or enhancing these complementary assets, but that they are more reluctant to do so when this requires sharing knowledge and learning experiences about their critical competencies. Once this balance of options is achieved – and this is a constantly moving target – competition and co-operation are no longer seen to be exclusive alternatives, but reinforcing avenues for advancing competitiveness.

GLOBALIZATION VS. LOCALIZATION: THE PARADOX OF SPACE

As the late nineteenth century witnessed the widening of local into national markets, and the emergence of foreign direct investment (FDI) as a significant form of international commerce, so the late twentieth century is seeing the regionalization and globalization of economic activity. The difference, however, between these two events is not just one of the size and character of markets – but the fact that, while a century ago, economic activity was largely conducted between independent buyers and sellers, the unique feature of the contemporary world economy is the deep structural integration and interdependence of cross-border transactions.

The extension of geographical space has not affected all activities to the same extent. While the markets for some goods (e.g. Coca-Cola, fast food, Levi jeans, Gucchi handbags) and some kinds of services (e.g. financial assets, music, television and sports) span the globe, others are restricted by the specificity of local supply capabilities, customs, tastes and government regulations. Similarly, while some parts of the value chain (e.g. those involving the electronic transmission of standardized data) acknowledge few geographical borders, others, in which trust-based relations, personal interface and complex, but non-codifiable, knowledge are at a premium, are having to pay more heed to spatially constrained capabilities and needs. Hence, we have the paradox of what Ann Markusen (1994) has referred to as 'sticky places within slippery space'. At the same time, the imperatives of much of contemporary product and production technology and the lowering of natural and artificial barriers to traversing space have most certainly enabled firms to take a more holistic stance to their foreign and domestic operations.

The liberalization of markets, more outward-looking development policies, and the current attractions of regional economic integration have all helped to push out the territorial boundaries of firms. While FDI is the main route by which this extension is being accomplished, increasingly, as I have already mentioned, cross-border alliances – varying from international subcontracting and *keiretsu*-type relationships, to R&D consortia among rival firms – have become more significant in the last decade, and seem likely to be a major feature of the capitalism of the twenty-first century.

If we can think of the spatial widening of economic activity as the 'yin' of globalization, the 'yang' is surely the increasing pressure on individuals, firms, nations and localities to reassert their distinctive traits and values. The paradox of regional economic integration – albeit it is often market driven – is that it introduces an economic uniformity into people's lives, which they wish to offset by emphasizing other, and more unique, characteristics of their individuality. In some cases – although we would hesitate to suggest this has been caused by the emergence of the global economy, however much it may facilitate it – it leads to ethnic and ideological schisms and to political disintegration and fragmentation. Just as there can be little doubt that the merger movement among corporations is going on alongside a regeneration in the role and prosperity of small businesses, so as countries group together better to attain their common economic aspirations, they are anxious to reassert their distinctive cultural and ethnic heritages. As John Naisbitt (1994) has put it, there is a rising conflict between universalism and tribalism, and between regional unification and fragmentation.

As the global economy favours the growth of the large MNE, so many of its spatial units are becoming smaller. The same may well be true of 'body politique'. The concept of subsidiarity is gaining widespread acceptance at all levels of governance, and the role of subnational region, district, city and town in affecting the location of economic activity would appear to be more, rather than less, important. Certainly, this is the view of Kenichi Ohmae, who, in his latest book (Ohmae 1995), argues persuasively that, in a borderless world, region states may well come to replace nation states as the ports of entry into the global economy and the centrepiece of economic activity.[8]

Once again, however, I would suggest to you that the contradiction between the globalization and the localization of economic space is more perceived than real, and that this is being amply demonstrated by the activities of the more successful MNEs. They know full well the axiom 'think globally but act locally', and of the need to balance the gains arising from the integration of scale-related technologies with those which stem from adapting world product production markets, techniques and work practices to local situations. They also appreciate that the ability to recognize these latter needs, and to co-ordinate them efficiently, are important competitive advantages in their own right. At the same time, the *kind* and *degree* of adaptation required in the late 1990s is very different from that of a century ago. Then, it was mainly based on the availability (and quality) of natural resources and of national consumer tastes. Now, it is based on the flexible use of created assets (namely, of innovations, production technologies and organizational structures), and on an acceptance of the fact that in a variety of quite subtle ways, the kind of product improvements sought by consumers reflects national and subnational, as well as international, physical and spiritual values.

In short, globalization is leading to a spatial reconfiguration of economic activity – and also the governance of such activity. In some cases, this is resulting in a harmonization, or homogenization, of the functions of firms and of the tastes of consumers the world over. In others, it is increasing the value of close spatial linkages between firms (such as that fostered in business districts and science parks) at a subnational level, while, at the same time, stimulating individuals and nations to differentiate themselves from each other and emphasize their discriminating characteristics. The 'yin' – or slippery space – of economic integration is then going hand in hand – indeed some would say giving rise to – with the 'yang' – or sticky place – of a re-evaluation of national or local cultural, religious and ethnic diversity. As long as these trends of globalization are treated as complementary, rather than substitutable for each other, then there is no real paradox of geographical space. And, as I have already suggested, the more successful MNEs are already demonstrating some of the ways in which spatially related tensions can be minimized and used to promote their global objectives. I accept, of course, that this task is a good deal more challenging for national and regional governments, but grapple with it they must if the full benefits of globalization are not to be destroyed by inter-country social and cultural strife. I shall return to this point towards the end of this chapter.

THE ROLE OF GOVERNMENTS: THE PARADOX OF 'LESS, YET MORE', AND THAT OF 'CENTRALIZATION VS. DECENTRALIZATION'

A century ago, there was comparatively little dispute about the role of national administrations – at least in Western economies.[9] The spiritual heritage of Adam Smith and the founding fathers of the American Revolution was very much alive. In economic matters, at least, the invisible hand of the market was thought superior to that of the visible hand of extra-market planning and government intervention. The duties of government were to defend the realm, to maintain internal law and order, to combat the unacceptable face of capitalism, to provide the legal and commercial framework in which property rights were respected and unfettered markets might flourish, and to alleviate unavoidable social distress.

There was no conflict in performing these tasks; they were not even regarded as competitive to those of other organizational forms. The fact that in some countries (e.g. France and Germany) governments pursued more paternalistic policies and were more interventionist than others (e.g. the UK), was accepted to reflect their distinctive institutional heritages, or their particular stages of development, rather than any differences in their economic philosophies. In any event, because of the immobility of resources and absence of any cross-border structural integration of economic activity, national administrations were able to follow largely autonomous economic and social strategies. Even what international commerce there was at the time was largely determined by a world order, namely the gold standard, although restrictions on some kinds of trade, and other forms of government intervention, were beginning to emerge.

Today, the optimum or appropriate role of government is hotly debated. In particular, the last twenty years have seen a blurring of the boundaries of the organizational modes of capitalist economies, while globalization has led to an intensification of the 'yin' and 'yang' of government intervention. On the one hand, as markets have become more liberalized and central planning has become discredited, the interventionist role of governments has lessened. On the other, as the economic prosperity of firms and nations has become more dependent on the continual upgrading of indigenous created assets – notably innovatory capacity, human resources and the commercial and communications infrastructure, many of which are within the power of governments to influence – the role of the state has become more critical.

I believe that, for the most part, globalization is *not* reducing the role of national governments. But it is changing its *raison d'être* and its content. And it is doing so within the context of deepening structural integration; the growing importance of public goods (e.g. crime prevention, health care, education and the environment); and the increasing ease with which corporations can avoid unpopular actions by their national governments by relocating their activities elsewhere (i.e. 'vote' with their feet).[10]

Another feature of globalization and economic change is that it is leading to a greater coincidence of interests between governments and the private sector in market economies. Even the arch-priest of market forces – the World Bank – has recognized this.[11] The 'yin' of a policing and umpiring, but otherwise non-interventionist, stance of governments is being supplemented by the 'yang' of governments as institution builders, facilitators of efficient markets and catalysts of dynamic comparative advantage, and managers of social conflict (Chang and Rowthorn 1995). Hence the paradox that a free market needs strong government – a paradox which scholars are only able to resolve by constructing a theory of state involvement which 'takes full account of uncertainty and innovation, institutions and political economy' (Chang and Rowthorn 1995: 46).

To date, the need for a reconstituted role of governments in the age of alliance capitalism has only been fully acknowledged – and put into practice – by some East Asian governments (Wade 1995). The competing or adversarial relationship between governments and private enterprise, which was (and is) a feature of hierarchical capitalism, remains strongly embedded in Western – especially US – cultures. But the phenomenon of the globalizing economy, the growing recognition that a nation's competitiveness rests as much on its ability to supply the location-bound assets necessary to attract or retain firm-specific mobile assets, as those assets themselves, and the acceptance that, *de facto*, governments *do* compete with each other for these latter assets, are combining to induce a 'sink or swim together' philosophy among all except the most extreme free market administrations.

Of the three paradoxes so far identified, that of the 'less' or 'more' of governments may be the most difficult to resolve. This is not only because of entrenched ideological views and institutional rigidities, but also because the costs and benefits of non-market intervention are extremely difficult to measure. So, if and when markets do fail, it cannot necessarily be presumed that government intervention will improve the situation, as the costs of such intervention may be greater than the benefits. Such evidence as we have (e.g. Bradford 1994, Wade 1995) suggests that the interaction between national governments, fiat governments and markets in countries such as Korea, Taiwan and Malaysia has led to a virtuous circle of growth and efficiency, while that in many parts of Latin America, at least until recently, has led to a vicious circle of low economic growth and social unrest.

Although there has been some research done on the kinds of government action which are most likely to improve economic performance,[12] for the most part our knowledge is woefully inadequate. Once again, however, there are some hints from the responses of MNEs to market failure and to the demands of globalization. In particular, there are major changes now taking place in the organizational structure of firms. Pyramids of hierarchies are being increasingly flattened as more heterarchical (and horizontal) relationships are being forged between decision takers and line managers. Nowhere is this being more clearly demonstrated than in the Swedish/Swiss MNE Asea Brown Boveri (ABB).[13] In this changed organizational scenario, the job of top management is less to control and take decisions, and more to orchestrate a strategic vision and set performance standards, to nurture organizational values and to encourage down-the-line entrepreneurship. The 'yin' of a centralized corporate strategy and the setting of targets is being accompanied by the 'yang' of devolved responsibility for achieving these goals, that is subsidiarity in action. Similarly, one can see globalization leading to a relayering of some of the traditional tasks of national governments to regional states or business districts and local authorities, while others (e.g. the harmonization of trade, FDI and competition policies, and the framing of technical and environmental standards) are increasingly becoming the responsibility of regional or supranational regimes. According to Charles Handy (1995:113), this is leading (and I quote his words) 'to the disappearing middle of national administrations'.

THE HUMAN CONSEQUENCES OF GLOBALIZATION: THE PARADOX OF BENEFITS AND DISBENEFITS

Perhaps the most transparent effect of globalization – or more accurately the economic forces associated with it – is that on the everyday lives of people the world over. While the 'yin' of structural economic interdependence and the liberalization of markets is undisputedly raising average living standards, offering new job opportunities, widening consumer choice, and, in a whole variety of ways, improving the lifestyles of large numbers of people, the 'yang', or downside, of globalization is no less dramatically portrayed in disturbingly high levels of unemployment – particularly among the younger unskilled workers – a personal sense of insecurity and foreboding associated with rapid technological change, the breakdown of traditional social mores, the resurgence of ethnic conflicts, and the easier cross-border movement of tangible or intangible *disbenefits*, for example organized crime, drug trafficking, international terrorism and unacceptable patterns of behaviour. It is downsides such as these which Klaus Schwab and Claude Smadja (1996) – two of the most prominent advocates of global trade and integration – had in mind when, at this year's Davos Forum, they referred to a 'mounting backlash against globalization'. Other commentators have gone further by asserting that, unless the less desirable consequences of globalization are tackled and, at least, partially resolved, the utopian vision – and I paraphrase Aldous Huxley's words – of a 'brave new economic world' could quickly be turned into a cauldron of social unrest, political upheaval, cultural fragmentation and ideological conflict between nations, or even civilizations.[14]

Such a stark paradox, I believe, was much less in evidence at the turn of the last century.[15] True, at that time there was much structural change, brought about, *inter alia*, by the advent of electricity, the telephone, the internal combustion engine and the introduction of the Fordist system of production. But economic growth, both in the older and newer capitalist economies of the time, was, in general, able to cope with the less desirable consequences; the jobs created were generally more congenial than those which they replaced; while, for the most part, improvements in education and vocational training were able to keep pace with the needs of the market-place. Moreover, most of the required social adjustments were contained within domestic economies, and it was not until after the First World War that FDI became a significant allocator of economic activity and, hence, jobs between countries.

At that time, too, there were far fewer non-economic claims on the resources and capabilities of countries than there are today. Most social welfare programmes were in their infancy, and very little attention was paid to environmental issues. In the main, the second industrial revolution of the late nineteenth century was accomplished with more observable benefits and fewer observable costs than those resulting from its predecessor of a century earlier, or (so it would appear) its successor a century later. Even the hierarchical system of managerial capitalism, although it had some adverse consequences on the fortunes of small family-owned enterprises, generally offered the ordinary worker more benefits and opportunities than it took away!

Again, the situation is totally different in the emerging global neighbourhood of the 1990s. This is apparent both at the level of the individual firm and that of the nation state. Almost daily, it seems, one reads about huge restructuring and relocation programmes of corporations, which frequently have traumatic effects on people's lives and livelihoods – not just in one country, but in several. Often the slogan 'one person's job is another person's dole' is all too true. Often, too, the benefits – as well as the costs – of McWorld are exploited by ethnic or religious fundamentalists to advance the course of Jihad.[16] There are both losers and winners in the globalization process, and the very pace of economic change often requires major adjustments even in the lives of the winners. Over the last two decades, I would suggest, there has been more reallocation of economic activity involving people-adjustment, both within and between countries, than at any other time since the late eighteenth century.

At the level of the nation state, globalization is requiring one of the basic tenets of comparative advantage – namely, the cross-border immobility of resources – to be questioned. Not only are many firm-specific assets and capabilities mobile across national boundaries, but the demands being made by the owners of these assets and capabilities on those which are locationally bound are changing. Thus, for example, in their choice of investment locations, both between and within countries, MNEs are being increasingly influenced by the presence of agglomeration economies of transport and communications infrastructure, and by the price and productivity of skilled labour.[17] As I have indicated, not only are these assets largely location bound, but their supply is strongly influenced by government action. If these policies are inappropriate, or are not perceived to be as congenial as those offered by other governments, then those assets which have the opportunity to do so will move elsewhere. In such an event, globalization may result in more economic disbenefits than benefits – certainly to the countries and the immobile assets – losing the economic activity. Equally, because of differences in age, structures, social policies and the competence of national administrations, the ability of countries to absorb the 'yang' of globalization will vary considerably.

How can one hope to reconcile the conflicting consequences of globalization – which, in the economic arena at least, are mainly distributional? I believe the first essential thing is to recognize that, barring natural or human catastrophes, the globalization of economic activity is largely irreversible. This is because it is the result of technological advances which, themselves, cannot be reversed. However, the pace and form of globalization can be affected as can the response of governments to some of its less welcome consequences. And, it is the extent to which countries can successfully devise new ways to minimize these costs by effective 'voice' rather than 'exit' strategies which will determine the net benefits they derive from globalization.

Since many of the less welcome effects accompanying the advent of the global village are non-economic, it might be thought that the actions of MNEs can be of only limited relevance to governments. This would be incorrect, and for two reasons. The first is that the more socially responsible MNEs are demonstrating that there need be no real conflict between the achievement of economic and social goals. Nowhere is this more clearly seen than in the area of environmental standards. Far from being exporters of pollution – as was once thought – MNEs are among the trail blazers of environmentally friendly, yet competitive-enhancing, innovations, and often set, rather than follow, the dictates of governments. Similarly, in their redeployment, retraining and pension schemes, the more progressive global companies offer a microcosm of the type of policies which governments would do well to study. Second, because they span the globe, many MNEs provide a salutary reminder to national administrations that 'best practice' techniques – particularly in minimizing the social hardships of structural change – are not always 'home grown', and there is much to learn from other cultures and institutional regimes.

I accept, of course, that, by themselves, corporations cannot – and, indeed, should not – be expected to resolve the challenges of globalization, although initiatives, such as the *Business Leaders Forum* set up by HRH the Prince of Wales in 1989 to consider the corporate response to the social, cultural and spiritual dimensions of globalization, are to be warmly commended. But, the potential for dialogue and collaboration between the main instruments of globalization and the stakeholders affected by it remains largely untapped. In this connection, I particularly welcome the recently published report by the Commission on Global Governance entitled *Our Global Neighbourhood*. The Commission – the brain-child of ex-German Chancellor Willy Brandt – was set up in 1992, under the joint chairmanship of the (then) Prime Minister of Sweden – Ingvar Carlsson – and Shridath Ramphal, the ex-Secretary General of the Commonwealth, and comprised twenty-eight very distinguished statesmen, business leaders, bankers, and presidents of international agencies from throughout the world. In its 'call to action', the report makes many astute recommendations on matters ranging from global security to managing economic interdependence and fostering a global civic ethic. It also urges the UN to convene a *World Conference on Global Governance* in 1998, to which (it suggests) should be invited not only the political leaders of the world, but those of 'the wider human constituency' who are 'infused with a sense of caring for others and a sense of responsibility to the global neighbourhood' (Commission on Global Governance 1995). Such a gathering of men and women of goodwill would, indeed, be an expression of the 'benefits' of international co-operation, which, I would argue, is needed to counter-balance some of the disbenefits of international competition.

CONCLUSIONS

To conclude: as we approach the twenty-first century, we do so with a mixture of optimism and pessimism, and of hope and trepidation. The future seems both more complex and more daunting than that faced by our forefathers a century ago. This, I have suggested, is for four reasons. The first is the increasing dichotomy between the territorial space open to individuals and corporations, and under the jurisdiction of governments. This is leading to a number of paradoxes and dilemmas – particularly as far as the intercountry distribution of the gains and losses of globalization is concerned. The second is the erosion of the boundaries of the leading institutions for organizing economic activities – and particularly those of firms, markets and governments. *Inter alia*, this is resulting in a more intricate and pluralistic network of interinstitutional arrangements, and to a new complementarity between the 'yin' of competition and the 'yang' of co-operation.

Third, improvements in standards of living – especially among wealthier nations – are increasingly taking the form of quality-of-life-enhancing goods and services (e.g. computer software, telecommunications, education, health care, environmental protection and the absence of crime, terrorism, etc.), the supply of which governments, by their actions or non-actions, strongly influence. The consequences of globalization are being increasingly evaluated by their effects on the availability, character and distribution of these 'public' products. In so far as communication advances and the cross- border integration of economic activity are being accompanied by a renewal of national or subnational (e.g. tribal) specific cultures and values, this is creating a range of interrelational tensions and dilemmas quite different in scale and effect from those arising from the second industrial revolution.

Fourth, while twentieth-century hierarchical capitalism has generally been accompanied by an expansion in the economic role of national governments, twenty-first-century alliance capitalism and the renaissance of the market economy seems likely not only to demand changes in the nature of that role, but to increase and deepen that of both subnational and supranational authorities.

In seeking to reconcile the paradoxes of globalization, I have further suggested that the ways, in which successful MNEs have adapted their organizational and economic strategies to the changes demanded of them by recent economic events bear close scrutiny by public authorities as they seek to reformulate their own policies. Moreover, the cross-border activities of firms – noticeably via FDI and strategic alliances – may, themselves, assist national governments not only to upgrade the competitiveness of their own firms and indigenous resources, but to do so in a way which promotes their longer-term economic and social goals. Of course, the strategies of MNEs, like those of governments, may be protective and result in a vicious circle of market–state interface, and the discouragement of these is as important as any positive competitive-enhancing actions which both firms and governments might implement.

Looking further ahead into the twenty-first century, as the Yale historian Paul Kennedy has recently done (Kennedy 1993), one cannot but be sobered by one final paradox which, in many ways, overarches everything I have been saying this morning. That is, currently the wealthiest 12 per cent of the world's population owns or controls 85 per cent of the world's stock of created assets, while the rest, that is 88 per cent of the population, owns or controls only 15 per cent of these assets. Moreover, virtually all of the 50 per cent increase in the world's population over the next thirty to thirty-five years is likely to occur in the less wealthy parts of the world. Clearly, the geographical imbalance between the current technology revolution and the population revolution – to use Kennedy's terminology – is a potential social time bomb. Whether or not the bomb is diffused will, I believe, largely rest on two factors. The first is the nature and pace of Indian and Chinese economic development, as, between them, these two super giants are expected to account for between 25 and 30 per cent of the world's population by 2025. The second is whether the peoples of the world and their leaders can summon up enough determination and emotional intelligence to reconcile the growing threat of ideological warfare which is epitomized by the Jihad vs. McWorld syndrome. For, I fear, unless this is done, our global dream could so easily turn into a global nightmare!

As a university educator and researcher, I should like to make one final remark. The future shape of our planet is now being fashioned by the decisions being taken in the board rooms of larger corporations, in the corridors and chambers of government departments, and around the conference tables of international agencies. Anything we, as international business scholars, can do to provide the decision makers with information about the costs and benefits of globalization, and what requires to be done at various institutional and decision-taking levels, is surely to be applauded. Indeed, it is our duty so to participate and to influence those who guide our destinies and those of our children.

NOTES

1 This chapter is based on the Tore Browaldh Lecture delivered by the author at the University of Götenborg in April 1996, and at the academy of International Business, UK Chapter annual meeting in April 1997. The first person singular has been retained throughout.

2 Some economists (e.g. Carlota Perez 1983) would go as far as to argue that both the 1880s and the 1980s heralded in a new Kondratiev cycle of techno-economic and socio-institutional change.

3 Eric Hobsbawn is a distinguished historian who has authored several books with titles depicting (what, to him, is) the key characteristic of the period he is writing about. Among these are *The Age of Revolution, 1789–1848, The Age of Capital, 1848–1875, The Age of Empire, 1875–1914* and *The Age of Extremes, 1914–1991* (1995).

4 Barber (1995). Jihad refers to an ideology of parochial ethnicity, which is often portrayed as extreme ethnic or religious fundamentalism. McWorld is the ideology of the global corporation, which is primarily interested in economic gain and would like to ignore all national or political boundaries.

5 Put more accurately, perceived paradoxes; we believe the paradoxes described are more 'imaginary' than they are 'real'.

6 And more than is commonly realized. For a contemporary account of the interventionist – albeit catalytic – role of the US government in the development of US industry – agriculture in the nineteenth century, see Kozul-Wright (1995).

7 The concept of core and complementary assets has been explored by several business scholars, but particularly by David Teece (1987).

8 See also a perceptive article on a related theme by Richard Florida (1995).

9 The same might well be true of most Eastern economies, but here the functions of government were viewed in a very different light to those in the West.

10 An expression first coined at the time of the American Revolution to reflect the extent to which firms and/or individuals could escape (through emigration) unacceptable taxes and other fiscal duties imposed by national governments.

11 See especially World Bank (1991).

12 As is reviewed, for example, in Dunning (1994) and Panic (1995).

13 As documented, for example, by Bartlett and Ghoshal (1994).

14 See Barber (1995) and Huntington (1993).

15 But, interestingly enough, it was in the years following the first industrial revolution. Indeed, as Paul Kennedy astutely observes, the disbenefits of the globalizing market economy of the late twentieth century fairly accurately mirror those of the *national* market economy of the first half of the nineteenth century, following the industrial revolution and the 'laissez faire' philosophies of some of the classical economists (Kennedy, 1993).

16 Barber (1995) gives some fascinating examples of how practical applications of the two starkly opposing ideologies often aid and abet each other, and that neither is complete without the other. For example, he points out that modern transportation and communication technologies, and the export to Jihad ideologies and practices, often lead to non-Jihad nations or regimes becoming more dependent on Jihad nations or regions for their economic well-being.

17 For a review of the literature, see Dunning (1993), Braunerhjelm and Svensson (1995) and Mariotti and Piscitello (1995).

REFERENCES

Baden-Fuller, C. W. F. and Stopford, J. M. (1992) *Rejuvenating the Mature Business*, London and New York: Routledge.

Barber, B. R. (1995) *Jihad vs McWorld*, New York: Times Books.

Bartlett, C. G. and Ghoshal, S. (1994) *Beyond the M-Form: Towards a Managerial Theory of the Firm*, Pittsburgh: Carnegie Bosch Institute for Applied Studies on International Management, Working Paper No. 94–6.

Bradford, C. I. (1994) *The New Paradigm of Systemic Competitiveness: Toward More Integrated Policies in Latin America*, Paris: OECD.

Braunerhjelm, P. and Svensson, R. (1995) *Host Country Characteristics and Agglomeration in Foreign Direct Investment*, Stockholm: Industrial Institute for Economic and Social Research (mimeo).

Chang, H.-J. and Rowthorn, R. (eds) (1995) *The Role of the State in Economic Change*, Oxford: Clarendon Press.

Commission on Global Governance (1995) *Our Global Neighbourhood*, Oxford and New York: Oxford University Press.

Dunning, J. H. (1993) *Multinational Enterprises and the Global Economy*, Wokingham, England, and Reading, MA: Addison Wesley.

——(1994) *Globalization: The Challenge for National Economic Regimes*, Dublin: The Economic and Social Research Council.

Florida, R. (1995) 'Towards the learning region', *Futures* 27(5): 527–36.

Handy, C. (1995) *The Empty Raincoat*, London: Arrow Business Books.

Hobsbawn, E. (1995), *The Age of Extremes 1914–1991*, London: Abacus.

Huntington, S. (1993) 'The clash of civilizations', *Foreign Affairs* 72, Summer: 22–49.

Kennedy, P. M. (1993) *Preparing for the Twenty-First Century*, New York: Random House.

Kozul-Wright, R. (1995) 'The myth of Anglo-Saxon capitalism: reconstructing the history of the American state', in H.-J. Chang and R. Rowthorn (eds) *The Role of the State in Economic Change*, pp. 81–113, Oxford: Clarendon Press.

Mariotti, S. and Piscitello, L. (1995) 'Information costs and location of fdis within the host country: empirical evidence from Italy', *Journal of International Business Studies* 26(4): 815–41.

Markusen, A. (1994) *Sticky Places in Slippery Spaces: The Political Economy of Post-War Fast Growth Regions*, New Brunswick Center for Urban Policy Research, Rutgers University Working Paper No. 79.

Naisbitt, J. (1994) *Global Paradox: The Bigger the World Economy, the More Political its Smallest Players*, New York: William Morrow.

Ohmae, K. (1995) *The End of the Nation State: The Rise of Regional Economies*, London: Harper Collins.

Panic, M. (1995) 'International economic integration and the changing role of national governments', in H.-J. Chang and R. Rowthorn (eds) *The Role of the State in Economic Change*, pp. 51–80, Oxford: Clarendon Press.

Perez, C. (1983) 'Structural changes and the assimilation of new technologies on the economic and social system', *Futures* 15: 357–75.

Schwab, K. and Smadja, C. (1996) *Start Taking the Backlash Against Globalization Seriously*, Address given to Davos Forum, January.

Teece, D. (1987) 'Profiting from technological innovation: implications for integration collaboration, licensing and public policy', in *The Competitive Challenge*, Cambridge, MA: Ballinger.

Wade, R. (1995) 'Resolving the state-market dilemma in East Asia', in H.-J. Chang and R. Rowthorn (eds) *The Role of the State in Economic Change*, pp. 114–36, Oxford: Clarendon Press.

World Bank (1991) *The World Development Report 1992*, Oxford and New York: Oxford University Press.

INDEX

For Product Safety Concerns and Information please contact our EU representative GPSR@taylorandfrancis.com
Taylor & Francis Verlag GmbH, Kaufingerstraße 24, 80331 München, Germany

www.ingramcontent.com/pod-product-compliance
Ingram Content Group UK Ltd.
Pitfield, Milton Keynes, MK11 3LW, UK
UKHW020022200926
475702UK00014B/2019
9781138879379